Brain and Perception
Holonomy and Structure in Figural Processing

Karl H. Pribram
Stanford University
and
Radford University

Appendices in collaboration with
Kunio Yasue *and* **Mari Jibu**
Notre Dame Seishin University
Okayama, Japan

LEA LAWRENCE ERLBAUM ASSOCIATES, PUBLISHERS
1991 Hillsdale, New Jersey   Hove and London

The studies reported and the manuscript were made possible by grants from the National Institutes of Health, the Office of Naval Research, Steven DeVore and his Sybervision Corporation, Walter Morris and his foundation, the Feldenkrais Foundation and Paul Larsen of the Summit Organization. Their support is gratefully acknowledged.

Lawrence Erlbaum Associates, Inc., Publishers
365 Broadway
Hillsdale, New Jersey 07642

Library of Congress Cataloging-in-Publication Data

Pribram, Karl H., 1919–
    Brain and perception : holonomy and structure in figural
processing / by Karl H. Pribram.
        p.   cm.
    Collection of nine lectures.
    ISBN 0-89859-995-4
    1. Brain.   2. Perception.   3. Cognition.   I. Title.
    [DNLM: 1. Brain—physiology.   2. Pattern Recognition.
    3. Perception.   WL 300 P945b]
    QP376.P674   1991
    612.8'2—dc20
DNLM/DLC
for Library of Congress   89-71539
                                                          CIP

Printed in the United States of America
10 9 8 7 6 5 4 3 2

One must conclude, as a firmly fixed scientific generalization, that the properties of the external world are rarely represented in a straight-forward way in the human responses triggered in that world. Should perception therefore be expected to be disorganized and chaotic? Not at all. . . . The reason for the apparent disjunction between external stimulus properties and those of the final percept is not hard to find. The physiological organism, standing between these two end terms, has dimensions of its own to contribute, makes its own transformations and creates its own . . . functional relationships in the devious paths from peripheral receptor processes to final response mechanism.

Frank Geldard, pp. 20–21
Sensory Saltation, Inaugural
MacEachran Memorial Lecture, 1975

There are two unavoidable gaps in any behavioral account: one between the stimulating action of the environment and the response of the organism and one between consequences and the resulting change in behavior. Only brain science can fill those gaps. In doing so it completes the account; it does not give a different account of the same thing.

B. F. Skinner (p. 18, 1989)

Contents

Lecture 6. Images of Achievement and Action Spaces: Somatic Processes in the Control of Action   121

PART 11: COGNITIVE ASPECTS

Lecture 7. Comprehension: Contributions of the Posterior Cerebral Convexity in Enhancing Processing Span   165

John M. MacEachran
Memorial Lecture Series

The Department of Psychology at the University of Alberta inaugurated the MacEachran Memorial Lecture Series in 1975 in honor of the late Professor John M. MacEachran. Professor MacEachran was born in Ontario in 1877 and received a Ph.D. in Philosophy from Queen's University in 1905. In 1906 he left for Germany to begin more formal study in psychology, first spending just less than a year in Berlin with Stumpf, and then moving to Leipzig, where he completed a second Ph.D. in 1908 with Wundt as his supervisor. During this period he also spent time in Paris studying under Durkheim and Henri Bergson. With these impressive qualifications the University of Alberta was particularly fortunate in attracting him to its faculty in 1909.

Professor MacEachran's impact has been signficant at the university, provincial, and national levels. At the University of Alberta he offered the first courses in psychology and subsequently served as Head of the Department of Philosophy and Psychology and Provost of the University until his retirement in 1945. It was largely owing to his activities and example that several areas of academic study were established on a firm and enduring basis. In addition to playing a major role in establishing the Faculties of Medicine, Education and Law in this Province, Professor MacEachran was also instrumental in the formative stages of the Mental Health Movement in Alberta. At a national level, he was one of the founders of the Canadian Psychological Association and also became its first Honorary President in 1939. John M. MacEachran was indeed one of the pioneers in the development of psychology in Canada.

Perhaps the most significant aspect of the MacEachran Memorial Lecture

Series has been the continuing agreement that the Department of Psychology at the University of Alberta has with Lawrence Erlbaum Associates, Publishers, Inc., for the publication of each lecture series. The following is a list of the Invited Speakers and the titles of their published lectures:

1975   Frank A. Geldard (Princeton University)
        "Sensory Saltation: Metastability in the Perceptual World"

1976   Benton J. Underwood (Northwestern University)
        "Temporal Codes for Memories: Issues and Problems"

1977   David Elkind (Rochester University)
        "The Child's Reality: Three Developmental Themes"

1978   Harold Kelley (University of California at Los Angeles)
        "Personal Relationships: Their Structures and Processes"

1979   Robert Rescorla (Yale University)
        "Pavlovian Second-Order Conditioning:
        Studies in Associative Learning"

1980   Mortimer Mishkin (NIMH-Bethesda)
        "Cognitive Circuits" (*unpublished*)

1981   James Greeno (University of Pittsburgh)
        "Current Cognitive Theory in Problem Solving" (*unpublished*)

1982   William Uttal (University of Michigan)
        "Visual Form Detection in 3-Dimensional Space"

1983   Jean Mandler (University of California at San Diego)
        "Stories, Scripts, and Scenes: Aspects of Schema Theory"

1984   George Collier and Carolyn Rovee-Collier (Rutgers University)
        "Learning and Motivation: Function and
        Mechanism" (*unpublished*)

1985   Alice Eagly (Purdue University)
        "Sex Differences in Social Behavior:
        A Social-Role Interpretation"

1986   Karl Pribram (Stanford University)
        "Brain and Perception:
        Holonomy and Structure in Figural Processing" (*in press*)

1987   Abram Amsel (University of Texas at Austin)
        "Behaviorism, Neobehaviorism, and Cognitivism in
        Learning Theory: Historical and Contemporary Perspectives"

1988   Robert S. Siegler and Eric Jenkins (Carnegie-Mellon University)
        "How Children Discover New Strategies"

1989   Robert Efron (University of California at Davis & Veterans
        Administration Medical Center)
        "The Decline and Fall of Hemispheric Specialization"

Eugene C. Lechelt, Coordinator
MacEachran Memorial Lecture Series

**Sponsored by The Department of Psychology, The University of Alberta
with the support of The Alberta Heritage Foundation for Medical Research
in memory of John M. MacEachran, pioneer in Canadian psychology.**

Preface

Motive

These lectures are motivated by several considerations. First among these is the desire to present in an integrated fashion the results of research in my laboratory as it applies to pattern perception. There are a considerable number of perceptual psychologists who feel that the results of brain research are still too crude to help understand the sophisticated issues that define problems in figural perception. At the same time, perceptual psychology texts often rely on incomplete and out-dated findings obtained by neurophysiologists. These lectures review the current state of the art in brain research to show that several lines of inquiry have been converging to produce a paradigm shift (Kuhn, 1962) in our understanding of the neural basis of figural perception.

The second motivation that has produced these lectures is the desire to update the holographic hypothesis of brain function in perception as developed in my laboratory (Barrett, 1969, 1972, 1973a, 1973b, 1973c; Pribram 1966, 1971, 1982b; Pribram, Nuwer, & Baron 1974). The earlier formalisms of the theory have been enriched by new neurophysiological data and by the emergence in the field of artificial intelligence of parallel distributed processing architectures (Rumelhart, McClelland, and the PDP Research Group, 1986). These "neural networks" or "connectionist" models are similar to OCCAM, a content address-able computational model that we (Pribram, 1971; Spinelli, 1970) developed in the late 1960s and stem directly from the content addressable parallel distributed procedures that characterize optical information processing such as holography (see e.g., Hinton, 1979; Willshaw, 1981).

A third motivation for the lectures stems from the desire to emphasize the fact that *both* distributed (holistic) *and* localized (structural) processes characterize brain function. For almost two centuries scientists have squabbled as to whether brain processes are localized (e.g., Broca, 1863; Ferrier, 1886/1978; Gall & Spurtzheim, 1809/1969; Munk, 1881) or distributed (e.g., Flourens, 1846/1978; Lashley, 1942; Walshe, 1948). The facts always have been and still are that both localized and distributed processing takes place in the brain and that it is our job to discern which processes are distributed and which are localized (see e.g., Pribram, 1982b).

A final motivation for these lectures is the desire to portray a neural *systems* analysis of brain organization in figural perception by developing sets of quasi-quantitative models; that is, to describe processing in terms of formalisms found useful in ordering data in 20th-century physical and engineering science. It is my conviction that it is only through the use of these formalisms that the psychological and neurological levels of inquiry regarding perception can become related. The relationship entails sets of transformations which, unless they are described precisely and formally, are apt to be misunderstood by both psychologists and neuroscientists. Chances of misunderstanding are less when communication takes the form of mathematics.

The lectures are divided into three parts. A Prolegomenon outlines a theoretical framework for the presentations; Part I deals with the configural aspects of perception, Part II with its cognitive aspects. There is therefore a considerably different tone to the three sections and the reader must be prepared to "shift gears" from (1) processing theory to (2) perceptions (such as color, form, motion) largely immune from intrusions by what the perceiver has come to know and lastly, to (3) those aspects of perception which entail such knowledge (tableness, flowerness, personness). Critical to understanding is the acceptance of evidence that brain perceptual systems operate as top-down as well as bottom-up processors. It is this evidence that my colleagues and I have spent almost a half century in amassing. Some 1,500 nonhuman primates, 50 graduate students, and an equal number of postdoctoral fellows have participated. The results of these researches have cast doubt on viewing brain perceptual processing as elementaristic, bottom-up, reflex-arc, stimulus-response—views that still characterize many texts in neurophysiology, psychology, and perception.

For the most part, tenets based on these exclusively bottom-up views are held implicitly and therefore felt to be fact rather than theory. Such opinions are thus extremely difficult to modify by only presenting evidence against them. The lectures are therefore composed in terms of an alternative theoretical structure which is presented in the Prolegomenon. This theoretical structure is, however, based on the rich set of data presented in the lectures composing Parts I and II.

There is too much here, and yet not enough. The lectures present a point of view, they review some data ordinarily secluded under the rubrics of memory research or the neurophysiology of attention. Still, many relevant psychophysical experiments and data gathered by studying illusions are barely mentioned. But as I have found no text that explains neural processing in perception in terms of the primate brain as I have come to know it—although bits and pieces of explanation abound—I have written down these lectures. As all authors are, I have been plagued by alternations of mood ranging from exhilaration as the text reflects insights previously barely acknowledged, to despair that these insights will not be shared because of inadequacies in my writing style or lack of an interested audience.

The term for the theory, *holonomic,* was first used by Hertz to describe linear transformations when they are extended into a more encompassing domain. I have here extended its meaning to cover the spectral domain. Holos refers to this domain and Nomos to the naming of the generalization. My greatest trepidation has been caused by the attempt to present the outlines of a formal holonomic theory, a set of models of brain processing in perception. I have, therefore, collaborated with Kunio Yasue and Mari Jibu who became intrigued by the theory and are far more coversant with mathematical modeling than I am. The results of our collaboration make up seven appendices that illustrate facets of the theory.

Clearly neither these mathematical models nor the theory as a whole are in any sense conceived to attempt a "final word" regarding brain processing in figural perception. A story best illustrates the actual purpose of the attempt: At the time of the 3rd neuroscience conference in Boulder, Colorado, Donald Broadbent, Colin Blakemore, Fergus Campbell, and I had climbed high into the Rocky Mountains. Coming to rest on a desolate crag, a long meditative silence was suddenly broken by a query from Campbell: "Karl, do you really believe it's a Fourier?" I hesitated, then replied, "No Fergus, that would be too easy, don't you agree?" Campbell sat silently awhile, then said, "You are right, its probably not that easy. So what are you going to say tomorrow down there?" I replied, this time without hesitation, "That the transform is a Fourier, of course." Campbell smiled and chortled, "Good for you! So am I." We needed no further explanation for our mutually chosen course of action. As scientists we shared Popper's (1962) injunction that scientific propositions need to be falsifiable. And we knew the Fourier relation, because of its relative simplicity, to be the most vulnerable to disproof. Thus far, however, nature has surprised us—she may well be more tractable than we dared hope.

The lectures therefore address those who are deeply interested in understanding how brain processes configure perception. Because of the transdisciplinary nature of the lectures, a number of language systems are inolved in integrating current knowledge: neurophysiological, perceptual, computational, and mathematical. The reader must therefore have the patience to become familiar with what to him is unfamiliar terminology—*Languages of the Brain*, Pribram, 1971 can be of help. As important, is a tolerance for naiveties in descriptions in the disciplines in which the reader is expert: As in parallel distributed processing networks, the tension (error signals) between these naiveties and expertise in each of the disciplines being integrated should improve the models presented in the lectures and therefore our understanding of brain organization in perception.

These lectures are thus but a beginning. The next step is to simulate computationally some of the models composing the theory as outlined mathematically in the Appendix. Insights obtained from the simulations should provoke new directions in brain research and as a consequence sharpen and modify the theory or even replace it with a more comprehensive one. To that end, these lectures are dedicated.

Acknowledgments

No man is an island: My first thanks go to Diane McGuinness without whose penetrating criticism of early drafts of the manuscript and painstaking help with later drafts, this book would certainly fail to communicate. As well, my heartfelt thanks go to Eloise Carlton who accompanied me in all the adventures that led to Part I and initially provided the mathematics necessary to make the theory formally realizable.

Herbert Bauer, Don Doherty and especially Niklas Damiris helped set the tone of the published lectures. They also fed me current articles ranging from quantum physics to neuro- and neurocomputer sciences which considerably sharpened my thinking and consequently the text. Brooke Armstrong, Lauren Gerbrandt, Alastair Harris, William Hudspeth, and Sam Leven contributed in a similar fashion at a later date, especially to Part II. Helga Wild, Helgi-Jon Schweizer, Ivan Blair, and Ray Bradley made the manuscript understandable by their careful attention to the language used and the concepts it represents. Jack Hilgard, Wayne Shebilski, and Brooke Armstrong provided much needed emotional support.

The roots of the ideas presented in these lectures, and therefore my indebtedness, extend deep into this century. Ralph Gerard introduced me to monitoring the electrical responses of the brain to sensory stimulation when as an undergraduate, I attended some of the earliest experiments in which such responses were obtained (Gerard, Marshall, & Saul, 1936). As a medical student I helped record the effects of transecting brain tissue on the transmission of D.C. currents (Gerard & Libet, 1940).

Karl Lashley was, of course, responsible for introducing me, in the course of a decade of close association, to the necessity for the flexibility that comes with distributed processing. He also introduced me to the possibility of cortical interference patterns (Lashley, 1942), a concept central to the theory developed in these lectures. When, therefore, Wolfgang Kohler asked me to record D.C. currents in monkeys and humans during sensory stimulation an opportunity was provided to examine in the laboratory several of Gerard's and Lashley's unorthodox ideas regarding cortical function. The results of these experiments (Kohler & Held, 1949; Stamm & Pribram, 1961) showed perception to be so resistant to disruption of brain electrical organization that repeated efforts toward understanding failed. Despite joint teaching seminars with Walter Miles and Lloyd Beck (where we actually considered a frequency based mechanism for figural perception) and intensive conversations with Jerome Bruner, Warren McCulloch, and Floyd Allport no plausible neurological frame for understanding perception emerged. Nonetheless, Allport's penetrating review of perceptual theory and his ideas on cyclic event structures (Allport, 1955) kept alive my interest in what at the time seemed an unfathomable mystery.

A series of encounters at the University of Alberta's Center for Theoretical Psychology with Karl Metzger and James Gibson sparked my interest in realism and renewed for me the issue of isomorphism which had occupied many evenings with Kohler and Lashley. This interest was pursued further in conferences (see e.g., *Cognition and Symbolic Processes, Vol. 2,* edited by Weimer & Palermo, 1982) with Robert Shaw, Michael Turvey and Walter Weimer as well as with Gibson himself (see Pribram, 1982a).

It took the advent of optical holography in the early 1960s to dispel the mystery for me (Pribram, 1966). Even then, the complex mathematical nature of the explanation posed difficulties: I recall an earlier seminal conversation with Georg von Bekesy where he characterized the explanation as some newfangled mathematics invented by Hilbert which defies understanding. A session with Dennis Gabor—over an excellent dinner and a memorable bottle of Beaujolais—regarding this mathematics while we both attended a UNESCO meeting in Paris produced three napkins full of equations that described a stepwise procedure for attaining a Fourier transformation, a procedure that I later used to describe processing stages from receptor to cortex (Gabor, 1968; see Lecture 4). The Fourier relation per se was not the answer Gabor warned me, as did Donald MacKay, in repeated further discussions on the topic. The warnings were heeded and I gathered groups of investigators of various persuasions to debate the issues at a series of symposia. For instance, William Uttal, Otto Creutzfeld, William Hoffman and I sought common ground at an international psychological congress in Paris in 1976 and thereafter.

The Boulder Neuroscience Conference of 1974 gave Fergus Campbell, Donald Broadbent, Daniel Pollen, and Colin Blakemore and me a unique opportunity to take a close look at "the state of the art." One of my graduate students, Terrence Barrett (1969b, 1972, 1973b&c) had made forays into Gaborian territory, had grappled with the problem of efficient processing and in general had developed the theme of cortical function as interferometry. All of these developments made it possible to openly discuss a radically different view of the perceptual process at a Neuroscience meeting in Minneapolis (1982) where Karen and Russel DeValois, Horace Barlow, David Hubel, and I aired our intuitions and presented the evidence on which they were based. The heat and light provided by these interactions began to mature my earlier formulations.

However, more complete understanding of the warning given by Gabor and MacKay had to await yet another set of circumstances: Frane Marcelja, a computer scientist working in my laboratory shared the enthusiasm generated by the formal presentation of the holographic hypothesis as an explanation for certain facets of perception and memory as put forward by Robert Baron, Marc Nuwer, and myself (Pribram, Nuwer & Baron, 1974). Unbeknownst to me, he transmitted this enthusiasm to his brother, a mathematician at the National University in Canberra, Australia. The mathematician-brother went to see for himself what visual processing entailed by attending experiments in Peter Bishop's excellent vision research laboratory in the same institution. The result was that he realized that a Gabor elementary function better described the cortical process initiated by sensory stimulation than did the Fourier relation (Marcelja, 1980).

Shortly thereafter, Daniel Pollen—who had in the early 1970s come to Stanford for a few months to teach us his techniques for recording Fourier-like visual responses from cells in the visual cortex (Pollen, 1974)—asked me to address his laboratory group at the Barrows Institute in New Mexico. After the lecture he showed me his "sine-cosine" recordings from neighboring cells in a cortical column—and also introduced me to Stepjan Marcelja, the mathematician, who, with his brother the computer scientist, came to visit me at Stanford a week later. If there is an episode that marks the inception of these lectures, it is this visit.

I first presented the ideas generated by these encounters in 1985 at the Center for Interdisciplinary Research (ZIF) of the University of Bielefeld, Germany. I had been invited by a former student, Bruce Bridgeman, to a meeting on the subject of Perception and Action honoring Ivo Kohler. Together with Eloise Carlton, a formal publication in Psychological Research was forged (Pribram and Carlton, 1986). However, the opportunity to fully realize and bring to completion the expression of these ideas, I owe to Terrence Caelli who initiated the invitation to present the MacEachran lectures and provided immeasurable help not only with data from his laboratory but by critically reading drafts of the manuscript. In this vein, I also acknowledge my indebtedness to those who worked behind the scene at the University of Alberta and its center for Theoretical Psychology, to Diane Kohlman, Barabara Smith, and Deborah Akers who typed and typed and typed once more the various revisions of the manuscript, and again to Deborah Akers and to Pierre Bierre and Lawrence Erlbaum and his staff who smoothed the way to publication.

Viewpoint

Before discussing the details of neural processing in perception, it is important to pause for a moment to consider how best to think about and address the contents of our awareness. More fundamental disagreement has plagued this issue than almost any other topic affecting the mind-brain relationship. At one extreme, is the common sense feeling that the contents of perception can be trusted to reliably inform the perceiver about the world in which he navigates—in philosophy this position is called naive or, when bolstered by evidence, direct realism (Gibson, 1979; Shaw, Turvey, & Mace, 1982).

At the other extreme is the feeling that we can never "really" be sure of anything, including the validity of our perceptions—in philosophy this position is called solipsism, or when specified by evidence, autopoiesis. Autopoieses is the view that our perceptual apparatus operates autonomously as a closed system (Maturana, 1969; Varela, 1979).

In between are compromise views and these also range from various materialisms (e.g., Bunge 1980) to phenomenalist, mentalist (e.g., Sperry, 1980; Searle, 1984) and constructional (e.g., Maxwell, 1976; Pribram, 1971) positions. A recent brief review of these issues is given by Epstein (1987).

When intelligent and deeply thoughtful scientists and scholars come to such disparate conclusions it is often fruitful to search for the specific data on which the conclusions are formed. When this is done it can usually be shown that each "position" has intrinsic merit when limited to its data base but becomes untenable when extended beyond these limitations (Pribram 1986a). What remains is the view that brain processes undergo a dynamic matching procedure until there is a correspondence between the brain's microprocesses and those in the sensory input.

The current lectures review evidence which indicates that the sensory aspects of perception entail brain processes separable from those involving the cognitive aspects. Realism fits the data that deal with sensory driven aspects of percepts; constructivism characterizes cognitively driven processes. Ordinarily the cognitive operations (noumena) operate back onto those (phenomena) that are sensory driven: Kant (1965 edition) was not far off in his constructional realism.

Within the province of realism a critical issue surfaces with regard to how the sensory array, the input to receptors, becomes processed. The difficulty arises in an attempt to specify how the input to the senses is related to receptor processing. In figural vision the issue comes center stage when scientists try to specify the nature of a "retinal image."

Many difficulties are resolved by focusing on the single fact that everyone agrees to: when a diffracting object is placed in the front focal plane of the optical apparatus (pupil, and converging lens), a Fourier transform exactly describes the optical "image" at the back focal plane within the eye (e.g., Taylor, 1978, p. 37). Thus the optical apparatus (especially the lens) operates as a phase adjuster integrating interference patterns among wave forms (due to diffraction) into an optical image. As discussed in detail in Lecture 3, taking this anchor of agreement as a starting point allows the concept of a retinal image to be separated into an "optical image" or "flow" and a "retinal process." From this beginning, clearcut differences can be readily identified in the organization of optic array, optical flow, and retinal process.

Taking the transformation performed by the sensory apparatus—the lens in the case of vision—as a starting point for the analysis of perception and other psychological functions is not new. Egon Brunswick (1966) based his probabilistic functionalism on what he called a "lens model." Patterns of energy become "scattered" in the environment and the sensory receptors "recombine" the scatter:

> The . . . strategy of the organism is predicated upon the limited ecological validity or trustworthiness of cues. . . . This forces a probabilistic strategy. . . . To improve its bet, it must accumulate and combine cues . . . Hence the lens . . . model . . . may be taken to represent the basic unit of psychological functioning. (1966, p.37)

As indicated by the vague wording "limited ecological validity or trustworthiness of cues," Brunswick did not have available the evidence presented in these lectures to analyze in depth the various sensory and neural systems and microprocesses that comprise his "lens-like" operation. Nor did he have available the ecological analyses in depth of the environmental patterns reaching the senses performed by Gibson, Johannsen, Cutting, Turvey, and Shaw. Moreover there was no formal theory available to relate these domains. However, Brunswick was a staunch advocate of such explorations into the more remote causal interrelations among layers of variables composing "manifolds" both external to and within the organism.

A good place to begin the study of these interrelations is Gibson's suggestion that we consider brain processes to resonate to the patterns that stimulate the senses, a suggestion in keeping with the harmonic analyses undertaken in the holonomic brain theory presented in these lectures. As will be detailed, taking Gibson's suggestion seriously commits one to realism. But the commitment entails accepting the full implication of the ecological, "layered," approach to perception by including the layers of brain processes largely ignored by Gibson.

REALISM

There are, therefore, areas of close agreement between Gibson's ecological approach and that taken in the holonomic brain theory. For example, Shaw, Turvey, and Mace indicate the broad implications of taking a realist stance:

> What are the major conceptual barriers to a successful realism? . . . [It is] the assumption . . . [(a)] that the mapping of distal object properties onto proximal stimulus properties is destructive; [(b) that] the structuring of the light by the laws of reflection does not preserve the structure of the environment. On this assumed failure of the proximal stimulus to specify the distal object, it is a simple matter to generate skepticism about an animal's knowledge of what is real. Given the non-specificity assumption, perception must be a matter of making propositions (about what the proximal stimulus stands for) with neither a guarentee of their truth nor any apparent way to determine their truth.
>
> A second related barrier to realism is raised by the mind-body subtheme of animal-environment dualism. It is the promotion of . . . two different and irreducible languages. . . . skepticism arises about the animal's ability to perceive what is real, because the perception of reality depends on . . . the physical and the mental being coordinated. It has seemed in the past a relatively trivial matter to show slippage between the object of reference and the object of experience.
>
> Animal-environment dualism thwarts realism in another, though more subtle, way: It invites a science of psychology largely separate from a science of physics and vice versa . . . Realism is hamstrung to the extent that the sciences hold distinct the knower and that which is known.
>
> Consider, however, a program of theory and research committed to realism. . . . Such a program would have to seek a definition of reality that would be animal-relative, but no less real for being so. (Shaw, Turvey, & Mace, 1982, pp. 160–161)

Taking the stance implied by realism ("a program of theory and research committed to realism") is akin to an act of faith: The initial sensory experiences of infants are disparate; even as adults, introspection yields perceptions differing in kind according to the sense involved. When we identify what we hear, see, and touch as referring to the "same" event, we resort to consensual validation. In humans this procedure is repeated when we identify "a red winged black bird," as the "same" object with the "same" attributes referred to by someone else. One makes a pragmatic existential choice early on, either to distrust the process of consensual validation and retreat into soipsism, or to trust and embrace a realist philosophy, and act accordingly.

Ecological psychology and the holonomic brain theory are both eminently compatible with a realist position. However, to state simply that perception is "direct" skips over several steps in the perceptual process that cannot be ignored.

One *must* confront the fact that the senses are stimulated by patterns of energy perceived as "light," "sound," and "touch" which do not have the same configural properties as do the objects with which they interface. This, however, does not mean that these patterns are composed of elements. Rather, a different process is at work: The configural properties that define objects become distributed and enfolded in the process of interfacing. They are thus *transformed* into an order which, as in a hologram, is recognizably different from the perceived configuration of objects but which, in some non-trivial sense, "contains" those configurations. More on this in Lecture 3.

COMPUTATION AND REPRESENTATION

Given the transformational aspect of the realist stance, the next issue that needs to be discussed concerns the nature of cognitive influences on percepts. This topic is best addressed under the heading "representations." Representation literally implies hierarchical levels of processing in which what is processed becomes "re-presented" at another level. A level or *scale* of processing can be defined as a presentation, a description of an *entity* that is simpler than if it were made in terms of the collection of constituents of that scale or level. Thus the entity at each level can be characterized by a description that is a presentation. Components are described in some different fashion than the entity as a whole. Furthermore, there would be no need for a presentation of the entity as a whole were it not in some basic sense, simpler, that is, more efficient in processing than that available to the components (see e.g., Pribram, 1971, chapters 4 & 13). For example, bytes are more efficient in use than the equivalent description in bits. A presentation of a program in Fortran is much more efficient than a presentation of the successive switch settings that form the hardware equivalent of the program. The question is whether psychological processes can, in the same manner, be considered to be re-presentations of functions of the brain.

In the sense of hierarchical levels of presentation, the analogy between computer software (programs) and hardware serves well. The psychological, mental level is described in presentations that are analogous to presentations at the program level. The "wetware" of the brain can be thought of as analogous to the hardware of the computer (Miller, Galanter, & Pribram, 1960; Pribram, 1986a). There is an equivalence between program and successive hardware switch settings. Can we say therefore that in some real sense the switch settings are represented in the program? If this is so, then in the same sense psychological processes re-present brain function.

This leads to a most tantalizing question: To what extent are the re-presented entities configured in a fashion similar to the entities they re-present? In other words, to what extent are presentation and re-presentation isomorphic to one another? The answer to this question obviously depends on reaching some consensus on the definition of isomorphic. Processes that map into each other in such a way as to preserve structure can be said to be either geometrically or algebraically isomorphic. For instance, although the Gestalt psychologists thought that the electrical fields of the brain have a geometric *shape* resembling that of perceived objects, evidence shows that perspective transformations display algebraic (i.e., secondary) not geometric isomorphism (Shepard & Chipman, 1970).

Isomorphism is a non-trivial problem when one assesses the nature of brain representations. Wolfgang Köhler (1964) attempted to show that the geometry of cortical electrical activity conforms not only to the geometry of the physical events that produce sensory stimulation but to the perceptions experienced by the organism. This line of reasoning suggested that brain representations literally "picture" the significant environment of the organism or at least caricature it. Experiments by Lashley (Lashley, Chow, & Semmes, 1951), Sperry (Sperry, Miner, & Meyers, 1955) and Pribram (reviewed in 1971) created a severe disturbance of the geometry of cortical electrical activity without disrupting behavior dependent on perception. Thus, geometric isomorphism between the gross aspects of brain electrical activity and perception has been ruled out.

By contrast, the computer program-hardware analogy suggests that significant *transformations* can occur between levels of presentation: indeed that the utility of re-presentations is derived from these transformations. According to the holonomic brain theory developed here, algebraically linear isomorphic (i.e., isoformal), nonlinear or paralinear transformational processing characterize the relations among brain representations. The computer analogy helped make understandable the results of neuropsychological research which showed that the search for "pictures" in the brain (e.g., Kohler's D.C. potentials, Kohler & Held, 1949) was misplaced. Understanding comes when the neurophysiologist searches for algorithms, such as computable transforms of sensory input.

In the same vein, Gibson (1966), and Shaw, Turvey, & Mace (1982), among others, have proposed that as the organism becomes attuned to its environment, the relationship between the two is one of "complementation," not representation. Thus, musical instruments "complement" the fingers of the hand, yet piano keyboards, violin strings, and clarinet stops have completely different configurations. Complements share common procedures, common functions, and there has been considerable debate (see Vol. 3, No. 1; 1980 of the *Behavioral and Brain Sciences* especially Fodor, pp. 63–110) as to whether the modeling of psychological processes should be complementary and functional (computational and procedural) or structural (representational).

The holonomic brain theory defines its formalism in terms of *transformational* procedures that specify the relationships among complements—presentations—*and* between re-presentations of these presentations. For instance, neuroscientists talk of the "representation" of the spatial ordering of receptors and effectors in the ordering of cortical inputs and outputs—this, despite considerable distortion.

Furthermore, there is good evidence from the work of Sokolov (1963) that brain events "model" sensory input patterns. When a sensory input recurs repeatedly, an organism habituates, that is, fails to react overtly to that input. Sokolov found that when he omitted a stimulus in a regularly recurring series, the organism dishabituates; an orienting reaction occurs. Similarly, if suddenly a signal of reduced intensity is presented within a series of signals of greater intensity, an orienting reaction marks the reduced signal. There must be some enduring brain process that is produced by an input if subsequent variations of that input are "sensed" (although this does not mean that the geometries of input and brain process are isomorphic). Reducing or omitting a signal produces a mismatch, which results in an orienting reaction. During habituation a "neuronal model," a "representation" of the input appears to be constructed and subsequent inputs are matched to this representation. More on this in Lecture 8.

Still, the representation need not be an immutable structure. Rather, re-presentation must be a process, the re-construction of a presentation. (For a sophisticated analysis of what is involved, see Hochberg, 1984). The issue can perhaps be grasped most readily by focusing on memory. Is memory structural in the sense that one may find in the brain an isomorphic form or figure corresponding to a subjectively remembered experience, or is such a "memory" the result of processing neural events stored in some other form? By using primes and probes, Fergus Craik in an elegant program of experiments (Craik, 1988), has shown that disturbances in remembering are almost always due to interference with process and not with a loss of stored items. Neuropsychological evidence (e.g., Pribram, 1986b; Weiskrantz, 1986) has also repeatedly demonstrated that "engrams" are not "lost" as such as a result of brain damage. Rather engrams are reconstructions that can appear as intrusion errors when amnesics are examined in a systematic fashion: that is, during recall, reconstruction of an engram occurs but in an inappropriate context.

The holonomic brain theory thus holds that the "deep structure" of memory (in Chomsky's 1965 sense which distinguishes deep from surface structure) is distributed, as in current image processing and PDP neural network computational models; that this distributed, dismembered store must be re-membered, assembled into an experienced "memory" by a content-addressable process. The process can be triggered internally or from a sensory input. In short, re-membering is a process that depends on *transforming* a deep structure, a dis-membered re-presentation, which is holonomically organized and thus of a form different from either the experienced memory or the sensory array that originated the process.

Formally, in terms of the holonomic brain theory developed in these lectures, the re-presentation occurs as a dynamical transformation in a distributed network of dendritic microprocesses. Smolensky captures the essence of this formalism as follows:

> The concept of memory retrieval is reformalized in terms of the continuous evolution of a dynamical system towards a point attractor whose position in the state space is the memory; you naturally get dynamics of the system so that its attractors are located where the memories are supposed to be; thus the principles of memory storage are even more unlike their symbolic counterparts than those of memory retrieval.

It is these dynamical transformations, these *transfer functions,* that critically distinguish current theories (including the holonomic brain theory) from earlier formalisms such as those of General Systems Theory.

Thus, the holonomic brain theory incorporates "representations" not as pictorial forms but as self-maintaining structures that act somewhat like the setpoints of thermostats. These setpoints serve as "attractors" in more or less temporary stable configurations which are subject to continuous adaptive change. Holoscapes defined in Lecture 2—mapping of isopotential dendritic polarizations—are such configurations. Physiology is replete with examples of self-maintaining structures: the skin remains "the same" despite constantly shedding cells which are replaced with new ones; red blood cells last only a month, yet the red blood cell count remains stable. You as a person, a structure, are recognizable over the years despite the fact that every cell in your skin, hair, and so forth has probably been repeatedly exchanged during the period of observation. Certainly every molecule in your body has been exchanged several times. This self-maintenance of structure is often called self-organization, autopoiesis (Maturana, 1969; Varela, 1979) because the organizing propensity generates the organization since it is genetically specified.

According to the views expressed in these lectures, structure and process are distinguished more by the level or scale of observation than by any intrinsic difference. At the seashore, breakers are processes; they exert considerable force, can move objects, and upset bodies. When viewed from 10,000 feet these same breakers appear as standing waves, a structure that delimits and represents the boundary between open sea and land.

In the holonomic brain theory, when viewed closely the "representations" that are coordinate with perceptions (or memories) are composed of fluctuating polarizations within the dendritic network—probablility amplitude modulated Fourier coefficients. At close range they, like the seashore at hand, are seething with activity that, however, exhibits structure (coordinate with images, objects, etc.) when viewed from the distance of sentient observation.

IN SUMMARY

The holonomic brain theory espouses a *transformational* and *constructional* realism and thus goes beyond the direct realism proposed by Gibson in specifying the ecological details of the sensory and brain processes involved in perceiving. Specification devolves on recognizing *transformations* that occur between *bottom-up levels* among brain systems. *Top-down* influences on processing procedures provide *structural constraints* on processing. That is what these lectures are about.

PROLEGOMENON

Before the connection of thought and brain can be explained, it must be stated in elementary form; and there are great difficulties about stating it. . . . Many would find relief at this point in celebrating the mystery of the unknowable and the "awe" which we should feel. . . . It may be constitutional infirmity, but I can take no comfort in such devices for making a luxury of intellectual defeat. . . . Better live on the ragged edge, better gnaw the file forever! (William James, 1950, pp. 177–179)

. . . it is entirely possible that we may learn about the operations of thinking by studying perception. (Irvin Rock, 1983, p. 1)

1 Aims and Origins

There is good evidence for the age-old belief that the brain has something to do with. . . mind. Or, to use less dualistic terms, when behavioral phenomena are carved at their joints, there will be some sense in which the analysis will correspond to the way the brain is put together. . . . In any case each time there is a new idea in psychology, it suggests a corresponding insight in neurophysiology, and vice versa. The procedure of looking back and forth between the two fields is not only ancient and honorable—it is always fun and occasionally useful (Miller, Galanter, & Pribram, 1960, p. 196)

AN INTRODUCTION

The explosion of data in the behavioral and neural sciences has made the study of the correspondence between the way the brain is put together and the carving behavioral phenomena at their joints even more intriguing and rewarding than when the introductory quotation was written. Exploring the way the brain is put together provides insights into how experience becomes processed. When the evidence from the brain sciences is ignored, the experiential phenomena guiding behavior are found to be so richly structured, and carving can proceed in such a multitude of ways, that the result has often been a purely descriptive phenotypical science in which descriptions constitute a tower of Babel. This is especially true of perception, which of necessity must come to grips with the simultaneity, subjectivity, and relative privacy of what is being experienced.

By contrast, as developed in these lectures, a neural systems analysis of the brain-behavior relationship, which takes into account processing levels, allows

1

the perceptual experience to be analyzed into basic functional modules that are at the same time separable and interpenetrating.

However, care needs to be maintained when identifying the functions of separate neural systems. It seems deceptively easy, but is inadmissable to completely identify neural system function with behavioral system function. The mistake of slipping into a category error plagues all of physiology. The function of the lungs is readily identified as respiration; but respiratory functions include those of red blood cells and the membrane exchange of O_2 and CO_2, as well as the lung's inspiratory/expiratory cycles that make the other aspects of respiration possible. The models that describe inspiration/expiration by the lungs are considerably different from those describing oxygen transport by the hemoglobin of red blood cells.

The issues are the same when it comes to relating the physiology of receptors and the nervous system to behavioral functions including those reported as perceptions. Perception entails the functions of receptors, primary sensory receiving stations, and those brain systems associated with them. There can be no simple model of "perception" or even "pattern recognition," any more than there can be a simple model of "respiration."

In the current lectures these issues are handled in two ways: (a) An attempt is made to sharply distinguish models based on observations made at the behavioral level of psychophysics and perception from those at the neural systems, neuronal and subneuronal levels. The distinction is implemented according to whether models describe *what* is being processed or whether they describe *how* processing is carried out by the nervous system; and (b) whenever possible, transformations, transfer functions, are described that relate the models at different levels to one another. It is the specification of these transfer functions that distinguishes current from earlier mathematical and general systems approaches. The nature of the transfer functions is adduced from data obtained in neuropsychological observations in which both the brain and the situational variables controlling the behavioral reports of perceptual experience are specified.

NEURAL SYSTEMS

When the neurophysiology of perception is considered, a set of processes emerges, each served by a separate neural system. These systems are shown to act in concert with other neural systems anatomically and/or biochemically related to them. Three major divisions can be discerned (see Fig. 1.1) in the sets of primate brain systems relevant to perception. The division is made on the basis of sense modality. In the posterior convexity of the cerebrum, processing is anchored in visual and auditory inputs ("distance" processing); in the frontolimbic forebrain, processing is anchored in olfactory/gustatory and in pain/temperature stimulation (thermochemical processing); midway, surrounding the central

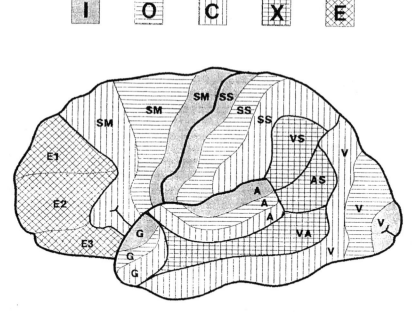

FIG. 1.1. Systems of cerebral structures which are coordinate with cognitive functions. The hierarchical organization is arranged in a top-down manner and designated by the indicated textures for: Executive (E), Cross-Modal (X), Cognitive (C), Object (O) and Image (I) functions. The image, object and cognitive functions apply to the sensory and motor processes such as Vision (V), Audition (A), Gustation (G), and the Somatic divisions. The Somatic division is partitioned into predominantly Motor (SM) and Somaesthetic (SS) compartments. Intrinsic cross-modal processes are represented by regions within which the principle sensory systems interact: Visuospatial (VS), Visuoauditory (VA) and Acousticosomatic (AS). The frontal executive functions are interconnected to other systems so that they can be regulated by Priorities (E1), Practicalities (E2) and Proprieties (E3). From: Hudspeth, W. J. and Pribram, K. H. (1990).

(Rolandic) fissure, processing is anchored in somatic sensibilities that allow the organism to be in proximate *touch* with the environment and, even more important, to directly *act* on, and thus alter it.

Within each division, there is a core of projection systems connected extrinsically, rather directly, with the receptors of the modality: these systems provide for sensory imaging. Surrounding these projection systems are perisensory systems that process the input by controlling movements related to that input: it is these systems that allow figure to be extracted from ground. Beyond these systems are others intrinsic in their connections, that is, they primarily receive their input from and operate back on the sensory-motor systems. The intrinsically connected systems themselves are hierarchically organized: One set of intrinsic systems is sensory-mode specific, extracting invariants from iterated images to produce object-forms. Another, still sensory-mode specific, makes categoriza-

3

tions possible. Yet another is involved in setting up computational spaces which relate processing in various sensory modes to one another. Finally, in humans, systems entailing language have developed as another intrinsically connected complex.

As reviewed in the body of these lectures, the systems responsible for extracting the invariances (constancies) that characterize object-forms, interpenetrate in a top-down, corticofugal fashion, those systems responsible for imaging. This top-down interpenetration is implemented by parallel connections. Such connections, now at a new level in the hierarchy, are found again when systems responsible for stimulus sampling and categorizing are considered, and once more when the systems concerned with relevance and inference are studied. Each level entails both feedforward and feedback operations: thus, the paradox of the separable yet unitary nature of the perceptual experience can be accounted for.

This characterization of the relations between brain systems differs from the traditional view that has been limited to bottom-up, forward propagation from sensory projections to higher order "associative" systems. In the nineteenth century, Flechsig (1900) had suggested that cognitions are derived exclusively by a process in which input from various senses becomes associated in the cortex of the posterior cerebral convexity—thus the term *association cortex*. Flechsig's view is still widely held despite overwhelming evidence (reviewed in Lecture 7) against it. (See e.g., Kuffler and Nichols, 1976; Luria, 1973; Mishkin, 1973; Shepherd, 1988).

As noted, in the alternative view the results of computation at the later level of processing are fed back to the earlier levels. These lectures are based on evidence for such *reciprocal* connectivity between hierarchically ordered neural systems, by means of which processing leads to a *selection* procedure in which input is matched against a resident microstructure (genetically or experientially produced memory). The result of the match acts like a set point on a thermostat (or homeostat) to *instruct* further processing. Of course the set point is not a point or single number as it is on a thermostat; rather, it is a set of "attractors" developed in a multidimensional complex, a temporary stable state, (Prigogine & Stengers, 1984) often referred to as an Image (e.g., a "motor image"). At the same time, the details of processing need not be specified in the match, a great savings in memory storage. Von Foerster (1965) described such operations as providing memory without record. Nonetheless, memory storage is involved, but it consists more of refining Images (Gibson & Gibson, 1955) than of detailing procedures.

In such a reciprocally acting set of systems, input *triggers* an operation that at any moment is largely self-determining. Further, the larger the amount of experience stored in the systems operating in a top-down fashion, the greater the self-determination. Thus Beethoven could compose the late quartets and the Eighth and Ninth Symphonies despite the fact that he was completely deaf at the time of composition.

In short, in systems characterized by bottom-up, top-down reciprocity, selection characterizes a microprocess in which sensory and central inputs are matched with a resident microstructure. The results of the match instruct and direct further processing. In systems endowed with memory storage, these interactions therefore lead to progessively more self-determination. Momentary input serves to trigger rather than specify the process.

NEURONS

Neurons are ordinarily conceived to be the computational units of the brain. Thus the majority of processing theories since the seminal contribution of McCulloch and Pitts (1943) have taken the axonal discharge of the neuron, the nerve impulse, as the currency of computation.

However, this framework for computational theory has led to considerable misunderstanding between neuroscientists and those interested in computational processing. Successful computational networks depend on highly—often randomly—interconnected elements. The more complex the computation, the more connections are needed: the law of requisite variety (Ashby, 1960). Neuroscientists know that neurons are connected nonrandomly, often sparsely, and always in a specifically configured fashion (see Crick & Asanuma, 1986, for a neuroscience view of connectionist computational theory). In short, current computational processing emphasizes a minimum of constraints in the processing wetware or hardware; in the current neuroscience framework wetware is highly constrained.

Misunderstanding is alleviated when the computational framework is broadened to include the microprocessing that takes place within dendritic networks. Not only are axonal-dendritic synapses that connect neurons subject to local influences in these networks, but innumerable local circuit operations provide the unconstrained high connectivity needed in computational procedures (Bishop, 1956; Pribram, 1960, 1971; Schmitt, Dev, & Smith, 1976). Local circuit neurons are found in many locations in the sensory and central nervous system (see Table, p. 9, in Shepard, 1981). The processing capability of such neurons (primarily inhibitory) is often dendro-dendritic. (See e.g., Rakic, 1976; Sloper, 1971.)

Junctions (axodendritic and dendo-dendritic) between neurons in the form of chemical synapses and electrical gap junctions occur within overlapping dendritic arborizations (Fig 1.2). These junctions provide the possibility for processing as opposed to the mere transmission of signals. The term neurotransmitters applied to chemicals acting at junctions is, therefore, somewhat misleading. Terms such as neuroregulator and neuromodulator convey more of the meaning of what actually transpires at synapses.

Nerve impulse conduction leads everywhere in the central nervous system to such junctional dendritic microprocessing. When nerve impulses arrive at syn-

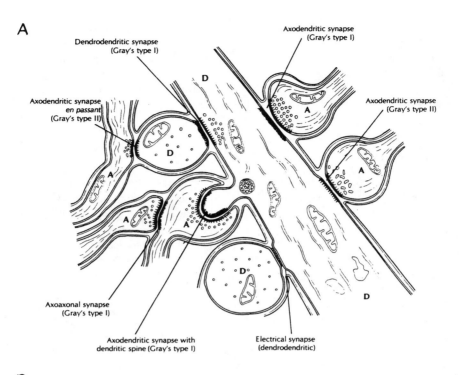

A

Dendrodendritic synapse
(Gray's type I)

Axodendritic synapse
(Gray's type I)

Axodendritic synapse
en passant
(Gray's type II)

Axodendritic synapse
(Gray's type II)

D

A

D

A

A

A

D

A

A

D

D

Axoaxonal synapse
(Gray's type I)

Axodendritic synapse with
dendritic spine (Gray's type I)

Electrical synapse
(dendrodendritic)

B

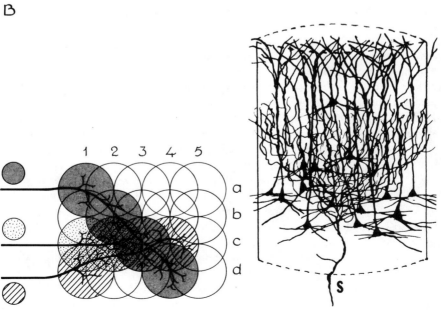

1 2 3 4 5

a
b
c
d

S

6

apses, presynaptic polarizations result. These are never solitary but constitute arrival patterns. The patterns are constituted of sinusoidally fluctuating hyper- and depolarizations which are insufficiently large to immediately incite nerve impulse discharge. The delay affords opportunity for computational complexity.

The dendritic microprocess thus provides the relatively unconstrained computational power of the brain, especially when arranged in layers as in the cortex. As developed in the next lecture, this computational power can be described by linear dynamic processes, in terms of quantum field neurodynamics.

Neurons (Fig. 1.3) are thresholding devices that spatially and temporally segment the results of the dendritic microprocess into discrete packets for communication and control of other levels of processing. These packets are more resistant to degradation and interference than the graded microprocess. They constitute the channels of communication not the processing element.

Communication via neurons often consists of dividing a message into chunks, labelling the chunks so that they are identifiable, transmitting the chunked message, and reassembling it at its destination. Neurons are labelled by their location in the network. This form of labelling is highly efficient because of the essentially parallel nature of neuronal connectivities.

Neuronal channels constrain the basic linear microprocess. These structural constraints can be topologically parallel, convergent, and divergent. An instance of a combination of these forms of constraint is the connectivity between retina and cerebral cortex, which is expressed as a logarithmic function of distance from the foveal center. Other constraints shape the time course of computations and lead to learning. Unveiling the manner in which constraints are imposed in the natural brain is the work of the neurophysiologist. Much of what is contained in these lectures describes the results of this work.

DENDRITIC MICROPROCESSING

Recognizing the importance of dendritic microprocessing allows a coherent theory to be framed regarding the neural functions responsible for perception. As Pribram (1971) initially stated in *Languages of the Brain*:

> Any model we make of perceptual processes must thus take into account both the importance of Imaging, a process that contributes a portion of man's subjective

---

FIG. 1.2A.   Ultrastructure of various types of synapse. (A) Axons. (D) Dendrites. From: Barr, M. L. & Kiernan, J. A. (1983). *The Human Nervous System,* Fourth Edition. Philadelphia, PA: Harper & Row.
FIG. 1.2B.   Diagram of microstructure of synaptic domains in cortex. The ensemble of overlapping circles represents the junctions between branches of input axons and cortical dendrites. Redrawn after Scheibel and Scheibel in Chow and Leiman, 1970. From Pribram, 1971.

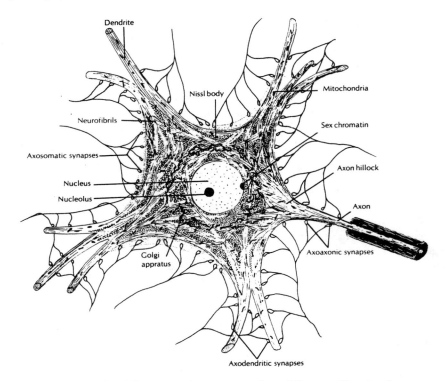

FIG. 1.3.   Semidiagrammatic representation of the constituents of a nerve cell. From: Barr, M. L. & Kiernan, J. A. (1983). *The Human Nervous System,* Fourth Edition. Philadelphia, PA: Harper & Row.

experience, and the fact that there are influences on behavior of which we are not aware. Instrumental behavior and awareness are often opposed—the more efficient a performance, the less aware we become. Sherrington noted this antagonism in a succinct statement: "Between reflex action and mind there seems to be actual opposition. Reflex action and mind seem almost mutually exclusive—the more reflex the reflex, the less does mind accompany it." (p. 104)

Languages then proceeds to detail the fact that nerve impulses in axons and junctional microprocessing in dendrites function reciprocally. An hypothesis was formulated to the effect that when habit and habituation characterize behavior that has become automatic, there is efficient processing of dendritic "arrival patterns into departure patterns." On the other hand, persisting designs of junctional patterns are assumed to be coordinate with awareness. The hypothesis is consonant with the view that we are cognizant of some, but not all of the events going on in the brain.

Nerve impulses arriving at junctions generate dendritic microprocesses. The design of these microprocesses interacts with that which is already present by virtue of the spontaneous activity of the nervous system and its previous experience. The interaction is modulated by inhibitory processes and the whole procedure accounts for the computational power of the brain. The dendritic microprocesses act as a "cross-correlation device to produce new figures from which the patterns of departure of axonic nerve impulses are initiated. The rapidly paced changes in awareness could well reflect the [pace of] duration of the correlation process." (Pribram, 1971).

Historically the issues were framed by Lashley, Kohler, and Hebb. Donald Hebb (1949) summed up the problem by pointing out that one must decide whether perception is to depend on the excitation of *specific cells*, or on a *pattern of excitation* whose locus is unimportant. Hebb chose the former alternative: "A particular perception depends on the excitation of *particular cells at some point* in the central nervous system."

As neurophysiological evidence accumulated (especially through the microelectrode experiments of Jung (1961); Mountcastle (1957); Maturana, Lettvin, McCulloch, and Pitts (1960); and Hubel and Wiesel (1962) this choice, for a time, appeared vindicated: Microelectrode studies identified neural units responsive to one or another feature of a stimulating event such as directionality of movement, tilt of line, and so forth. Today, textbooks in psychology, in neurophysiology, and even in perception, reflect this view that one percept corresponds to the excitation of one particular group of cells at some point in the nervous system.

Profoundly troubled by the problem, Lashley (1942) took the opposite stance:

> Here is the dilemma. Nerve impulses are transmitted over definite, restricted paths in the sensory and motor nerves and in the central nervous system from cell to cell through definite inter-cellular connections. Yet all behavior seems to be determined by masses of excitation, by the form or relations or proportions of excitation within general fields of activity, without regard to particular nerve cells. It is the pattern and not the element that counts. What sort of nervous organization might be capable of responding to a pattern of excitation without limited, specialized paths of conduction? The problem is almost universal in the activities of the nervous system and some hypothesis is needed to direct further research. (p. 306)

Wolfgang Kohler also based his Gestalt arguments on such "masses of excitation. . . within generalized fields of activity" and went on to prove their ubiquitous existence in the decade after the publication of Hebb's and Lashley's statements. A series of experiments in which I was involved established the existence of generalized fields but showed that, although they were related to the speed with which learning took place, they were unrelated to perception as tested by discrimination tasks (see *Languages of the Brain*, chap. 6, for a review of these studies).

Lashley was never satisfied with either Hebb's or Kohler's position. His alternative was an interference pattern model which he felt would account for perceptual phenomena more adequately than either a DC field or a cell assembly approach. He did not, however, have a clear idea of how the process might work. He never specified the fact that the interference patterns were generated by arrivals of nerve impulses nor how such patterns provide a computational scheme for perception. Thus he never developed an argument for the existence of a dendritic microprocess responsible for the computational power of the neuronal mechanism.

According to the views presented here and in keeping with Lashley's intuitions, this computational power is not a function of the "particular cells" and the conducting aspects of the nervous system (the axonal nerve impulses), nor is it necessarily carried out within the province of single neurons. At the same time, the theory based on these views does not support the notion that the locus of processing is indeterminate. Rather the locus of processing is firmly rooted *within regions of dendritic networks* at the junctions between neurons.

As summarized by Szentagothai (1985, p. 40):

> The simple laws of histodynamically polarized neurons . . . indicating the direction of flow of excitation . . . came to an end when unfamiliar types of synapses between dendrites, cell bodies and dendrites, serial synapses etc. were found in infinite variety. . . . A whole new world of microcircuitry became known. . . culminating in a new generalized concept of local neuron circuits (Rakic, 1976; Schmitt et al., 1976).

The ubiquity of such local circuit neurons indicates that computation is strongly influenced by local circuit interactions that modify the postaxonal dendritic processes. Perceptual processing depends therefore on network properties that extend beyond the purview of the dendrites of a single neuron. It is the synaptic event, rather than the neuron per se, that serves as the computational element.

The sub- and superneuronal aspect of the dendritic microprocess, its potential to extend beyond the single neuron, provides explanatory power for both older and recently accumulating evidence that brain processes coordinate with perception are *distributed*. This evidence is reviewed in lectures 2 and 4. In a distributed process, perceptual events are represented not by single neurons but by *patterns of polarization* across ensembles of synapses.

On the basis of their extensive studies Thatcher & John, (reviewed in 1977) came to a similar conclusion:

> The spatiotemporal patterning of these cooperative processes . . . [involve] ionic shifts . . . with extrusion of potassium ions and ionic binding on extracellular mucopolysaccharide filaments. If we focus our attention not on the membranes of single neurons, but upon charge density distributions in the tissue matrix of neurons, glial cells, and mucopolysaccharide processes, we can envisage a complex,

three-dimensional volume of isopotential contours, topologically comprised of portions of cellular membranes and extracellular binding sites and constantly changing
over time. Let us call this volume of isopotential contours or convoluted surfaces a
hyperneuron. (pp. 305–306)

Basic to this new view of the neurology of perception is the fact that propagated nerve impulses are but one of the important electrical characteristics of neural
tissue. The other characteristic is the microprocess that takes place at the junctions between neurons. Hyper- and depolarizations of postsynaptic dendritic
membranes occur at the junctions between neurons where they may even produce
miniature electrical spikes. However, these minispikes and graded polarizations
also differ from axonal nerve impulses in that they do not propagate. As discussed in Lecture 4, the influence of these minispikes and graded polarizations
on further neuronal activity is by way of *cooperativity* among spatially separated
events. Cooperativity is mediated by the cable properties of dendrites and the
surrounding glia (see e.g., Poggio & Torre, 1980) This type of interaction is
called nonlocal because the effect is exerted at a distance without any obvious
intervening propagation. By analogy the effect is also called *jumping* or *saltatory*
as in saltatory conduction by myelinated nerve fibers. It is this saltatory nature of
the interactions as captured by perceptual experiences that fascinated Frank
Geldard, experiences so clearly described in his inaugural MacEachran Memorial Lecture (1975).

RECEPTIVE FIELDS

The neurophysiologist can readily study the output—spike trains—of neurons
when they act as channels, but he has only limited access to the functions of the
interactive dendritic junctional architecture because of the small scale at which the
processes proceed. A major breakthrough toward understanding was achieved,
however, when Kuffler (1953) noted that he could *map* the functional dendritic
field of a retinal ganglion cell by recording impulses from the ganglion cell's axon
located in the optic nerve. This was accomplished by moving a spot of light in front
of a paralyzed eye and recording the locations of the spot that produced a response
in the axon. The locations mapped the extent of the responding dendritic field of
that axon's parent neuron. The direction of response, inhibitory or excitatory, at
each location indicated whether the dendrites at that location were hyperpolarizing
or depolarizing.

The resulting maps of dendritic hyper- and depolarization are called *receptive
fields*. The receptive fields of retinal ganglion cells are configured concentrically:
a circular inhibitory or excitatory center surrounded by a penumbra of opposite
sign. This center-surround organization has been shown to be due to the operation of horizontally arranged dendritically endowed neurons that produce "later-

al" inhibition in the neighborhood of excitation and vice versa. The center-surround organization thus reflects the formation of a spatial dipole of hyper- and depolarization, an opponent process fundamental to the organization of the configural properties of vision.

Utilizing Kuffler's techniques of mapping, Hubel and Wiesel (1959) discovered that at the cerebral cortex the circular organization of dendritic hyper- and depolarization gives way to elongated receptive fields with definite and various orientations. They noted that oriented lines of light rather than spots produced the best response recorded from the axons of these cortical neurons. They therefore concluded that these cortical neurons were "line detectors." In keeping with the tenets of Euclidean geometry where lines are made up of points, planes by lines and solids by planes, Hubel and Wiesel suggested that line detectors were composed by convergence of inputs from neurons at earlier stages of visual processing (retinal and thalamic—which acted as spot-detectors due to the circular center-surround organization of the receptive fields.)

The Euclidean interpretation of neuronal processing in perception became what Barlow (1972) has called the neurophysiological dogma. The interpretation led to a search for convergences of paths from "feature detectors" such as those responding to lines, culminating in "pontifical" or "grandfather" cells that embodied the response to object-forms such as faces and hands. The search was in some instances rewarded in that single neurons might respond *best* to a particular

FIG. 1.4. Two dimensional map of points on the retina at which a light spot produces responding in a particular lateral geniculate cell in the brain of a monkey. After Spinelli and Pribram, 1967.

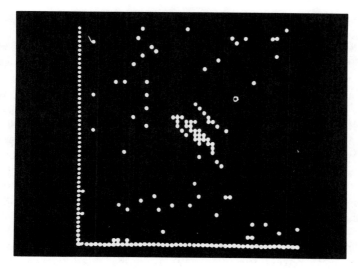

FIG. 1.5. Two dimensional map in the visual field at which a light spot produces responding in a particular striate cortex cell in the brain of a monkey. After Spinelli and Pribram, 1967.

object form such as a hand or face (Gross, 1973). However, response is never restricted to such object-forms. As detailed in Lectures 4 and 5, such "best" responses can also occur in parallel networks in which convergence is but one mode of organization.

About a decade after the discovery of elongated visual receptive fields of cortical neurons, new evidence accrued that called into question the view that figures were composed by convergence of Euclidean features. For instance, in our laboratory at Stanford University we mapped the architecture of cortical dendritic fields by computer and found cortical receptive fields that contained multiple bands of excitatory and inhibitory areas (Spinelli & Barrett, 1969; Spinelli, Pribram & Bridgeman, 1970). In Leningrad similar observations were made by Glezer (Glezer, Ivanoff, & Tscherbach, 1973), who remarked that these cortical neurons responded more like "stripedness" (than line) detectors (Fig. 1.5). The critical report, however, was that of Pollen, Lee, and Taylor (1971), who interpreted similar findings to indicate that the cortical neurons were behaving as Fourier analyzers rather than as line detectors.

At the same time Campbell and Robson (1968), initially on the basis of psychophysical, and subsequently, on the basis of neurophysiological experiments, developed the thesis that vision operates harmonically much as does audition except that the visual system responds (by virtue of a Fourier process) to *spatial* frequencies. The details of these experiments and their intepretation makes up the content of Lectures 2 and 4. Here I want to introduce the critical difference between Euclidean-based geometric and Fourier-based harmonic approaches.

For those using the geometric approach, spots and lines are seen as elementary features that become combined in ever more complex forms as higher levels of the neural mechanism are engaged. When a harmonic analysis is taken as the approach, the elongated receptive field organization of cortical neurons suggests that neurons act as "strings" tuned to a limited bandwidth of frequencies. The ensemble of strings compose resonators or active filters as in musical instruments. A century ago, Helmholtz proposed that sensory receptors are akin to a piano keyboard; that a spatially isomorphic relation is maintained between receptor and cortex as in the relation between keys and strings of a piano, but that each cortical "unit" responds (resonates) to a limited bandwidth of frequencies as do the strings attached to the piano's sounding board. From the operation of the total range of such units, magnificent sounds (in the case of the piano) and sights (by means of the visual system) can become configured (Fig. 1.6).

The geometric and harmonic views differ significantly with respect to the composition of a percept. Irwin Rock (1983) described this difference as follows:

> One confusion here may be with the meaning of "feature." A feature could refer to an identifiable part or unit that must first be extracted or detected, and then along with other features assembled into an overall pattern. Or "feature" could refer to an identifiable emergent characteristic of the form once it is achieved rather than as one of the parts that produces it. (p. 96)

The details of the neurophysiological data as reviewed in Lectures 4 and 5 show that features such as oriented lines, movement and color are best conceived as identifiable emergent characteristics of form because they are already conjoined in the receptive field. Furthermore such features become activated *either by sensory input or by central process to configure a percept*. This evidence, makes the "resonating string metaphor" more reasonable than the feature detector approach.

There are four critical reasons for preferring tuned frequencies to detected features: (a) Neurons in the visual cortex respond to several features of sensory input and there is no evidence that the different features are represented by separate neurons, as would be required if it acted as a detector; (b) the receptive field properties of such neurons can be accounted for by considering them as spatial and temporal differentiations of tuned frequency; (c) tuned frequencies provide a potentially richer panoply of configuration (e.g., texture, paralax), and (d) perceptual research has clearly shown that lines (and therefore line detectors) composing contours are inadequate elements with which to account for the configural properties of vision.

Rock (1983) summarized the evidence and argument as follows:

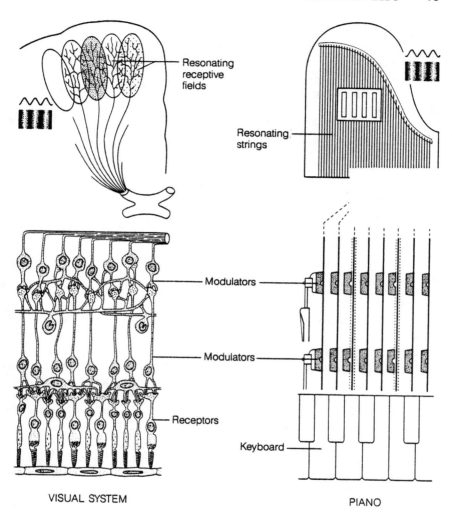

Resonating
receptive
fields

Resonating
strings

Modulators

Modulators

Receptors

Keyboard

VISUAL SYSTEM

PIANO

FIG. 1.6. Diagram of essential connectivity of the initial stages of visual sensory processing and its similarity to the connectivity of a metaphorical piano to illustrate the principles of harmonic analysis.

The emphasis on contour detection is entirely misplaced because, as far as form is concerned, a contour simply marks or delineates a location. What matters for form perception is the set of all such locations; and if these can be delineated without contours, contours are not necessary. That is why, in addition to depth, we perceive regions of particular *shapes* in two random dot patterns viewed binocularly despite the absence of any physical contours (Julez 1971). Illusory contours . . . also support this conclusion. (p. 43)

Rock provided the results of innumerable experiments to document his insight that the configural properties of vision are due to a "process of directional integration" (p. 47). The most critical is the demonstration that "the perceived direction of a point with respect to ourselves. . . is a joint function of retinal locus and eye position" (p. 46). The details of the evidence for this approach are presented in lecture 3.

In summary, sensory cortical receptive fields are considered analogous to resonating strings in a piano. The functional relationship among strings (among the receptive fields of the sensory cortex) and with the keyboard (with the sensory receptors) is spatially organized and provides a macrolevel of perceptual processing. The functional relationship among resonant frequencies, characteristic of overlapping functions of the receptive fields of the cortical neurons, provides a microlevel of perceptual processing. It is this cooperative microprocess that allows one to assume that indeed a specific brain process is coordinate with the richness of experience that is perception.

PLASTICITY

Cooperativity, implemented in the dendric microprocess, makes possible parallel distributed processing of considerable flexibility within a single processing layer. Moreover, in multilayered networks *selective* modification can occur provided the *presynaptic* network becomes influenced by iterations of input. Such an arrangement is often referred to as the Hebb rule because Donald Hebb (1949) captured the imagination of the broad scientific community when he called attention to the fact that *selective* modification is dependent on presynaptic effects. The importance of this presynaptic requirement had been familiar to many neuroscientists for a half-century: For example in his *Project for a Scientific Psychology* (1895/1966), Freud ascribed selective learning to the restricted lowering of certain synaptic resistances by the absorption of energy (precathexis) at the presynaptic site due to repeated use. It is *the actual mechanism* by which such selective changes can occur that has taken a century to unravel (see e.g., Stent, 1973; and discussion in Kimble, 1965).

The holonomic brain theory presented in the next lecture is based on a *radical* extension of this rule: A microprocess is conceived in terms of *ensembles* of mutually interacting pre- and postsynaptic events distributed across limited extents of the dendritic network. The limits of reciprocal interaction vary as a function of input (sensory and central) to the network—limits are not restricted to the dendritic tree of a single neuron. In fact, reciprocal interaction among pre- and postsynaptic events often occurs at a distance from one another, that is, in a saltatory fashion. More on this in Lectures 2 and 4.

Perceptual learning is extremely rapid—three to five iterations usually suffice (Kimble, 1967). This type of rapid learning is achieved when several layers of cooperative networks are cascaded—as in cortical layers—so that feedback and feedforward procedures can be implemented. In feedforward computations are fed to all subsequent processing layers in parallel (with possible delays due to longer paths). Feedback implements the results of computation at each layer by back propagation to layers closer to the input source.

These layered networks simulate layered neural configurations such as those characterizing the retina and cerebral cortex. Other neural configurations such as those characteristic of the basal ganglia and brain stem nuclei are better simulated by clusters of interconnected units described in graph theory by "cliques," "hypercubes," and so forth (Fig 1.7). Brain systems are configured by composites of clustered and layered processors related by topologically discrete parallel connections.

Both layered and clustered processors are implementations of dynamical principles more appropriate for modelling the configural aspects of perception than the digital finite-state principles that guided earlier theories concentrating on symbolic processes. The similarity of these current processing theories to neurodynamics and the success such programs are having in simulating the psychological and neurological aspects of perception indicates that the time is ripe for

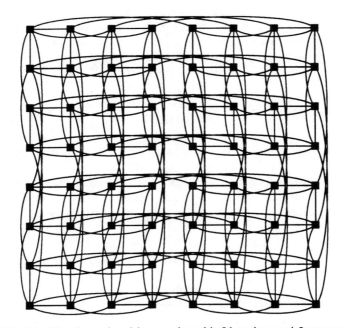

FIG. 1.7.   Six dimensional hypercube with 64 nodes, and 6 connections per node. Computer generation by Conrad Schneiker. From: Hameroff, S. R. (1987). *Ultimate Computing*. Amsterdam: Elsevier Science Publishers.

brain theory to be formally realizable whenever possible. However, just as in computer science, the level of description becomes critical in determining the model—that is, the code, the language—in which a particular procedure is to be invoked.

The interesting and often difficult problems are those that specify the transfer functions, the transformations that relate one level, one code, to another: The necessity to deal with these transfer functions is immediately apparent in computer science where one must have available (often at considerable cost) the software that encodes the "transfer functions" connecting machine to machine-language and this to assembler language, assembler to operating system, and so forth. A computational neural theory of perception must specify the relationship between operations of the subneuronal to the neuronal level; those at the neuronal level to those at the neural systems level; and, as well, those at the neural systems level to those at the perceptual level.

Cooperative networks, even when layered, have limitations as well as strengths. Cooperativity, in sensory systems, given iterative inputs provided by movement, is powerful in correlating, in developing perceptual constancies, and is self-organizing. For other kinds of computation, structured constraints must be imposed on the networks. These constraints can come directly by way of sensory input or they can be imposed from within the brain. The centrally imposed top-down constraints are generated by a variety of brain systems that preprocess at the midbrain and thalamic level the input to the primary sensory cortex. These top-down preprocessing procedures, organized by prior experience, are those that constitute the cognitive aspects of perception.

PARALINEARITY

The cooperative stages of sensory processing are described in the theory presented in the next lecture as paralinear computations. Nonlinearities enter only as auxilliaries that sharpen the computational process. The locus of entry of nonlinearities can thus be identified without jeopardizing the advantages that accrue to the overall linearity of the operation of the brain systems involved in configuring percepts.

A beginning in making the distinction between overall linearity and the entry of nonlinearities comes from analyzing the relevant dynamics of neural processing. The input to the brain is in the form of modulations of nerve impulse trains, modulations initiated in receptor activity.

Similarly, the output to muscles and glands is in the form of spatially and temporally patterned trains of nerve impulses. There are, of course many stages of processing intervening between input and output. At each of these processing stations, four types of transformation take place. Walter Freeman (1989) described these stages in the following passages:

At the first stage pulses coming in to a set of neurons are converted to synaptic currents, [patterns of hyper-and depolarizations] which we call waves. Second, these synaptic currents are operated on by the dendrites of the neurons. This involves filtering and integration over time and space in the wave mode. Third, the wave activity reaching the trigger zones is converted back to the pulse mode. Fourth, it then undergoes transmission, which is translation from one place to another, delay, dispersion in time, etc. The operations of filtering, integration and transmission can be described with linear differential equations. Pulse to wave conversion at synapses is commonly thought to be nonlinear, but in fact in the normal range of cortical operation it is linear. Multiplication by a constant suffices to represent the conversion from a density of action potentials (pulse density) to a density of synaptic current (wave [i.e. polarization amplitude]). But the operation of wave to pulse conversion is nonlinear, and the trigger zone is the crucial site of transformation that determines the neural gain over the four stages. (personal communication)

These passages contain the key elements of the holonomic brain theory presented in the next lecture, in which "the operations of filtering, integration, and transmission can be described with linear differential equations" and "pulse to wave conversion at synapses is commonly thought to be non-linear, but in fact, in the normal range of cortical operation is linear." It is only at the axon hillock where nerve impulses are generated that "wave to pulse conversion is non-linear." (Fig. 1.8) In the holonomic approach, the configural aspects of perception are coordinate with synaptic and dendritic processing; modelling can therefore take advantage of the practical features of linearity. This leaves to conducted nerve impulse activity the role of imposing nonlinear constraints and of communicating the results of processing at one brain location to another such location. Signal transmission with its attendant gain control (as indicated by Freeman) necessitates the introduction of nonlinearities. But (again, as Freeman noted) pulse to wave conversion at synapses once more linearizes the system. Thus the unconstrained dendritic computational microprocess in perception is essentially linear.

Understanding the neural basis of the imposition of nonlinearities in constraining the linear junctional microprocesses is illustrated by the work of Poggio. Poggio, Torre & Koch (1985) came to the following views:

[An] analog parallel model of computation is especially interesting from the point of view of the present understanding of the biophysics of neurones, membranes and synapses. Increasing evidence shows that electrotonic potentials play a primary role in many neurones. Mechanisms as diverse as dendrodendritic synapses, gap junctions, neurotransmitters acting over different times and distances, voltage-dependent channels that can be modulated by neuropeptides and interactions between synaptic conductance changes provide neurons with various different circuit elements. Patches of neural membrane are equivalent to resistances, capacitances and phenomenological inductances. Synapses on dendritic spines mimic voltage

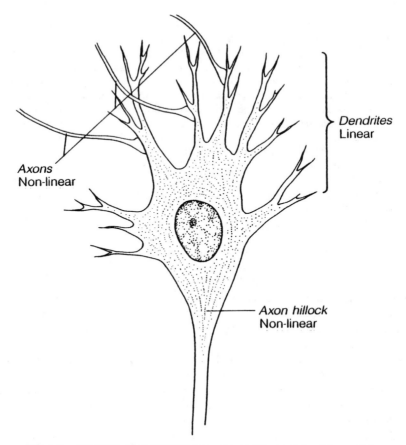

FIG. 1.8.   Diagram of an idealized neuron as it is conceived to participate in the processing of signals.

sources, whereas synapses on thick dendrites or the soma act as current sources.
Thus, single neurons or small networks of neurons could implement analog solutions. (p. 317)

When the constraints on processing are asymmetrical, as for instance, when
excitatory and inhibitory inputs are spatially or temporally asymmetrical (Pog-
gie, Torre, & Koch, 1985) directional selectivity results. Such asymmetries
impose nonlinearities on the basically linear analog microprocess.

The issue of linearity with regard to cortical processing in visual perception
has been addressed in a comprehensive review by Shapley and Lennie (1985):
"The idea [that within patches of receptive field, linearity is maintained] is an

attractive one because it is consistent with the narrow spatial frequency tuning and spread of best frequencies of cortical neurons but is weakened to the extent that the neurons behave non-linearly" (p. 572).

As noted, these nonlinearities are a function of the outputs of neurons that depend on gain control at the axon hillock. The nonlinearities are thus introduced primarily into the perceptual microprocess in the form of overall retinal to cortical mapping that is spatially logarithmic (Schwartz, 1977). However, in addition to the effects on the perceptual macroprocess, "the nature of some of these nonlinearities suggests that they are precisely what make the cells highly tuned spatial frequency filters" (Shapley & Lennie, 1985, p. 575).

To anticipate the theme detailed in Lectures 2 and 4, the configurations (i.e., the internal architecture) of the receptive fields of visual cortical neurons can be described in terms of *spatial* frequency: Recordings of axonal impulse responses of the cortical neuron show that the stimulus that best engages these cortical neurons is a (sine wave) grating (composed of regularly spaced bars of widths equal to those of the spaces), which is drifted across the visual field. The spatial frequency of the gratings that engages the spatial frequency of the receptive field is determined by the widths of the bars making up the grating and the spacings between them. The range of spatial frequencies to which the cortical neuron responds determines the bandwidth of the tuning curve. This bandwidth is approximately an octave ($\pm$ 1/2 octave) (see review by DeValois & DeValois, 1980).

These experimental results have led to the view that the neural processes involved in spatial vision are kin to those involved in audition. Harmonic analysis is therefore an appropriate tool for developing a computationally realizable theory of the neural processes involved in the configural aspects of perception.

The simplest and most fundamental of the tools of harmonic analysis is the Fourier decomposition, which represents a spatial or temporal pattern by a set of regular oscillations differing in amplitude and frequency. Each regular oscillation is in turn decomposed into sine and cosine components, which differ only in that they are 90° out of phase. The phase of each of the regular oscillations with respect to the others differing in frequency, is encoded by a ratio called the *Fourier coefficient*. Computation of the Fourier representation of *oriented gratings* in terms of their coefficients has more successfully predicted the responses of cortical neurons, than has the display of oriented *single* lines or bars of various widths (DeValois, Albrecht, & Thorell, 1978). At the neural microprocessing level, the holonomic brain theory is thus not only computationally simpler, especially with respect to calculating correlations, than nonlinear theory, but is more accessible to test.

However, each of the sinusoidal Fourier components extends to infinity. Cortical receptive fields are bounded. The limit on the functional receptive field of cortical neurons is produced not only by the anatomical extent of the dendritic field of a single neuron, but also by inhibitory (hyperpolarizing) horizontal networks of dendrites that interpenetrate overlapping excitatory (depolarizing) fields. Lecture 10 deals with the way inhibitory networks modify the functional dendritic field.

These bounded receptive fields provide the data reviewed by Shapley and Lennie (1985), which were obtained using harmonic analysis. They noted that the existence of nonlinearities has caused advocates of the Fourier approach "to propose that the spatial image may be analyzed into spatial Fourier components over small patches of visual field." This "patch" technique of Fourier analysis was pioneered for radioastronomy by Bracewell (1965) and then applied to neurophysiology by Pollen, Lee, & Taylor (1971); Pribram (1971); Robson (1975); and Glezer (1985). For the brain cortex each patch is configured by a simple cortical receptive field.

STATE OF THE ART

Currently, several formalisms have been adopted to construct theories of perception similar in character to the holonomic approach taken in these lectures. These theories differ from the holonomic brain theory in that they do not address the role of each of the various *brain systems* involved in perception. In fact, most of the theories—for example see Ginsberg (1971), Caelli (1984), Watson and Ahumada (1985), Hoffman (1984), Dodwell (1984), Cutting (1985), Cavanagh (1984, 1985) and Palmer (1983)—are based primarily on psychophysical data. Their encoding schemas aim to explain in one model the full range of phenomena involved in pattern recognition by a variety of correlational methods (e.g., those of Anderson, Silverstein, Ritz, & Jones, 1977; Kohonen, 1977), holographic filters (Cavanagh 1975, 1976), or Lie group manifolds (Dodwell & Caelli, 1984; Hoffman, 1984).

Kronauer and Zeevi (1985), have summarized the essentials of the *neural* microprocesses on which the holonomic brain and similar theories must be based:

> The operation in question obviously cannot be a global Fourier transformation or, for that matter, any simple harmonic decomposition scheme, since we are dealing with a space (position) dependent system whose characteristics are inhomogeneous. At best, therefore, we may consider a possible "short distance" spectral decomposition analogous to the time-frequency domain spectrogram so widely used in speech analysis (Flanagan, 1972). (p. 99)

Flanagan (1972) and before him Gabor (1946) showed that in a communication there is a tradeoff between accuracy in the spectral domain and accuracy in the time domain. In fact the unit they found to be most useful to represent and analyze a communication (e.g., speech) was a time-limited sinusoid (repetitive waveform) of specified frequency. It is this unit that forms the basis of the holonomic brain theory as developed in the next lecture.

For vision, the sinusoid is place limited (as well as time limited). As Kronauer and Zeevi (1985), have noted, the tradeoff between space and frequency has consequences:

> Thus, as every engineer well knows, sharpening up the spatial resolution results in a spread of the spatial-frequency characteristics, and vice versa. Does this conclusion, based on pure communication theory considerations, bear any relevance to better understanding of cortical engineering design and signal processing in the visual system? Recent studies indicate that, in fact, cortical neurons in area 17 respond in a way that is localized both in space and in spatial frequency (Maffei & Fiorentini, 1973; Andrews & Pollen, 1979; Tootell, Silverman, & DeValois, 1981; Movshon, Thompson & Tolhurst, 1978), in the sense that a cell's stimulus domain exists in a certain well-defined region of visual space (the so-called receptive field) and is also localized in spatial-frequency to a limited range of luminance-periodicity-modulation. Proceeding from photoreceptors through ganglion- and LGN-cells to cortical simple cells, one finds a progressive loss in localizability of positional information (at the single cell level of operation) and a decrease in spatial frequency bandwidth. (pp. 99–100)

This relationship between space and frequency is fundamental. A convenient way to picture it is to recall the metaphor of a piano (described in a previous section) as developed by Helmholtz (1863) and Ohm (1843) to describe the auditory system. At a macro level of organization, the keys of the keyboard (the receptors) are spatially arranged with respect to one another and this spatial arrangement is maintained in the connectivity between keyboard and the strings of the sounding board. It is at the micro level of individual strings (the receptive fields of cortical cells) that the frequency mode of response occurs: each string resonates at a limited bandwidth of frequency. We are well acquainted with the richness of sensory experience that can be generated by such an arrangement.

Furthermore, Kronauer and Zeevi (1985) indicated that this micro level frequency response is carried out within the functional receptive field, that is, the dendritic microprocess of junctional polarizations.

> The response characteristics of a cortical simple cell can conveniently be described in terms of a receptive field profile (the cell's kernel) that specifies its excitatory and inhibitory substructures. Typically there appear to be two major subclasses of simple-cell receptive field profiles: bipartite ("edge" type) and tripartite. Careful analysis of the receptive fields, reconstructed from spatial-frequency selectivity measurements, indicates additional "ringing" reminiscent of Gabor's elementary function (Andrews and Pollen 1979). Most interesting, however, is the finding that pairs of simple cells that are adjacent in the cortical tissue and have the same preferred orientation are tuned to the same spatial frequency and respond to drifting sine wave gratings 90° out of phase, spatially (Pollen and Ronner 1980). Thus, the

fact that cortical neurons balance the position/frequency trade-off by possessing both some spatial retinotopic localization and, at the same time, a spatial frequency bandwidth of about one octave with matched sine and cosine (phase quadrature) cell pairs, suggests that important kinds of visual processing are going on in both domains (Zeevi and Daugman 1981).

One of the advantages of processing in both spatial and frequency domains is economical coding. This is due to the efficiency of encoding when uncertainty with regard to frequency and place (in space and time) are minimized. Kronauer and Zeevi (1985) pointed this out in the following passage:

> Some recent theoretical studies have emphasized the principle of economical coding (minimal representation) for the cortex (e.g., Sakitt and Barlow 1982). In view of the high-functional multiplicity found in the cortex, this emphasis seems misplaced. Yet, it is true that, from several view points, the processing is economical. The receptive field patterns of simple cells come very close to minimizing uncertainty in the four-dimensional space comprised of two spatial and two frequency coordinates (Daugman 1980, 1984). Moreover, it seems that no two cells perform the same functions, so there is no wasteful redundancy in the simple sense. (p. 100)

As detailed in the next lecture, this type of economical encoding, is achieved by an *ensemble* of receptive fields. The advantages of such coding are critical: Transformations between frequency spectrum and spacetime are readily accomplished because the transform is invertable. This makes the computing of correlations easy. In addition, the property of projecting images away from the locus of processing (as by a stereo system and by a hologram) and the capacity to process large amounts of information are inherent in holonomic processing. As these properties are also the ones that characterize figural awareness, they make a good point of departure for constructing a theory of brain organization in perception.

2 Outline of a Holonomic Brain Theory

Fourier's theorem is probably the most far-reaching principle of mathematical physics. (Feynman, Leighton, & Sands, 1963)

Linear systems analysis originated in a striking mathematical discovery by a French physicist, Baron Jean Fourier, in 1822 . . . [which] has found wide application in physics and engineering for a century and a half. It has also served as a principle basis for understanding hearing ever since its application to audition by Ohm (1843) and Helmholtz (1877). The successful application of these procedures to the study of visual processes has come only in the last two decades. (DeValois & DeValois, 1988 p. 3)

INCEPTION OF THE FORMALISM

This lecture outlines the holonomic brain theory. The theory has several roots. As noted in the introductory lecture, historically it developed from Lashley's (1942) concern that the specific connectivities of the nervous system cannot account for the observation that "All behavior seems to be determined by masses of excitation, by the form or relations or proportions of excitation within general fields of activity, without regard to particular nerve cells" (p. 306). Lashley drew on suggestions by Loeb (1907) and Goldscheider (1906), that the configurations experienced in perception might derive from excitation in the brain resembling the "force lines" that determine form during embryogenesis. Goldscheider suggested that similar lines of force are developed when sensory input excites the brain. Lashley noted that such lines of force would form interference patterns in

25

cortical tissue. However Lashley remained perplexed regarding the neuro-physiological origins of these interference patterns and how they might generate the configurations of the experiences and behavior under consideration.

The limitations of understanding the interference pattern model began to yield to further inquiry with the advent of optical holography. This invention made it possible to specify how interference patterns could account for image (re)con-struction and for the distributed nature of the memory store (Van Heerden, 1963; Julez & Pennington, 1965; Pribram, 1966, 1971, 1975). A holographic hypoth-esis of brain function in perception was developed into a precise computational model of brain function on the basis of the mathematics that had made hologra-phy possible (see e.g., "The Cortex as Interferometer" by Barrett, 1969a; "The Holographic Hypothesis of Brain Function in Perception and Memory" by Pri-bram, Nuwer, & Baron, 1974). The computational promise and firm neu-rophysiological base of this model was perceived by many scientists as a starting point for what has become the "connectionist" parallel-distributed processing approach to modelling brain function in perception and learning (e.g., Anderson & Hinton; Willshaw; both in Hinton & Anderson, 1989).

Despite this acknowledgment of promise, objections, some more precisely stated than others, were raised regarding the holographic model. Certain initial objections were based on an incorrect analogy between the *paraphenalia* of early optical information processing techniques (such as coherent reference beams) though these were shown very early on to be unnecessary (Leith 1976; Pribram, Nuwer & Baron 1974). Other objections derived from a misidentification of the "waves" involved in holography as somehow representative of the brain waves recorded from the scalp. Macroscopic waves cannot possibly carry the amount of information necessary to account for the processing requirements involved in perception. On the other hand, spatial interactions among junctional micro-processes occurring in dendritic networks can provide the basis for extremely complex processing (Pribram, 1971, chap. 8).

A more germaine objection came from the fact that the mathematics involved in holography as developed by Gabor (1948), centered on the Fourier theorem. In psychophysics, therefore, it was sometimes held that the transfer function com-puted by the sensory system was a global Fourier transform, thus spreading the input over large extents of cortex. This was shown to be an untenable position for psychophysics (Caelli & Julez, 1979). However, the neurophysiologists who had initially formulated the hypothesis with regard to brain function had *always* noted that the transfer functions involved are limited to particular receptive fields and that more complex relations determine processing of ensembles of such fields (Pollen & Taylor, 1974; Pollen, Lee, & Taylor, 1971; Pribram, 1966; Pribram, Neuwer, & Baron, 1974; Robson, 1975).

However, the fundamental difficulty for understanding has to do with the nature of the Fourier relation itself. The Fourier theorem holds that any pattern can be analyzed into a set of regular, periodic oscillations differing only in frequency, amplitude, and phase. The Fourier transform of such a pattern is described as a spectrum composed of coefficients representing the amplitudes of the intersection (quadriture) of sine and cosine components of the various frequencies present in the pattern. The medium of optical holography, the silver grains of the photographic film, encodes these coefficients. The effects of reinforcement and occlusion at the intersections among wave fronts are encoded, not the wave fronts themselves. The sites of intersection form nodes of varying amplitude, which are represented numerically by Fourier coefficients. A rainbow displays a spectrum of colors diffracted by discrete drops of moisture - the wave forms that compose the display are not seen as such. Thus, the holographic model of brain function had to be described in terms of a complex spectral representation. Often description was erroneously made solely in terms of wave forms per se; sometimes, because of its counterintuitive nature, the spectral representation was discounted.

Much of the confusion was due to confounding two dualities: a wave vs particle duality, on the one hand, with a space-time (configural) vs energy-momentum (spectral) duality on the other. The Fourier transformation expresses only the space-time vs energy-momentum duality.

Dirac (1951) introduced a concept, extended by Feynman, (1985), which is used in the holonomic brain theory to relate these two dualities to one another (see Appendix B). The concept is called the *least action principle*. This is an optimization principle. It claims that the *path* of a particle (a configuration) will tend toward the least expenditure of energy. This occurs because energy and momentum are conserved in any physical interaction (the conservation laws).

Holographic theory is based solely on the "either-or" Fourier duality between spacetime and spectrum. The holonomic brain theory incorporates this duality but is additionally based on the delineation by Gabor of a "phase space" in which the complex of space-time *and* spectrum become embedded. In such a phase space, space-time considerations constrain an essentially spectral computation. It is in this complex coordinate space that the least action principle is applied.

The holonomic brain theory thus aims to go beyond the earlier formulations of the holographic hypothesis and to extend the scope of computability. The term *holonomic* was chosen to distinguish it from holographic and still connote that it is holistic and lawful (Webster's *3rd International Dictionary* defines holo as whole; nomic as having the general force of natural law, i.e., is generally valid). In mathematics the term holonomic was first used by Hertz. As such it referred to structural constraints by which a set of original coordinates can be expressed by more generalized (Lagrangian) coordinates. In this usage the term was applied only to space (and time) coordinates. Here usage is extended to include the spectral domain (which as noted is the Fourier transform of space-time). In contrast to a purely holographic theory, therefore, the inclusion of space-time coordinates in the holonomic theory incorporates the operation of structural constraints in processing.

The formal, mathematical foundations of the computations contributing to the holonomic brain theory rest on four fundamental concepts and the relations between them. Only one of these basic conceptions is familiar—that of space-time, and even here, only in the 20th century has it been formally realized that space and time are intimately related through movement. The second basic conception is a generalization of the application of the concept of a spectral domain: Not only colors and tones can be analyzed into their component frequencies of oscillation. Processing of all exteroceptive sensations including those dependent on spatiotemporal configurations (such as the shapes of surfaces and forms) can be understood as amplitude modulations of these oscillations. As noted, it is this spectral aspect of processing that was the foundation of the holographic hypothesis of brain function in perception. In the case of surfaces and forms this aspect is described in terms of *spatial* frequencies of oscillation. In fact, due to the Fourier transformation, spectra enfold the ordinary conception of both space and time.

A third concept derives from plotting spectral and space time values within the same frame. It turns out that when this is done, there is a limit with which both frequency and space-time can be concurrently determined in any measurement. This *uncertainty* describes a fundamental **minimum** defined by Gabor (1946) as *a quantum of information*. This minimum is a sinusoid variably constrained by space-time coordinates and thus differs from the unit of information defined by Shannon, usually taken as a bit (a binary digit), a Boolean choice between alternatives (Shannon & Weaver, 1949). However, Shannon also defined information as a **reduction of uncertainty**. This uncertainty relationship provides a link between Gabor's and Shannon's definitions and allows for an explicit convergence of information processing theories. Furthermore, the distinction between Gabor's and Shannon's formulations provides the basis of the distinction between the configural and the cognitive aspects of perception.

The fourth concept basic to the holonomic brain theory emphasizes the manner in which optimization is achieved in perception. Dendritic microprocessing is conceived to take advantage of the uncertainty relation to achieve optimal information processing. The holonomic brain theory concerns the efficiency with which processing proceeds—efficiency based on spectral resolution obtained by sharpening the tuning of receptive field properties.

THE HOLOSCAPE: SPACETIME, SPECTRA, AND QUANTA OF INFORMATION

The holonomic brain theory is based on the Fourier and Gabor relationships. As noted, Fourier's theorem states that a pattern can be decomposed into components representing the relationships among sets of regular (i.e., periodic) oscillations each of which has been further decomposed into oscillations 90° out of phase. Components encode frequency, amplitude, and phase (the relations be-

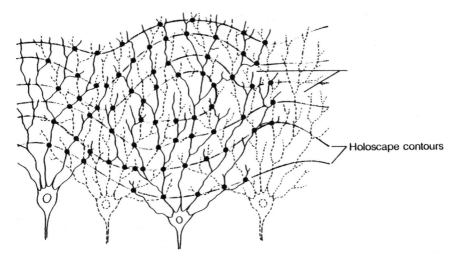

FIG. 2.1.   An idealized portrait of a holoscape.

tween oscillations). These components are quantified as Fourier coefficients. The ensemble of such coefficients, when embodied in physical form, becomes palpable as an optical hologram. When coefficients of identical value are connected as in a contour map, the resulting schema is what in the holonomic brain theory is called a holoscape (Fig. 2.1). The contours forming such a holoscape are embodied in the microprocess of polarizations occurring in dendritic networks, thus constituting a sub- and transneuronal manifold.

Furthermore, the Fourier theorem states that the original pattern can be reconstituted by performing the inverse transform. This invertibility is one of its most attractive features. (For others, see Weisstein, 1980; Weisstein & Harris, 1980; Yevick, 1975.) There is, therefore, a computational gain were brain processes to follow the rules of the Fourier relationship. Actuality is somewhat more complex.

Perceived patterns are ordinarily described in space and time. When the Fourier analytical procedure decomposes a space-time pattern into an ensemble of components representing the interactions among frequencies of oscillations from which the pattern can be reconstructed, the decomposition is described as the spectrum of the pattern. Thus (a) space-time, and (b) spectrum are differentiated by the Fourier procedure, whereas in the Gabor relation they become two orthogonal sets of coordinates (see Fig. 2.2).

Gabor's interest in a joint space-time/spectral domain stemmed from telecommunication. Whereas telegraphy depended on a Morse or similar code that was readily seen to be composed of discrete elements, telephone communication utilized the spectral domain. It took some time to realize that efficient com-

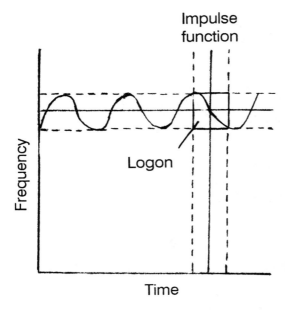

Impulse
function

Logon

Frequency

Time

FIG. 2.2. An idealized graph of a Hilbert space showing a Logon (Gabor elementary function; quantum of information). Visualize the sinasoid as perpendicular to the graph. In visual processing the time axis would be supplemented by the two axes of coordinate space.

munication in this domain entailed signals coded as Fourier coefficients. In addition, signal transmission takes time. Nyquist (1924) and Kupfmueller (1924) pointed out that there is a relation between the rate of transmission and bandwidth. Hartley (1928) formalized this relation by noting that to transmit a given "quantity of information" a product of bandwidth x time is required. Hartley's formulation not only anticipated Gabor but also Shannon: He proposed that information was selective in that communication depends on a preexisting alphabet of possibilities, and furthermore, that the selective process is logarithmic. (For an excellent review of this history see Cherry, 1978, and Bracewell, 1989).

Note that with Hartley, communication and process begin to merge: The processing of information depends on communication and communication depends on processing. In communications systems that depend on processing it is practical to ask how efficient a process can be in order to facilitate communication.

Hartley's law indicates that there is a tradeoff between bandwidth and the time taken to process-communicate a set of signals: The greater the number of frequencies utilized, the more densely the signals are packed per unit time, and the less time (or distance along a medium) is required. This distance-density relation is fundamental to many levels of processing in the holonomic brain theory and appears repeatedly in subsequent lectures.

Gabor (1946) noted that there is a limit to the efficiency with which a set of signals can be processed and communicated. This limit is due to a limit on the precision to which simultaneous measurement of spectral components and [space]time can be made. It is this limit, defined by residual bandwidth of frequencies and the probability of an occurrence within a range of [space]time, that proscribes the efficiency with which the system can operate. In effect, therefore, the Gabor relation describes the composition of a communication/processing channel, and the residual uncertainty defines the limits of channel processing span.

Processing efficiency was handled by Gabor in terms of a measure he termed the *Logon*. Today we often refer to these Logons as "Gabor elementary functions." In Gabor's two dimensional scheme the Logon was a unitary minimum. This minimum describes an area surrounding the intersection of frequency and a temporal impulse (Dirac or delta) function.

Gabor's mathematics paralleled that used by Heisenberg to describe experimental findings in the field of quantum physics. In essence, therefore, the mathematics found so useful in understanding relationships in quantum physics was generalized to deal with issues in psychophysics, and Gabor termed the Logon a *quantum* of information. An *ensemble* of such quanta, processing channels, is dealt with by what mathematicians call a phase space or "Hilbert space," as Hilbert originally devised the mathematics used by Heisenberg and Gabor.

There are, however, some pitfalls inherent in the Gabor approach. Gabor's use of the Hilbert space representation deals only with steady states, when what needs to be represented is a process. The holonomic brain theory avoids this pitfall by generalizing the Gabor function and adhering to the reality implicit in the Fourier relation: There is in fact good evidence (see Lecture 10) that the Gabor elementary function can be pushed toward the spectral domain (as in holography) or toward the space time domain (as in ordinary photography) almost, if not quite, to the limit. Iterations of successive applications of the Fourier transform; differences of offset Gaussians; Gaussians times Hermite polynomials and, in general, four dimensional informational hyperspaces based on Jacobi delta functions (Atick & Redlich, 1989) or Wigner distributions (Wechsler, 1991) are thus, in empirically determined situations (e.g., Stork & Wilson, 1990), often a better representation of process than the Gabor elementary function (see Appendix B to these lectures). Structural (space-time) constraints can thus operate not only as initial conditions as in the Gabor representation, but also as ongoing operations constraining the dendritic microprocess (Daugman, 1985).

Nonetheless, on the basis of the neurophysiological evidence (see e.g., Field & Tolhurst, 1986), the holonomic brain theory takes as its starting point, the description of Logons (Gabor elementary functions), which are composed of several receptive fields. As noted in the previous lecture, Pollen and Ronner (1980) found adjacent neurons in the visual cortex to respond best to gratings 90° out of phase. These neurons make up a couplet, a sine-cosine quadrature pair. Thus a module of receptive fields encodes the quadrature relation (i.e., the sine and cosine components that make up Fourier and Gabor coefficients). Each

Logon, that is, each such receptive field module, is a channel. According to Gabor, the ensemble of such channels is a measure of the degrees of freedom, the number of distinguishable dimensions or features (e.g., spatial and temporal frequency, degrees of orientation, preferred direction of movement, color). The minimum uncertainty relation expressed by Gabor elementary functions sets the limits on the information processing competence of each of these channels.

The holonomic brain theory, by generalizing both the Gabor and the Fourier theorems, allows for the operation of a process. In addition, the theory further develops Gabor's insight, and goes on to encompass ensembles in which multiple minima must be achieved by uncertainty reduction. The theory thus converges on thermodynamic and Shannon (Shannon & Weaver, 1949) information processing modes of explanation. The next sections discuss these relationships.

THE OCCAM NETWORK AND THE BOLTZMANN ENGINE

Given an ensemble of channels with Logon properties, there are as many minima of uncertainty as there are channels. This provides the theory with an additional important root. Recently, Hopfield (1982) and also Ackley, Hinton, and Sejnowski (1985)—who called their model a Boltzmann engine—proposed implementations of statistical mechanics and thermodynamics in computational models of parallel- processing arrays. These implementations address the problems of learning, memory storage and retrieval, which are developed in their relationship to the cognitive aspects of perception in Part II of these lectures. The thermodynamic processor is one of several current "connectionist" models, which are implemented as content-addressable multilevel parallel-processing arrays. (See review in Rumelhart, McClelland & the PDP Research Group, 1986). They are thus similar to a content addressable network called Occam, which was developed and implemented in our laboratory in the 1960s. (Pribram, 1971; Spinelli, 1970)

Occam described modules (Fig. 2.3) consisting of cortical columns each of which is composed of input and operator neurons, and of interneurons and test cells. An input to overlapping receptive fields of input neurons becomes distributed to the receptive fields of interneurons, which in turn connect to those of operator neurons. The receptive fields of interneurons are tunable - that is, they adapt and habituate, they have memory. Each interneuron thus acts like a bin in a computer that stores the averages of the part of the patterns of input to which it is exposed. The ensemble of receptive fields (bins) stores the averaged pattern. Only when a pattern is repeated does structured summation occur—nonrepetitive patterns simply raise the baseline and average out. Thus the receptive fields of operator neurons, sensitive solely to *patterns of averages*, are activated only when input patterns are repeated.

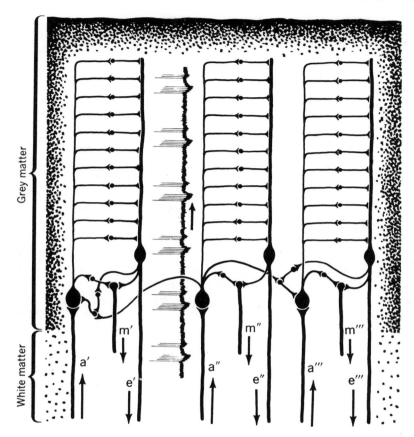

FIG. 2.3. Spinelli's OCCAM. See page 32 for explanation. Input neurons: a; output neurons: m. From Pribram, 1969b. *On the Biology of Learning,* © 1969 by Harcourt Brace Jovanovich, Inc. and reprinted with their permission.

This procedure provides a primitive implementation of the least action principle: The paths by which polarizations are matched become "shortened" as processing proceeds. This shortening of the processing path is enhanced by feeding the output from the operator neuron *back* onto the receptive fields of the input cells via test neurons that compare the pattern of neural activity in the input and operator neurons. When a match is adequate, the test cell produces an exit signal, otherwise the tuning process continues. In this fashion, each cortical column comes to constitute a *region* of minimum uncertainty, an engram (a memory trace), by virtue of its specific sensitivity to one pattern of neural activity.

Each cortical column is connected with others by horizontal cells and their basal dendrites, which are responsible for inhibitory interactions. Whenever these horizontal cells are activated asymmetrically, as they are by directional sensitive inputs, a temporary structure composed of several columns becomes functionally connected. These extended structures or *modules* are thus dependent for their extent on dendritic hyperpolarizations in local circuit neurons and not on nerve impulse transmission.

The current connectionist models have a similar, though more generalized architecture. They are also composed of three or more reciprocally acting layers. Most compute the pattern to be stored by taking the least mean square of the difference between the stored and the input pattern. This enhances optimization (the least action principle) by doing away with the necessity of raising a baseline as in the earlier model. The recent connectionist models are therefore error-driven and go a step beyond Occam in that Occam models only the initial template (the "adaptation level" of the response to input), which, in current connectionist procedures, becomes the goal of processing.

The thermodynamic version of the connectionist models consists of elements (conceived to be neurons interconnected by synapses), which constitute an array in which neighboring elements *mutually* influence one another in a more or less symmetrical fashion. Ordinarily, the generation of an impulse (a nerve impulse) is considered a "+" and the suppression of an impulse a "−". A more neurologically sophisticated version would identify the "+" with depolarization and "−" with hyperpolarization. And the holonomic brain theory would place the entire computational structure in the synaptodendritic microprocess rather than in the interaction among pulsatile outputs of neurons. What is interesting is that the "+" and "−" are identified in the theory as directional polarizations due to "spin" in the computation:

With respect to a directional component in the polarizations occurring in the dendritic microprocess, Pribram, Nuwer, and Baron (1974) presented a preliminary outline of a model that can profitably be enriched and extended on the basis of current knowledge.

Perturbation in the postsynaptic domain is a function of differences in distribution of hyper- and depolarizations produced by the arrival of input patterns. Lecture 4 describes in detail the structure of dendritic spines and their activation that creates such voltage differences in dendrites. When neighboring spines become locally hyper- and depolarized, the effect is to produce a pair of vertically oriented electric dipoles at the surface of the dendritic membrane, which becomes superimposed on the horizontal fields already present (Fig. 2.4). The net effect is to produce electrical polarizations that can be conceived to display direction somewhat akin to spin (see Appendix A).

The likelihood that neighboring postsynaptic events form a dipole consisting of hyper- and depolarization is enhanced in those structures endowed with many local circuit neurons such as the cerebral cortex. These neurons are responsible for "lateral inhibition" by way of ubiquitous connections interspersed among those provided by input neurons.

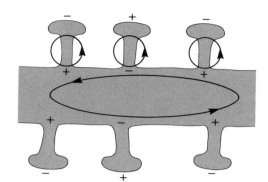

FIG. 2.4. Diagram of the perpendicularly oriented dipoles of polarization assumed to be generated at spines within the parent dendrite.

The contribution of any pair of synaptic dipoles is small, but when many identical effects throughout the dendritic microprocess are summed, the physiology of the network is significantly affected. As described in Lecture 4, not only adjacent but remote synaptic events sum cooperatively and the effects of such cooperative interactions have been computationally modeled.

In the holonomic brain theory, computations proceed in collective cooperative ensembles constituting a holoscape. The holoscape is composed of vertically oriented spine-produced dipoles embedded in horizontal dendritic polarization fields. The computations in the holonomic brain theory are therefore formally equivalent to computations in quantum field theory and thus constitute quantum neurodynamics (See Appendix A for formal treatment). However, formal similarities do not necessarily imply that the processes at the neural level can be identified substantively with those described in quantum physics. The holonomic brain theory does not imply that neural processes are quantum mechanical, although this is not ruled out as indicated by specific suggestions such as those proposed by Fröhlich (1978, 1983, 1986), Hameroff (1987) and others, reviewed in the epilogue to these lectures.

The computations in quantum neurodynamics differ somewhat from those developed in the thermodynamic models. In the thermodynamic models computations are driven by "the principle of least action" to energy minima (Hamiltonians), which comprise an equilibrium (Hamiltonian) state. By contrast, on the basis of evidence that efficiency in processing is a function of band-width, not energy, the holonomic brain theory substitutes entropy minima for energy minima: Experiments by Caelli and Hubner (1983) have shown that the resolving power of the visual system is determined by its spatial frequency resolution and not by the amplitude modulation of the system.

Caelli and Hubner (1983) compared an original image with one that had been "filtered" in different ways by a computational procedure, a procedure used by

Ginsberg (1978) to demonstrate the possible origins of a variety of perceptual illusions. In these experiments:

> The Fourier transform is first applied. Average amplitudes are then determined for each of the specified two-dimensional frequency regions, and all composite frequency components are assigned this value. The inverse transform is then computed to result in a new image which should not be discriminable from the original—if the bandwidths are chosen to be consistent with the lower bounds . . . of approximately 5 [orientation increments] and 1/8 octave [frequency bandwidth]. From a psychophysical perspective, these lower bounds correspond to bandpass regions in the two dimensional frequency domain whose elements cannot be discriminated.

> We have computed these transformations for a variety of different bandwidths (Fig. 2.5). Clearly as the bandwidth approaches zero, the approximation to the original image improves. From our results with two images (texture and face) the $1/4$ octave width and 10° orientation bandwidth result in an image almost impossible to discriminate from the original. [This despite the fact that]. . . the amplitude coding reduction is considerable. . . . [The] amplitude (and so energy) coding reduction is 98.3% [!].—- [This makes] the $1/4$ octave 10° wide amplitude code . . . approximately 60 times more efficient than the baseline (digital) frequency code [that of the original image]. (p. 1053)

Such considerations of processing efficiency have led Daugman (1988a) to reconstruct a remarkably realistic portrait from a complete discrete two dimensional Gabor transform network at only 2.55 bits/pixel. The network was composed of overlapping Gabor elementary functions—the entropy (Fig. 2.6) of the ensemble of pixels is "little different from that of noise with uniform density since it does not exploit their intrinsic correlation structure" (p. 1170).

The results of these experiments clearly indicate that image processing is a function of the efficiency of the spectral resolution of ensembles of Gabor elementary functions based on bandwidth and not on the average amplitudes of the processes. Average amplitude is a statistical measure of the amount of energy it takes to drive the process, whereas the efficiency of spectral resolution (which utilizes amplitude coefficients for each bandwidth of frequency) is measured in terms of the amount of ordering of energy, that is, entropy. It is reasonable, therefore, to suggest that efficiency or entropy, rather than energy, is the critical element in perceptual processing: that entropy (uncertainty) minima rather than energy minima characterize the computational terrain.

ENERGY, ENTROPY AND INFORMATION

The relation between measures of efficiency and measures of information (i.e., entropy and negentropy) has been discussed at length by Shannon (Shannon &

Face　　　　　　　Texture　　　　　　Spectrum

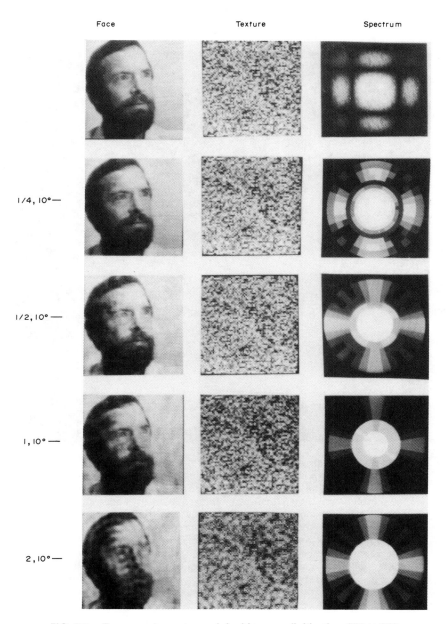

1/4, 10°—

1/2, 10°—

1, 10°—

2, 10°—

FIG. 2.5.　Top row shows two original images digitized as 256 × 256, 4-bit pixels and the amplitude spectrum for the texture. Rows 2–5 represent the inverse Fourier transforms of the amplitude averaging process illustrated for the texture case in the middle column. The unit radial frequency widths (octaves: RF) and orientation tuning (deg:) are shown on the left (RF, 0). Note the importance of the spectral dimension. From: Caelli and Hubner (1983).

37

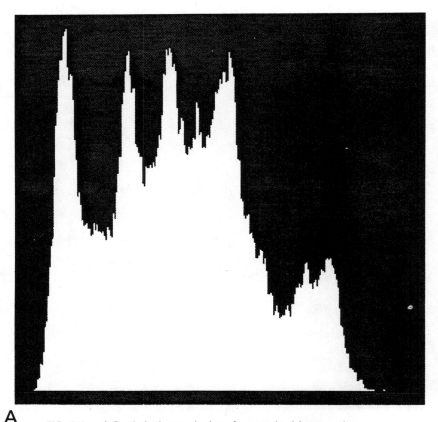

A

FIG. 2.6. a) Statistical complexity of a standard image when represented point-by-point, as if by retinal photoreceptors. In this pixel histogram the entropy, or mutual self-information, is $S = 7.57$ for the
ensemble. A point-by-point image representation does not extract the
intrinsic redundancies and correlations which distinguish structure
from noise. b) Histogram of the coefficients comprising a complete 2-D
Gabor representation of the same image as described by a, with the
same number of degrees of freedom (65,536) and the same quantiza-
tion (8-bits). Compared with the statistical complexity of the distribution of (a), this distribution has an entropy reduced by five binary log
units to $S = 2.55$, but it nonetheless represents a complete encoding of

Weaver, 1949), Brillouin (1962), and Mackay (1969). However, these authors
came to somewhat different conclusions: Shannon equated the amount of information with the amount of entropy, MacKay and Brillouin with the amount of
negentropy. A conciliation of these views comes from the holonomic modification of the thermodynamic model. The conciliation results in a definition of
entropy as potential information: The reasoning is similar to that which moti-

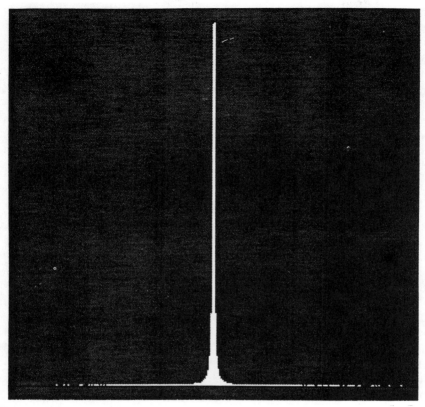

B   FIG. 2.6.   (continued)
the image. Nearly all the image structure is carried by a small fraction
of the 2-D Gabor coefficients, namely those which are far out on the
tails of the distribution. Assuming that 2-D Gabor functions are a good
model for cortical simple cell receptive fields profiles, the implication
for biological image coding is that for any *given* image, most of the
information load is carried by a very small subset of the cells, while the
majority are essentially quiescent. From: Daugman, J. G. (1990). An
Information-Theoretic View of Analog Representation in Striate Cortex. In E. Schwartz (Ed.), *Computational Neuroscience.* Boston, MA:
MIT Press.

vated Shannon. The structure within which information processing occurs is
called uncertainty. It is this structure that allows for a measured amount of
information to emerge. Shannon's use of the term *uncertainty* can thus be seen to
be equivalent to "potential information," the term used in the holonomic brain
theory. In outline, the argument runs as follows:

Thermodynamic connectionist models are conceived to produce a Hamiltonian state characterized by energy minima. However, the models are sensitive to the entropy in the system measured as an amount of noise. In thermodynamics the amount of entropy is measured as temperature. At 0 temperature a thermodynamic system acts like a ferromagnet (it has, at best, 2 minima). If the temperature is too high, the system acts as a "spin glass"—that is, there are multitudes of minima. For connectionist models to perform with optimal efficiency—that is, for optimal information processing—a "window" or "bandwidth" of noise must be added in. The amount and bandwidth is decided upon on the basis of trial and error (simulated annealing, Hinton & Sejnowski, 1986; Hopfield, 1982). In short, the system can be *tuned* to perform optimally in recognizing patterns to which it had previously been exposed. Efficient, informative pattern matching, occurs in a region between total randomness and total organization.

Note that "informative pattern matching" is an active process. As detailed in Lecture 3, "information" is a function of a participating processing agency, ordinarily a living creature or its surrogate. Information does not exist per se in the absence of such an agency any more than sound or sight exists without a sentient being equipped with the capability to select and interpret patterns "existing" in the physical environment.

Shannon (Shannon & Weaver, 1949) and Lila Gatlin (1972) noted that the efficiency of information processing depends not only on the presence of noise (measured in information theoretic models as redundancy) but also, by virtue of pattern matching, by actively structuring the redundancies. George Miller (1956) called attention to the importance of such structuring, which he called "chunking." Lectures 8 and 9 review the evidence that the frontolimbic portions of the forebrain are critically involved in structuring redundancy and thus in enhancing the efficiency of information processing.

The holonomic brain theory holds that efficiency in processing entails a "polarization pattern path-integral" whose trajectory determines optimization, that is least action. The Hamiltonians became operators (defining paths) in a Hilbert space. In this space the amount of entropy is described as an amount of potential constraint. Therefore, the path of uncertainty reduction is described, much as in Shannon's (Shannon & Weaver, 1949) definition of an amount of information, by a content addressable match between two patterns of constraining probabilities, two polarization pattern pathways. These patterns constitute two domains where the amount of entropy reduction achieves the minimum possible entropy; that is, the process reaches Gabor's definition of a quantum of information. In the holonomic brain theory, these quanta are idenitified as polarons.

Two examples can help the exposition of these concepts, which have posed such difficulty for thoughtful scientists. I have an evening of leisure and wish to catch up with my reading of books that have recently arrived. They are stacked "randomly". By this I mean that the order in which the books are placed fails to reflect some other order that might be currently relevant to me. Randomness does not reflect disorder, however. The books are structured elements and one might wish to select one "at random"—say one with a red cover. The attributes that make for a book, for a cover, and for a color must all be present for me to make that "random" selection.

Einstein was wrong in expression if not in intent when he stated his view that God does not play dice with the universe. Indeed he does, and has six-sided cubes (numbered at that), or perhaps 10-dimensional superstrings with which to play. Playing with marbles would only get him Hamiltonians: The marbles would accumulate in equilibrium structures composed of sinks of least energy. In my evening's search for relevant information, in Einstein's search for determinate structure, the books and dice are constraining initial conditions. Randomness is as much a consequence of the structure of these initial conditions as it is of the processes of shuffling the books or throwing the dice.

What is perceived as disorder with respect to some particular activity ordinarily results, however, from the shuffling and throwing process. On closer scrutiny, randomness could be seen to reflect the structure of the initial conditions as they become processed in shuffling, throwing, or selecting (Pribram, 1972, 1986).

In the holonomic brain theory these initial conditions and the continuing control procedures that constrain processing compose structures that determine the degrees of freedom which characterize the potential for actions to be taken in the situation. It is in the process of shuffling different constraining structures that both Shannon's BITS of information (reductions of uncertainties) and Gabor's quanta of information (minimum uncertainties) are produced.

Thus, amount of structure in the initial condition and amount of residual structure (the result of entropy reduction) are reciprocals of one another. If entropy is a measure of the amount of initial structure, the initial degrees of freedom, then the amount of residual structure is the amount of information achieved. In the brain the entropy reduction process involves a match between an input pattern and a pattern inherent in the synaptodendritic network by virtue of genetic or learning experience. In the holonomic brain theory, both the input and inherent patterns provide initial conditions. The match between them is probabilistic and is expressed as changes in the probability amplitude weighting functions of synaptodendritic polarizations.

In recognizing that entropy provides a variety of potential paths for the reduction of uncertainty (and thus for the accretion of information), an additional possibility is presented for convergence among theoretical formulations, a possibility that can be described as follows: In information measurement theory, there is the concept of *requisite variety* (Ashby, 1956). Requisite variety is an optimization principle claiming that the reduction of uncertainty devolves on a tradeoff between equivocation and information density. Equivocation is defined as the sum of noise and redundancy. For the holonomic modification of the thermodynamic process this means that not only noise but structure, as inherent in redundancy, can be added to the system in order to maximize efficiency (Attneave, 1954; Garner, 1962; and especially Gatlin, 1972). And redundancy can be structured by experience as for example, in chunking (see Lecture 10). This indicates once again, that for information processing the measure of efficiency, that is, of entropy, denotes not only randomness but tacit structure.

Daugman (1988b) has made some additional observations relevant to an information theoretical approach to figural perception. He pointed out that retinal and geniculate processing decorrelates the optical image. Daugman also noted that Gabor proved that one could completely represent any arbitrary signal by expanding it in terms of ensembles of elementary functions (although he could not actually prescribe a way to do this). Daugman's contribution has been not only to generalize Gabor functions to two dimensions (independently achieved by Carlton in Pribram & Carlton, 1986), but to find a method to accomplish expansion when the Gaussian envelope is scaled proportionally according to spatial frequency. He related his implementation to sampling in the theory of oriented wavelet codes. More on this in appendix A.

A final point: Hopfield (1982) used Liapunov functions in his analysis of the development of stabilities in neural networks. These are the same functions used by Prigogine (Prigogine & Stengers, 1984) to model dissipative structures that more or less "spontaneously" develop stabilities far from equilibrium. As such these processes are represented by nonlinear equations. As Kohonen pointed out (Kohonen & Oja, 1987) this nonlinearity depends on an a priori assumption that the network connectivity be proportional to the wanted state vectors. In its initial form the thermodynamic processor is therefore incomplete. Brain processes are to a considerable extent optimally self-maintaining and even self-organizing (a point also made by Maturana, 1969 and by Varela, 1979) - and not subject only to the vagaries of input organization nor to spontaneous, unpredictable organization. Of course, occasional spontaneous innovative reorganizations can also occur. In more ordinary circumstances, Kohonen noted, where synaptic couplings are formed adaptively, (thus continuously relating input and central state values), the output state can relax to the linear range or to saturation. In Kohonen's model (1972, 1977) learning takes place in the linearized mode. Modifications of the thermodynamic models by Hinton, McClelland, Sejnowski, and Rumelhart (Hinton, McClelland & Rumelhart, 1986; Hinton & Sejnowski, 1986) used similar continuous feedback ("back propagation") processes to overcome the limitations of nonlinearity. More of this in Lectures 3 and 10. Only when "bifurcations" produce alternatives as in Prigogine's approach and decisions are made among those alternatives does the theory need to become sharply non-linear. It is such cognitive influences on perception that are dealt with in part II of these lectures.

With respect to sensory driven aspects of perception the models point to the importance of successive iterations of the process. These successive iterations can readily serve an optimization principle. In the holonomic brain theory successive iterations are based on movement which produces polarization pattern paths in computational space, paths that proscribe the efficiency with which perceptual processing occurs. These polarization pattern paths are described by the least action principle in terms of mathematical group theory. Lecture 5 describes, in such terms, the construction of object-forms and object spaces by correlations among iterations of images, correlations that result in group theoretic processing structures.

SUMMARY

The thermodynamic models fit well into the frame of holonomic brain theory (see, e.g., Psaltis, Brady, Gu, & Lin, 1990). However, a modification based on the Gabor relation needs to be made. In the Hopfield networks and the Boltzmann engine, computations proceed in terms of attaining energy minima, while in the holonomic brain theory computations proceed in terms of attaining a minimum amount of entropy and therefore a maximum amount of information. In the Boltzmann formulation the principle of least action leads to a space-time equilibrium state of least energy. In the holonomic brain theory the principle of least action leads to maximizing the amount of information, defined as an ensemble of minima of least entropy. Such minima, defined by isovalent contours representing junctional polarizations (polarons) of equal value, can compose a temporarily stable holoscape far from equilibrium. In short, the holoscape is a dissipative structure, composed of ensembles of uncertainty minima. These ensembles, which serve as attractors, define the boundary conditions for further processing. (For review of the functions of attractors see Prigogine & Stengers, 1984).

Thus, the holonomic brain theory can account for the fact that organisms such as primates and especially humans are, on occasion, information (i.e., entropy minima) seeking "informavores" (Miller, personal communication; Pribram, 1971). The implementation of this aspect of the theory in terms of evidence at the neural systems level makes up the content of Part II of these lectures.

I CONFIGURAL ASPECTS

Objects are not fleeting and fugitive appearances [images] because they are not only groups of sensations, but groups cemented by a constant bond. It is this bond alone, which is the object in itself, and this bond is a relation.

—(Poincare, 1905b)

3 Transformational Realism: The Optic Array, The Optical Image and the Retinal Process

Instead of postulating that the brain constructs information from the input of a sensory nerve, we can suppose that the centers of the nervous system, including the brain, resonate to information. (Gibson, p.267)

INTRODUCTION: THE WHAT OF PERCEPTUAL PROCESSING

This lecture concerns the initial sensory mechanism, which in the eye consists of the optics of pupil and lens and the receptor processes of the retina. In vision, I hope to show that making a distinction between the optic array, optical images, or flows, and retinal process (and specifying the transformations involved), resolves several hitherto intractible issues. These issues are: (a) the grain problem, that is, determining the scale of the origins of sensory configurations; (b) the existence or nonexistence of a retinal image; and (c) the dimensionality of the initial sensory process.

Interpretations regarding this initial level of processing are critical to understanding what it is that is being perceived. As a result, the interpretations have been the subject of considerable controversy. Of primary concern, has been "the grain problem," because the input to receptors is described at two very different scales: One of these scales is *microphysical* and based on analysis by physical instruments, the other is *macropsychological* and based on reports of introspection. Eddington described this issue in terms of two tables: one is composed of atoms and subatomic particles; the other is used to serve a meal. Psychophysics describes the relation between these modes but does not deal with the fact that physical descriptions are made in microterms of patterns of energy, entropy, and information (probability amplitude-modulated frequencies), whereas reports of introspection yield macroconfigurations such as tables and chairs. The gap in scale or "grain" of the psychophysical pair is immense and has hitherto seemed insurmountable.

The holonomic brain theory addresses the grain problem by specifying the transformations that occur between processing stages in the same terms as those used in physical measurement (energy, entropy, information) without neglecting the configural properties of the percepts being described. The key to achieving such specification lies in the transformational nature of the Fourier and Gabor relationships enfolding and unfolding configuration into and out of the spectral domain.

As suspected by Gibson in the epigram introducing this lecture, the grain problem has been addressed in two ways: Either (a) percepts are *constructed* from simpler elements or (b) regions in the brain *directly* resonate to configurations already present in the input to the senses. The resolution to the problem presented in the holonomic brain theory is orthogonal to these views and therefore somewhat unexpected: The initial sensory process is neither constructive nor direct. As detailed shortly, sensory processes are *transformational*. The initial processing stage is not a construction from elements but consists of reordering a distributed, enfolded array that forms the content of the sensory input. Neither are the initial levels of processing—the image and object-form levels—direct. Rather, they involve transformation. However, construction becomes a part of the perceptual process as a result of cognitive operations. These operations inform the image by preprocessing the input channels via the brain's corticofugal pathways.

For vision, the controversy regarding grain has centered on the existence of a "retinal image" and other such representations in more centrally located brain regions. Resolution of the controversy comes in the holonomic brain theory by unpacking the concept "retinal image." This is done by showing that an optical image is formed from the optic array by the pupil/lens system, whereas, a retinal process performs operations much more complex than those that register an image in ordinary photography.

Optic array, optical image, and retinal receptor process all differ in their configuration. Each processing step transforms, changes the form of what is being processed. How then can one ascertain what is being processed, the critical features that characterize a percept? The answer to this question is: By ascertaining that which remains invariant across processing stages. Such invariants are discovered by a procedure that is an extension of that used in psychophysics: Constraints are placed on processing by manipulating a situation that can be described in the computational language of physics or engineering. The limits within which the subjective report of the ensuing perceptual experience remains unchanged provide an indication of the invariant features of that situation.

Such experiments have shown that *relations* between perceived parts of images and object-forms are the grist of the perceptual mill. The classical experiments by Stratton (1896, 1897) in which he continuously wore lenses that inverted the optical image, only to find that within a week everything was once more experienced as right side up, demonstrated this beyond doubt. The experiments by Richard Held (1968) and Ivo Kohler (1964) showed that moving about was critical to this adaptation of phenomenal experience.

Given that relations are basic to what is being processed, the next question becomes, "Relations among what?" Mach concluded, on the basis of his observations (see review by Ratliff, 1965) that what is being processed are the spatial and temporal relations among the magnitudes of infinitesimally small points of radiant electromagnetic energy, the spatial and temporal derivatives of luminance. As described later in this lecture, a more comprehensive but related formulation of this approach has been used by Sejnowsky and Lehky (1987) to compute configuration using "the second derivative of the tangent vector to the surface along a line" (p. 18).

THE OPTIC ARRAY

What must be taken into account when describing the initial stages of processing can be illustrated by examples taken from research on visual perception. An ecological view of perception was developed by James Gibson on the basis of his extensive research, which clearly showed that visual form perception is initially three-dimensional (or even four, that is, space and time dimensional) and not composed of elementary lines and two-dimensional planes. This led Gibson to view perception as direct or immediate rather than constructional (with the exception of the cognitive influences on perception).

Although the holonomic brain theory supports Gibson's intuitions, the tenets of the theory were not acceptable to Gibson. Both he and his colleagues (as well as many others) suspected that its constructional aspects implied construction from elements (elementarism). These suspicions become groundless once it is understood that the initial perceptual processes are transformational and not elementaristic. In accord with Gibson's view, the constructional aspects of perception are top-down cognitive operations, such as those involved in learning: for example, the progressive differentiation of the sensory input (see e.g., Gibson & Gibson, 1955, and Lectures 7–10).

Some philosophers (e.g., Putnam, 1973) and scientists, such as Gibson and Turvey, are puzzled by the fact that whereas "perceivers are primarily sensitive to higher order variables of stimulation, light which lacks macroscopic structure provides no information to a visual system." (Fowler and Turvey, 1982). As noted earlier, this is known in philosophy as "the grain problem." The choice must clearly be made for a perceptual system responsive to higher order variables. These are, in fact, provided by reflected and diffracted patterns of radiant energy. Gibson and Turvey as well as most scientists fail to distinguish between radiant energy and "light" that is produced when patterns of such energy stimulate appropriate receptors. Nor do Gibson or Turvey realize that reflected radiant energy provides such patterns. This is because patterns are not discernable in the ambient diffracted "scatter" produced by reflection from objects.

A simple demonstration suggested by C. A. Taylor (1978) in a small volume on Imaging, prepared for instruction at the 6th form level in England, illustrates what is involved. Taylor placed a slide in a slide projector and projected it after removing the lens. "Technically the pattern on the screen with no lens in the projector is called a hologram. . . . the term simply means that each point on the screen. . . is receiving information from *every* point on the object" (p. 2).

Taylor went on to demonstrate that indeed each section of the screen receives information from every point on the object (the slide) by performing the following experiment: The projector is placed a few feet from the screen and then a converging (magnifying) lens is used to form a reduced image of the slide on the screen. The reduced image of the whole slide can be produced with the lens at any position within the patch of light, demonstrating that all sections of the illuminated screen contain information about all points on the slide (Fig 3.1).

This demonstration makes clear that incident radiation becomes diffracted, "scattered," by an object—scatter being defined as an organized bouncing of incident radiation off the object so that the organization of the radiation becomes distributed. It takes a lens to transform this organized scatter into what we are able to recognize as a (space-time) image. Taylor rightly pointed out that "the simple ray diagrams of geometrical optics hide a great deal of the complexity of this operation" (p. 3). In short, image formation depends on the recombination of incident radiation "scattered" by reflection and diffraction from surfaces and objects.

Thus, the dilemma posed by ecological optics is not really a dilemma after all. With respect to vision, reflected patterns of radiant energy that enter the pupil appear to lack macroscopic structure, but appearances are deceiving: The structure is hidden because it becomes diffracted: enfolded and spread, distributed, into a form displaying "nonlocality." Just as in a hologram, or in the placement of a radio receiver tuned to a broadcast, every location potentially contains the essential information necessary to reconstruct the macroscopic structure. Pupil and lens then unfold this potential into a recognizable optical image that interfaces with the retinal process (Fig 3.2).

As with Gabor's insights that led to the invention of optical information-processing systems such as holography, the holonomic brain theory holds that ambient patterns of energy that appear as "scatter" actually enfold and distribute macroscopic structure into a new order or organization (Fourier transforms entail sets of operations called "point spread functions"). This order serves as a potential to be re-transformed into a space-time image by the optics of the eye.

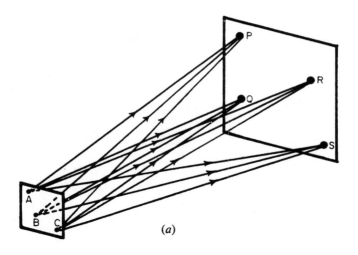

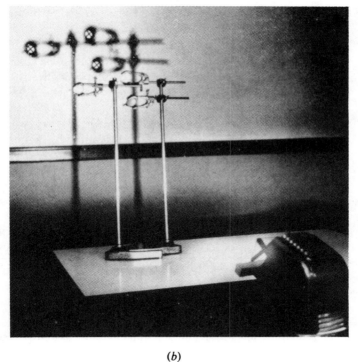

FIG. 3.1.   a) The hologram relationship: each point of the slide contributes scattered light to each point of the screen. b) The hologram
relationship: wherever the lens is placed a *complete* image of the slide
is produced. From: Taylor, C. A. (1978). *Images: A unified view of
diffraction and image formation with all kinds of radiation.* New York:
Wykeham Publications (London) Ltd.

51

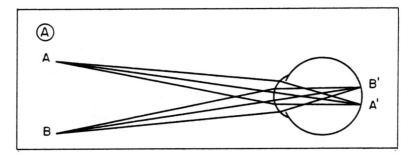

FIG. 3.2. A simplified drawing of the path of light rays through the eye's optical system, ignoring refraction by the lens. *Note that due to reflection and diffraction, A and B would not represent isolated points on a figure but nodes in a distributed array.* From: DeValois, R. L. and DeValois, K. K. (1988). *Spatial Vision.* New York: Oxford University Press.

Configurations hidden by the distributed nonlocal reordering of the input (as in a hologram) can be unfolded by the pupil and lens performing an inverse transformation.

THE OPTICAL IMAGE AND OPTICAL FLOW

How do these arguments regarding image formulation relate to the issue of the existance of a retinal image? Gibson (1979) claimed that no such representation of the object world need be involved in the perceptual process. The holonomic brain theory on the other hand, because it necessarily incorporates all the stages of processing as performed by the organism, begins with the observation that, in the stationary eye, the optics do in fact create recognizable images of objects. The fact that this is so tells us something about the system and cannot just be dismissed.

There is a sense in which even Gibson would admit such images:

If we could think of an image in the derived sense as a complex of relations, as the invariant structure of an arrangement, in short as information, there would be no great harm in extending the original meaning of the term. But this is hard to do, for it carries too much weight of history. It is better not to try. It would surely be false to say that there is a phonograph record in the ear, and the same error tempts us when we say that there is an image in the eye.

Thus, in ecological optics, the optic array, the optical image (or flow), and the retinal process become confounded. Gibson argued rightly that the retinal process differs from a photograph and that the optic array external to the eye conveys the complexity necessary for perception to occur. However, he ignored the transformational steps that characterize the optics of the eye and the distinction between the resulting optical image and the retinal process.

A realist stance toward both the momentary optical (moving, informative) image and the optic array identifies their difference. Thus, as noted, the optic array is considered to consist of a spectral manifold (an enfolded, distributed form of radiant energy), which is a transform of the patterns defining objects. The optic array thus resembles a holographic film—or a cross section of the waves carrying radio and television programs that have been broadcast (cast-broadly). By contrast the optical image is a three or more dimensional flow in the unfolded, space-time sense. To an observer of an excised eye it appears much as does a photograph taken by a camera; under natural conditions, flow patterns constitute an occulocentric space.

A further argument has been made to the effect that although the eye is a camera that focuses an image on the retina, it is we, with our visual apparatus who "see" that image, that we cannot know the actual design that the optical apparatus projects onto the retina. But the same considerations hold for a photographic print. Are we to deny the reality of the photograph as we perceive it to be? The holonomic brain theory considers optical images (flow) as real but distinguishes it clearly from the retinal process that transduces that flow by virtue of its neurochemical and neuroelectric properties.

The medium that operates on (records) the optical flow is different from that which records a photograph. The photographic medium is sensitive only to the intensities (amplitudes) of energy at any given point. By contrast, as Selig Hecht (1934) and others (Sakitt, 1972) have shown, retinal receptors are sensitive to single quanta of electromagnetic energy. Therefore, the quantal aspects of incident radiation must be considered in any representation of the receptor process. Mathematically, the holonomic brain theory therefore represents the receptor process not only by a real number representing the amplitude of the energy at a particular location but by a complex number that takes into account attributes of the quantum, that is, a number with direction. Thus, the retinal receptor processing of the optical flow is sufficiently multidimensional to allow visual experience to be three and even four or more dimensional.

There is an interpretation of the function of the pupil/lens system, presented in several texts on physiological optics (e.g., Hecht & Zajac, 1974) that differs completely from either Gibson's or the position taken here. Although the transformational description of the aperture/lens system is the same in this approach as in that taken in the holonomic brain theory, what differs is the interpretation of what is being transformed. In most interpretations other than those used in ecological optics or formalized by the holonomic brain theory, the events occurring on both sides of the aperture/lens system are described in complementary fashion, that is, in either space-time or spectral terms depending on which description is the most convenient. Such approaches do, of course, distinguish between holograms (a spectral representation) and ordinary photographs (a space-time image), but only with respect to how each is formed and not in relation to stages of perceptual processing. Complementarity in psychophysics is akin to complementarity in quantum physics (the Copenhagen solution to the Heisenberg duality). "Meaning," interpretation, are eschewed.

Complementarity in description sounds sophisticated and is appealing to many scientists who do not want to become enmeshed in philosophical issues. However, careful consideration of the complementarity stance strongly suggests that it leads to something akin to solipsism. At best such an approach yields "many worlds" (many different explanations are equally valid) at worst an "any worlds" (any explanation will do) interpretation. This approach unnecessarily complicates explanation—especially in studies of perception (take a look at most texts in this field).

By contrast, the remaining sections of this and the ensuing lectures describe the functions of sensory and various brain systems in terms of a hierarchy—better termed a "lowerarchy"—of nested subroutines (control processes). These subroutines operate (in the case of brain function, often in parallel, see e.g., Sperling, 1984) on the sensory process. This top-down operation by *sub*routines avoids "the insoluble paradox of an infinite regress" of *super*ordinate little men in the brain that so troubled Gibson. All that is necessary is a system of allocation, initiated either by the sensory input per se, or by ongoing physiological stimulations. (See e.g., Chap. 4 in *Plans and the Structure of Behavior* by Miller, Galanter, & Pribram, 1960). When these are inadequate, an "executive," decides on the basis of prior experience which subroutine is to operate when. The role of the frontal cortex of the forebrain in executive processing has been reviewed extensively (Pribram 1961b, 1973, 1987a) and is the subject of Lecture 10.

RETINAL RECEPTOR PROCESSES

The disassociation of optical image, understood as flow, from retinal receptor processing clarifies a considerable number of points that have been raised by those interested in the perceptual process. First, as noted, Gibson's intuitive mistrust of the notion of a two-dimensional picturelike image can be taken into account without denying the existence of a moving optical image, that is an optical flow. Second, the optical and retinal processes are, therefore, not constrained to two dimensions. Third, the details of the retinal process become accessible to interpretation as modulations of the spontaneous activity of this structure by both (a) the full multi-dimensional richness of the optic array as transformed into a spatiotemporal optical flow and (b) central control processes.

Cutting (1986), with several penetrating descriptions, reviewed the types of

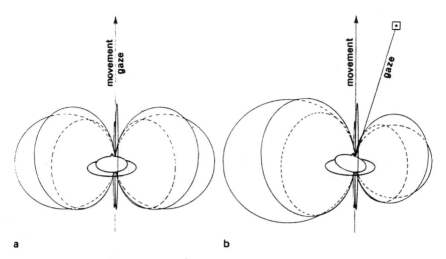

FIG. 3.3.   (a) A three-dimensional instantaneous isoangular displacement contour for linear movement with gaze fixed along the movement path. This shape is a toroid, or figure eight rotated in the third
dimension along the path of movement and gaze. (b) The same contours for an observer looking somewhat off to the side. The toroid has
deformed into a shape more like a lopsided bagel. From: Cutting,
James E. (1986). *Perception with an Eye for Motion.* Cambridge, MA:
The MIT Press.

relations that, at a minimum, must enter into computations performed by the
retinal process. To begin, the retinal surface is curved, conforming nearly to a
section of a sphere. Thus the interface of the optical flow with the retina must be
curved and the type of geometry used to describe this interface must be spherical
rather than plane, a distinction first made by Leonardo da Vinci. As a consequence, the processing units established with reference to the optical flow are
lines across curved surfaces, that is, arcs. Such arcs (and tangents to such arcs)
can become grouped into cones, and measured in terms of solid visual angles.
Cutting provides "rules of thumb and fist": The width of one's thumb at arm's
length is about 2° degrees whereas that of the fist (without thumb) is about 10°.

Second, the eyes move in their sockets in such a way that the retinal surface
moves with respect to the optical array to cause transformations in the retinal
coordinates. The relationship between such transformations and the dimensionality of the optical array is expressed in terms of occulocentric concentric toroids
(Cutting, 1986, p. 195).

As an example, Cutting analyzes motion parallax, which provides a plausible
means for determining one's direction of movement. As noted, occulocentric
concentric toroids are observer-related descriptions of potential optic motions.
Thus

Any object or texture in three dimensional space can be assigned an optic vector with one assumption and three variables. The assumption is that the objects in the world are not moving, and the variables are the object's instantaneous distance and direction from the observer and the observer's trajectory through the environment. These specify all flow. (p. 218)

Lectures 5 and 6 describe the neural processes that become involved in processing optic flow. Here, it is sufficient to note that computations regarding parallax (as well as other related phenomena such as the Doppler effect) come naturally and simply when the spectral domain as well as the space-time domain are addressed in the computations.

This type of analysis of relationships among surfaces constitutes projective geometry. Johansson (Johansson, Van Hofsten, & Jansson, 1980, p. 31) emphasizes the relational nature of projective geometry: In "projective geometry metrics has no meaning. Instead certain relations, the so called projective properties, which remain invarient under perspective transformations of a figure, are abstracted. One example [of] such invariance under form change is the cross ratio." The cross-ratio is, in most computations, the polar projection of four colinear points.

Cutting details how computing cross-ratios can account for the rigidity and flatness of perceived figures. When extended to such related techniques as density indices, all four space-time coordinates are handled, giving rise to three-dimensional images. As already indicated, in the holonomic brain theory the optical image is already three- or more dimensional as is retinal processing. Furthermore, it is the optical image that veridically represents the properties of surfaces and objects in space-time, not the optic array. Thus, the value of Cutting's approach, which is based on prior work by both Johannsen and Gibson, is not as Cutting conceives it, to show how a two-dimensional retinal image can be processed into a three-dimensional experience, but to show how two-dimensional pictures and displays on an oscilloscope screen become experientially perceived as three- or more dimensional. The two-dimensional display can be thought of as similar to the experiment in mechanics where a ball rolling down an inclined plane is used to determine the basic laws that govern bodies in motion.

The cross ratio has limitations: It "is confined to colinear or coplanar points . . . [and] is confined to four and only four elements" (p. 115). Cutting indicated that these limitations are overcome by generalizing the cross ratio technique to a distance-density model as proposed by Krumhansel (1978). The cross ratio changes more when a moving element is in a region that is more densely packed. Krumhansel devised formal methods by which distance information could be permuted into measures of density.

Cutting shows that in order to perceive flat rigid surfaces rotating in space—what in these lectures are considered to be images—the distance-density model specifies the invariance processed by the perceptual system. For situations in which the organism approaches or recedes from such surfaces, distance-density models fail and flow vectors specify the invariant. Lecture 6 describes the neural system involved in this sort of "looming" processing and the evidence that ensembles of neurons actually compute such vectors.

Here the distance-density model for image processing is more relevant. Cutting utilized several forms of the model and found that, when he used an exponential form, an infinitely dense array of points yields a density distribution that is uniform throughout—in other words, the density distribution is little different from the perceived shape of the image.

Cutting (1986) cautions, however:

> I do *not* contend that index 4 [the exponential form] is a computational algorithm used by the visual system. I suggest only that it captures constraints on the information used for making perceptual judgments. I assume that the visual system performs some structure-through-motion analysis, perhaps along the lines proposed by Ullman (1979). I assume further that densities at various points in space around and on the object correspond to the sensitivities of the algorithms for determining a unique three-dimensional interpretation. In regions of high density the algorithm— whatever form it takes—should be sensitive to any point not in rigid relation to others, and in regions of low density it should be less sensitive. In other words, density measures predict the tolerance of the human visual system for small perturbations in the registration of the locations of particular points in the array. (p. 129)

Two possibilities for understanding brain function in perception result from this assessment: (a) The fit of the exponential form of the model reflects the logarithimic form of the retinal configuration: "retinal fovea to periphery" in the cortical representation, and (b) the requirements of the human perceptual system can be expressed in terms of spatial frequency as well as density—high density equals high spatial frequency, low density equals low spatial frequency. Discussion of the relation between the distance-density model and the holonomic brain theory is resumed in the next lecture.

THE HOW OF PERCEPTUAL PROCESSING

Note that Cutting sharply distinguishes between the constraints used by the visual system, the "what is being processed" from the "how of processing." The question therefore arises as to whether the distance-density model has any relevance to neural processing in vision. If the approach taken in these lectures is correct, the answer is yes. What needs to be found is the set of transformations between the description of the invariants constraining the perceptual process and those constraining the description of the neural process.

When our interest lies in how processing takes place, we must look from the world of what is being processed as would an outside observer. Helmholtz (1863) stated the issue clearly:

> Let me first remind the reader that if all the linear dimensions of other bodies, and our own, at the same time were diminished or increased in like proportion, as for instance to half or double their size, we should with our means of space-perception be utterly unaware of the change. This would also be the case if the distension or contraction were different in different directions, provided that our own body changed in the same manner.
>
> Think of the image of the world in a convex mirror. The common silvered globes set up in gardens give the essential features, only distorted by some optical irregularities. A well-made convex mirror of moderate aperture represents the objects in front of it as apparently solid and in fixed positions behind its surface. But the images of the distant horizon and of the sun in the sky lie behind the mirror at a limited distance, equal to its focal length. Between these and the surface of the mirror are found the images of all the other objects before it, but the images are diminished and flattened in proportion to the distance of their objects from the mirror. The flattening, or decrease in the third dimension, is relatively greater than the decrease of the surface-dimensions. Yet every straight line or every plane in the outer world is represented by a straight line or a plane in the image. The image of a man measuring with a rule a straight line from the mirror would contract more and more the farther he went, but with his shrunken rule the man in the image would count out exactly the same number of centimetres as the real man. And, in general, all geometrical measurements of lines or angles made with regularly varying images of real instruments would yield exactly the same Euclidean results as in the outer world, all congruent bodies would coincide on being applied to one another in the mirror as in the outer world, all lines of sight in the outer world would be represented by straight lines of sight in the mirror. In short I do not see how men in the mirror are to discover that their bodies are not rigid solids and their experiences not good examples of the correctness of Euclid's axioms. But if they could look out upon our world as we can look into theirs, without overstepping the boundary, they must declare it to be a picture in a spherical mirror, and would speak of us just as we speak of them; and if two inhabitants of the different worlds could communicate with one another, neither, so far as I can see, would be able to convince the other that he had the true, the other the distorted relations.

Helmholtz's observation is relevant to the thesis of these lectures: He notes that when two inhabitants of different worlds, in our case the worlds of psychophysics and neuroscience, try to communicate with one another, each would have difficulty in convincing the other that he had the undistorted view. Communication can only occur when both frames of reference, both worlds are acknowledged by discovering the transformations (e.g., the convexity of the mirror in Helmholtz's example) that connect them.

Movement is critical to the determination of the transformations that characterize the relationship between psychophysics and neuroscience. But more than movement is involved. As noted in Lecture 1, visual processing is ordinarily (see e.g., Hubel & Wiesel, 1962; Marr, 1982) assumed to result in images by way of a procedure similar to that proposed by Euclid: that is, the formation of lines or contours from points, the formation of two-dimensional surfaces from contours, and the formation of three-dimensional object-forms from surfaces. This assumption is fed by recourse to experiments in which two-dimensional pictures of three-dimensional forms are used—and the illusions resulting from such use. The assumption also follows from the erroneous belief that a two-dimensional "retinal image" is formed by the optics of the eye. As noted, the optical image is a flow composed of at least three-dimensions, the retinal receptor surface is curved, and nystagnoid movement continuously changes the relationship of the optical flow to that which is being imaged. How then do the retinal receptors process the optical flow? Rock, (1983), suggests that because of movement,

each stimulated retinal point signifies a distinct direction. Therefore one can interpret the outcome even of the typical conditions of form perception in terms of the collectively perceived occulocentric directions of the parts of a figure. This would already be a departure from the current emphasis on contour detectors. But we can take a step further. In humans and other species that move their eyes, the perceived direction of a point with respect to ourselves (referred to as egocentric or radial direction) is some joint function of retinal locus and eye position.

We performed the following simple experiment (Fig. 3.4) (Rock & Halper, 1969). Condition 1: The observer fixates one luminous point while another moves around in a particular path in a dark room. Since the latter point traces an extended path over the retina, we can safely predict that its path will be discerned. However, the speed of the point is relatively slow, so that we should not expect a simultaneous iconic image of the entire path. Observers have little difficulty in perceiving the path in this condition. They are able to draw an accurate picture of it. Condition 2:

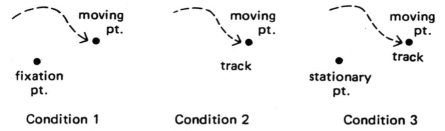

FIG. 3.4.   Three conditions of experiment on the perceived path of a moving point. Condition 1: Observer fixates a stationary point. Condition 2: Observer tracks the moving point. Condition 3: Observer tracks the moving point but judges the path of the stationary point. From: Rock, I. (1983). *The Logic of Perception*. Cambridge, MA: The MIT Press.

The observer tracks a single luminous point as it moves along the same path as in condition 1 with no other point visible. Here no image is spread over the retina. Only a small region of the fovea is stimulated. However, by taking account of changing eye position, the perceptual system is able to detect the changing ego-centric directions of the point. The result is that observers perceive the path of the moving point as well in this condition as in the first. Condition 3: The observer tracks the moving luminous point but tries to note the path of a second stationary point. The stationary point here produces an image that is successively spread over the retina. But the observer is unable to use this information and has no impression whatsoever of a path traversed by the stationary point. Position constancy obtains, which means that path perception is governed not by changing local sign but by changing egocentric direction. The stationary point does not change its egocentric direction. Therefore, no motion path is seen.

A simple method of performing this kind of experiment is to move a narrow slit in an opaque surface over a luminous figure seen in the dark. Then only a single point of the figure will be visible at any time. This method is essentially one that has been referred to as the "anorthoscopic" procedure. (p. 46)

The results of this type of experiment contradict the common assumption that form perception follows the rules of Euclidean Geometry where points compose lines, lines compose planes, and planes compose solids. The primitives of form perception are not points or contours but relations between changes in oculocentric and egocentric direction. The occurrence of these directionalities implies the existence of oculocentric and egocentric frames of reference, that is, "spaces," which must be constituted in a top-down fashion. Their constitution is described in Lectures 5 and 6. To repeat: Lines and edges are not the primitives that configure the perceptual process; lines and edges result from the perceptual process, they do not determine it.

A COMPUTATIONAL IMPLEMENTATION

A similar conclusion was reached by Sejnowski and Lehky (1987), who devised a most ingeneous *computational* model that takes advantage of the full richness of the optical image:

One of the primary properties of a surface is its [three dimensional] curva-ture. . . . The curvature of a surface along a line through the surface can be computed by measuring the second derivative of the tangent vector to the surface along the line. The principal curvatures at a point on the surface are defined as the maximum and minimum curvature, and these are always along lines that meet at right angles. The principal curvatures are parameters that provide information about the shape of a surface, and they have the additional advantage of being independent of the local coordinate system. Hence it would be helpful to have a way of estimating principle curvatures directly from the shading information in an image. (p. 9)

After reviewing the failure of other attempts to compute the shape of a surface from its shading, Sejnowski and Lehky decided to base their computation on the known properties of receptive fields of neurons in the ganglion cell layer of the retina. An input layer was constituted to consist of two superimposed hexagonal arrays of units, one array being made up of "on" and the other of "off" units. Thus each point of the image is sampled by both on and off units. The response characteristic of the receptive field of each unit is the Laplacian of a two-dimensional Gaussian, in other words, the typical center-surround organization of receptive fields recorded from the optic nerve. Responses of these input units to an image were determined by convolving the image with the units' receptive fields. This procedure was used by Rodieck (1965) to describe the functions of the retina on the basis of actual recordings (Rodieck & Stone, 1965) and formed one of the cornerstones of holographic theory (Pribram, Nuwer, & Baron, 1974).

Simulation of these procedures in a computational model adds considerably to our ability to portray just how the sensory process operates: "Besides being biologically plausible, choosing these particular input receptive fields was advantageous from a computational view . . . : the responses of these center-surround receptive fields, acting as second derivative operators, tended to compensate for changes in appearance in the object [illuminated] from different directions" (Sejnowski, 1976). I am sure Ernst Mach (see e.g., Ratliff, 1965) would be especially pleased to see this aspect of the model in operation.

The model programs the receptive fields of the output layer in terms of graded responses, which are a function of both the value of the principal curvatures as well as their orientations: in short, the phenomenological descriptors of the image. This accords with the assumption made in the initial lecture that phenomenal experience is coordinate with the junctional dendritic microprocess, which is composed of graded polarizations.

However, a problem emerged in that the signal from each unit is ambiguous: There are an infinite number of combinations of curvature and orientation that give rise to an identical response. "The way to [re]solve this ambiguity is to have the desired value represented in a distributed fashion, by the joint activity of a population of such broadly tuned units in which the units have overlapping receptive fields in the relevant parameter space (in this case curvature and orientation)" (Sejnowski & Lehky, 1987, p. 11).

This kind of distributed representation is found in color vision. The responses of any one of the three broadly tuned color receptors is ambiguous, but the relative activities of all three allow one to precisely discriminate a very large range of colors. Sejnowski and Lehky (1987) noted the economy of coding such an arrangement: "It is possible to form fine discriminations with only a very small number of coarsely-tuned units, as opposed to requiring a large number of narrowly-tuned, nonoverlapping units" (p. 11).

From the neurophysiological viewpoint the most interesting aspect of the model is the development of receptive field configurations in the middle, hidden, layer of the model. Recall that only the first layer of the model was programmed according to physiological constraints, that is, those that configure the ganglion cell layer of the retina. The configurations of the unprogrammed middle layer come to show a remarkable resemblance to those in the primary visual receiving region (the striate visual cortex). Many of these units had oriented receptive fields. Two classes of such fields were identified on the basis of their connections with output units: those that discriminated for the direction (vertical columns), and those that discriminated the magnitudes of the principal curvatures (horizontal rows).

Koenderink (1989) has shown that the "receptive field" of a point operator is a 2 or more dimensional Gaussian envelope. By receptive field is meant the geometric differentiation of the point. In this manner a bilocal entity such as direction encoded as a vector has as its "receptive field" an edge finder and its second derivative maps into a "bar" configuration. Koendrik has shown that the range of receptive fields mapped in the primate visual cortex can be described within the first four orders of differential geometry. The layers of the network, artificial and natural, appear to be performing operations of this sort.

As noted by Sejnowski and Lehky, from the standpoint of understanding the neurophysiology of perception, there is a critical conclusion to be drawn from these experimental and mathematical analyses: The network model provides an alternative to the usual interpretation of these properties: shape can be derived from shading rather than [from] edges.

Shading is spatially four-dimensional because it varies over height, width, depth, and time with movement. Retinal processing, if shadings (and textures that can be conceived as microshadings) are to be utilized, must therefore be more than two-dimensional. As noted, retinal receptivity is in the range of photons, quanta of radiant electromagnetic energy, and therefore sensitive to phase—that is, direction. This gives the process sufficient degrees of freedom to allow the type of multidimensional processing espoused by Sejnowski and Lehky. As they reported, the model must still overcome some remaining difficulties: "In the curvature domain, unlike the orientation domain, we have a set of non-overlapping tuning curves, and therefore curvature is not well represented in the model in its present state." The curvature domain should be sampled more densely. This is certainly the case in the actual retina and the quantal approach of the holonomic brain theory directly addresses this issue; the issue of grain that was the theme of the early parts of this lecture.

SUMMARY

The facts of optical processing by lens and pupil are agreed upon and therefore make a good starting point for an examination of the perceptual process. Distinguishing between processing performed by the optics of the eye from that performed by the retina allows for the occurrence of a moving optical image, that is, an optical flow. This flow is not two-dimensional, but richly multidimensional. The multidimensionality is complemented by the richness of the retinal receptor process. A computational approach to modelling the retinal process is not only feasible but has been begun with results that lead to the simulation of the receptive field properties of cortical neurons in the visual system. The computations are based, not on the construction of two-dimensional stick figures from lines and edges, but on shadings of curved (and colored) three-dimensional moving images as they are experienced.

The transformational processing of apparently "scattered" radient energy into the optical flow as preserved and complemented by retinal processing resolves "the grain problem" but poses an additional hurdle for direct perception. As Cutting (1986) pointed out, Gibson's program of identifying invariants leads to a plethora of dimensions potentially useful in perception. This means that selection must occur at the various processing stages. Selection can be passive, as by filtering, or active and directed by the accumulation of the results of prior selections. According to the evidence that makes up the foundations of the holonomic brain theory, sensory driven, essentially passive selection characterizes the configural aspects of perception. On the other hand, because of the amount of memory storage involved, cummulative, directed selection characterizes the cognitive aspects. As noted in the previous lectures and brought out more fully in those to come, the results of prior selections become stored not only in the primary projection systems but also in neural systems separate from these primary systems. These "higher order" systems are *triggered* by current sensory input to initiate directive procedures that operate back on the sensory driven processes by way of top-down neural connectivity: Thus directive and selective neural processes interpenetrate. Perception results from the transformational character of these interpenetrations.

The theme of the lecture has taken us inward from the optic array to the first stages of neural processing. The remaining lectures are devoted to further stages of perceptual processing by the various systems of the brain.

4 Imaging: Cooperativity in Primary Sensory Systems

If we could find a convenient way of showing not merely the amplitudes of the envelopes but the actual oscillations of the array of resonators, we would have a notation (cf. Gabor 1946) of even greater generality and flexibility, one that would reduce under certain idealizing assumptions to the spectrum and under others to the wave form . . . . . The analogy . . . [to] the position-momentum and energy-time problems that led Heisenberg in 1927 to state his uncertainty principle . . . has led Gabor to suggest that we may find the solution [to the problems of sensory processing] in quantum mechanics. (Licklider, 1951, p. 993)

In 1957 it was possible to say '. . . These considerations also lead us to the suggestion that much of normal nervous function occurs without impulses [emphasis in original] but mediated by graded activity, not only as response but also as stimulus' (Bullock, 1957). The notion had appealed to me for some time (Bullock, 1945) and in 1947 I wrote in a review 'The far-reaching implications of the assumption that neurons can affect each other by means distinct from classical impulses in synaptic pathways are obvious'. I referred to Bremer (1944) and Gerard (1941) who influenced me the most in this view, which remained for a long time ignored in the conventional orthodoxy. [Currently, therefore,] I propose that a 'circuit' in our context of nervous tissue is an oversimplified abstraction involving a limited subset of communicated signals; . . . that in fact there are many parallel types of signals and forms of response, often skipping over neighbours in direct contact and acting upon more-or-less-specified classes of nearby or even remote elements. Thus the true picture of what is going on could not be drawn as a familiar circuit; and specified influence would not be properly called connectivity, except for a very limited subset of neighbours. Instead of the usual terms 'neural net' or 'local circuit' I would suggest we think of a 'neural throng', that is, a form of densely packed social gathering with more structure and goals than a mob. (Bullock, 1981, p. 269, 281)

INTRODUCTION

The previous lecture focused on the distinction between optic array, optical flow, and retinal process. The relationship between these stages of processing was conceived in terms of transformations. In this lecture the focus is on the transformations that characterize the brain processes involved in imaging. Evidence derived from psychophysical, perceptual, and neurophysiological research is reviewed. This evidence leads to specifying the transformations in formal terms. In order to restrict this focus, it is necessary to clearly separate the experience of imaging discussed in the current lecture from those of object-form perception and categorizing discussed subsequently. What is it then, that we can identify as imaging?

I am sitting on a roof patio of the outer quad at Stanford University. The scene before me is strikingly beautiful in the January sun. The upper part of the scene forms a curved deep blue surface that becomes less saturated at its juncture with a deep violet-green surface with undulating margins. In the foreground are splotches of tile-red interspersed with splotches of dark green. I am writing on a yellow rectangle lined with blue, placed on a slate grey circular surface. The same scene can also be described in a different way: a blue hemisphere sitting astride a circular plane from which arise large undulating masses and smaller masses topped with three-dimensional shapes at various angles with one another and covered with semicylinders. Interspersed with these shapes are others, more rounded and composed of swaying round and elongated shimmering small objects. What I am looking at are, of course, the sky, the Santa Cruz hills, the rooftops of the quadrangle of buildings intermingled with trees.

These three descriptions of the same scene represent three distinguishable experiences that ordinarily interpenetrate. Some people have difficulty making a separation among *image* (the first description), *object* (the second), and *category* (the third). The easiest way to see the distinction is to move: Images change when there is relative movement between oculocentric and egocentric frames; objects remain objects over a wide range of movements; categories deal with the relationship among prototypical objects.

Distinguishing between image, object, and prototypes is important because each is processed by a separate brain system. The experience of interpenetration results from reciprocal connectivities within and between hierarchically arranged systems that make possible top-down constraints on lower level (e.g., imaging) systems. Top-down connections from higher order systems (e.g., those involved in categorizing) penetrate into thalamic, brain stem, and even receptor levels thus preprocessing the input to the primary sensory projection cortex.

That top-down constraints operate on perception is well documented in experimental psychology. When experimental psychologists turn to neurophysiology, however, they almost always accept uncritically the dogma of bottom-up reflex-arc type processing, which has been shown to be in error even at the spinal reflex level (Miller, Galanter, & Pribram, 1960; Pribram 1960, 1971). The fact of reciprocal connectivity within and between brain systems needs to be emphasized and accepted—the brain really is as it ought be, given our perceptual reality.

Currently, cognitive psychologists and some neurophysiologists (see e.g., the excellent review by Marrocco, 1986) are grappling with the problem of specifying the transformations between configurations at various processing levels. The issues involved are usually discussed under the rubric of bottom-up vs top-down models, issues also addressed in Lecture 1. Some (e.g., Broadbent, 1977; Deutsch & Deutsch, 1963; Norman, 1964; Treisman, 1969) have ultimately opted for a compromise between the two extreme positions. However, even in these compromises, bottom-up processing is conceived as a combination of elementary features. In the same vein top-down processing is conceived as "integrating" the lower order into higher order forms. According to the holonomic brain theory both conceptions are in error. The misconceptions are due to an incomplete understanding of data gathered at the neurophysiological and neurobehavioral levels of inquiry.

As is detailed shortly, both bottom-up and top-down processing are *directed* (i.e., instructive) and *selective*. The perceptual process, by virtue of receptor and brain systems inputs, is directed toward selecting some features (or dimensions) from a genetically determined neuronal ensemble that more or less arbitrarily conjoins such features. This lecture deals with conjunctions perceived as images, conjunctions selected by a sensory input. The computation is accomplished by means of reciprocal input-output connectivities. The resulting brain processes occur within the "primary" sensory projection systems that compute and invert a Gabor elementary function.

AN EXPERIMENT

When a grating consisting of bars of equal width and spacings is moved across the visual field of an immobilized cat or monkey, the response from single neurons in the visual cortex can be recorded. Response consists of discrete impulses of axonal activity referred to as a spike train. The size and spacings of the grating are measured as spatial frequency; the velocity of the movement by temporal frequency. Luminance and orientation of the bars can also be specified. Neurons in the visual cortex are selective with regard to all of these dimensions of the stimulus (and also to acceleration, color and, as detailed shortly, other stimulus and behavioral response dimensions). Thus a particular neuron's preferred spatial and temporal frequency, preferred orientation, and other dimensional preferences can be determined. Ordinarily, determination depends on listening by way of a loudspeaker or watching an oscilloscope face for the density (often called frequency) of spikes in the spike trains—that is, how closely (or distantly) spaced the nerve impulses are to one another. Greater spike density indicates greater response to the stimulus.

According to the approach taken in these lectures, the invariant described in the previous lecture by the distance-density model for image processing should be reflected in the density of spikes in a neural spike train when images are moved in a planar surface as in Cutting's experiments. For single neurons, however, the exponential form of the model would not necessarily apply because that form incorporates the results of processing by the entire visual system.

Each neuron could nonetheless approximate the distance-density model in its own fashion. Gerstein and Mandelbrot (1964) suggested that the firing pattern of single neurons made such an approximation by a random walk. A modification of their earlier suggestion yields what is, in fact, a form of the distance-density model. In this random walk version, distance is set by a barrier height that limits the distance of each step in the walk. Barrier height is determined by the polarization of axonal membrane. The density parameter is determined by a drift rate due to the rate of repolarization after depolarization.

An analysis of records of spike trains of visual cortical neurons was made while the spatial frequency and orientation of moving bars was parametrically changed. The analysis showed that distance indexed by barrier height varied as a function of changes in orientation, whereas drift rate is more generally determined and especially reflects changes of spatial frequency (Fig. 4.1, Berger, Pribram, Wild, & Bridges, 1990).

In terms of the random walk form of the spectral-density model, the density function is represented by drift rate which is determined by the ratio of co-spectrum (essentially, sine components) to quadspectrum (essentially, cosine components), in other words by Fourier coefficients. As shown by Pollen & Ronner (1980) this quadrature can be recorded from neurons within a cortical column. Neurophysiologically, the value of polarizations within such an ensemble of receptive fields is represented by these coefficients whose weighting is determined by the spatial frequency of the displayed patterns. The coefficients are cross multiplied by probability which are represented by amplitudes, boundary conditions determined by the orientation of the display. The result is, of course, the probabilities amplitude modulated set of Fourier coefficients, which describe a class of four-dimensional informational hyperspaces such as Hermite polynomials constrained by Gaussians, of which the Gabor function is an elementary example. (See Appendix A for formalism.)

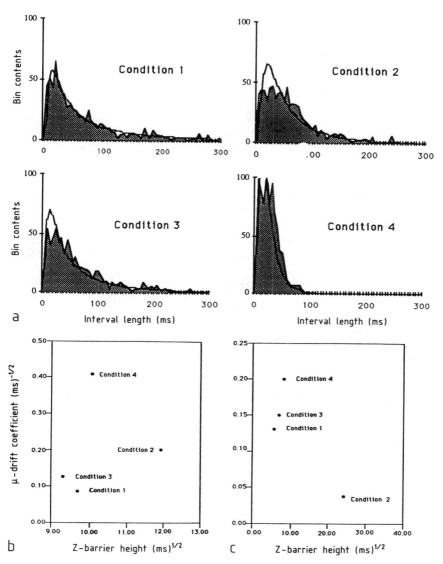

FIG. 4.1. a) The interspike interval histograms for the four stimulus conditions are shown by the shaded areas. The solid line shows the calculated curve for the first passage time of random walk with positive drift with the same mean and variance as the measured histograms. b) The barrier height and drift coefficient for the cell with the interspike interval histograms illustrated in a is shown. c) Another cell is presented which shows a large increase in barrier height for the 90 degree orientation change of Condition 2. From: Berger, D., Pribram, K., Wild, H., & Bridges, C. (1990). An analysis of neural spike-train distributions: determinants of the response of visual cortex neurons to changes in orientation and spatial frequency. *Experimental Brain Research, 80,* 129–134.

THE GABOR ELEMENTARY FUNCTION

The quotation from Licklider introducing this lecture comes from Steven's *Handbook of Experimental Psychology* written almost a half century ago. The passage presages the essence of how processing is dealt with in the holonomic brain theory. In the theory, the function of cortical receptive fields is defined, on the basis of data to be reviewed, in terms of ensembles of Gabor functions that are especially sensitive to the processing of the shadings, coloring, and textures of surfaces that constitute images (see e.g., Caelli & Moraglia, 1985).

As described in Lecture 2, Gabor developed the main points of a holonomic, quantal, psychophysics that was inspired by the mathematics invented by Hilbert in the early part of the century. This mathematics was the same as that applied by Heisenberg to deal with the phenomena of quantum mechanics. But as Gabor (1946) pointed out, his contributions "are merely an acknowledgement to the [quantum] theory which has supplied us with an important part of the mathematical methods" (p. 452). Events at the quantum level are not necessarily responsible for the psychophysical (and neurophysiological) processes involved, although as described in the epilogue to these lectures, this remains a distinct possibility (see e.g., Margenau, 1984; Frohlich, 1968, 1983, 1986, and especially Hameroff, 1987).

Gabor's discovery was based on the fact that the Fourier theorem opposes two different orders, two different ways in which signals become organized. In Lecture 3, we became acquainted with these two domains as characterizing the input to and output from a lens that performs a Fourier transform. On one side of the transform lies the space-time order we ordinarily perceive. On the other side lies a distributed enfolded holographic-like order referred to as the frequency or spectral domain.

Gabor (1946), as had Heisenberg and Hilbert before him, chose to represent the spectral and space-time orders by orthogonal coordinates, thus forming a phase space. Gabor was intrigued by the fact that in psychophysics, as in quantum physics, one could accurately determine either frequency (e.g., of a tone) or time (e.g., of its occurrence) but not both. Thus an uncertainty principle holds for psychophysics as well as for quantum physics:

> Fourier's theorem makes of description in time and description by the spectrum, two mutually exclusive methods. If the term "frequency" is used in the strict mathematical sense which applies only to infinite wave-trains, a "changing frequency" becomes a contradiction in terms, as it is a statement involving both time and frequency.
>
> The terminology of physics has never completely adapted itself to this rigorous mathematical definition of "frequency." For instance, speech and music have a definite "time pattern" as well as a frequency pattern. It is possible to leave the time pattern unchanged, and double what we generally call "frequencies" by playing a

musical piece on the piano an octave higher, or conversely, it can be played in the same key, but in different time.

Let us now tentatively adopt the view that both time and frequency are legitimate references for describing a signal and illustrate this—by taking them as orthogonal coordinates. In this diagram harmonic oscillation is represented by a vertical line. Its frequency is exactly defined while its epoch is entirely undefined. A sudden surge or "delta function" (also called "unit impulse function"), on the other hand, has a sharply defined epoch, but its energy is distributed over the whole frequency spectrum. This signal is therefore represented by a horizontal line. (p. 431)

With the advent of frequency analysis in studies of the figural processing pioneered by Schade (1956), Kabrisky (1966), and Campbell and Robson (1968), the term "spatial frequency" has become commonplace in the visual sciences. This term emphasizes the mathematical relation between frequency and space-time, as noted by Gabor (1946), who, however, took the additional step of using the Fourier relation to compose a Hilbert space, changing from a function of either

[Space]time *or* frequency—[to] a function of two variables—[space]time *and* frequency—. [Thus] we have the strange feature that, although we can carry out the analysis with any degree of accuracy in the [space]time direction or the frequency direction, we cannot carry it out simultaneously in both beyond a certain limit. In fact, the mathematical apparatus adequate for treating this diagram in a quantitative way has become available only fairly recently to physicists, thanks to the development of quantum physics.

The linkage between the uncertainties in the definition of "[space]time" and "frequency" has never passed entirely unnoticed by physicists. It is the key to the problem of the "coherence length" of wave trains, ... But these problems came into the focus of physical interest only with the discovery of wave mechanics, and especially by the formulation of Heisenberg's principle of indeterminancy in 1927. This discovery led to a great simplification in the mathematical apparatus of quantum theory, which was recast in a form of which use will be made in the present paper. (p. 432)

In the pages that follow Gabor developed his theme. He introduced the complex exponential for operations with simple sine and cosine functions. This allows for an effect of phase, adding computational power. The introduction of complex variables is necessary because:

If we had operated with the real signal . . . the weighting function would have been even, and the mean frequency always zero. This is one of the points on which physical feeling and the usual Fourier methods are not in perfect agreement. But we could eliminate the negative frequencies only at the price of introducing a complex signal. (p. 434)

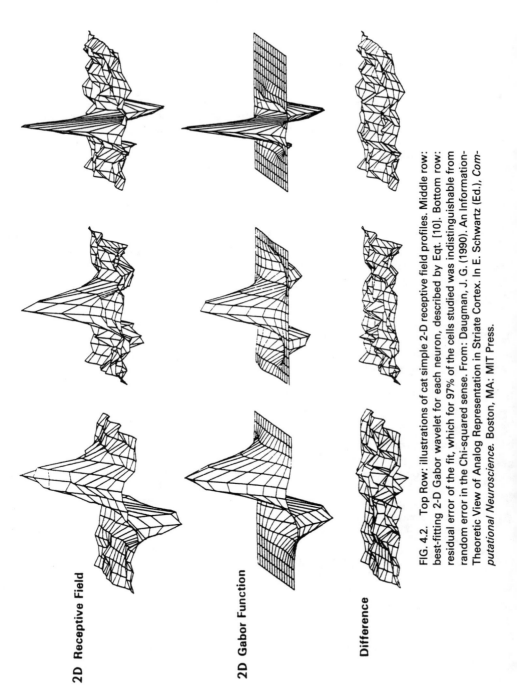

2D Receptive Field

2D Gabor Function

Difference

FIG. 4.2. Top Row: illustrations of cat simple 2-D receptive field profiles. Middle row: best-fitting 2-D Gabor wavelet for each neuron, described by Eqt. [10]. Bottom row: residual error of the fit, which for 97% of the cells studied was indistinguishable from random error in the Chi-squared sense. From: Daugman, J. G. (1990). An Information-Theoretic View of Analog Representation in Striate Cortex. In E. Schwartz (Ed.), *Computational Neuroscience*. Boston, MA: MIT Press.

Finally, Gabor defined his elementary function, the *logon*:

> The signal which occupies the minimum area is the modulation product of a harmonic oscillation of any frequency with a pulse of the form of a probability function. . . . The probability signal has always played an important part in the theory of Fourier transforms. But its minimum property does not appear to have been recognized. (p. 435)

ACHIEVING THE TRANSFORM

In addition to the contributions to mathematical psychophysics already noted, Gabor (1968) described a method by which a Fourier transform can be achieved by way of a set of transfer functions each of which convolves two adjacent stages of signal processing. This stepwise procedure is especially relevant to the manner in which the neural apparatus achieves the spectral domain in the configural aspects of sensory processing.

Before tracing these steps, however, it is reasonable to ask: What advantage does the organism gain by processing in the spectral transform domain? The answer is efficiency: the fact that correlations are so easily achieved by first convolving signals in the spectral domain and then, inverse transforming them into the space-time domain (see Kronauer & Zeevi quotation, Lect. 1 p. 23). Thus, in statistics, the Fast Fourier Transform (FFT) procedure has become a and modifications of the Fourier process are the basis of computerized tomography, the CT scans used by hospitals to (re)construct images of brains and other organs of the body. As to the stepwise procedure of convolving adjacent levels of neural processing, the retina of the visual system once more makes a good starting point.

In the range of ganglion-cell receptive fields Enroth-Cugell and Robson (1966) demonstrated a variety of relationships between center and surround patterns of excitation and inhibition. This variety can be explained on the assumption of an opponent mechanism—separate excitatory (depolarizing) and inhibitory (hyperpolarizing) retinal processes, each process displaying an essentially Gaussian distribution.

Where do these separate excitatory and inhibitory processes take place? Dowling and Boycott (1965), among others, have shown that, prior to the ganglion cell layer, few if any retinal neurons generate nerve impulses. All interactions are performed by way of graded polarizations. These are of two opposing types— depolarizing excitations and hyperpolarizing inhibitions. Intracellular recordings (Sveactichin, 1967) suggest that the excitatory polarizations are generated along the input transmission paths (bipolar cells) of the retina, whereas the inhibitory polarizations are due to the horizontal layers (amacrine and horizontal cells) that cross the transmission channels. This lateral inhibitory process has been studied extensively and has become the basis for quantitative descriptions of sensory interaction by Hartline (see Ratliff, 1965) and by von Bekesy (1959) in their treatment of the Mach band phenomenon. The equations they invoke are similar to those used by Rodieck (1965) in his description of ganglion-cell receptive fields.

Essentially these experimental analyses point out that the retinal mosaic becomes decomposed into an opponent process by depolarizing and hyperpolarizing analog, graded potentials. The mosaic is transformed into more or less concentric receptive fields in which center and surround are of opposite sign. The difference of two overlapping Gaussians (DOGs) fully describes this transformation.

The next group of cells in the visual pathway is the lateral geniculate nucleus of the thalamus. The receptive field characteristics of the neurons of this nucleus are in some respects similar to the somewhat less complete concentric organization obtained at the ganglion cell level (Spinelli 1966). The concentric organization of geniculate receptive fields is more symmetrical, the surround usually has more clear-cut boundaries and is somewhat more extensive (e.g., Spinelli & Pribram, 1967). Furthermore, a second penumbra of the same sign as the center can be shown to be present, though its intensity (density of nerve impulses generated) is not nearly so great as that of the center. Occasionally, a third penumbra, again of opposite sign, can be made out beyond the second (Hammond, 1972; confirmed by Pribram, personal observation).

Thus, another transformation has occurred between the output of the retina and the output of the lateral geniculate nucleus. In the frequency domain, this transformation can be described as changing of a quadrature (sine, cosine) relationship from asymmetric to symmetric: each geniculate receptive field acts as a peephole "viewing" a part of the retinal mosaic. This is due to the fact that each geniculate cell has converging upon it some 10,000 ganglion cell fibers. The receptive field peephole of each geniculate cell is made of concentric rings of opposing sign, whose amplitudes fall off sharply with distance from the center of the field.

Pollen, Lee, and Taylor (1971) emphasized that the geniculate output is essentially topographic and punctate, is not frequency specific, and does not show translational invariance—that is, every illuminated point within the receptive field does not produce the same effect. Furthermore, the opponent properties noted at the retinal level of organization are maintained and enhanced at the cost of overall translational invariance. Still, a step toward a complete Fourier transformation has been taken because the output of an *array* of rod or cone receptors is the origin of the signal transformed at the lateral geniculate level.

CORTICAL RECEPTIVE FIELDS

When the output of lateral geniculate cells reaches the cerebral cortex, further transformations take place. One set of cortical neurons was christened "simple" by their discoverers (Hubel & Wiesel, 1968), as their response is maximal when a line in a certain location at a certain orientation is presented to the visual system. This selective responsiveness to oriented lines was assumed to be due to the convergence of axons from lateral geniculate cells literally arranged along a line.

The central part of the simple-cell receptive field is accompanied by side bands of opposite and the same sign as that of the central field. Pollen, Lee, and Taylor (1971) showed that more than one such side band characterizes these receptive fields, a characteristic that becomes especially evident when the field is plotted in terms of space and time coordinates (Morrone, Burr, & Maffei, 1982; Watson & Ahumada, 1985). This stripedness of the receptive field suggested that gratings made up of several lines of given width, spacing, and orientation drifted across the visual systems would serve as a better stimulus than single lines. Hubel and Wiesel (1968) had proposed that these simple receptive fields serve as line detectors in the first stage of a hierarchical arrangement of pattern detectors. Pollen and colleagues (1971) countered Hubel and Wiesel's proposal with the suggestion that an ensemble of simple receptive fields would act much as the strip integrator (a patch hologram) used by astronomers to cull data from a wide area with instruments of limited topographic capacity. Whether in fact strip integration occurs, the linelike arrangement could be conceived as a preparatory step in Fourier or related spectral type processing (Fig. 4.2).

Another class of cortical receptive fields was christened "complex" by its discoverers, Hubel and Wiesel, and thought by them (as well as by Pollen) to be the next step in the pattern recognition hierarchy. Their relatively short latency of response has raised some doubt (Hoffman & Stone, 1971) as to whether all complex receptive cells receive their input from cells with simple receptive fields. Whether their input comes directly from the geniculate, colliculus, or by way of simple cell processing, however, the output from cells with complex receptive fields displays transformations of the retinal input clearly characteristic of the spectral domain. This is due to the fact that complex cell receptive fields are composed of subfields, each of which displays excitatory and inhibitory bands (Movshon, Thompson, & Tollhurst, 1978b).

More recently Maffei (1985) demonstrated that the output of cells with complex receptive fields is actually inhibitory on cells with simple receptive fields. Cells with complex fields respond to stimuli such as shaded surfaces. Maffei found evidence that their inhibitory effect on simple receptive fields functions to make the simple receptive fields especially sensitive to contours (see also Henry & Bishop, 1971). The results of these experiments indicate that cells with complex receptive fields, may in fact process signals prior to or in concert with processing by cells with simple fields, thus at least partially reversing the hierarchy as originally proposed. A reciprocal simple-complex receptive field interaction is most likely on the basis of all the evidence available.

A series of experiments by Fergus Campbell and his group showed that populations of cells in the visual cortex are tuned to limited bandwidths of spatial-frequency. Initially, Campbell (Campbell & Blakemore, 1969; Campbell and Robson, 1968) showed that the electrical potential changes evoked in man and cat by gratings of certain spacings adapted not only to that grating but also to other gratings which turned out to be in harmonic relation to the original. Campbell concluded that the visual system must be encoding spatial frequency (perhaps in Fourier terms) rather than the intensity values of the grating (1974). He then showed that when a square wave grating was used, adaptation occurred not only to the fundamental but to its third harmonic as well, as would be predicted by Fourier theory. Finally, he found neural units in the cat's cortex that behaved as did the scalp recordings.

Pollen (1974) had by this time also presented evidence that indicated that these spatial-frequency (and temporal frequency—see Burr, Ross, & Morrone, 1986) sensitive receptive fields were those Hubel and Wiesel classified as complex. Later both his work and that of Maffei and Fiorentini (1973) found that simple receptive fields also are sensitive to a selective band of spatial frequencies. These findings have been amply confirmed in a number of laboratories (e.g., Campbell, 1974; DeValois & DeValois, 180; Glezer, Ivanoff, & Tscherbach, 1973; Movoshon, Thompson, & Tollhurst, 1978; Pribram, Lassonde, & Ptito, 1981; Schiller, Finlay, & Volman, 1976). The data on the spatial frequency sensitivity of cortical neurons have been comprehensively reviewed by DeValois and DeValois (1980, 1988) and by Shapley and Lennie (1985).

The most telling of this experimental evidence in favor of a Fourier-like description of the receptive fields of neurons in the striate cortex is that of DeValois and his colleagues. In one experiment (DeValois, Albrecht, & Thorell, 1978) receptive fields were shown to be narrowly tuned (to $1/2$ octave) to spatial frequency while they responded equally to an edge or a broad stripe of over $10°$ visual angle. In another experiment (DeValois, DeValois, & Yund, 1979) receptive fields were tested for preferred orientation of a set of stripes. A second pattern was then designed in which the original stripes were crossed with others to form checkerboards and plaids. The Fourier transforms of these patterns were then constructed by computer scans. The patterns (which are similar to Walshe patterns) were presented to the monkey and the response of the cortical neuron determined:

> The result of measuring the orientation tuning of cells was quite unequivocal: knowing the orientation tuning of a cell to a grating, one can predict its orientation tuning to the various checkboards from the orientations of the fundamental components of the patterns, but *not at all* from the orientations of their edges. . . .

> Tests with checkboards of various length/width ratios make this point even clearer. Such checkerboards obviously all have edges of exactly the same orientations. If it is edge orientation to which cells are tuned, then they should respond to these patterns in exactly the same orientations. If, however, it is not edge orientation, but the orientations of the two-dimensional spatial frequency components that are

critical, then quite different orientation tuning would be expected to these various checkerboard patterns. As can be seen in Figure 4.3A, gratings and checkerboards of various length/width ratios give quite different orientation tuning where the "orientation of the pattern" is taken as the orientation of its edges. If, however (Figure 4.3B), one plots the same data with respect to the two-dimensional Fourier fundamental orientations, it can be seen that the cell's orientation tuning is the same for all these patterns. The orientation tuning of the cell to various patterns thus *cannot* be predicted from the edge orientations at all, but can be precisely predicted if one considers the orientation of the two-dimensional spectra of each pattern. These tests were carried out on a sample of 41 cat and monkey simple and complex cells. Not one cell showed the orientation tuning one would predict from edges; every one responded as predicted from the orientation of the Fourier fundamentals. (DeValois & DeValois, 1988, p. 281–282)

DeValois (1982) interpreted his findings in the following way:

> Since different cells receiving from the same region in the visual field are tuned to different spatial frequencies and orientations, the ensemble of such cells would fairly precisely encode the two dimensional Fourier spectrum of a patch of visual space (address to APA).

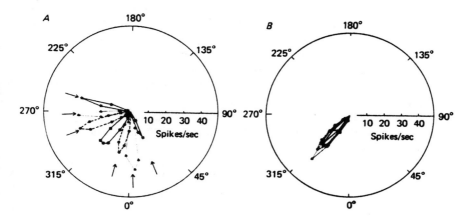

FIG. 4.3. Orientation tuning of a cat simple cell to a grating (squares and solid lines) and to checkerboards of various length/width ratios. In A the responses are plotted as a function of the edge orientation; in B as a function of the orientation of the Fourier fundamental of each pattern. In can be seen that the Fourier fundamental but not the edge orientation specifies the cell's orientation tuning (from K. K. DeValois et al., 1979. Reprinted with permission). From: DeValois, R. L. and DeValois, K. K. (1988). *Spatial Vision*. New York: Oxford University Press.

Equally compelling have been the results obtained by Pollen and Ronner (1980), who simultaneously recorded from two neurons within the same cortical column. The descriptions of the receptive fields of these neurons indicated that they functioned as a quadrature, (essentially a sine-cosine pair), and thus could function as important ingredients of the complex exponential in a Fourier analysis.

The Fourier results are not the final word, however, as noted in the Lecture 2. Constraints on the Fourier description become necessary when a precise mathematical analysis of receptive field profiles is undertaken. A series of ingenious studies by Henry and Bishop (1971) showed that simple receptive fields are exquisitely tuned to the edges (luminance contrast) of lines independent of line width, much as the DeValois experiments noted earlier. Some are tuned to the leading, some to the trailing edges. Responses to luminance contrast are of two types, excitatory and inhibitory, and very often show opponent properties; that is, when the edge is moved in one direction across the receptive field the effect (e.g., excitation) is the converse of that (e.g., inhibition) produced when the edge is moved in the opposite direction. (Incidentally, the effect is binocularly activated. Only when the excitation zones are in phase is an output signal generated. This occurs exclusively when the image on the two retinas superimposes; that is, when "objects" are in focus.)

Marcelja (1980) and Kulikowski, Marcelja, and Bishop (1982) understood these and similar observations to show that the unlimited Fourier description of these receptive fields is constrained by a Gaussian envelope. This Gaussian constraint on spatial frequency is most likely due to lateral inhibition (Creutzfeld, Kuhnt, & Benevento, 1974; Lassonde, Ptito, & Pribram, 1981; Sutter, 1976). Taken together with the results obtained by Pollen noted previously, a module consisting of quadrature pairs modulated by orientation selective inhibitory constraints. The result is readily described by a Hilbert space characterized by the inner product (the integral of the product) of the receptive field profiles of the cortical cells and the incoming sensory signals.

The dendrites of cortical neurons and therefore their receptive fields overlap. The extent to which an input becomes distributed is thus dependent on the controls operating on the elementary informational channels. Obviously, there is no global Fourier transform (Caelli & Julez, 1979; Pribram, Nuwer & Baron, 1974) that "spreads" the input over the cortical surface in one pass. Nor, however, because of overlap, is the spread necessarily limited to a single cortical receptive field covering only a few degrees of visual angle. In a series of experiments, Moyer (1970) demonstrated that recognition at a previously nonexposed retinal locus is impaired when an unfamiliar pattern is tachistoscopically presented once to a restricted retinal locus. Even a single repetition of the exposure with no change of locus will, however, significantly enhance recognition at a distant locus. Rehearsal is obviously a potent source of distribution of information. Evidence that such multiple copies occur has been obtained: Small macroelectrodes or microelectrodes were implanted over the visual cortex of monkeys and electrical activity recorded in a discrimination experiment. In randomly distributed locations over the visual cortex, localized electrical activity was reliably found to be related not only to the stimulus but also to response and reinforcing events (Bridgeman, 1982; Pribram, Spinelli, & Kamback, 1967).

In summary Gabor and similar elementary informational transforms are achieved at the visual cortical microprocessing level by way of integration over the retina. The initial stages of integration are achieved by convolving the optical image with the receptive field profiles of retinal neurons. Subsequent stages convolve the output of the ganglion cells of the retina with receptive field profiles of geniculate cells. The geniculate output is convolved with the profiles of ensembles of cortical receptive fields whose output is, in turn described by the class of informational transforms; the Gabor elementary function is the prime example.

CLASSIFICATION OF RECEPTIVE FIELD PROPERTIES

The holonomic approach to imaging depends on understanding another aspect of the results of microelectrode analysis of the receptive field properties of neurons in primary sensory areas such as the visual cortex. Many attempts were made to classify the results of recording from units, cells, in the visual cortex according to their properties. Beginning with the seminal work of Hubel and Wiesel (1959, 1962) in the late 1950s, it was the cortical cells that were assigned to categories such as concentric, simple, complex, and hypercomplex. However, a series of studies begun in our laboratory during the mid–1960s (Phelps, 1973, 1974; Spinelli & Barrett, 1969; Spinelli, Pribram, & Bridgeman, 1970) led to a different conclusion. We attempted to make a quantitative assessment of the properties defining these categories by using a computer-controlled experimental situation in which single, double, and multiple spots and lines were drifted across the visual field of cats and monkeys. In this way the receptive field of a cell could be accurately mapped because the computer "knew" where the spots or lines were located and could assign the response of the neural unit to the location in a set of bins that represented the possible locations in which the spot(s) or line(s) might appear. In addition, elementary sensitivities of the cells to such stimuli as color, and the direction and velocity of movement, were assessed.

The most striking result of these and subsequent experiments (Pribram, Lassonde, & Ptito, 1981) was the fact that each cell in the primary visual projection cortex has multiple propensities, and that the cells differed in the combination of these propensities. Thus it became impossible to classify the cells on the basis of single features. In fact, it is only the properties of a network of receptive fields that are amenable to specification and classification. These properties are to a large extent, though not exclusively, characterized by the elementary stimuli used to study the receptive field network. In short, each neuron in the primary

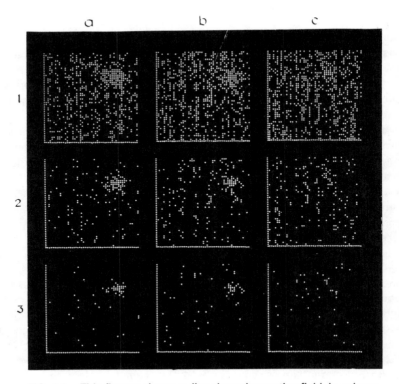

FIG. 4.4.   This figures shows a disc-shaped receptive field. In column
'a' the unit was mapped with both eyes open; in columns 'b' and 'c'
with the left and the right eye respectively. Rows 1, 2 and 3 represent
regions where the unit fired 1, 2, 3 times or more respectively. From:
Spinelli, D. N., Pribram, K. H., & Bridgeman, B. (1970). Visual receptive
field organization of single units in visual cortex of monkey. *International Journal of Neuroscience,* 67–74.

visual cortex has already conjoined sensory properties in some characteristic
combination.

The following are some examples: Henry (1977) noted that in several thousand explorations of primary visual cortex, hypercomplex properties (i.e., an
inhibition when elongation of the receptive field extends beyond certain limits)
were found only rarely. Furthermore, when present, the receptive field also
showed either complex (i.e., responsive to an elongated stimulus anywhere
within its receptive field) or simple (i.e., showing excitatory and inhibitory
regions within its receptive field) properties. Schiller, Finlay, and Volman (1976)
found so many properties for each neuron examined that they attempted classification via a multidimensional statistical analysis. Though not undertaken by

them, Henry's and Schiller's approach, drawn to its logical conclusion, results in a classification of network properties rather than a classification of single neurons (Pribram, Lassonde, & Ptito, 1981).

Thus any conceptualization based on the idea that sensory feature elements are kept isolated in the primary visual projection systems must take these data into account. Whatever the nature of feature analysis and of channel separation, it is not due to a limited line, neuron-to-neuron mechanism.

Let me repeat this point once again, because it is critical to any understanding of the issue: It is often assumed that imaging results from the conjoining of features each of which is initially isolated by a single cell; the output of these "feature detections" cells then converge on other single cells, the so-called pontifical or grandfather cells. According to the results reviewed here this is not correct. If the feature detecting cell, rather than the feature per se, were the basic representational unit to be classified, a cell might, for example, be complex or hypercomplex, but not both. The fact that a cell can simultaneously be both, and in addition be color- and direction-specific, as well as velocity and luminance-sensitive, indicates that the representations of these properties, features, are already conjoined within the receptive field of the cell. Some of these cells in the visual cortex are even differentially tuned to acoustic frequencies (Spinelli, Starr, & Barrett, 1968). Groups of neurons and even single cells show late responses (ca 300–400 msec after a stimulus is presented) only to a stimulus that has been rewarded in a problem-solving situation (Bridgeman, 1982; Pribram, Spinelli, & Kamback, 1967). Thus a cell's response is defined by a congerie of properties, not a single feature.

This conjoining of representations of properties in a receptive field of a neuron in the primary visual cortex does not mean, however, that each neuron represents those conjunctions that characterize any particular image or object. At this initial processing stage no pontifical "grandfather" or "grandmother" cell has been found whose output is uniquely specified by an object. It remains possible that such specificity becomes encoded in the pattern of the output of a neuron, for example, a pattern that can be specified by an interresponse interval histogram or burst profile.

We have attempted by various statistical manipulations to discover whether a particular output code reflecting a specific input is continuously present in the spike trains of visual cortical neurons. As described earlier, differences in the conditions modulating spike generation can be determined, for example, by utilizing a random walk model. We used such a model based on two parameters, drift rate and barrier height, and were able to show that changing the orientation of a drifting display of bars changes the boundary conditions while changing the spatial frequency of the display changes drift rate (Berger, Pribram, Wild, & Bridges, 1990). This result confirms results obtained by Ramoa, Shadlen, Skottun, and Freeman (1986) using entirely different techniques and, as noted, supports the tenet of the holonomic brain theory: The cells' output is governed by its resonant

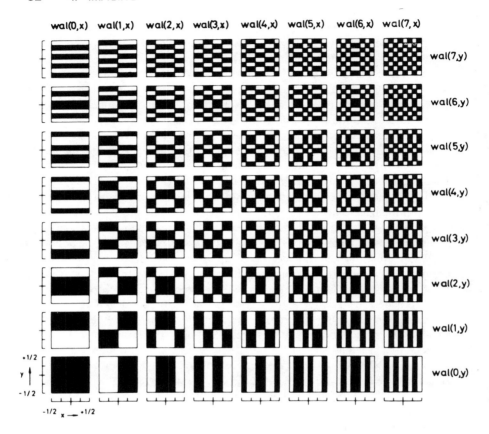

FIG. 4.5. Set of "Walsh" patterns used by Richmond and Optican in their experiments. From: Richmond, B. J., & Optican, L. M. (1987). Temporal encoding of two-dimensional patterns by single units in primate temporal cortex. II. Quantification of response waveform. *Journal of Neurophysiology, 57*(1), 147–161.

frequency modulated by the space-time constraints of orientation selectivity.

The results of this analysis tell us about the modulation of spike trains by the dendritic network, but not about the code carried in the spike train pattern that identifies a stimulus pattern. Identification has been accomplished when a brief sensory stimulus is used to evoke a response and small macroelectrodes or microelectrodes are used to record from populations of cells (Bridgeman, 1982; Pribram, Spinelli, & Kamback, 1967). In such experiments the initial burst of spike activity is correlated with stimulus features followed shortly by components that reflect the response made (e.g., to a left or right panel) and to whether the response was correct (a reinforcement obtained) or in error.

The initial 300–500 msec of a spike train of a single neuron codes a conjunction of stimulus (as well as response and reinforcement) features. Richmond, Optican, and their colleagues (Richmond, Optican, Podell & Spitzer, 1987) used two-dimensional Walsh patterns (see Fig. 4.5) as stimuli and found that in the first 300 msec of each spike train features are segregated in the components of the spike interval histogram of the train. Thus, every spike train encodes both the spatial frequency and orientation of the lines in the Walsh pattern. As noted, the origins of this code can be modelled by a random walk in which drift rate— representing speed of repolarization—is determined for the most part by the spatial frequency of the stimulus, and, barrier height—representing the boundary at which depolarization results in a spike—is determined by the orientation of the stimulus (Berger, Pribram, Wild, & Bridges, 1990).

Moreover, Richmond and Opticon showed that each spike train transmits only about one half bit of the information necessary to identify the stimulus pattern. At least three neurons must be involved, therefore, in the transmission of each bit of information. Neurons do not behave as feature detectors: There is no one-to-one correspondence between a stimulus feature and the spike train of a specific neuron. It takes a group of neurons, each with multiple propensities, or an ensemble of neurons of related propensities to encode a feature.

PATTERNS OF ACTIVITY IN POPULATIONS OF RECEPTIVE FIELDS

These results make it likely that during continuous processing, features become encoded in the output of populations of cells in the primary visual cortex. A metaphor illuminates this type of coding. In a classroom, ask everyone wearing blue jeans to raise a hand. A spatial pattern of hands can be recorded. Next ask those wearing glasses to raise their hands. A different spatial pattern characterizes the property "wearing glasses." Finally, ask only those who are wearing blue jeans and glasses to raise their hands. A more restricted and still different pattern of hands emerges. If one were to multiply features or properties—such as "also wearing red sweatshirts," "having blond hair," "being female," and so forth, one might (or might not) end up with a single person in the class who answers to the totality of conjunctions of properties—a true "grandmother-type" "cell."

There is direct evidence that, in fact, the output of spatially distributed populations of cells do encode "properties." Gray and Singer (Singer, 1989; Gray & Singer, 1989; Gray, König, Engel, & Singer, 1989) have shown that neurons in cat primary visual cortex, responding to optimally oriented light bars, show spatially distributed oscillatory responses in the range 35–45 Hz which are tightly correlated with the phase and amplitude of a local field potential. These synchronous oscillations of an ensemble of coactive neurons lead to coherent periodic patterns of activity which enable columns of cells in different parts of the cortex, representing different parts of the visual field, to corelate their respective activity patterns.

Mountcastle (Motter, Steinmetz, Duffy, & Mountcastle, 1987; Steinmetz, Motter, Duffy, & Mountcastle, 1987) has also been concerned with the mechanism by which spatially distributed populations of neurons encode properties that relate input to output:

> A general problem in neurophysiology is whether precise signals of events may be coded in population patterns of neuronal activity, when only imprecise signals of those events are provided by any single neuron of the population. Some mechanism of this sort appears necessary to account for the common observation that sensory and motor performances are more exact than would be predicted from the signal imprecision of single neurons. (p. 188)

Specifically, incorporating certain reasonable assumptions Mountcastle devised a viable explanatory population model of the effects of axial body motion on visual space similar to the linear type of model proposed in the holonomic brain theory.

> The . . . assumption is that there exist neuronal mechanisms for . . . linear vector summation. No such mechanisms have, to our knowledge, been described, but their existence appears to us more plausible than the alternative, i.e., that summations of this kind are made by single neurons or even by small groups of neurons. It seems more likely that the flow-through of brain activity from inputs to outputs occurs by the interfacing of large neuronal populations, although little is presently known of the nature of those interfaces. (p. 188)

The details of Mountcastle's model are presented in Lecture 6. With respect to vision, of interest here is that—though the responses of individual receptive fields are tuned to sinusoids, the Fourier fundamentals, and not to vector sums (DeValois, DeValois, & Yund, 1979)—it is the vector summation of a population discharge that can account for such phenomena as illusory conjunctions described by Treisman (Treisman & Schmidt, 1982): for example, the observation that in brief exposures the wrong color can be assigned to an object when that color is available somewhere in the display. In the light of the neuronal physiology that shows that features are already conjoined in receptive fields, sensory perception results not from processes that conjoin properties, but rather from processes that direct the selection of these properties from a pool in which they are already to some extent conjoined (much as in the example of the classroom noted at the beginning of this section).

Directed selection would account in a novel fashion for the distinction between perception and sensory processes. Both bottom-up and top-down theories admit readily to such a distinction, and in fact are based on it: in these theories sensory properties combine into percepts for bottom-up; percepts configure sensory properties for top-down. The holonomic brain theory differs from these alternatives in that both percepts and properties are directively selected from some more primitive matrix in which conjunctions already abound. Input from the senses to this matrix drives the system to abstract sensory qualities; perceptions of prototypical object-forms are constituted by operations on the matrix driven by input from brain systems (usually called association or intrinsic) associated with the sensory systems.

The directively selective nature of the neural processes raises two questions: First, how does the process activate some features and not others? Second, how do the representational properties of the receptive field matrix originate? The next section examines the first of the questions, whereas the section following examines the origin of representational properties.

ACTIVATING THE JUNCTIONAL MICROPROCESS

Receptive fields in the sensory cortex are composed by the junctional polarizations occurring in the dendritic networks of cortical neurons (see Pribram, 1971; Schmitt, Dev, & Smith, 1976). According to the holonomic brain theory these polarizations collectively interact to produce the receptive field properties resemble little cilia, or hairs, protruding perpendicularly from the dendritic fiber. These spines have bulbs at their endings, knoblike heads that make contact with branches of axons and other dendrites to form synapses (see Fig. 4.6). Activity in axons and in other dendrites such as those stemming from reciprocal synapses produce depolarizations and hyperpolarizations in the dendritic spines. The postsynaptic effects are ordinarily invoked by chemical transmitters whose action is modified by other chemicals that act as regulators and modulators.

Shepherd, Rall, Perkel, and their colleagues (see, e.g., Coss & Perkel, 1985; Perkel, 1982, 1983; Perkel & Perkel, 1985; Shepherd, Brayton, Miller, Segey, Rindsel, & Rall, 1985) modeled the process whereby these postsynaptic events occurring in spine heads interact. The issue is this: The stalks of the spines are narrow and therefore impose a high resistance to conduction (active or passive) toward the dendritic branch. Spine head depolarizations (as well as hyperpolarizations) must therefore interact with one another if they are to influence the action potentials generated at the axon hillock of the parent cell of the dendrite. The interactions (dromic and antidromic) among dendritic potentials (by means of

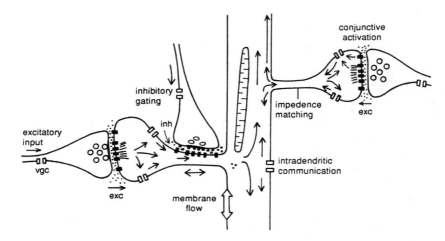

FIG. 4.6.   Diagram illustrating the concept of the dendritic spine as the smallest neuronal microcompartment capable of providing for a complete input-output operation of a synapse. Two spines are shown, arising from a dendritic branch. Excitatory (exc) input on the left, coming through impulses (voltage-gated channels: vgc) in presynaptic axons, activates the spine. The synaptic response can be amplified by voltage-gated channels and gives rise to second-messenger actions. Its transmission to the dendritic branch can be gated by inhibitory (inh) synapses on the spine stem. The spread of the response into the dendritic branch and from there into neighboring spines, as on the right, can depolarize those spines. By this means, electrotonic depolarization of spines receiving excitatory synaptic input can provide for conjunctive activation of Hebb-like mechanisms. Communication between spines and parent dendrite depends on impedance matching of electrotonic properties (rall and Rinzel, 1973); activity-dependent changes in these properties could contribute to mechanisms for learning and memory. Proteins move within the plasma membrane, and may distribute differently between dendrite and spine (Horwitz). (For reviews of spine properties and complete references, see Coss and Perkel, 1985; Shepherd and Greer, 1987). From: Shepherd, G. M. (1988). *Neurobiology.* New York: Oxford University Press.

which the signal becomes effective at the next stage of processing) thus depend on the simultaneous activation of both pre- and postsynaptic sites. According to Shepherd and colleagues (1985) several advantages accrue from this form of activation:

First the relative efficacy of distal dendritic inputs would be greatly enhanced. Second,. . . the transients within the model spines and dendrite are rapid and do not have the slow, low amplitude time course of synaptic potentials recorded experimentally at a distance from the cell body. Within the distal dendrite, information might thus be processed through precise timing of specific inputs to different neighboring spines . . . These precise interactions would greatly increase the complexity of information processing that can take place in distal dendrites. (p. 2194)

A prime virtue of this enhanced complexity is the potential for selectivity allowed by such a process:

"it has been shown that [post]synaptic polarization in a spine head can spread passively with only modest decrement into a neighboring spine head. If the neighboring spine is presynaptic, transmitter release could be evoked Shepherd et al., 1985." (p. 2192)

Thus effects on the presynaptic neuron can occur, effects critical to selectivity in learning (see e.g., Freud, 1895; Hebb, 1949, Stent, 1973).

Active spines appear to provide a basis not only for multiply contingent processing of synaptic inputs as outlined above but also for storage of information. The spine stem resistance as a parameter for varying the effectiveness of spine input to parent dendrite has been recognized as a locus for plasticity underlying learning and memory. (opiciti p. 2193)

And the spine stems have actually been seen to change their length and thickness under different processing conditions (Perkel & Perkel, 1985).

Important for the holonomic brain theory is the finding that the activation of interacting polarizations occurs in parallel, is distributed and discontinuous: "Thus, the active propagation. . . was discontinuous and resembled in this respect the saltatory conduction that takes place from node-to-node in myelinated nerve" (Shepherd et al., 1985, p. 2193). In the holonomic brain theory such parallel distributed and discontinuous processing is described as nonlocal and cooperative and is represented by a Hilbert space. The mathematical similarity between the quantum and neural mechanics can have a basis in neurophysiological reality: For instance, as described in the Epilogue to these lectures, the microtubular structure of dendrites can serve to provide cooperativity by way of boson condensation to produce soliton or phonon patterns of excitation practically instantaneously (Fröhlich, 1968, 1983, 1986; Hameroff, 1987). Spine heads are immersed in microtubule rich glia, which can serve as the conducting medium. Changes in the microtubules of glial cells can be the locus of the effects of activation registered by a tremendous increase in the metabolism of RNA as discerned in the experiments of Hyden (1969; reviewed by Pribram, 1971, chap. 2).

FEATURES EXTRACTED FROM NOISE

There is a considerable body of evidence supporting the conception that at least some feature properties of the receptive field manifold are inborn (see, e.g., Chow, 1961, 1970; Ganz, 1971; Wiesel & Hubel, 1965a, 1965b). These properties must be exercised in an ordinarily rich environment lest they deteriorate and/or develop abnormally (Pettigrew, 1974; Wiesel & Hubel, 1965a, 1965b). And there is some additional tuning that can occur as a result of specialized environmental inputs (Blakemore, 1974; Hirsch & Spinelli, 1970). In the context of perception, these data can be taken to indicate that a feature representational matrix is a relatively stable property of the organism's sensory (receptor to cortical) system. Tuning of elements in that matrix by sensory input from the environment is feasible, but the properties to be tuned are characteristic of the organism.

An additional experimental result bears on this issue: In our laboratory, we identified a cortical unit with simple receptive field properties and then stimulated it with visual white noise (which looks like "snow") by presenting many spots appearing and disappearing on a TV monitor (Sutter, 1976). The experiment was undertaken to determine whether the response of the cell was linear (i.e., whether all of the variance of the stimulus-response relationship could be accounted for by the first kernel of a Wiener polynomial). Within 30 msec the cell mapped those spots within its receptive field that had previously been mapped by the conventional method of presenting a luminous line at a particular orientation. Ten msec later an inhibitory flank became evident, as would be predicted for simple receptive field properties on the basis of intracellular recordings (Creutzfeldt, Kuhnt, & Benevento, 1974). In short, the cell actually extracted the features "elongation" and "orientation" from noise on the basis of its own propensities. Similar results were obtained for frequency selection in the auditory system (Hosford, 1977). Clearly, the cells are selecting from the multiform sensory input only those properties to which they are sensitive.

It is interesting to note that computational simulations such as Alopex (*Algorithm for Pattern Extraction;* Hart, 1976), have shown just such emergent organizations of receptive fields in layered cooperative networks (Linsker, 1987; Lehky & Sejnowski, 1990; Sejnowski & Lehky, 1987). Orientation selective units appear in middle layers of such networks even in the absence of space-time patterned input. When the input is patterned, the cooperative dendritic algorithm acts as a generic optimization principle. It tends to maximize the accuracy with which input patterns can be inferred given only the output of the cell.

On the basis of these results, a caveat is in order: Our perceptions of the display (snow) and the selective response of the receptive field (an elongated excitatory band flanked by an inhibitory one) are different from one another. This indicates that the responses of single neurons in the primary visual cortex fail to reflect the perceptual response. How then is the experiencing of perceptual images constituted?

ACHIEVING THE PERCEPTUAL IMAGE

Up to this point the lectures have remained close to available data in constructing the holonomic brain theory. There remains an issue, however, which demands a different approach. The issue is joined when we consider the perceptual experiences coordinate with the cortical receptive field microprocesses. Essentially these micro processing patterns consist of Gabor elementary functions. Macro-space-time considerations such as orientation enter the computations as constraints on the spectral domain. By contrast, our experience of images is primarily in macro-space-time terms. There must be some operations performed on the cortical activity patterns so that images are perceived (the "grain" problem, Lecture 3).

Fading and annihilation of the perceptual image by stabilizing the optical image on the retina provides the basis for an hypothesis regarding these operations: The micrometer movements of the eye can be conceived to perform an inversion of the Gabor transform so that the essentially "quantal" micro process becomes reconverted into a macro image. When such oscillatory movements are stopped or counteracted, sensory adaptation takes place and sensations fail to be experienced. In vision, producing stabilization by scleral mirrors and other devices (Ditchburn & Ginsberg, 1952; Heckenmueller, 1968; Kelly, 1983; Riggs, Ratcliff, Cornsweet, & Cornsweet, 1953) has proved to be a powerful research tool for analyzing visual processes.

Thus, according to the holonomic brain theory, patterns in Hilbert space are formed when the sensory input selectively addresses and is selectively addressed by the conjoint receptive field properties of cortical neurons. Inversion into macro images is hypothesized to occur when the motor apparatus of the organism provides a scan over the sensed environment. With respect to this first stage of perception, oscillatory movements of receptor surfaces are critical: tremors for touch (Fowler & Turvey, 1978), respiration in olfaction (Sheer & Grandstaff, 1970), the movement of cochlear hair cells in hearing (Bekesy, 1960), nystagmoid displacements of the retina in vision.

In support of the hypothesis is the finding noted earlier, that the information contained in a spike train occurs in the initial milliseconds after a sensory stimulus evokes a neural response. The ongoing activity recorded from a paralyzed visual system displays a high degree of stationarity and serves primarily as a background upon which change produced by movement produces a signal (Bierre, Wild, Bridges, & Pribram, in prep.).

Cells in the visual cortex that display "simple" receptive fields, by virtue of their obvious excitatory and inhibitory elongated subfields, are especially sensitive to such micrometer movements. However, cells with complex receptive fields are also likely to be sensitive to micrometer eye movements since Movshon and colleagues (1978) showed them to be composed of subfields, each of which shows simple properties.

The holonomic brain theory postulates that inversion occurs by way of corticofugal pathways that reach subcortical processing stations. Lecture 5 deals with such pathways as they are involved in object perception; with respect to imaging, corticofugal connections from the primary sensory receiving areas provide the circuitry that reaches geniculate and even retinal processing stages (Spinelli, Pribram, & Weingarten, 1965; Spinelli & Weingarten, 1966).

Harth, Unnikrishnan, and Pandya (1987) developed a computational model in which the corticogeniculate pathways serve to modify sensory input so as to enhance and complete images, suppress irrelevant features, and generate imaginal configurations when input stimulation is weak or absent. The computation devolves on an optimization process akin to that used in the thermodynamic models described in Lecture 2. The spontaneous activity of the retinal receptors provides the requisite noise to keep the system from premature stabilization. The model is nonlinear so that the ensuing percept is the result of the emergence of a single component and is not formed by superposition of many weaker responses.

In this respect, the holonomic brain theory differs: With respect to imaging, linearity is maintained. Weaker aspects of a pattern of signals are, after all, perceived. Information is not dropped out. Even when the weaker signals remain unattended for the moment, one can become aware of them when attention to them is "paid" (Posner, 1987; Lecture 10). Nonlinear summation is relegated to cognition, the directive and inferential processes imposed by the systems of the temporal and frontal lobes as discussed in lectures 7 and 10. However, in keeping with Harth and Pandya's model, the locus of entry of nonlinear processes is primarily tectal and influences the geniculate secondarily (via the perigeniculate nucleus, which is part of the thalamic reticular nucleus.)

The importance of maintaining linearity at this stage of processing is critical. If indeed nonlinearities were introduced as integral to the process, momentarily unattended aspects of an image would be lost to further processing. This is clearly not the case: "Latent learning" would not be possible and shifts in attention toward "weaker" aspects of the image would never occur.

In fact, the potential combinations of possible selections from multiform inputs appear to be legion. The resulting sensory process reflects input, that is, receptor-driven selectivities that engage invariances in the relationship between input, receptor variables, and thalamo-cortical system variables. The invariants become projected onto the environment.

What determines projection? Bekesey's ingenious experiments (1960, 1967) with artificial cochleas hold the clue to an answer. By lining up five vibrators on one's forearm, Bekesey was able to produce the feeling of a single spot that could be moved up or down by changing the phase of vibrations between the vibrators.

When a second artificial cochlea was placed on the opposite forearm, the feeling of a spot could be made to jump from one arm to the other. With practice the spot was finally "projected" away from the receptor surface of the skin much as sound is projected from two stereophonic speakers.

However, bilaterality is not a necessary condition for projection. When phase relations between fingers are adjusted, a spot can be projected outward from them. One feels the paper on which one is writing at the tip of one's pencil, not at the tip of the fingers holding it. Under certain conditions projection occurs: specifically movement in space and movement in time, such as vibration. More on this later.

To return to the hypothesis posed at the beginning of this section, that micrometer movements, by way of reciprocal connectivity in the sensory pathways, are responsible for inversion of the Gabor transform: Experiments in our laboratory, some using electrical stimulation of cortex and recording at geniculate and optic nerve locations demonstrated the existence of the centrifugal influences so critical to perceiving (Spinelli, Pribram, & Weingarten, 1965; Spinelli & Weingarten, 1966). In addition, and most significantly, in one set of optic nerve recordings it was shown that whereas about 8% of the nerve fibers in the optic nerve carry signals to the retina, these 8% modulate the input in 80% of the input fibers in the optic nerve.

There is also direct evidence that such corticofugal influences are involved in imaging. Eason, Oakley, and Flowers (1983; see also Eason, Flowers, & Oakley, 1983; and a more recent review by White & White, in prep.) asked subjects to respond verbally (counting) to stimuli presented at various locations in the visual field while attempting to ignore stimuli at other locations. Retinal responses were measured with electrodes placed at the inner canthus of the eye. Retinal responses were larger to the attended than to the ignored stimuli. In the same as well as another set of experiments from the same group of investigators (Eason, 1981; Eason, Harter, & White, 1969; White & White, in prep.) it was shown that the early (80–100 msec) positive wave of an event-related cortical potential is influenced in the same fashion as the retinal response. These results can be taken as circumstantial evidence that the reciprocal connections of the retinal-geniculo-striate-retinal circuitry are critically involved when stimuli are actively perceived as images.

CONCLUSION AND SUMMARY

This lecture set out to describe image processing in the visual system, utilizing some basic neurophysiological data. The data indicate that both bottom-up sensory and top-down cognitive operations address features already conjoined in cortical receptive fields. As sensory perception depends on micrometer movement, the theory entails sensory-motor reciprocity in perception.

Mathematically, the conjoined feature space is described as a multidimensional vector space determined in part by the cortical receptive field properties of orientation and spatial frequency. The processing of figural patterns as demonstrated by Pollen and Feldon (1979), and by Marcelja (1980), was shown to involve Gabor elementary functions mapped over a four-dimensional vector space. Gabor functions are one example of a set of functions describing vectors in a four-dimensional hyperspace. Sensory processing can best be described more generally in terms of this larger set of functions.

As Gabor (1968) noted, the Fourier aspect of the elementary function can be composed by convolving successive processing stages. Pollen and Taylor (1974) and Pribram, Nuwer, and Baron (1974) detailed the neural systems responsible for each stage of convolution.

Retinal processing is best described in terms of convolving pupillary input with receptor activity (Rodieck & Stone, 1965) to obtain a DOG, a difference of Gaussians (Enroth-Kugel & Robinson 1966); processing at the geniculate is portrayed in terms similar to near field Fresnel optical image processing; whereas the cortical process is found to be most appropriately modeled in Hilbert space. Hilbert space activity is characterized by the inner product (the integral of the product) of the receptive field profiles of the cortical cells and the incoming sensory signals. This produces, in the cortex, a highly redundant distributed representation of that input.

The approach taken here differs from that taken by some others interested in computational modelling (e.g., Marr, 1982) in that the full measure of sensory input (generated by the retinal process) reaches the cortical level. No sketch pad image-processing stage is demanded: Whatever constraints are imposed are due to subsequent stages, which preprocess the activity in the retino-geniculo-cortical system.

What has occurred as a result of processing the optical image by retina and primary visual cortex is an invertible transformation from a space-time image to a processing domain of at least eight dimensions: four in space-time and four spectral. Inversion results from the operations of corticofugal influences on the spontaneous nystagmoid movements of the eye. The psychophysical transformation is in accord with the suggestion made by Gabor in the quotation from Licklider introducing the lecture.

5 Object Forms and Object Spaces: Sensory-Motor Reciprocity in Perisensory Systems

Thus, by our movements *we find it is the stationary form of the table in space which is the cause of the changing image in our eyes. We explain the table as having existence independent of our observation because at any moment we like, simply by assuming the proper position with respect to it, we can observe it. (Helmholtz, 1909/1924, p. 31)*

INTRODUCTION

In this lecture we come to grips (literally) with objects as distinct from images. Try the following demonstration: Have someone repeatedly touch the palm of your hand with a pocket knife or other object while your eyes are closed. You feel the touching, rubbing, pressure—subjective sensory qualities and perhaps patterned sensory images. Now grasp and manipulate the knife and suddenly its "objectivity" materializes.

The idea that perception involves a motor process is not new. Sperry (1947), Festinger, Burnham, Ono, and Bamber (1967), and Held (1968) each have taken an extreme position, holding that all of perception is a motor response to a sensory input. In part this suggestion stems from the fact that neurons are sensitive to transients, and, as noted in the previous lecture, movement produces transients. However, if our perceptions are purely responses, why are we unable to change them at will?

In the holonomic brain theory, as developed here, the motor systems are assigned a more restricted role, that of developing object (especially shape) constancies. When an organism actively moves about in an environment—

whether with eyes, head, hand, or whole body—a set of images results. These images become sorted into figure and ground. Furthermore, invariances must be extracted from the set of figures to coalesce into phenomenally constant perceptions, that is, objects. In vision and somesthesis object-forms result from this process. In audition, such invariances produce tones, vowels, and consonants. For example, consonants are thought to become constituted largely by articulation (this is known as the motor theory of speech—see Liberman, Cooper, Shankweiler, & Studdart-Kennedy, 1969), and phoneme construction can be described in a manner similar to that developed here for object-form perception. Such a formulation is based on a theory of vowel construction by a "center of gravity" determination (Syrdal, 1985), much as that developed for object-form perception later in this lecture. Taste and smell form flavors and odors by swirling a substance across the tongue and by sniffing. Here, a description of the neural circuitry entailed in the production of invariances in vision is undertaken.

In primates two neural systems beyond those discussed so far are involved. The first is a peristriate system (defined cortically by area 18, V2). The peristriate cortex surrounds the striate (defined cortically by area 17, V1), which was the main subject of the previous lecture. When the peristriate system is electrically stimulated, head and eye movements are obtained. The movements allow iterations of images to be operated upon by way of interconnections between striate and peristriate systems that form an intimately interlinked couplet. As is described later, these operations result in the perception of figure/ground relationships within an occulocentric reference frame.

The second more anterior but adjacent system, the prestriate (defined cortically by area 19), is less well-circumscribed at its cortical terminus and consists of clusters of cells each of which shows special selectivities (e.g., for color, shape, movement). This prestriate system is involved in extracting constancies from among figures to allow the perception of object-forms within an object-centered "space."

A space is that part of ground that frames, provides more or less local context—a Mondrian—within which perceptual constancies, properties such as those that define object-forms, are achieved. Constancies within object-centered spaces are the result of operations dependent on the intimate interconnections between prestriate and peristriate systems that allow the results of prestriate computations to be fed back onto the peristriate-striate couplet.

According to the holonomic brain theory, object constancy is achieved through movement by iteratively impressing on the primary visual circuitry sets of samples that must be matched to produce constancy. In turn, samples are produced by matching sensory input to centrally generated representations based on previous iterations of input. The locus of the match and the nature of the matching process form the substance of the current lecture.

WHAT IS PROCESSED IN ACHIEVING CONSTANCY

The perception of objects is possible only because there is constancy; according to the holonomic brain theory, constancies emerge as invariances obtained from the superposition of sensory patterns produced by movement. As noted in Lecture 3, movement defines the relationship between an optical image and retinal (sensory) processing. The optical image changes as a function of changes in the layout of environmental surfaces producing an optical flow.

As an immediate consequence of changes in the optic flow, certain aspects of the flow are perceived as occulocentric figures, whereas other aspects become ground. The organizational rules whereby changes in layout produce figure/ground relationships are several and have been adduced from experiments by Gestalt psychologists and their followers (for review see Gibson, 1966; Rock, 1975). The operation of these rules make some aspects of the input hang together and stand out as figures.

An argument can be made that the operation of these rules is intrinsic to the layout of the optic array: The layout, the distal stimulus, is made up of real textured surfaces and objects, not of an unorganized or disorganized unpatterned reality. Only the luminous input reflected and refracted from real surfaces and objects becomes "scattered." And that "scatter" is transformed into images of the surfaces and objects by the optics of the eye, as indicated in Lecture 3.

Gibson (1966, 1979) was the first to emphasize the view that constancies result from relative movements of the layouts of environmental surfaces as specified in the optic array. When organisms move, environmental surfaces move with respect to one another to provide an invariant input to the organism: In this scheme invariance, "information," resides entirely in the environment and the major contribution of the organism to object perception is that he is moving.

But patterned organization intrinsic to the layout, though primary, is not all that is involved in perceiving. Learning and memory and therefore brain processing can be critical. An experiment by Rock (1983, pp. 126—127) illustrates this dramatically. He used the illusion in which a triangular figure is formed by three filled circles with triangular cutouts arranged as if they were the apexes of the illusory figure. The illusion is readily seen when a set of transparent oblique stripes is interposed between viewer and figure (which is also displayed on a transparent medium). When, however, the stripes are placed behind the illusory display, the illusion is never seen: We have all learned that a solid figure precludes seeing what is behind it. When the stripes are seen behind the display, the illusion cannot be sustained. Some aspects of figure-ground relationships are prone to influence by learning.

There is obviously some mechanism within the perceptual systems of the organism that aids the extraction of invariances. Not only illusory images attest to the presence of such a process. Subjectively, as one moves about, one can simultaneously perceive the differences between ordinary sensory images produced by an object and the extracted invariant that identifies the object-form as object. According to Gibson, only the invariant should be perceived; yet this is not so. Furthermore, the environment contains all sorts of invariant patterns, but only some are processed as figures that provide "information." To repeat an old adage, a tree that falls in the woods perturbs its surrounds, but the making of a "sound" by a falling tree depends on having a sentient organism within earshot. Sentience, whether of a sound or other informative input, depends on being endowed not only with appropriate sense organs but also with a complementary central processing competence.

As detailed in the next section, this central processing competence must, at a minimum, be composed of connectivities that correlate the variety of sensory patterns relating a series of events to one another. Processing must proceed in such a way that only those invariances remain that define the figures that compose an object. These invariants which result from relative movements of environmental surfaces with respect to one another provide a good starting point for inquiry.

Bernstein (1967) and Johansson (1978) developed techniques that display the effects on perception of coordinated motion of one part of the environmental layout with respect to another. These investigators have used dots and lines displayed on a two dimensional surface and have succeeded in giving precise renderings of the observed phenomena in terms of Fourier and vector analysis. Gibson, however, voiced reservations regarding the use of dots and lines as elements in such an analysis. These reservations are clearly stated by Gibson (1977) as follows:

An optic array can be thought of in two quite different ways, as a set of elements or [alternatively] as a manifold of parts. It might consist of spots or points in an otherwise empty extent or it might consist of adjacent forms in a wholly filled structure. The spots or points would correspond to bodies or atoms in space. The adjacent forms would correspond to the faces and facets of opaque surfaces in the terrestrial environment. In the first case space is empty, a vacuum. In the second case space is filled, a plenum. It is interesting to note that Democritus' theory of atoms in a void was appealing to early physicists because the atoms had vacancies to move in, whereas the parts of Aristotle's plenum could not move. The atoms of a surface in modern optics correspond one-to-one with the focus-points of an image, whereas the faces and facets of surfaces in ecological optics correspond to the nested forms of a structure. The former correspondence is produced by a bundle of rays intersecting in a common point, a "pencil" of rays in projective geometry, whereas the latter correspondence is produced by a manifold of visual solid angles all having a common apex at the point of observation. The latter conception is unfamiliar, especially inasmuch as the solid angles are nested and each is unique.

An optic array consisting of solid angles is very different from an optic array consisting of lines.

The motions of optical elements in an array can be compared to the motions of material bodies in space, and then the powerful mathematics developed for mechanics and kinetics is available for the analysis of an array. This is what Johansson has developed with such success, together with his students, beginning with his monograph on "Configuration in Event Perception" (1950). It has only to be assumed that motions in two dimensions are related to motions in three dimensions by projection. One perceives depth through motion. Just as points are grouped into an object by proximity so moving points are grouped into a moving object by their common motion. One of the great achievements of Johansson was to take Wertheimer's vague law of "common fate" and give it precision and elegance by vector analysis.

In contrast to this precise analysis, the alternative that I have been struggling to formulate can only suggest that an optic array undergoes disturbances of structure including parts that come and go in various ways, some of them reversible and some not. Neither the motions of points nor the transformations of forms will describe these disturbances. They are brought about by the coming into sight and the going out of sight of surfaces (at occluding edges or at the horizon of the earth) during the locomotions of an observer and the motions of objects. They are reversible. And optical disturbances are also brought about by the going out of existence and coming into existence of surfaces during the death and destruction or growth and creation of objects. Difficult as it may be to formulate the parameters of all these optical disturbances it seems to me that we should try to do so. (pp. 161–162)

But from the vantage of the holonomic brain theory, Gibson's and Johansson's views are not that far apart. Johansson's elements are not features such as lines or edges: The emphasis is on relations (see e.g., Johansson, 1978, p.275).

From this perspective, Johansson's two-dimensional displays are simulations using dots and lines. In the holonomic brain theory, these dots and lines serve as "centers" seen to be produced by the interactions among surfaces (Gibson's "optic flow") whose tangent vectors (solid angles) determine the centers. In describing biological motion, Johansson (1978) used harmonic analysis, conceiving the human skeleton to consist of

a hierarchical system of connected pendulums. Only the endpoints of each of the displayed pendulums, mainly those of the limbs, are presented by a bright spot . . . These pendular motions are severely distorted by a great number of higher harmonics. Also the amplitudes and phase relations are strictly subordinated to the system as a whole. (p. 98).

The system as a whole frames the set of pendulums, and the motion of each pendulum frames each endpoint.

Additional evidence for the operation of such "frames" comes from Weisstein and Harris (1974, 1980), who found that accuracy in identifying lines was greater when the lines were enclosed by overlapping surfaces demarcated as squares—a function they have labeled an "object-superiority effect" because accuracy is even greater when lines are presented as part of object-forms. In the spectral domain, Gibson's "disturbances of structure" become calculations that produce invariance; Johansson's dots and lines describe optimal paths that characterize changing relationships among surfaces according to the least action principle. These paths are manifest in the space-time domain, but are processed in the phase-space domain, that is, in terms of probability amplitude-modulated spectra. The nature of these processes is described in the remainder of this lecture.

FIGURE AND GROUND IN AN OCCULOCENTRIC SPACE: STRIATE-PERISTRIATE-TECTAL CIRCUITRY

One of the characteristics of the development of the mammalian brain is the progressive separation of motor from sensory cortex. This separation allows for an addition of cortico-subcortical loops to the more local cortico-cortical symmetrical connectivities of the projection cortex (Burgess, Wagner, Jennings, & Barlow, 1981; Pribram, 1960). The separation is especially noticeable for the somato-sensory-motor system (see Pribram, 1982a, for review). In the visual system the separation is not as complete. But even here, it is primarily electrical excitation of the peristriate cortex that produces eye movements by way of corticofugal pathways to the brain stem (the tectum, especially the superior colliculus).

Movement involves corticofugal pathways from both the striate cortex (V_1), and the peristriate cortex (V_2). The striate (V_1) and peristriate (V_2) cortices are reciprocally connected and there are only minor, though important, differences in their receptive field properties. One of these is a marked increase in receptive fields sensitive to vergence (especially convergence) and fields sensitive to the disparity between optical images due to the separation between the eyes (Poggio & Fisher, 1977). These receptive field properties signal relative distance from and between surfaces and objects. Furthermore, relative movement of surfaces is dependent on distance and allows for the segmentation of scenes by virtue of separating the common direction of motion of "elements" and surfaces of the scene. Parallax is dependent on such differences in the common directions which delineate surfaces in a scene. Disparity and especially parallax lift figure from ground.

Another difference between the receptive fields in striate and peristriate cortex is an increase in the number of receptive fields that are sensitive to endstopping (inhibition due to lengthening of an elongated stimulus) (Hubel & Wiesel, 1977).

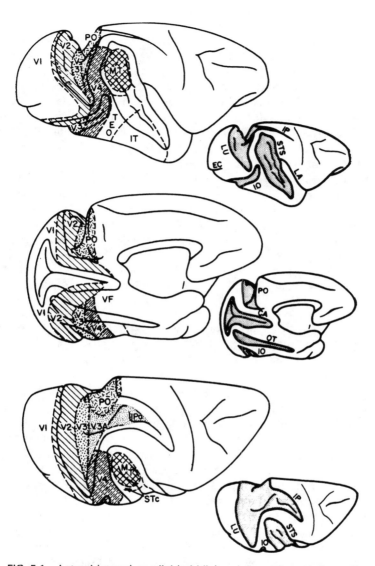

FIG. 5.1.   Lateral (upper), medial (middle) and dorsal (lower) views of
a brain with the sulci partially opened (stippled areas in right drawings). Left drawings show the location of the striate, peristriate, and
prestriate visual areas. V3A refers to in the annectant gyrus, and Stc
refers to STS color area. In right: CA, calcarine sulcus; EC, external
calcarine s.; IO, inferior occipital s.; IP, intraparietal s.; LA, lateral s.;
Lu, lunate s.; OT, occipito-temporal s.; PO, parieto-occipital s.; STS,
superior temporal sulcus, the movement area. Cortical Visual Areas of
the Macaque: Possible Substrates for Pattern Recognition Mechanisms. In C. Chagas, R. Gattass, & C. Gross (Eds). *Pattern Recognition
Mechanisms.* Berline: Springer-Verlag.

This implements an increase in dimensionality by enhancing computations based on disparity and others dependent on the opponent nature of an exitatory center flanked by inhibition. Such opponent processes aid significantly in separating figures, which are multidimensional, from ground. In fact, single-cell recordings in monkeys have shown that neurons in peristriate visual cortex (V2), but not primary striate visual cortex (V1), respond selectively to stimuli that humans perceive as contours, despite no actual line being present (Peterhans & von der Heydt, 1989; von der Heydt & Peterhans, 1989).

In the holonomic brain theory, striate (V_1) and peristriate (V_2) are considered to be a closely coupled interactive system by virtue of both reciprocal cortico-connectivity and their connection to the brain stem tectal region. It is upon this closely coupled system that more complex perceptual processing converges. The locus of convergence is the brain stem tectal region surrounding the colliculi, which in turn connects to the colliculi. For vision, the connections from the superior colliculus to those neurons in the striate cortex (V_1), which display complex receptive fields, complete the circuit (Graybiel, 1973; Stone, 1983).

OBJECT CONSTANCY IN OBJECT-CENTERED SPACES; PROCESSING SIZE, COLOR AND SHAPE BY PRESTRIATE-PRETECTAL CIRCUITRY

The prestriate system is the first level of systems operating on the basic V_1 -V_2 reciprocally connected couplet. The prestriate cortex is reciprocally connected both to the basic couplet, and in turn, to higher order processing systems. The neurons of the prestriate cortex compose a somewhat ambiguously defined region, which contains clumps of neurons with large receptive fields. The feature selectivities of these receptive fields segregate to some extent the properties conjoined in the receptive fields of the neurons of the striate cortex (see Van Essen, 1979; Van Essen & Maunsell, 1983 for review).

One set of receptive fields is especially sensitive to processing movement in the visual input, especially relative movement of one part of the input with respect to another. This sensitivity to relative movement is critical to the formation of object-centered spaces and is dealt with in the last sections of this lecture. A second set is especially sensitive to relative movement between visual and somatosensory inputs. The receptive fields of these neurons are directly involved in the formation of egocentric action spaces and are covered in the ensuing lecture.

The receptive fields of other aggregates of neurons (labelled V_3, V_p, and V_4) respond especially to color (V_4), and to the spatial frequency and orientation of gratings (V_p and V_3). It is these receptive fields that are involved in the computation of object constancies. The receptive fields differ from those in the striate cortex (V_1) not only in their large size but also in that they encompass both the

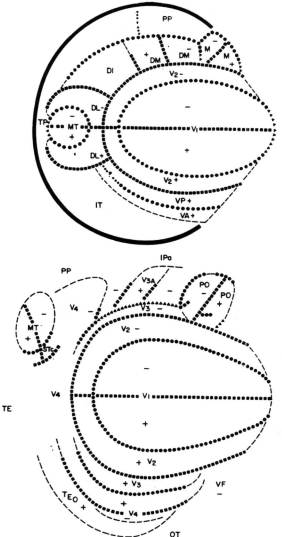

FIG. 5.2. Flattened representation of the striate peristriate and prestriate areas of New (upper) and Old (lower) World monkeys. Vertical meridian (dots, horizontal meridian (square) and periphery (triangles). For details, see text. From: Gatass, R., Sousa, A. P. B., and Covey, E. (1985). Cortical Visual Areas of the Macaque: Possible Substrates for Pattern Recognition Mechanisms. In C. Chagas, R. Gattass, & C. Gross (Eds). *Pattern Recognition Mechanisms.* Berline: Springer-Verlag.

101

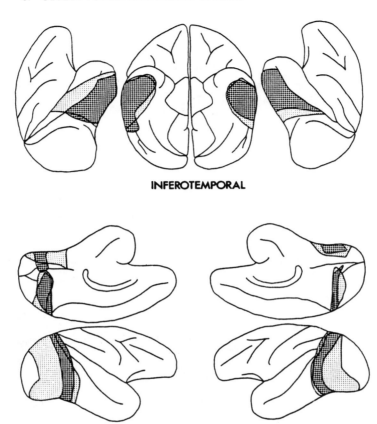

INFEROTEMPORAL

PRESTRIATE

A

FIG. 5.3.   a) Minimum and maximum extent of cortical damage for
monkeys sustaining inferotemporal and prestriate lesions. b) Effects of
pulvinar, prestriate, and inferotemporal lesions on retention of the size
constancy problem. Mean saving scores on preoperative and
postoperative retention tests, analyzed separately for the equal (Stage
I) and unequal (Stage II) distance phases of the problem, were computed according to the formula: (Trials to Learn − Trials to Relearn)/
(Trials to Learn + Trials to Relearn). The control bars shown in the
figure are based on the preoperative data of all eight monkeys, c)
Observed distribution of size constancy errors on Stage II trials of the
problem following lesions of prestriate and inferotemporal cortex.
From: Ungerleider, L. G., Ganz, L., and Pribram, K. H. (1977). Size
constancy in Rhesus Monkeys: Effects of Pulvinar, Prestriate and Inferotemporal Lesions. *Experimental Brain Research, 27,* 251–269.

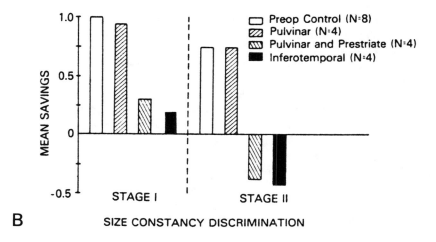

B   SIZE CONSTANCY DISCRIMINATION

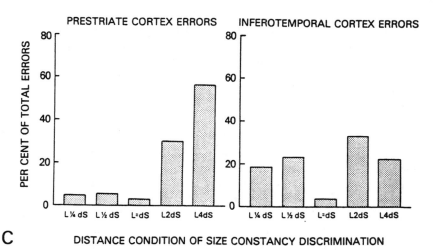

C   DISTANCE CONDITION OF SIZE CONSTANCY DISCRIMINATION

FIG. 5.3.   (continued)

contra- and ipsilateral hemifields: they extend across the midline of the visual field. Furthermore, many of these receptive fields respond only to gratings of particular length, that is, they are sensitive to endstopping, the hypercomplex property that, as noted in the previous lecture, is only rarely found in the selectivities of neurons in the striate (V_1) cortex.

Direct evidence has been obtained that the peri- and prestriate cortex are involved in processes that result in at least one type of invariance entailed in object constancy: Size constancy was shown to be dependent on these neural systems. The results were obtained in an experiment (Ungerleider, Ganz, & Pribram, 1977) in which square panels were placed at different distances in a highly patterned alley. The monkeys were trained to pull in the square that appeared to them to be the larger. After extensive resection of the peristriate and prestriate systems (including destruction of their thalamic portions), monkeys respond exclusively to the optical image size of an object, ignoring the contextual and vergence factors responsible for constancy that had guided their responses prior to surgery (Fig. 5.3).

Specifically, one of two squares placed at various distances within an alley had to be drawn in by an attached string. The sides of the alley were painted with stripes so that distance cues were enhanced by the apparent convergence of the lines as distance increased. The correct response consisted of drawing in the square that was perceived (by us and by the monkeys) to be the larger. Preoperatively, all the monkeys always pulled in the square that was physically larger—irrespective of distance up the alley. After removal of the peri-prestriate systems, the monkeys pulled in the square that—because of proximity—produced the larger optical image. That is, the monkeys now responded on the basis of images rather than on the basis of objects.

Direct evidence that the prestriate system is involved in the processing of perceptual constancies is available only for size, but conjectures regarding color and shape constancies have been developed. The receptive fields of V_3, V_p, and V_4 are especially suited to extraction, not only of size invariance, but also of other properties of visual input such as color and shape. A description follows of preliminary models of how neural processing of color and shape invariance can result in the perception of object-forms.

Color provides an introduction anticipating in simplified form the model for processing shape discussed in greater detail in subsequent sections of this lecture. Color often defines the limits of an object—colors ordinarily do not appear independent of objects or surfaces—and changes in color considerably aid in setting the boundaries between figure and ground (see DeValois & DeValois, 1988 for review). For such changes to be perceived, the color must remain invariant within those boundaries. But color constancy is dependent on the entire extent of the perceived space. There are parallels in the changes of organization of this processing space for color and for shape from retina to striate-peristriate and prestriate systems.

The processing space for color at the receptor level is essentially trichromatic (e.g., Wald, 1964), much as Helmholtz (1909/1924) had envisioned it. In an elegant series of studies, De Valois recording from neurons in the lateral geniculate nucleus, showed that by this level an opponent process was operative. For instance, the response of neurons would be increased to red and decreased to green. The idea that color perception is based on such an opponent process was proposed by Hering (1964) and modified by Hurvitch and Jameson (1957). Two color pairs are involved: red-green, blue-yellow. Two further dimensions orthogonal to the color pairs and to each other describe and black and white (Sokolov & Ismailov, 1980). The opponent processing space is maintained and enhanced at the striate cortex (V_1). A double opponent process was found operative for receptive fields in V_4 (and sometimes in V_1) (Zeki, 1980). Double opponent processing entails the finding that the excitatory region and its inhibitory flanks respond in an opposite manner to a particular color and its opponent. This doubles the dimensionality of the color space (for an excellent review see DeValois & DeValois, 1988).

To achieve color constancy depends on utilizing the double opponent processing capabilities for the three sets of color pairs. Hurlbert and Poggio (1988) used computational techniques to simulate color constancy in color spaces composed of Mondrians of different reflectances. Their implementation utilized parallel processing in simple analog networks composed of the linear units devised by Poggio noted in Lecture 1. One of these implementations uses a "gradient descent" method that, over iterations, minimizes the least mean square of the error between actual and desired output (as determined by psychophysical experiment). This method is similar to that employed in Occam and the thermodynamic models described in Lecture 2. As Hurlbert and Poggio pointed out, this procedure is closely related to optimal Bayesian estimation. In their computations they used vectors to represent sample input sequences of Gaussian stochastic processes with zero mean (similar to the difference of Gaussian, DOGs discussed in the previous lecture). The property (e.g., Blue) is then fully specified by a computation similar to a regression equation.

It is necessary that the operator in this computation be space invariant, that is, it must not change with a change in location. This is accomplished by processing in the spectral domain (Fourier transforming). The calculation thus becomes "equivalent to the formation of an optimal [matched] filter" (p. 239). The calculation utilizes the power spectrum (amplitude-modulated frequencies) of the inputs. From an ensemble of such inputs, the cross power spectrum is calculated. These calculations are familiar to the holonomic brain theory.

Hurlburt and Poggio (1988) point out that:

> The significance of our results lies not so much in the specific estimation technique we used, but in the form of the filter we obtain. It is qualitatively the same as that which results from the direct application of regularization methods exploiting the spatial constraints on reflectance and illumination . . . The Fourier transform of the filter . . . is approximately a bandpass filter that cuts out low frequencies due to slow gradients of illumination and preserves intermediate frequencies due to step changes in reflectance . . . The shape of the filter is suggestive of the "non-classical" receptive fields that have been found in V_4, a cortical area implicated in mechanisms underlying color constancy (Desimone et al 1985; Wild et al 1985; Zeki 1983). (p. 13)

As these authors note, their calculations are similar to Land's (1986) most recent retinex operator. This operator divides the image irradiance at each pixel by a weighted average of the irradiance of pixels in a large surround—again suggestive of the receptive field structure in V_4. The double opponent nature of these receptive fields, with their large surrounds, highlights the relational nature of color constancy with respect to the total color space in which the color occurs: The calculations are shifted from contrast enhancement (cutting out low frequencies and enhancing intermediate frequencies by producing step-functions), which is produced by a single opponent process. The shift is to a relational space in which ratios of at least four values of an opponent pair enter into the computation.

Livingstone and Hubel (1984, 1988) also emphasize the fact that the varieties of hues composing such a multidimensional space operate relationally rather than just in an opponent fashion. This relational multidimensional space was beautifully demonstrated by Land at an invited lecture to the Society for Neurosciences (1986). On this occasion Hubel noted that a change from an opponent to a double opponent and then to a relational color space shifts the intersection of the axes of the color space from external to that space, to a location within that space. In this respect, the shift from color imaging to color constancy is akin to the shift in figural perception from Gabor's Hilbert space to a space in which "group operators" structure the dimensions in the space.

It is in this manner that the spatial frequency and movement tuned neurons of V_p are directly involved in the creation of spaces centered on their own forms; that is, in shape constancy. How such spaces and forms are composed by virtue of eye movements is the topic of the following sections.

CENTERS OF SYMMETRY AND REFERENCE FRAMES

Eye movement studies (e.g., Mackworth & Otto, 1970; Stark & Sherman, 1957) have demonstrated a concentration of eye fixations on contours and on "informative centers" of an image. Blum (1973, 1974), Gauthier (1977) and others (Schwartz, Desimone, Albright, & Gross, 1983) devised precise mathematical models that can extract geometric descriptors of shape from series of such figure-ground observations.

Whitman Richards and Lloyd Kaufman (1969) pointed out the relevance of "center of gravity" tendencies that occur for spontaneous optic fixations onto figures in the presence of flow patterns of visual background. They suggested that each pattern boundary (contour)

> sets up a wave [in the cortical receptive field matrix] which is propagated at a constant velocity. The point at which all waves converge together will be the

apparent position of the whirlpool [the fixation point]. For simple figures with no invagination, this position will be the center of gravity of the figure (p. 82).

Richards and Kaufman concluded by stating that they would like to consider the possibility that a "center of gravity" analysis, "which regulates oculomotor activity may be occurring at the same time that the form of the pattern is analyzed. . . . Thus, it is the flow pattern and not the form of the pattern which is the principal correlate of the fixation behavior." And the flow pattern is, of course, determined by movement. Movement-produced flow patterns initiate interference effects in the dendritic microprocess that, when transformed are the basis for the perception of contours. Fixation points (whirlpools, centers of gravity) are determined from the intersections of tangents to the contours.

The "center of gravity" fixations tend to coincide with foci of zero velocity in contour-directed flow patterns of visual background in small figures (with less than 5 lobes). This indicates some sort of symmetry seeking by the saccadic eye movement control system. In another study involving angular patterns outlined by dots, Kaufman and Richards (1969) obtained the same fixation tendencies as with line figures. From this, they concluded that

it isn't simply the discontinuity of brightness at a corner which reduces the effect on fixation. . . . It might, therefore, be concluded that cortical representation of shape, rather than local properties of the shapes, is the determiner of fixation. . . . It is the already organized cortical representation of shape which governs fixation, rather than peripheral input per se. (pp. 85–88)

The cortical representation of the retinal process in the form of Gabor transforms can provide the information used by the superior colliculus system to direct saccades. These in turn provide continuously changing sensory patterns to the cortex. The independent, simultaneous analysis of this flow of patterns by projection to and from the striate-peristriate coupled system (as described earlier) with summation of the resulting cortical patterns, culminates in the perceived invariances that constitute an "object."

An illustration serves to portray this process. When recordings are made of the brain electrical activity by a sensory stimulus, each individual recording (each image) is so complex that it is hard to identify the specific pattern related to the stimulus. Simply by summing the recordings in synchrony with the stimulation, a summary pattern (the object form) specific to the stimulus emerges.

Summation through superposition of "images" is, of course, somewhat more complex. In their analysis, Richards and Kaufman (1969) borrowed from an earlier theory of Pitts and McCulloch (1947). These authors had also suggested that the superior colliculus carries out a "center of gravity" analysis in order to direct saccades. In their theory the superior colliculus calculates the spatial coordinates of the center of brightness of the visual field, the eyes are moved so as to bring these spatial coordinates to the "origin of the visual axes" (pp. 142–146). Richards and Kaufman (p. 83) suggested that patterns of contours are "translated into directional apparent movement," perhaps perpendicular to the contour, which orients the fovea to the point of zero velocity. They relate this type of analysis to Blum's (1973) "symmetric disc coordinates," which are the two-dimensional coordinates of maximal discs centered on an axis equidistant from the boundaries of a given figure.

In terms of spatial coordinates of the visual field these calculations are inordinately complicated. By contrast, the least action principle of the holonomic brain theory assures that the saccadic system seeks the center of symmetry of the Gabor transformed optical image.

As in the case of imaging, object constancy is achieved by calculations largely in the spectral domain rather than in space-time: centers of symmetry rather than centers of gravity; Fourier descriptors (tangent vectors) of contours rather than boundaries; the extraction of invariances by superposition to form groups among transformed patterns. This is discussed in more detail in the next section.

By way of the inverse transform, these calculations result in cross correlation among ratios of shadings of surfaces so that invariances are extracted. The inverse transform is accomplished by virtue of corticofugal operations of the peristriate-striate system: The perception of object-form thus entails the execution of a third Gabor transform (the first by the optics of the eye; the second by the retino-cortical system).

To summarize, the approach taken here makes a distinction between sensory image and perceived object (there can be several images of a single object). At the same time, both imaging and object perception are the resultants of processes going on in the manifold of receptive fields in the primary visual cortex: Sensory imaging results from the selection operations of the sensory input on the cortical receptive field properties. Object-form perception, constancy, results from the selection operation of the perisensory motor systems on the striate cortical activity patterns: The peristriate cortex and superior colliculus, while producing variety in the sensory input, are set their own processing limits by massively parallel feedback from the prestriate cortex. Object-form perception is thus driven by movement which initiates a reciprocal motor-sensory process.

GROUP THEORY

The selection operations that result from superposition among tangent vectors of contours, characterize the neural processes by which object-forms become perceived. The results of superposition are represented mathematically by the theory of groups. Groups can be used to represent temporary stabilities. Such stabilities in polarization form in the receptive field manifold of the striate cortex by virtue of processes initiated by movement. As noted, movement involves the peristriate-tectal-geniculostriate circuit (the striate-peristriate couplet). The operation of group processes, based on recurrent input from the prestriate system, can be conceived to highlight this or that receptive field property much as a program highlights certain bulbs in a running advertisement or news display (as in Times Square). Any letter, cipher, or figure in such a display is an "object-form" in the sense used here.

The lighting of these bulbs is akin to Johanssen's experimental demonstrations of perceptual grouping discussed earlier. Recall that in these experiments it was shown that moving points of light become perceptually grouped according to definite principles: First, any movement common to the entire group is quickly picked up. More interesting, local groupings of lights around a single focal point or around several such foci are perceived as belonging to a "rigid" object that is highlighted, and represented by the individual lights. Thus a light on an axle and another on the rim of a wheel identify the wheel in motion. When the light on the axle is omitted, the other light appears to jump forward, without a circular motion. Fewer than a dozen lights strapped to joints, navel, and forehead readily identify their wearer as a single "object" who is climbing stairs, walking, or dancing.

These and even earlier observations on the power of grouping led to the formulation of a precise mathematical conception of the group. Specifically,

In the 1860's von Helmholtz demonstrated that the axioms of Euclidean geometry could be deduced from the laws of motion of rigid bodies, along with the assumption that a space of any number of dimensions is determined by that number of coordinates; similarly, non-Euclidean geometries are the laws of motion of other sorts of bodies. It was essentially the lack of rigor of von Helmholtz's results that spurred Lie in 1867 to begin developing the subject of continuous groups of transformations. As Lie wrote to Poincare in a letter of 1882: "(Riemann and) v. Helmholtz proceeded a step further [than Euclid] and assumed that space is a Zahlen-Mannigfaltigkeit [manifold or collection of numbers]. *This standpoint is very interesting; however, it is not to be considered as definitive* (italics in original)". Thus, instead of studying in an approximate manner how geometries are generated by rotations or translations of rigid bodies, Lie developed the means to analyze rigorously how points in space are transformed into one another through infinitesimal transformations—that is, the subject of continuous groups of transformations. Helmholtz, 1876; Lie, letter of 1882 to Poincare. (Footnote 4, p. 61, chap. 1, *Imagery in Scientific Thought*, Arthur I. Miller 1984, Birkhauser, Boston, MA)

This promising beginning was all but forgotten until Cassirer (1944) independently rediscovered the relevance of the group concept for understanding perceptual constancy. Then, as described earlier, Pitts and McCulloch (1947) modelled a neural network for computing group invariants. More recently Gibson (1966, 1979) and Johansson (1978; Johansson, von Hofsten, & Janssen, 1980) discussed the importance of grouping and invariance for object perception. The rediscovery of the utility of the Lie algebra for perception had to await the interest of a mathematician, William Hoffman (1966, 1978), who, in conjunction with Peter Dodwell and Terrence Caelli, presented a comprehensive and formal theory of visual perception based on the Lie algebra. Once again, however, their theory is limited to the space-time domain and thus differs in fundamental ways from the holonomic brain theory presented in these Lectures.

In a comprehensive review Palmer (1983; see also 1988) noted that not much attention has been paid to group theoretic ideas by mainstream perceptionists, perhaps because group theoretical language is not widely understood in psychology. He suspected, however, that group theoretic approaches to perception will prove invaluable in future theorizing about perceptual organization. I agree, but suggest that an understanding of Gabor elementary functions as descriptors of receptive field properties of visual cortical cells are equally essential to such future theorizing. Earlier group theoretic formulations based solely on feature detection and the impulsive mode of neural activity may well have failed to capture attention because they insufficiently reflected actual brain processes.

Mathematically, in order to adequately deal with perceptual phenomena, groups are used because they display the following properties: closure, associativity, identity and inversion. Closure means that composition of group elements results in another element of the group. The identity transformation leaves the underlying space unchanged: That is, the inverse of a transformation or operator, composes with that transformation to give the identity transformation. Finally, associativity is satisfied when the order in which elements of a given product are composed has no effect on the resultant.

HOLONOMIC TRANSFORMATIONS
AND GROUP THEORY

The particular group involved in image-object transformations is the Euclidean group generated by translations and rotations of three-dimensional Euclidean space. When these two types of transformation are combined, they result in helical transformations. The method of composing groups by such transformations has been generalized to other attributes of the image-object relationship, such as reflection (mirror images) and dilation (radial expansion and contraction). The study of abstract transformation groups is a form of harmonic analysis.

In the holonomic theory, harmonic analysis involves the operations of Euclidean groups on a Hilbert space of Gabor functions. Recall that this "space" is composed of (square) integrable functions defined on the spectral and space time domains. As reviewed in lecture 4, Gabor elementary functions parametrized by spectral and spatial (probability amplitude) variables describe the configural receptive field properties of single neurons in the striate cortex. Thus the manifold of receptive fields is represented mathematically as the domain of functions composing a Hilbert space. The operations on this manifold of receptive fields, by the reciprocal sensory-motor processes responsible for object-form perception, are represented mathematically by the theory of groups and can be implemented in harmonic analysis.

Palmer (1983) began a harmonic analysis of perceptual organization by showing that shape constancy can be handled by transformations applied to two-dimensional space. By contrast, the holonomic brain theory emphasizes, in agreement with Gibson, that percepts are initially, at minimum, three-dimensional and in fact four-dimensional (i.e., include movements through space, thus time). But as Palmer noted, there is no inherent difficulty in applying transformational analysis to more dimensions:

> Applying this transformational analysis to two-dimensional figures in the frontal plane is straightforward . . . the set of image transformations over which shape equivalence extends . . . consists largely of the group of projective transformations that form the basis of projective geometry. Thus the transformational analysis of shape constancy in two and three-dimensional space is identical at the "object" level and closely related even at the 'image' level. (p. 274)

What then are these transformations? There are four that, in various combinations, account for object constancy: Two of these transformations relate to translational invariance; two involve transformations around some central "point." Translational invariance is the property of an image or object to remain invariant across space-time; the transform producing it is also critical to reflection: The representation yielded by an inverse Fourier transform is translationally invariant; further, both "real" and "virtual" space-time images (which are mirrors of one another) are obtained.

Rotations and dilations (radial expansion and contraction), the other two transformations, demand a "fixation" point within the outlines of an object. Here also, the computations in the spectral domain simplify the process. As detailed earlier, such a central point for an object is best computed in the spectral domain through a series of superpositions of image transforms that inherently compute a common center of symmetry that is, their invariance. Rotations are discussed in detail later in the lecture. With respect to dilations, computations based in the spectral domain make up the subject of fractal geometry (Mandelbrot, 1977). Jean-Claude Perez (1988) at IBM Montpellier, France, developed a computational model using parallel-distributed processing architectures to construct a fractal "holographic" memory. The holographic aspects of the model are the encoded Fourier coefficients. Interestingly, the model incorporates not only fractal geometry, but "self-organizing" properties that manifest an entropic order. Perez described his model as "holography emergent from fractal chaos."

INVARIANCE AND REFERENCE FRAMES

Another simplification that the transformational model makes possible relates two approaches that dominate the constancy literature: The invariant feature and the reference frame hypotheses. Palmer (1983) stated the case as follows:

> The invariant features hypothesis, then, suggests that shape is represented by detecting just those properties of objects that do not change over the relevant set of transformations. As argued above, the set that underlies shape constancy is just the similarity group. Thus, angle-size, relative length of lines, number of lines, number of angles, closedness, connectedness and the like are possible candidates for invariant features of perceived shape because they are all invariant over the similarity group. This means that any pair of figures that have the same shape will be identical with respect to these figures. . . .

> The reference frame hypothesis makes use of the underlying transformation group in a somewhat different way. Rather than ignoring properties that vary over the transformations of the group, it assumes that the effects of transformations are neutralized by imposing an "intrinsic frame of reference" that effectively "factors out" the transformation, thereby achieving shape constancy. The "intrinsicness" of the frame simply means that the frame is chosen to correspond optimally with the structure of the figure rather than being imposed arbitrarily. (pp. 275–276)

As indicated, choosing a frame that corresponds optimally with the structure of the figure comes naturally to the holonomic model when centers of symmetry and Fourier descriptors are computed. For Palmer the virtue of the reference frame theory lies in the fact that "the frame effectively absorbs transformational variation." This is accomplished because orientation, size, position, and shape all become relative to the frame. In the holonomic brain theory these calculations are performed by way of a Fourier descriptor reference-frame scheme that automatically processes Fourier transforms from centers of symmetry (See Appendix B). Invariance is thus doubly assured because it is relative to the frame provided by the set of figures (images, perspectives) of the object.

As an example of the necessity for a reference frame, Palmer cited the experiments on "mental rotation" using Shepard figures. Whether one subscribes to the "coding" hypothesis (Pylishin, 1983) or the "minds eye" (Kosslyn, 1980) as explanatory of the findings, the invariant feature hypothesis is inadequate.

In the Shepard experiment, pairs of two-dimensional figures of various object-forms are presented at different orientations and subjects are asked whether or not the figures are identical (Fig. 5.4). When the orientations of presentations vary in the plane of the figures, the amount of their difference in angular rotation hardly influences response time. This finding is compatible with the invariant-feature hypothesis. When, on the other hand, the pair of figures differs in reflection, (that is, the figures are rotated only in a plane perpendicular to the plane of the figures) reaction time is linearly related to the amount of rotation

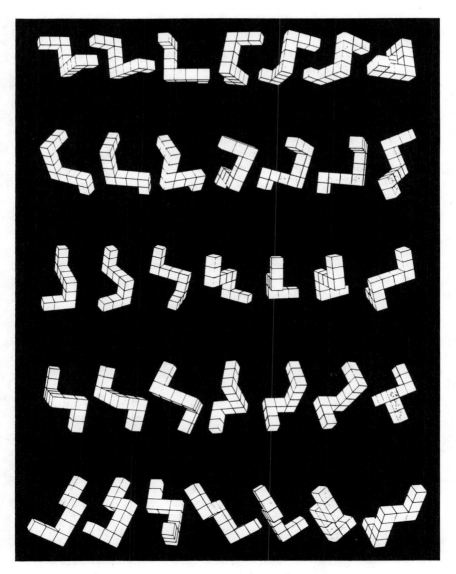

FIG. 5.4. Three-dimensional shapes rotated in space are depicted in computer-generated perspective drawings. When the subjects were shown pairs of line drawings portraying the same shape in different orientations, the time they took to recognize that the shapes were identical was proportional to the angular difference in the orientations shown. The linear increase in comparison time with difference in orientation suggested that subjects had to imagine one shape rotated into the orientation of the other in order to check for a match. From: Cooper, L. A. and Shepard, R. N. (1984). Turning Something Over in the Mind. In: *The Mind's Eye: Readings from Scientific American,* pp. 102–108. New York: Freeman.

required to mentally or physically superimpose the figures. This finding—and a similar finding for figures that differ in size (Bundesen & Larsen, 1975)—indicates that the figures cannot be readily compared until they are "mentally placed" into the same frame. Palmer (1983) noted:

> It seems, then, that certain kinds of shape comparisons can only be made when figures have the same orientation and size. This is what would be expected from the reference frame hypothesis. The mental transformations sound very much like operations that would be performed to align two frames so that their contents could be compared directly. (p. 279)

COMPUTATION IN JOINT OCCULOCENTRIC AND OBJECT CENTERED FRAMES

Carlton and Shepard (1988) carefully analyzed some of the possible types of "space," which will account for the observed facts of rotation of objects. It is the fact that mental rotation of objects mimics actual rotation (indicated by reaction time, for example) which establishes the reality of an internal, that is, brain, representation of a processing space. Once again, however, a distinction must be made between what it is that needs to be processed and the way in which processing proceeds. This section deals with characterizing the motions and frames that need to be processed; the next section describes computational procedures that can account for processing.

According to Carlton and Shepard (1988) the three-dimensional occulocentric frame in which translations of objects occur, must be supplemented with another three dimensions (an object centered frame) to allow for rotations:

> Students of perception and internal representation have long focused primarily on the perception and representation of static stimuli—perhaps because the static case was thought to be simpler and thus more suited to initial investigation than the dynamic case. Increasingly, however, the view has been emerging that it is not objects but their transformations that may be primary (e.g., Freyd, 1987; Leyton, 1988; Pribram and Carlton, 1986; Shepard, 1981). Even a static object is perceptually interpreted not as an imutable sui generis but, rather, as a member of a set of natural alternatives (Garner, 1974; Shepard, 1987). In a very general class of cases, moreover, the natural alternatives are just those to which the given object is related by psychologically simple transformations (Cassirer, 1944; Leyton, 1986a, 1986b, 1986c; Palmer, 1982, 1984; Shepard, 1981, 1988). (p. 5)

Carlton and Shepard (1988) resort to the principle of least action as instanced by geodesics, the shortest paths taken by points moving within the joint translational and rotational space.

> Minimum principles have been prominent in perceptual psychology since the advent of Gestalt theory (see Hatfield & Epstein, 1985). In relation to the representation of motion their most fundamental analogue in physics is the principle of *least*

action enunciated by Maupertuis; refined for classical mechanics by Euler, Lagrange, and Hamilton; and extended to relativistic and quantum physics by Einstein, Tomonaga, Schwinger, Feynman, and others. They are related to the notion, in geometry, of a *geodesic*—when the geodesic is interpreted as a path determined by the variational principle that between any two points along the path, arc length (if definable) be minimum. (p. 17)

They initially represented these geodesics by a Euclidean group but now intend to generalize to a Poincare group. Specifically Carlton and Shepard search for fundamental principles that give rise to the "psychologically most natural" paths through which rigid objects may move. They suggest that certain select principles have been internalized through evolution. Candidate principles include: (a) laws of kinetic physics, which specify that in the absence of perturbing forces, an inertial object will follow a least-energy path in which the center traverses a straight line while any rotation is about that rectilinearly translating center; (b) principles of kinematic geometry, which specify that in the absence of symmetries of the object (and without regard to physical concepts of inertia or energy), the simplest transformation is a screw displacement that carries the object over a helical path around a uniquely determined axis in space; (c) principles of kinematic geometry extended to take account of symmetries of the object, which permit screw displacements around different axes in space, and even rotation around an axis of symmetry that is itself undergoing a screw displacement in space; or (d) various other possible extensions or combinations of these principles.

These alternatives are mathematically formulated in terms of the geodesic paths. Each path prescribes the closest analog of straight lines in the appropriate curved manifold of possible positions of the object in space. Comparisons with emerging experimental data so far suggest that the more abstract geometrical principles dominate the more concrete physical principles in the internalized mental mechanics.

Abstractly formulated, the problem becomes one of comparing alternative one-dimensional curves in the full six-dimensional manifold of possible positions and of specifying which paths of motion are simplest. In order to make such comparisons and specifications, however, the manifold must be endowed with a rich topological structure. A structure is needed to permit the identification of those paths that, like great circles on the surface of a sphere, are, in the resulting six-dimensional curved manifold, the closest analogs of straight lines. The simplest motions would then be taken to be those that correspond to these shortest paths, the geodesics.

THE PROCESSING MODE

Carlton and Shepard also noted that a representation similar to that used in the quantum physics would elegantly solve the computational problem posed by the rotation of objects by representing that rotation by six dimensions.

Such a solution is clearly consonant with the holonomic brain theory based on a generalization of the mathematics used in the quantum physics as applied to psychophysics and neurophysiology in terms of the Gabor relation. The following history of the relevance of a quantum-like computational process is detailed:

> As we noted, Cassirer (1938/1944) made an early proposal that perception might be best understood through an extension of Klein's (1893) *erlangen* program for basing geometry on the transformations that leave geometrical objects invariant. Such a proposal was not seriously pursued in psychology, however, until Hoffman (1966) set forth, in some detail, how Lie groups and their one-parameter subgroups might account for a number of known perceptual illusions and other phenomena. In subsequent extensions of the application of group theory to real and apparent motion, Caelli, Hoffman, and Lindman (1978a, 1978b) introduced the *Lorentz group* of relativity physics, to which we shall return. . . .
>
> Foster (1975) evidently was the first . . . to report evidence that an extended object alternately presented in just two positions yields apparent rigid motion over a curved path. On the basis of this finding, Foster (1975; see also Foster, 1978) made what appears to have been the first explicit proposal that apparent motion of an extended object follows geodesic paths in the rotation group SO(3). Like Hoffman, however, Foster seems not to have explicitly treated . . . more general cases.
>
> [With regard to the least action principle,] . . . In 1844, W. R. Hamilton . . . announced a succesful generalization of algebra beyond both real numbers, x (each of which consists of but one component), and complex numbers, z (each of which consists of two components, x and y). Having found that elements consisting of three components were precluded by their inability to satisfy the required rules of vector multiplication, Hamilton introduced *quaternions* q, each of which consists of four components, q_1, q_2, q_3, q_4 (Hamilton 1844). Quaternions turned out to provide a particularly felicitous representation for rigid rotations in space (Cayley, 1845; Hamilton, 1853). For this reason, quaternions have been advocated in recent years for the control of the orientation of a physical space vehicle (e.g., Ickes, 1970), for the interpolation of intermediate frames, in computer animation, between frames portraying a rigid object in two different orientations in space (e.g., Shoemake, 1985), and even for mental transformations (see Oshins, 1984, Oshins and McGoveran, 1980). Indeed, interpolation in computer animation clearly bears a close affinity to the problem of mental interpolation, and we in fact take advantage of the computationally efficient way in which quaternions handle rotations. However, because the spherical metric of the noncommutative group of unit quaternions is the same as the angular metric of the orthogonal group SO(3) that we have already considered (Misner, et al, 1973), the paths of rotation that naturally arise from quaternions (see Shoemake, 1985) are identical to the great-circle paths we have already discussed for SO(3). Moreover, in order to accommodate general rigid motions, which include a translation as well as a rotation, the quaternions need to be extended by R^3 (see Carlton, 1988).

As described in the previous sections, the iterative application of certain elements of a group implements the least action principle. As pointed out by Carlton and Shepard, implementation turns out in certain cases to demand a rotation of 720° rather than 360° to return an object to its original position with respect to occulocentric space. Oshins (personal communication, 1978) demonstrated that 720° rotations, though counterintuitive, are often necessary. The human hand is such an object. The hand is connected to the human body by a nonrigid but impenetrable link, the arm. The hand can be brought back to its original position relative to the body only by a motion that results in a 720° rotation. Such 720° rotations are staples in the quantum domain (Wigner 1939). In implementation, therefore, the processing mode demands an extension into Hilbert Space of any purely space-time representation of extremal paths.

As to directions that future research might profitably take, Carlton and Shepard (1988) proposed that:

> We hope to explore the theoretical and empirical implications of formalizing mental transformations in terms of the Mobius rather than the Euclidean group and, also, in terms of more general (projective or conformal) groups. We also hope to assess the usefulness of representations—such as biquaternions (Clifford, 1882)—that naturally arise from such groups. . .
>
> In the cases of apparent and also of real motion, a fully adequate account of the chronometric data may . . . require, in place of the six-dimensional manifold of possible positions considered up to this point, a higher-dimensional position-time manifold. As originally implied by Hoffman (1966) and elaborated by Caelli, et al (1978b), the perceptual representation of motion should then be subject to laws resembling the Lorentz transformations of relativity theory. The Euclidean group E^+, which has so far served as the basis for our formalizations, might have to be replaced, in particular, with the more general Poincare group (Dirac, 1930; Wigner, 1939), requiring a manifold of as many as ten dimensions. We have begun a more formal exploration of these ideas, but regard them as insufficiently worked out or tested to present at this time. (p. 42)

If we indeed accept quantum computation as a possibility, then the internalized laws of kinetic physics and the principles of kinetic geometry provide a detailed description of what it is that must be computed, not the manner in which the computations are achieved. In fact, Carlton (1988; see also Pribram & Carlton, 1986) resorted to processing in a Hilbert space of complex valued functions of four real variables, which, as we have seen above and throughout these lectures, is a mathematical structure similar to that used by Heisenberg in quantum physics. Carlton already formally described the brain processes represented by geodesics in terms of the action on the Euclidean (three spatial dimension) group. As Carlton noted, this approach must be generalized to four-dimensional space-time (endowed with a Minkowski metric) in order to account for the time aspect of movement. The generalization must be accomplished by replacing the Euclidean group with the Poincare group of space time isometries, the relativistic analogues of geodesics according to both kinetic physics and kinematic geometry.

In the holonomic brain theory the geodesics would, therefore, describe the shortest path between isovalent contours in the neural holoscape. As detailed in the appendeces, this is a general property of such calculations: they achieve maximum efficiency, that is, minimum entropy. Thus the physiological processes described by a holoscape provide readily for geodesics.

INVARIANCE AS RELATIVE TO FRAME

The model developed by Carlton and Shepard and in the holonomic brain theory makes it unnecessary to choose between invariance and reference frame. The very same operations that determine centers of symmetry also determine the Fourier descriptors that define the frame of the perceived object.

Palmer (1983) came close to this view when he stated that "reference frames seem to be established so that they coincide with intrinsic geometric regularities in figures" (p. 300); thus, for example, "the stimulus variables that control the establishment of the position and size of the frame is inexorably attracted to the same values for the same shape" (p. 301); and again:

> The reference frame hypothesis requires additional assumptions to account for the exceedingly small number of ambiguous alternatives. This can be handled by proposing that the frame is "data driven": it is largely determined by the structure of the figure rather than being arbitrarily imposed. There are few cases of naturally occurring ambiguity because there are few figures for which the frame can be established in more than one way. In short, the processes that underlie frame selection are powerful heuristics rather than fail-safe algorithms. Their fallibility is revealed in what I have called reference frame effects.

> What do these reference frames have to do with transformations and symmetries? We have already mentioned that one of the most powerful rules for selecting the reference orientation is reflectional symmetry. I suspect that other sorts of symmetries are used in selecting other parameters of the reference frame. For example, the origin of the frame might well be established by selecting the point about which there is maximal rotational symmetry. (p. 306)

These observations are important because they take the proposals of the previous sections a step further: invariance, constancy, is seen to be, in a fashion, relative rather than absolute. This conclusion returns us to the theme which introduced this lecture: Movement, by superposing images, results in sensitivity to a frame, a Mondrain that provides local context.

At this point in the argument, in anticipation of the remaining lectures, the reciprocity between constancy and reference frames or spaces needs to be discussed. This reciprocity results from the fact that ordinarily movement produces a variety of perspectives from which an object is observed. In the mental rotation experiments the subject examines the object from the perspective of different images of that object. Posner (1987), Kosslyn (1980), and Attneave (1968), as well as Palmer, discussed this choice of perspective as involving visual attention. Palmer suggested that this "form of visual attention. . . is driven primarily by stimulus structure" (p. 321). In other words there is a selection of one of the images (at a time) from which the object was constructed and this image provides the perspective from which the object is "viewed." In Palmer's (1983) model:

> An attentional frame can be conceived as a pointer that selects the central defining analyzer [i.e., image]. To this pointer is "attached" the transformational structure of the frame. It maps the retinally-based system of analyzers [images] into the frame-based system [of objects] effectively decoupling the stimulus from its relationship to the sensory surface. Thus, the perceptual reference frame can be modeled as a mechanism that is positioned within the analyzer space. The output of the frame, then, is just the same as the input to it from some other image that is a similarity transformation of the stimulus. The position of the frame in the analyzer space determines which similarity transformation the input image implicitly undergoes as a result of the "positioning" of the frame.

> In this way stimulus transformations can be factored out simply by moving the attentional frame around within the analyzer space. Movement along the orientational dimension produces rotations; movement along the resolutional dimension produces dilations; movement along the positional dimensions produces translations; and movement along more than one of these dimensions produces various composite transformations. *The underlying reason that such movements result in output constancy is that they effectively produce the inverse transformations on the image.* For example, when attention moves from a smaller to a larger frame, the effective size of a constant stimulus relative to the frame is reduced. However, the effective size of a stimulus that enlarges at the same rate the frame does will remain invariant relative to the frame. This is an example of a "visual algebra" in which transformations are counteracted by their inverses to achieve the identity transformation. (p. 321)

Note the sentence emphasized by Palmer: Movements effectively produce inverse transformations on the image. Conversely, perspective regains the image (by producing the inverse transform on the object) by way of selective attention.

Neurons in V_3 are practically insensitive to movement per se, but respond to what can be thought of as movement of "the mind's eye"—attention. Experiments by Gross et al. (1985) and Desimone et al. (1985) demonstrated that when monkeys were shown two objects, one of which was consistently rewarded and therefore presumably relevant to the monkey and attended by him, responses were obtained from V_3 cells only when the relevant object appeared within the receptive field of the cells. When the relevant object was placed outside the cell's receptive field, responses were inhibited. Placement of the irrelevant object within or beyond the receptive field had no effect.

For the most part, as detailed in Lecture 7, selective attention though triggered by sensory input as Palmer so clearly describes, is controlled by input from memory based processing stages. Several of the subsequent lectures are concerned with such higher order neuropsychological control systems. Suffice it here to note that groups can be formed on the basis of relations other than those that form objects. Thus, for example, a body-centered egocentric frame is provided by the somatic sensory-motor system. Cells in the parietal cortex of monkeys respond when an object appears within reach of the animal, whether or not he actually reaches. If the object appears beyond reach no activity is generated (Mountcastle, 1957). The neural systems that include these cells have been identified (Mishkin & Underleider, 1982; Pribram & Barry, 1956; Wilson, 1975) to deal with where an object is located with respect to body space. These systems are addressed in the next lecture.

CONCLUSION AND SUMMARY

The perception of visual object-forms entails a procedure that extracts invariants from successive sensory inputs. According to the holonomic brain theory, this procedure is described by operations carried out in phase (Hilbert) space and involves the formation of groups. The procedure is carried out jointly by a coupled striate-peristriate and by the ventral portion of the prestriate visual system (V_p and V_3) with the consequence that eye movements scan the input in such a way that centers of symmetry and Fourier descriptors of the object-forms are processed. These procedures simultaneously establish the relations that describe the object-form and its frame, the object-centered space.

Object-forms in their object-centered frames are related to egocentric space by operations involving the dorsal portion of the prestriate and by parietal systems. The next lecture describes the brain processes involved in processing a corporeal self, an egocentric action space.

6

Images of Achievement and Action Spaces: Somatic Processes in the Control of Action

The singleness of action from moment to moment. . . is a keystone in the construction of the individual whose unity it is the specific office of the nervous system to perfect. (Sherrington, 1911/1947)

INTRODUCTION

The brain processes discussed in most of these lectures provide for amply endowed perceptions some of which are sensitive to modification by experience. But an organism so endowed remains a passive spectator unable to act in any way within a universe so richly perceived. Furthermore, the distance senses provide no direct contact with that universe. Contact is made by the somatic systems. The current lecture reviews evidence regarding somatic processing systems. The brain organizes these systems in two ways: (a) by processing relatively unpatterned grasping, "prehension," and (b) by processing targeted action.

Prehension results in the perception of object-forms as in the observations described at the beginning of the previous lecture. Constancies and object-centered spaces are developed much as in vision. Also as in vision, motor aspects of somatic sensory processing are crucial to the perception of object-forms. In contrast, as is developed in this lecture, the processing of targeted action is a unique function demanding a somewhat different neural organization. In primates the pyramidal tract, the major direct corticofugal pathway to muscles, originates from both pre- and post-Rolandic cortex; thus movement can be placed at the service of either prehension or targeted action. As a corollary, electrical stimulation of both pre- and post-Rolandic cortices produces movement; and

121

damage to both produces impaired motor capacity (Kruger & Porter, 1958; Peele, 1944).

However, just as in the case of the striate and peristriate visual systems, there is considerable functional separation of input and output systems as gauged by electrical recording. The portion of the pyramidal tract that originates in post-Rolandic cortex is involved in "holding" the prehended object, not in processing an achievement: for example, a selective negativity is, in brain electrical activity, recorded from the post-Rolandic parietal cortex *while* a monkey holds down a lever preparatory to receiving a peanut when he lets go. On the other hand, the portion of the pyramidal tract originating in the pre-Rolandic cortex is involved in targeted action: Brain electrical activity is recorded *prior* to the manifest muscle contractions involved in the action (Kornhuber, 1974; Donchin, Otto, Gerbrandt, & Pribram, 1973).

With regard to imaging and the perception of object-forms, there is considerable similarity between the somatic systems and those concerned with vision. Electrical stimulation of the post-Rolandic gyrus in humans results in the report of images such as pressure and movement. These occur in a part of the body corresponding to the location of stimulation in the homunculus that represents the body surface in the post-Rolandic system (Fig. 6.1). Resections of the post-Rolandic cortex result in astereognosis, an inability to perceive object-forms by manipulation. Also clusters of neurons in the post-Rolandic cortex are selective to one or another submodality of somatic sensation (Mountcastle, 1957). This is also true in vision where color and form selectivities are to some extent segregated (in about 20% of the receptive fields) in different aggregates (DeValois & DeValois, 1988; Hubel & Livingstone, 1981).

There is evidence that processing in the somatic, as in the visual and auditory modalities, entails the frequency domain. When the body or tendon of an immobilized muscle is mechanically vibrated, an illusion of movement is produced (Jones, 1988; Lackner, 1988). Resections of the parietal (including the post-Rolandic) cortex in monkeys produces an impairment in discriminating between frequencies ranging from 10–50 Hz produced by mechanical sinusoids delivered to the contralateral hand, especially for frequencies ranging between 24–36 Hz (LaMotte & Mountcastle, 1979). Also, clusters of neurons in the post-Rolandic cortex have been shown to respond selectively to such periodic stimulation (Mountcastle, Talbot, Sakata & Hyvarinen, 1969). As is described shortly, frequency selective neurons are also found in the pre-Rolandic cortex.

The advantages of processing in the frequency domain in the somatic modality are similar to those operating in vision. As noted in previous lectures, one such advantage is projection, that is, experiencing an object-form away from the sensory and brain process involved in computing that experience. As is described shortly, in contrast to vision, projection in the somatic modality operates as much in time as in space (see e.g., Lashley, 1951). This is especially true when objects perceived by virtue of the operations of the distance senses are apprehended and acted upon.

The contents of this lecture indicate that this difference between the somatic and visual systems is due to the primacy of the pre-Rolandic motor over the post-Rolandic sensory aspects of processing in the somatic modality. When the pre-Rolandic somatic motor systems are considered, a major difference from the visual system becomes evident: Whereas the motor process in which the peristriate visual systems partake is exclusively at the service of the visual sensory mechanism, the pre-Rolandic motor process controls the effectors that make it possible for the organism to act on and thus effect changes (over space and time) in the environment. The action systems are therefore more complex in their organization than the motor systems are in vision. In addition, actions are responsible for the construction of egocentric spaces, and additional brain systems have been identified that construct joint egocentric and occulocentric spaces. It is the action systems, therefore, that are the major concern here. The central theme, however, purports that action is guided by "images of achievement" processed in much the same fashion as the images processed by the distance senses.

This theme differs considerably from another which holds that forebrain control of action is guided by what neuroscientists refer to as "motor programs." Ordinarily such programs are thought to provide step-by-step instructions for sequences of muscle contractions and relaxations, instructions that guide movements. But most computer programs, especially those that implement parallel-distributed processing, are constructed hierarchically and it is only the lowest level of the hierarchy that implements the instructions in hardware.

With regard to fleshware, as described here, even at the lowest level, motor control is excercised largely by way of control over receptors. Hierarchically arranged levels thus embody controls that act much like those embodied in thermostats in which tests match an input against a setpoint, a set of attractors in a temporarily stable system. Mismatch produces a destabilization that transfers control to lower levels of operation that aim to restore stability. The operations can take a variety of forms. The set-point (which in regard to action systems is composed of sets of Images-of-Achievement) is the temporally projected target of the operation. Control, the Test-Operate-Test-Exit (TOTE) sequence is maintained until stability is achieved. Then control shifts to another TOTE—usually the shift is due to a movement produced variation in input (Miller, Galanter, & Pribram, 1960).

The projection of achievement by target images implies that the action systems, just as the perceptual systems, are driven by a cascade of reciprocally organized central controls on receptor processes (see e.g., Hoffer, 1982). However, the receptor processes for action and the central controls on them differ considerably from those involved in other modalities. Therefore, much of this lecture is devoted to specifying the details of muscle receptor function as well as

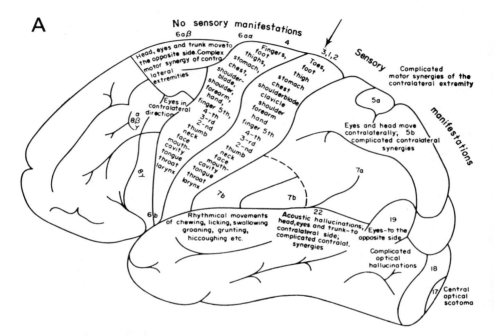

A

No sensory manifestations

6aβ · 6aα · 4 · 3,1,2 · Sensory

Head, eyes and trunk move to the opposite side. Complex motor synergy of contralateral extremities

Eyes in contralateral direction

8β
γ

8γ

Fingers, thighs, foot stomach, chest, shoulder, shoulder-blade, forearm, hand, finger 5th, 4-th, 3-rd, 2-nd thumb, neck, face, mouth-cavity, tongue, throat, larynx

Toes, foot thigh stomach chest shoulderblade clavicle shoulder forearm hand finger 5th 4-th 3-rd 2-nd neck face mouth-cavity tongue throat larynx

Complicated motor synergies of the contralateral extremity

5a

Eyes and head move contralaterally; 5b complicated contralateral synergies

7a

manifestations

6b

7b · 7b

Rhythmical movements of chewing, licking, swallowing groaning, grunting, hiccoughing etc.

22
Acoustic hallucinations; head, eyes and trunk-to contralateral side; complicated contralat. synergies

19
Eyes-to the opposite side

Complicated optical hallucinations

18

17
Central optical scotoma

FIG. 6.1. (a)Summary of data given by Ottfried Foerster on results of stimulation of various points of the human cortical hemisphere (1926). From Bernstein, c 1967. Reprinted with permission from Pergamon Press Ltd. (b)Motor representation on precentral cortex of man. (lower right)Diagram of surface of left cerebral hemisphere, showing location of precentral gyrus. (left)Precentral gyrus isolated, enlarged, and viewed from the same aspect as in lower right. (upper right)Medial aspect of the precentral gyrus. Actually there is considerable overlapping and variation in individual cases but the order is constant. From data on electrical stimulation of precentral cortex and observations of the resulting movements obtained by Foerster, Penfield and Boldrey and others. Redrawn after Krieg, 1966.

124

B

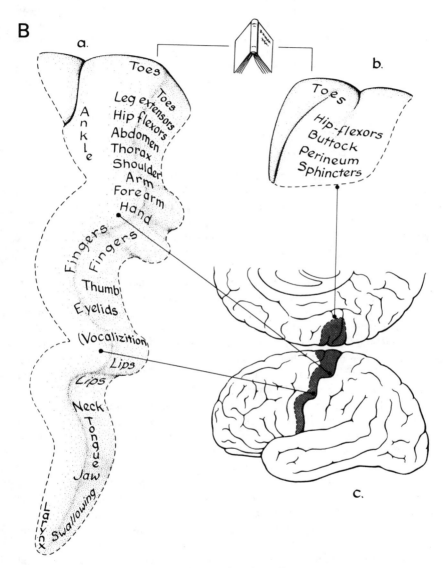

a.

Toes
Toes
Leg extensors
Hip flexors
Abdomen
Thorax
Shoulder
Arm
Forearm
Hand
Ankle
Fingers
Fingers
Thumb
Eyelids
(Vocalizition)
Lips
Lips
Neck
Tongue
Jaw
Larynx
Swallowing

b.

Toes
Hip-flexors
Buttock
Perineum
Sphincters

c.

FIG. 6.1. (continued)

the sets of central controls on these receptors. Action, the environmental consequence of such processing, is critical to the development of the full range of
attributes of perception. In the previous lecture it was already shown that the
perception of object-forms depends on movement. In subsequent lectures, the
cognitive aspects of perception are shown to depend on remembering the consequences of movement, that is, actions. In a very real sense, therefore perception
and action interrelate reciprocally, each providing constraints that define the
other.

SOMATOMOTOR CONTROLS: SPINAL, BRAIN STEM, BASAL GANGLIA AND CEREBELLAR

Acts carried out by muscle contractions are monitored by two types of receptors:
Spindles that lie parallel to contractile muscle fibers and tendon organs, which,
as their name implies, are embedded in tendons and thus connected in series with
the muscle fibers. Although both types of receptors are stimulated by muscle
contractions (and relaxations), only the response of muscle spindles is tuned by
signals reaching them (via two types of motoneurons, "dynamic" and "static")
from the central nervous system.

The central tuning of muscle spindles is effected by parallel systems of hierarchically organized control (Fig. 6.2). These controls operate on the spinal cord
level, where constantly hyperactive signal generators serve to excite both the
contractile muscle fibers (via motoneurons) and spindles. (Neurons in general are
spontaneously active, but spinal cord neurons have a much higher rate of spontaneous discharge than do those of the brain.) The spinal generators are modulated by inhibitory local circuit neurons in such a way that the resultant activity
can be modelled in terms of "coupled ensembles of limit cycle oscillatory processes" (Kelso & Saltzman, 1982). As a result, muscular contraction is oscillatory: Fine, almost subliminal, tremors characterize normal movement, tremors
that become gross and readily observable only under pathological conditions.
(See Grillner, 1974, 1981, and 1985 for review).

The spinal cord ensemble of oscillators is in turn organized by brain systems
that consist of cholinergic and adrenergic sets of neurons. The cholinergic set
regulates the frequency of a wide range of tonic rhythmic activities such as those
involved in locomotion, respiration, cardiovascular responses, and sleep. This
cholinergic system is coupled to the adrenergic set of neurons that segment the
rythmic activities into episodes (Garcia-Rill & Skinner, 1988). Both systems can
be considered to be part of an overall set of dopaminergically controlled basal
ganglia regulatory systems.

Malfunctions of the basal ganglia produce "tremors at rest," "cogwheel"
rigidity and difficulties in initiating movements. These difficulties are, as noted,
to a large extent, due to malfunction of control over the rhythmic tonic contrac-

tibility of the musculature, in other words, how tense rather than how long or short a muscle is to become. Tonicity supplies sets of stabilities, the reference frames, that specify equifinal paths of action within the context of postural settings. (For an excellent review and discussion, see MacLean, 1990).

The other set of brain stem regulatory systems centers on the cerebellum. Damage to the human cerebellar hemisphere disorganizes the metric lengthening and shortening of muscles during intended actions—at a minimum, causing intention tremors. When the difficulty is fullblown and the patient is asked to place his forefinger on his nose, his face must be protected from violent swings of his arm and hand. Ordinarily, cerebellar function assures that, once begun, actions proceed smoothly. This unperturbed flow has been likened to the trajectory of missiles and the cerebellar process is therefore referred to as ballistic (e.g., Kornhuber, 1974). Ruch (1951) was the first to point out that closed-loop feedback cannot account for such a process. Rather, what is involved is the type of parallel open-loop feedforward proposed by Helmholtz for voluntary eye movements (as described in the previous lecture).

There is good evidence that a comparison between current receptor input and current central process occurs in the cerebellar cortex (Fig. 6.3). These comparisons can be represented as a tensor matrix that matches current receptor input vectors to control vectors (Pellionisz & Llinas, 1979). The comparison is not altogether different from that which characterizes sensory systems: reference frames as well as targets are taken into account. In addition, the processing capacity of the cerebellar cortex is vast and unique: A massive inhibitory wave wipes the cortex clean every 500 msec (Eccles, Ito, & Szentagothai, 1967). This characteristic suggests that the cerebellar cortex acts as a buffer where the intended trajectory is extrapolated; that is, the results of the extrapolation are sent to the rest of the motor system to anticipate the trajectory of an entire act the moment it is initiated. By analogy to vision, each intended act initiates a saccade that, to some extent at least, achieves its intention. Should the saccade miss its mark a new saccade incorporating the degree of miss is initiated.

A great deal of interest has been centered on the functions of the cerebellum in classical conditioning and the learning of motor skills (see e.g., Thompson, 1986 for review). There is good evidence (Fig 6.4) that a circuit is involved which is composed of the inferior olive, the cerebellar nuclei (especially the n. interpositus) and the red nucleus: The role of the cerebellar cortex in operant conditioning and skill learning is less certain: Excision often leaves the conditioning process intact; but this lack of effect has been challenged (Russell personal communication, reviewed by Thompson 1986). Most likely, the cerebellar cortex receives the results of prior learning by way of feedback loops from the cerebral cortex which in turn receives its input from the cerebellar nuclei. Then, as described above, the cortical input is compared with the inputs from peripheral stations and the "saccad", the intended trajectory, is computed.

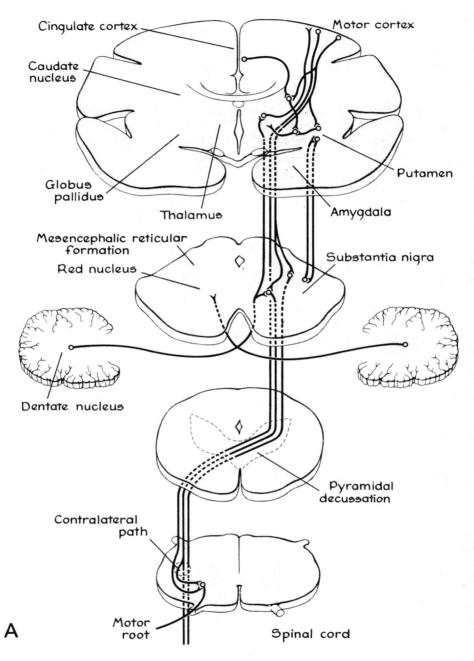

Cingulate cortex

Motor cortex

Caudate
nucleus

Globus
pallidus

Putamen

Thalamus

Amygdala

Mesencephalic reticular
formation

Substantia nigra

Red nucleus

Dentate nucleus

Pyramidal
decussation

Contralateral
path

A

Motor
root

Spinal cord

FIG. 6.2.

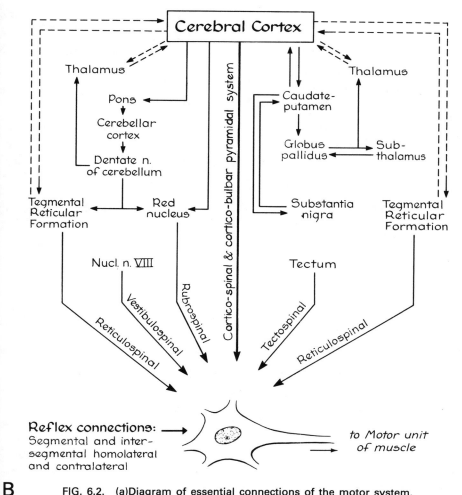

B

FIG. 6.2. (a)Diagram of essential connections of the motor system. (b)A few of the many descending systems influencing the activity of the "final common path," the motor neuron. Modified from Ranson and Clark, 1959. Compare with (a) for anatomical location of structures referred to.

A

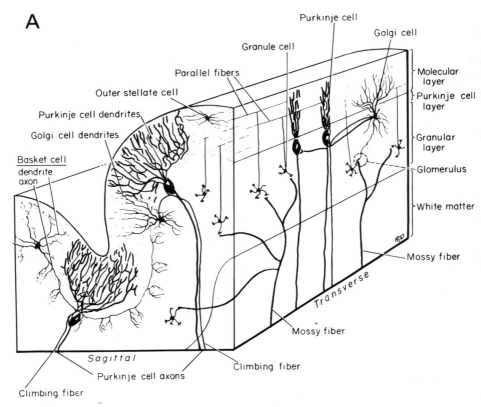

Purkinje cell

Golgi cell

Granule cell

Parallel fibers

Outer stellate cell

Purkinje cell dendrites

Golgi cell dendrites

Basket cell
dendrite
axon

Molecular
layer

Purkinje cell
layer

Granular
layer

Glomerulus

White matter

Mossy fiber

Transverse

Mossy fiber

Sagittal

Purkinje cell axons

Climbing fiber

Climbing fiber

FIG. 6.3.   (a)Schematic diagram of the cerebellar cortex in sagittal and
transverse planes showing cell and fiber arrangements. From Truex
and Carpenter, 1969. *Human Neuroanatomy*, 6th ed. © 1969 the
Williams & Wilkins Co., Baltimore, Md. (b) Diagram illustrating the
extension of inhibitory fields (shadowed areas) in the case that a narrow beam of parallel fibers be excited. The upper part of the diagram is
a transverse section of the folium and the lower part a view at the
folium surface from above. It is assumed that there is a "minimum
effective beam" of simultaneously excited parallel fibers, which is
more likely to stimulate a row of Purkinje, stellate, and basket cells.
Golgi cells having a much larger dendritic spread would be more likely
to be excited by broader bands of simultaneously excited parallel fibers. Effective stimulation of the Golgi cells would then in turn tend to
stop—as a negative feedback—all mossy input. Thus the Golgi cell
system can be considered as a "focusing" device restricting—or giving preference to—granule neuron (parallel fiber) activity in relatively
narrow bands. From Eccles, Ito, and Szentagothai, 1967.

130

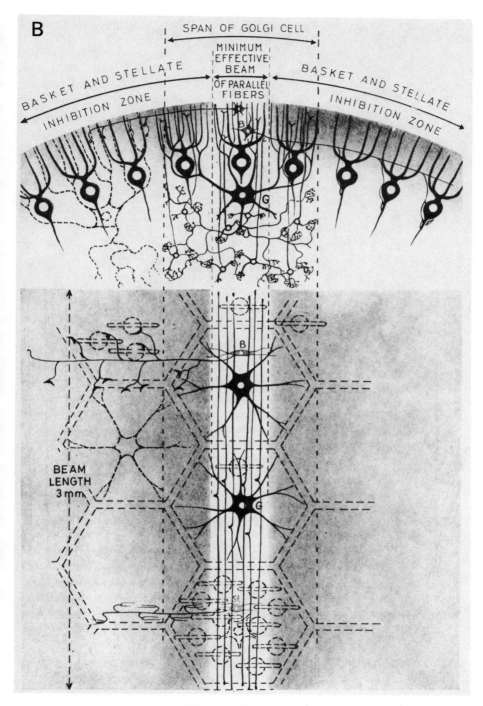

FIG. 6.3. (continued)

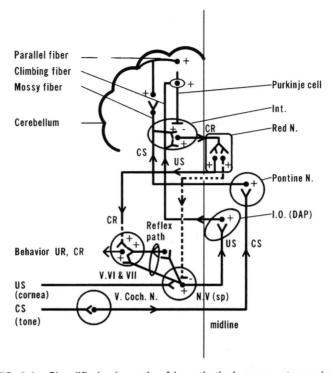

FIG. 6.4. Simplified schematic of hypothetical memory trace circuit
for discrete behavioral responses learned as adaptations to aversive
events. The US (corneal airpuff) pathway consists of somatosensory
projections to the dorsal accessory portion of the inferior olive (I.O.)
and its climbing fiber projections to the cerebellum. The tone CS pathway consists of auditory projections to pontine nuclei (Pontine N) and
their mossy fiber projections to the cerebellum. The efferent (eyelid
closure) CR pathway projects from the interpositus nucleus (Int) of the
cerebellum to the red nucleus (Red N) and via the descending rubral
pathway to act ultimately on motor neurons. The red nucleus may also
exert inhibitory control over the transmission of somatic sensory information about the US to the inferior oliver (IO), so that when a CR
occurs (eyelid closes), the red nucleus dampens US activation of
climbing fibers. Evidence to date is most consistent with storage of
memory traces in localized regions of cerebellar cortex and possibly
interpositus nucleus as well. Pluses indicated excitatory and minuses
inhibitory synaptic action. Additional abbreviations: N V (sp), spinal
fifth cranial nucleus; VI, sixth cranial nucleus; VII, seventh cranial nucleus; V Coch N, ventral cochlear nucleus. From: Thompson, R. F.
(1986). The Neurobiology of Learning and Memory. *Science, 233,* 941–
947.

TARGETS: THE COMPUTATION OF SOMATOMOTOR CONSTANCIES

The cerebral somatomotor cortex integrates the processes of the cerebellum and basal ganglia. The nature of this cortical integration is the concern of the current lecture. Earlier conceptualizations derived from Newtonian mechanics have proven inadequate whereas powerful explanations can be formulated in terms of cascades of the layered distributed processes. The necessity for such a shift is outlined by Partridge (1982) as follows:

> Motor control, like operations of other mechanical systems has been treated in terms of force, velocity, position, and mechanical impedence. It is almost never described in other equally valid coordinate systems,. . . those with dimensions such as momentum, power, work, kinetic energy, potential energy, etc. (e.g., Brooks 1981). In favor of such an alternative coordinate system is the constancy, over a wide range of velocities, of the relationship between neural drive and power output from muscle. . . . Evidence from the study of receptor responses indicates that, at least at the input level, mechanical information is carried in a non-Newtonian frame of reference. (1982 p. 561)

As noted, Kelso and Saltzman (1982) have proposed, on the basis of their research, that such a coordinate system is implemented by coupled ensembles of limit cycle oscillations. These authors as well as Stelmach and Diggles (1982) point out that such ensembles provide distributed control systems. The ensemble of cortical neurons

> . . . are viewed as control surfaces from which the spatiotemporal patterns for movement may be derived. Neural maps are used as control surfaces about the topographical relationship one item shares with several others. Thus information from one item will provide relative information about other items, suggesting a certain economy in storage and a basis for cooperative computation. It is then plausible that a layered motor controller exists in which position of input on the control surface, determined by the 'center of gravity' of an array of activation points, encodes the target to which [the] musculature will be directed. In this manner each activation point contributes to target determination, and responsibility for the course of movement is distributed among these points. (p. 556)

In the holonomic brain theory the distributed activation points are identified as isovalent postsynaptic polarizations in the dendritic receptive fields of somatomotor cortical neurons. Stelmach and Diggles' reference to a "center of gravity" of an array of activation points is reminiscent of Richards and Kaufman's (1969) description of a "center of gravity" determination of visuomotor activity discussed in the previous Lecture.

What is missing in Stelmach and Diggles' as in Richards and Kaufman's model is a relatively straightforward determination of constancies. As developed in the previous lecture, in the holonomic brain theory these "targets" can be provided by processing in the frequency domain and this determines centers of symmetry rather than centers of gravity.

In the visual system, the target computed by the reciprocal sensory-motor process is an object-form. As the earlier example of handling a pocket knife indicates, objectification and object identification are also resultants of sensory-motor processing in the somatic sensory processing mode. However, as noted in the introduction to this lecture, in the primate brain somatic motor processing is not only at the service of the somatic sensory mechanism but is the mechanism by which the organism manipulates and acts on the environment. Thus an independent set of action systems has developed. It turns out that processing of both somatic percepts and somatic acts depends on reciprocal input-output connectivity (Kruger & Porter, 1958; Malis, Pribram, & Kruger, 1953). In contrast to vision, in the case of the somatic system this fact has as its consequence that a separate target computed by somatic motor processing is produced by action. As noted, the target "object" computed by the post-Rolandic somatic sensory system is like the "object" of visuomotor processing. The experiments reviewed in the next section identify the "targets" of the pre-Rolandic somatic motor process as imaged achievements.

THE SENSORY ASPECTS OF THE ROLANDIC MOTOR CORTEX

Two views of the nature of the organization of the central motor system have been held for at least a century. Some (e.g., Woolsey & Chang, 1948) maintained that anatomically a point-to-point representation of muscles and even slips of muscles exists in the motor region. According to this view, the motor cortex is the keyboard upon which all other cerebral activity—and indeed all willed action—plays. By contrast others (e.g., Lashley, 1929, 1951; Phillips, 1965; Walshe 1948) have pointed out that the receptive fields of neighboring cortical units cover a wide sample of muscles although most of the fields recorded at any one location relate to a particular joint. Consonant with this observation is the fact that electrical excitations of the motor cortex in awake individuals produce movements, integrated sequences of muscle contractions; and that the movement produced by a particular excitation depends in part on the state of the brain and the position of the limbs to be influenced by the stimulation. These neurophysiological data were interpreted to mean that movements, not muscles, were represented in the motor areas.

Some years ago I reexamined these views by repeating many of the critical experiments and extending the observations by using some additional techniques (Pribram et al., 1955–1956).

The results of these experiments and observations showed that extirpation of the motor regions of the cortex disrupted neither the control of individual muscles nor of specific movements. Rather, the motor cortex seemed to play some higher order role in directing action—action defined not in terms of muscles, but in terms of the achievement of an external representation, a target. This result led me to suggest that the central motor mechanism is akin to a sensory system: Damage to the motor cortex produces "scotomata of action," using the analogy of the scotomata, the holes, in the visual field produced by damage to the visual cortex.

An hypothesis as to how movement becomes transformed into imaged action suggests that imaging must occur by virtue of processes occurring in the motor cortex. The "image" must be momentary and contain all input and outcome information necessary to the achievement of the next step. This is feasible because the input to the motor cortex arrives via the dorsal thalamus. This brain stem structure lies (as its name implies) dorsally and is an extension of the dorsal horn of the spinal cord, which receives what Bell (1811) and Magendie (1822) found to be the "sensory" part of peripheral nerves.

The anatomical puzzle of the "sensory" nature of the "motor" cortex was dramatized during the course of some experiments performed in my laboratory in which electrical potential changes were evoked in the cortex by electrical stimulation of peripheral nerves. Quite by accident such potential changes were observed to be evoked in the motor cortex. At first these observations were too unexpected to believe. Later, it turned out that other investigators had observed the same effects but had failed to report them. Only one footnote mentioned them, and only as possible artifacts. It became evident from our experiments (Malis, Pribram, & Kruger, 1953) and those of others (Albe-Fessard, 1957; Penfield & Boldrey, 1937) that indeed input does arrive at the motor cortex from the periphery. This input is routed through the dorsal thalamus, and does not come by way of any hitherto identified sensory areas such as the adjacent somatosensory cortex. Furthermore, this input was independent of the cerebellum. Surprisingly this input to the "motor" cortex originated not only in those nerve fibers that innervate muscle but also in those that connect exclusively with skin.

Evidence from other observations and experiments also emphasized the sensory nature of the motor cortex. Monkeys and men who had suffered removals of this cortex were able to make any and all movements provided the circumstances were right: War veterans whose hands had been paralyzed for years by motor cortex injury would, under duress such as the outbreak of a fire in their ward rotate door knobs with that hand. After motor cortex removals, monkeys were examined by slow motion movies. These showed clumsiness in performing the skilled sequence of opening latches on boxes containing peanuts. However, exactly the same hand and finger movements were performed without undue difficulty while climbing the wire mesh sides of their cages or during grooming.

Only some acts, some achievements, were difficult, and the difficulty had little to do with the specific movements required (Pribram et al., 1955–1956). How then is the motor cortex involved in transforming movement into action?

TRANSFORMING MOVEMENT INTO ACTION

Deciphering the nature of the cerebrocortical computations that make possible such skilled actions as riding bicycles and playing the piano, began with a classical experimental analysis performed during the 1930s by Bernstein (1967) in the Soviet Union. Bernstein's analysis was made from cinematographic records of performances such as walking, running, hammering, filing, or typing. Human subjects were dressed in black costumes outfitted with white tapes and dots to mark the limbs. The filmstrips would therefore be composed of a continuous pattern whose wave form could be mathematically analyzed (Fig. 6.5). For instance, Bernstein found that any rhythmic movement could be represented

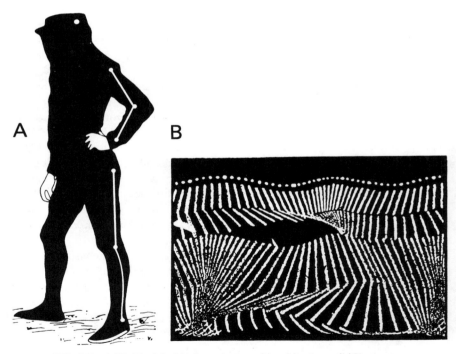

A   B

FIG. 6.5.   (a)Subject in black costume with white tape. (b)Cinematograph of walking. Movement is from left to right. The frequency is about 20 exposures per sec. reprinted with permission from N. Bernstein, *The Co-ordination and Regulation of Movements.* © 1967 Pergamon Press Ltd.

by a rapidly converging trigonometric series. Furthermore, he showed that the next step in such movements could be predicted "to an accuracy of within a few millimeters in the form of a sum of three or four harmonic oscillations, the so-called Fourier trigonometric sums."

The fact that these activities could be represented formally in terms of a Fourier decomposition led me to realize that their brain representation could also be organized by that sort of transformation. However, this realization did not as yet provide the particulars of neural processing.

Bernstein's observations suggest that constancy can be achieved in action regardless of the particular movements or the amount of contraction of any particular muscle or muscle group. In fact the action can be performed because the control of movements becomes attuned to the field of external loads operating on the muscle receptors at the moment. Constancy results from the adjustments and compensations to external loads, and its cortical representation must include these parameters. In fact, a great deal of the central neural mechanism is involved only in these adjustments and compensations; the central representation must therefore be a complement, a "mirror image" as it were, of the field of external loads.

Specific evidence that indeed the neurons of the motor cortex, especially the pyramidal neurons giving rise to its output, are sensitive to the loads acting on muscle contraction comes from another series of studies. In these experiments Edward Evarts (1967) trained monkeys to manipulate levers that were loaded with various weights to oppose their movement. (Fig 6.6) Once the monkeys had learned to move the lever, unit recordings were made from neurons located in their motor cortex, while the monkeys performed the task. The experiments showed that these neurons were sometimes activated even before external evidence (myographic recording) of the initiation of movement occurred. Careful analysis showed the electrical activity to be a function of the amount of the load imposed on the lever rather than the amount of required displacement of the lever. Furthermore, the units reacted most to the change of load, although some activity relating to the required magnitude could not be ruled out.

Thus the motor cortex is best conceived to be a sensory cortex sensitive to environmental load and change in load. It participates in the modulation of states of readiness to changes in load via its connections with the basal ganglia and in addition anticipates states-of-achievement by processing changes in load via its participation in the cerebellar circuit. The formation of the resulting "image" of load is dependent, as elsewhere in the cortex, on what we have come to recognize as the neural holoscape, "a highly selective channeling of activity in the horizontally running intracortical networks which excite and inhibit the corticofugal neurons" (Phillips, 1965).

That this motor representation is not to be conceived as a keyboard but as the strings in a sounding board similar to those formed in the visual cortical systems has been ascertained from studies of the receptive fields of units. These experimental results (Welt, Aschoff, Kameda, & Brooks, 1967) show that "sensory

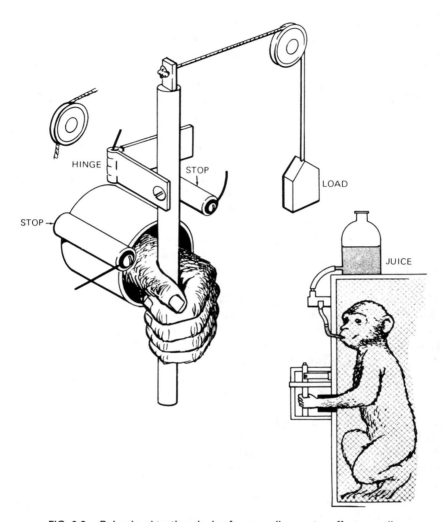

FIG. 6.6. Behavioral testing device for recording motor effect on cells in precentral cortex. The monkey's left hand protrudes from a tube in a lucite panel attached to the front of the home cage. In order to receive a fruit juice reward, the monkey is required to grasp the vertical rod attached to the hinge and to move it back and forth. The monkey is required to move the handle through the arc between the stops. Breaking contact with one stop and making contact with the other must be achieved between 400 and 700 msec, and the previous movement in the other direction must also fall within these time limits in order to operate a solenoid valve which delivers a reward. From Evarts, 1968, in Milner, 1970.

138

convergence into the motor (sensory) cortex is superimposed on topographically uniform output organization in radial arrays, the diameter of which is estimated to be 0.1 to 0.4 mm. Thus, neurons with fixed local receptive fields provide a radially oriented framework [a reference system] for common peripheral inputs. . . . Interspersed with these cells having local fields, constituting three-fourths of the total, there were neurons with wide, stocking-like, or labile fields that overlapped with the local fields". [p. 285]

In order to provide support for the idea that the computations performed by the somatic motor cortex are indeed similar to those in visual and auditory systems and thus compatible with the holonomic brain theory, an experiment was undertaken to discover whether there are neurons that respond primarily to the spectral dimensions (frequency, amplitude, and phase) of movements (Pribram, Sharafat, & Beekman, 1984). Recordings from single units in the head of the caudate nucleus and in the somatic cortex of the left hemispheres of cats were made while their right forepaw was passively moved up and down by an apparatus designed to hold the paw and to assure that its movement was sinusoidal. The period of the sinusoidal movement was controlled making it possible to administer 9 distinct frequencies in pseudorandom order. The results of these experiments are critical to the theme of these lectures, thus a fairly complete summary follows.

FREQUENCY TUNING

As can be seen in Fig. 6.7, the receptive fields of a sizeable number of cells in both caudate nucleus and sensorimotor cortex are selectively responsive to only a limited range of the frequencies with which the forelimb is moved. The response can be either in the form of increasing or decreasing the average spontaneous spike activity when a movement with a certain frequency occurs. The receptive fields of 33 out of 144 cells (approximately 23%) in the caudate nucleus and 35 out of 162 cells (approximately 22%) in the somatic sensorimotor cortex were narrowly tuned to a specific bandwidth. A receptive field was defined to be narrowly tuned when, at a specific frequency, its maximum or minimum activity is at least 25% higher (or lower) than the average baseline activity. Moreover, narrowly tuned receptive fields were defined as responding only with a bandwidth limited to less than 1/2 octave.

In examining the movement-frequency tuning curves of receptive fields, we found a wide range of maxima (minima). This range in tuning would be necessary if one were to build a system of band pass movement-frequency filters covering the whole range of frequencies. In support of such a filter model we found that all of the receptive fields that were not narrowly tuned to a single frequency band showed maxima (minima) within several frequency bands.

Of 35 narrowly tuned receptive fields in the sensorimotor cortex, 18 (11%) of

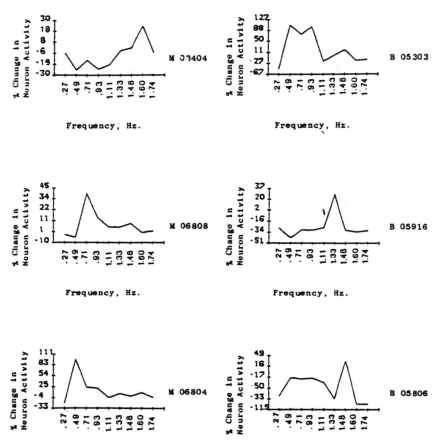

FIG. 6.7.   Frequency tuning curves for narrowly tuned cells. The frequency of the mechanical sine wave generated by the motor is represented on the x axis; the % change in response over baseline is represented on the y axis. The six letter/digit alphanumeric code at the righthand side of the tuning curve gives the following information. Recording site: M16212 Cell number for this site B: Basal Ganglia M: Sensorimotor Cortex.
From: Pribram, K. H., Sharafat, A., & Beekman, G. J. (1984). Frequency Encoding in Motor Systems. In H. T. A. Whiting (Ed.), *Human Motor Actions,* (pp. 121–156). North-Holland: Elsevier.

the total of 162, showed inhibitory responses to their tuned frequencies; that is, they acted like a notch filter. Most of these (16) and those that showed biphasic responses were obtained from placements shown postmortem to be located in the postcruciate gyrus. Only 8 out of 44 or 5.5% of the total of 144 receptive fields in the caudate nucleus showed similar behavior.

There is thus no question that some receptive fields in the caudate nucleus and some receptive fields in the somatic sensorimotor cortex of the cat responded selectively to only a limited range of movement frequencies. The number of such receptive fields compares favorably with the number of receptive fields in the visual system classified as having simple or complex properties (Hubel & Wiesel, 1959; Spinelli, Pribram, & Bridgeman, 1970), properties that, as noted in Lecture 4, have been shown to be related to the spatial frequency of visual patterns (DeValois, Albrecht & Thorall, 1978; Pribram, Lassonde, & Ptito, 1981; Schiller, Finlay, & Volman, 1976). In the visual cortex approximately 10%–12% of receptive fields are frequency-specific, tuned to a range of 1/2 to 1–1/2 octaves; in the sensorimotor cortex approximately 20%–22% of receptive fields are tuned to 1/2 octave bandwidth of the frequency of forearm movement.

Consequently, it is clear that some receptive fields in the motor system "resonate" to movements at certain frequencies. However, the results presented so far do not distinguish between the possibility that (a) these resonances are spurious in the sense that other variables conjoin to produce the effect, or (b) these resonances reflect the encoding of frequency per se. The second alternative would be demanded by the model of a set of band pass filters for movement, as proposed earlier. In order to initiate the search for variables other than frequency to which these receptive fields might be responsive, three likely candidates were chosen: velocity, length, and position. The results of observations on these variables follow.

VELOCITY AND LENGTH

In order to test whether the frequency-tuned receptive fields were responsive to other variables, the neuronal activity of narrowly tuned receptive fields was plotted against (a) position in the cycle of movement, (b) velocity of movement within cycles of various frequencies, and (c) the tension at different frequencies. As can be seen in Fig. 6.8, the minimal increase in activity when velocity or length are plotted, is spread over all frequencies, and fairly broadly within each frequency (especially at the higher frequencies). Velocity and length vary as a function of frequency, thus the nonspecificity of even this minimal increase in activity indicates that the receptive fields were not responding to these variables. To make this clear, picture the velocity of movement when the frequency of the cycle is low: If velocity is also low, the forelimb moves slowly. Now we increase the frequency of the movement cycle: Velocity is now high, the muscles of the forelimb are shortening and lengthening rapidly. If velocity (or acceleration) were being encoded by these receptive fields this would be reflected in a region of selective increase in their activity. Such a region would have to be restricted to a portion of the recording within each frequency. The location of the restricted portion of increased activity would have to move in a systematic fashion across the various frequencies. This effect was not observed.

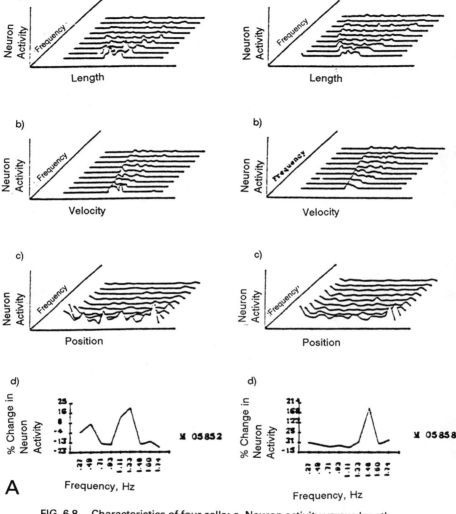

FIG. 6.8.   Characteristics of four cells: a. Neuron activity versus length for each frequency b. Neuron activity versus velocity for each frequency. c. Neuron activity versus position for each frequency. d. Tuning

The same argument applies to changes in length. Response to lengthening should be reflected in a localized increase in receptive field activity that systematically moves across the various frequencies. This phenomenon was not detected. The frequency-selective receptive fields are insensitive to velocity and

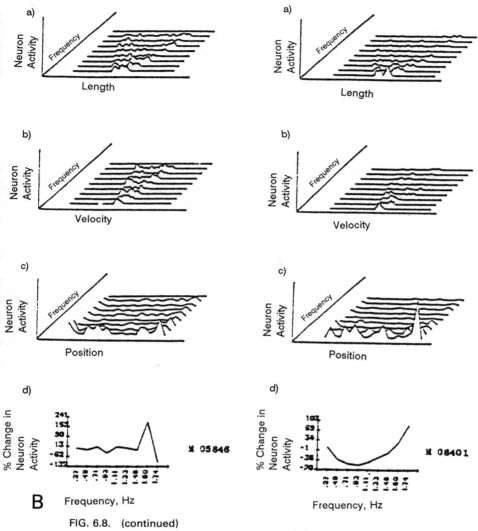

B

FIG. 6.8.   (continued)
curves as in Fig. 6.7. From: Pribram, K. H., Sharafat, A., & Beekman, G.
J. (1984). Frequency Encoding in Motor Systems. In H. T. A. Whiting
(Ed.) *Human Motor Actions*, (pp. 121–156). North-Holland: Elsevier.

lengthening that has been passively imposed on the muscles of the forelimb. This
result appears to differ from results obtained from others (Brooks, Horvath,
Atkin, Kozlovskaya, & Uno, 1969; Evarts, 1968), who have found velocity
sensitive cells in the motor system. However, in their experiments, active rather
than passive movement was involved. Furthermore, in the current experiments

no search was made for cells that selectively encode velocity. Thus, a different population of cells may be involved as even the nonnarrowly tuned receptive fields of the current sample were subjected to the same procedure and no velocity or length specificity was found. With regard to the purpose of this part of the experiment it had been accomplished: It was established that the frequency selectivity observed for this population of receptive fields is not an artifact of their selective sensitivity to velocity and/or lengthening.

POSITION IN THE MOVEMENT CYCLE

Whereas the frequency-selective receptive fields are insensitive to velocity and changes in length, these receptive fields show, as in Fig. 6.9, sensitivity to the position of the forelimb in the movement cycle. This sensitivity occurs almost always at the ends of the cycle of movement where the maximum phase shift is taking place. But it must be emphasized that these cells are not sensitive to phase shift (or change in direction) per se because the increase in the cell's activity does not occur at all frequencies. Rather, these cortical receptive fields encode phase shift, that is, position in the cycle, for a particular frequency band.

The encoding of phase shift was found to be a property primarily of cortical cells. Only one cell of the total population of those recorded in the caudate nucleus was found to encode position in the cycle and that cell was not max-

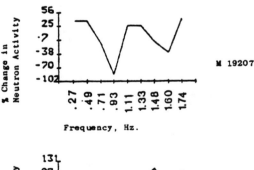

FIG. 6.9. Frequency tuning curves for narrowly tuned "notch filter" type cells. From: Pribram, K. H., Sharafat, A., & Beekman, G. J. (1984). Frequency Encoding in Motor Systems. In H. T. A. Whiting (Ed.) *Human Motor Actions*, (pp. 121–156). North-Holland: Elsevier.

imally responsive to the ends of the cycle where the maximum phase shift occurs. Once again, this result is reminiscent of results in the visual system where cortical cells but not those below cortex show a selectivity to the orientation in space of a pattern. The results of the current experiments can be similarly expressed: Below the cortex the cells encode the frequency of movement regardless of phase; at the cortex, shift in phase—in the orientation of the movement at a certain frequency—is an additional consideration.

In summary, the results of the experiment showed that the receptive fields of a 20% portion of a total of 306 cells sampled are tuned to a narrow (1/2 octave) band of the range of frequencies. (Tuning is defined as an increase or decrease in the cells' activity at least 25% over baseline spontaneous activity.)

Variables such as velocity, change in velocity (acceleration), as well as length, and change in length in isolation were found not to account for the frequency selective effects. This does not mean that the receptive fields of other cells in the motor system are not selectively sensitive to velocity and changes in length. But it does mean that the frequency selectivity of the receptive fields described is dependent on a higher order computation of the metric and tonic changes imposed on the foreleg musculature by the external load.

By contrast, position in the cycle of movement is encoded by cortical receptive fields (but not by caudate nucleus cells). Position is encoded only at the site of phase shift and only for a particular frequency, consequently the hypothesis is supported that the cortical receptive fields are in fact frequency selective: Any sensitivity to phase shift presupposes an encoding of phase and therefore of frequency. Furthermore, the fact that the cortical receptive fields respond to position suggests that they are directly involved in the calculation of the vector space coordinates within which actions are achieved.

Thus, the holonomic brain theory is equally applicable to understanding neural processing involved in action as to understanding the figural aspects of perception. What remains to be discussed is the nature of the target being determined. As noted, the position of the target becomes encoded by phase-shift. But what is it that remains invariant across phase shifts?

A VECTOR SPACE: FORCE DEFINED IN TERMS OF LOAD

The results of the Evarts' and our experiments ordinarily would be interpreted to mean that pyramidal neurons encode "force." In Newtonian mechanics force is defined to vary as a function of the acceleration of a mass. Thus, in physiology, force has been conceived as the product or resultant of the organism's metric motor activity: "Force can be looked upon as the body's basic output quantity: velocity is thus the single integral of this and displacement the double integral" (Bates, 1947). But if one takes displacement as basic to a measure of force,

Evarts' (1966, 1967, 1968, 1969) and our failure to obtain responses to displacement argues against the interpretation that force is being represented. Rather, as Evarts (1967) and Houk and Rymer (1981) pointed out, muscle tension, not change in length, must be thought of as the generator of force. In such a view, muscle tension is conceived as the equivalent of mass. Hoffer (1982) suggested that changes in tension are represented as a function of their mechanical impedance reflecting their elasticity and viscosity. Just as it is not mass but the acceleration of mass that defines force, it is not tension per se but changes in tension measured as its derivative (and even its second derivative—changes in changes of muscle tension) that produce the best correlation with the responses of pyramidal neurons. Thus, differentiation of muscle tension, that is, changes in tension with respect to space and time, become the target of computations.

More operationally, this target is represented in terms of load and changes in load. Load adjusting mechanisms are well-known in the sensory domain: In vision the mechanism of retinal adaptation to the varying loads imposed by differences in ambient luminance (see Dowling, 1967); in audition the mechanism of adaptation to changes in ambient sound level mediated by the olivocochlear system (see Dewson, 1968). In the motor mechanism that function has been ascribed, as we shall see later, to the gamma system of muscle spindle control (Matthews, 1964).

Changes in load are reflected either as changes in tension or in the length of muscle fibers or both. One way to determine whether these load changes will result in a compensatory change in the innervation of muscle fibers is to look at the ratio of change in muscle tension to muscle length. This ratio has been labelled "stiffness" by Houk and Rymer (1981), who have found it is dependent on the elasticity and viscosity of the muscle. In a series of well-conceived experiments Houk has found that fluency of control leading to a change in stiffness, is determined by the ratio of change of the sensitivities of muscle spindles to that of tendon organs.

According to the results obtained by Houk (reviewed by Houk & Rymer, 1981) there is an equality between the ratio of change of muscle tension to muscle length on one hand, and the ratio of the activity in muscle spindle and tendon organs, on the other. Thus, when one considers how the central nervous system encodes placement or displacement of limbs, coding can be seen to occur without the need for any consideration of motor-unit (muscle fiber) innervation that results in placement or displacement. Rather, placement and displacement can be controlled fluently by encoding the changes in stiffness. As the ratio determining stiffness is equal to the ratio of the sensitivities of muscle spindles to tendon organs, these, then, become the reference ratios. According to the evidence reviewed by Houk and Rymer (1981), the brain encodes reference ratios in the following manner:

As noted, at the spinal cord the activity recorded from, for example, alpha motorneurons is cyclic and can be thought of as constituting sets of relaxation oscillators (Grillner, 1974, 1981). The oscillatory activities are brought under cortical control via the pyramidal and extrapyramidal pathways. These pathways function by encoding only the terminal position to which the limb segment must be moved. It is this terminal position that is the target. Specifically, it is a stabilized point between tensions of agonist and antagonist muscle groups (Asratyan & Feldman, 1965; Bizzi, Polit, & Morasso, 1976, Bizzi, Dev, Morasso, & Polit, 1978; Schmidt & McGowan, 1980). When more than one limb segment is involved the target must also encode the timing or phase-relationships among different limb segments or different limbs in order to specify new points of stability for each joint (Schmidt, 1980).

Each stabilization is determined by the intersections of tension-length relationships between agonist and antagonist muscle groups. It is, therefore, easy to infer that these points of stabilization actually correspond to the mechanical stiffness of the muscle groups and are equivalent to their reference ratios. However, the organism does not encode a reference ratio once and stop, but continuously encodes new reference ratios. Fluency is thus described by the rate of change from a current reference ratio to a new reference ratio.

In the reference ratio the sensitivity of the tendon organs is fixed and very high (see e.g., Houk & Henneman, 1967; Jami & Petit, 1976; Stuart, Mosher, Gerlach, & Ranking, 1972). By contrast the sensitivity of the muscle spindles is variable. Dynamic gamma fusimotor-axons greatly sensitize the primary endings of the muscle spindle to dynamic stimuli, whereas the static fusimotor-axons greatly sensitize both primary and secondary endings to static stimuli (Matthews, 1981). Thus by means of gamma motoneuron innervation changes are made in the sensitivity of muscle spindles and, as a consequence, new reference ratios are created.

As already noted, the cyclical activities of the spinal central pattern generators are brought under brain stem and cortical control. This implies a higher order encoding of the reference ratio. Changes in muscle length, as well as changes in the sensitivity of muscle spindles, operate within the context of fixed values of the sensitivity of the tendon organs, so the changes are effected solely by the descending pathways projecting onto the gamma motoneurons. The higher order encoding of changes in the reference ratio is therefore due entirely to the representation of changes in the sensitivity of muscle spindles.

Conceived in this fashion, the interpretation that cortical units are unresponsive to spatial position in Evarts' (1966, 1967, 1968, 1969) experiments needs to be revised. Such an interpretation reflects a bias that position must be defined in terms of changes in muscle length rather than in terms of muscle tension. In the holonomic brain theory, muscle tension is represented by a vector space constituted of reference ratios that can specify position in terms of phase. This vector space of reference ratios composes a set of targets that, when transformed, results in an image-of-achievement. The vector space reflects, as we have seen, the sensitivities of muscle spindles operating within the context of sensitivities of Golgi tendon organs.

Reference ratios are related to Bernstein's Fourier analysis of joint motion as follows: For a body in simple harmonic motion (motion under the influence of an elastic restoring force in the absence of friction), adjusting the reference ratio (which in the holonomic brain theory are the probability amplitude-weighted Fourier coefficients), controls the frequency of motion around a joint to a temporary stability that reflects anticipated changes in the external load.

A most interesting consequence results from this analysis: A biological definition of force different from Newton's physical definition becomes necessary. Newton defined force in terms of a mass accelerating (changing velocity) in space time. When this definition is applied to the neurophysiology of action the expectation would be that the metric lengthening and shortening of muscles would be registered whenever force is applied. As noted, experiments have failed to uncover a relation between metric muscle contraction and the activity of units in the precentral motor cortex. Instead a correspondence between neural activity and the load placed on the system was found. Load translates into tonicity in the neuromuscular system. Rate of change of tonicity is, in fact, experienced as "force."

The tremors at rest and cogwheel rigidity of Parkinson's disease as well as other evidence reviewed earlier in the lecture, attest to the fact that tonicity is controlled in the spectral domain. In this domain, expenditure of energy per unit time is measured as power. Biologically, "force" is therefore measured as a rate of change in power. Definitions that work for classical mechanics, do not translate readily into the neuropsychology of action.

IMAGES OF ACHIEVEMENT

Targets are composed of Images of Achievement much as objects are composed of visual and tactile images. Images of Achievement are temporary stabilities that reflect anticipated changes in load. Thus they serve as attractors in the processing of acts. Skills such as riding a bicycle, skiing, golfing, musical performances, and writing all depend for their execution on the development of appropriate images of achievement. It is characteristic of such skills for achievement to be essentially invariant across movement: Entirely different movements carry out writing on a pad of paper than those that carry out writing on a blackboard. Nor is writing dependent on using familiar musculature: Try writing your name on sand with your left big toe (if you are right handed) next time you are at the beach. The result will be amazingly recognizable as your signature. Or hold a piece of chalk between your teeth and write on a blackboard. It is the words that are imaged (consciously or unconsciously); different sorts of movements are equivalent in producing the imaged consequence, the act.

The distinction between movement and action is important and is often confused in scientific writing. For instance, the term *behavior* is used by ethologists to describe particular sequences of movements such as those involved in egg rolling by birds. By contrast, in experimental psychology, behavior is the act: the environmental consequence of movement. As Skinner once said, the behavior of organisms is the cumulative record of performance that he could take home each night to study. The experimental psychologist is not concerned whether that record was produced by the pecking of a bird, the pressing of a pedal by a rat, or the pulling of a lever by a monkey.

Images of achievement become constructed much as other percepts. Such achievements as those leading to walking and eating are to a large extent genetically programmed. Achievements such as swimming and talking are intermediate and achievements such as writing are almost totally learned. Scarr (1978) noted that to the extent that skills, achievements, come readily to a species to that extent the achievements are innately determined. When skills are difficult to achieve, the learning component is high. More on this in the next sections.

NEGLECT AND APRAXIA: DISTURBANCES IN BODY IMAGE

Disturbances of imaging, more pervasive than loss of a particular skill, follow extensive parietal lobe damage in humans, especially damage to the right parietal lobe. Patients with such lesions often display a neglect syndrome: They can be completely unaware of their disabilities (For review see Heilman & Valenstein, 1979). I had a patient once whose arm, stuck in the bedclothes, kept her from sitting up. She searched at length to find the cause of her confinement. When I found the arm for her, she was puzzled as to what it was doing there—that it was actually attached to her. The arm had become solely a visual object no longer a part of her body image.

Interestingly, neglect follows left parietal lobe damage only rarely. This suggests that "body image" can be coded verbally, not only via the somatic senses. Lecture 8 reviews data that yet other brain systems are involved when the appreciation of self is dependent on incorporating episodes of experience into what has become familiar.

A disability, less severe than neglect, that follows less extensive parietal lesions is apraxia, a loss in proficiency. The resulting awkwardness is more pervasive than a loss of skill, however. It is interesting to note that apraxia (as well as neglect - see Heilman & Valenstein, 1972) can follow damage to the frontal as well as to the parietal cortex. This poses difficulties for diagnosis of the site of lesion but is explained by the fact that apraxias occur in primates whenever there is injury to a band of frontoparietal cortex surrounding and split by the primary somatic sensory motor cortex of the central (Rolandic) fissure. The next section describes the evidence for the existence of such a split band of cortex and the section following discusses the relevance of praxis (and the apraxias) to perception.

SKILL VS. PRAXIS: A ROLANDIC VS. EXTRA-ROLANDIC DISTINCTION

That, in primates, a split has occurred in a band of cortex that is continuous in other species can be seen from an analysis of the precise arrangement of thalamocortical projections and from comparing nonprimate with primate cortical anatomy. In tracing the thalamic projections to the precentral cortex, a surprising finding came to light. The dorsoventral arrangement of terminations, both pre- and postcentrally, is diametrically opposite to the arrangement of the projections further forward and further back (See Fig. 6.10). The dorsoventral terminations of the Rolandic projections reflect a lateral-medial origin from the thalamus; the dorsoventral terminations both forward and back of the peri-Rolandic cortex reflect a medial to lateral origin (Chow & Pribram, 1956).

In view of the fact that no such reversals are seen elsewhere in the systems of the posterior cerebral convexity, this finding is surprising. However, comparison of nonprimate with primate cortical anatomy clarifies what has happened phylogenetically. In nonprimate species such as the carnivores, the suprasylvian and

FIG. 6.10. Digrammatic drawing to show the general plan of cortical projection of the ventrolateral nuclear group. Straight line with arrow indicates the medial to lateral direction within a nucleus; interrupted line with arrow, the anterior to posterior direction; solid triangle, V1, roughly the n. ventralis anterior; solid circle, V2, roughly the n. ventralis lateralis; open circle, V3, roughly the n. lateralis posterior; solid square, V4, roughly the n. ventralis posterolateralis; cross, V5, roughly the n. ventralis posteromedialis. From: Chow, K. L., and Pribram, K. H. (1956). Cortical projection of the thalamic ventrolateral nuclear group in monkeys. *The Journal of Comparative Neurology, 104*(1), 57–75.

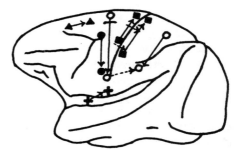

ectosylvian gyri extend the full length of the lateral surface of the cerebral convexity. The cruciate sulcus, the homologue of the Rolandic fissure, is mainly found on the medial surface of the hemisphere with only a minimal extension onto the lateral surface. It appears that in the evolution of primates this sulcus has migrated laterally to become the prominent central fissure (Fig. 6.11).

Such a migration would have split the supra- and ectosylvian gyri into anterior and posterior segments. That such a split has occurred is supported by the fact that terminations of thalamocortical projections to the anterior and posterior segments originate in adjacent parts of the ventrolateral nuclei. Furthermore, the frontal and posterior segments are intimately interconnected (Goldberg, 1985; Schwartz & Goldman-Rakic, 1984). Should the conjecture regarding a split be correct, it would go a long way in accounting for the difficulty in making a differential diagnosis between apraxias due to frontal and those due to parietal lobe damage.

That damage to both parietal and frontal systems can produce apraxia was shown in the laboratory by a study that quantified changes in the kinetic pattern of movement (Pribram, 1987a). Monkeys were trained (using peanuts as rein-forcements) to move a lever in a T-shaped slot beginning at the juncture of the arms of the T with its stem. The movements were then to be directed to the right, to the left, and finally down and up, in that order. Records were kept of the monkeys' ability to perform the movements in the correct order and the number and duration of contacts with the sides of the slots that formed the T. (This was done by having the sides and the lever lined with copper and wiring them so that contact could be recorded.)

Resections were made (a) of precentral cortex, (b) of the cortex of the anterior inferior parietal lobule, (c) of the lateral premotor cortex, (d) of the latter two lesions combined, and (e) of the entire lateral and medial premotor cortex. Precentral resections led the monkeys to make many more and briefer contacts along the path of the lever within the T slot, a loss of fine-motor skill. No change in overall sequencing occurred. By contrast, both the parietal and premotor resections had the effect that the monkeys carried out the same movement re-petitiously before proceding with the next step in the sequence. This persevera-tion was interpreted as evidence of apraxia. There was no observed difference between the effects of the anterior and those of the posterior resection and the overall order of the act was not disturbed. When the parietal and premotor resections were combined, the deficit was enhanced; still there was no change in overall ordering of the action until the far frontal (and in two monkeys, the cingulate) cortex were additionally resected. Control over overall ordering by the frontal system is discussed more fully in Lecture 10.

On the basis of similar evidence in human patients Goldberg (1985), proposed that the occurrence of apraxia devolves on faulty feedback processing. The repetitions that the lesioned monkeys made in the task might well have been a response to the necessity for gaining additional sensory feedback before proceed-

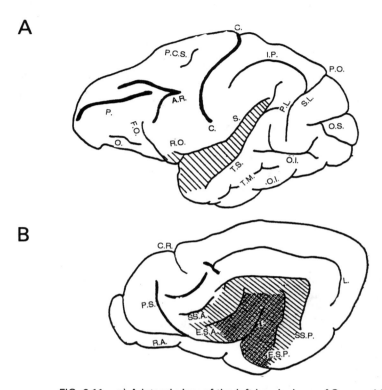

A

B

FIG. 6.11.   a) A lateral view of the left hemisphere of Semnopithecus showing the location of the motor centers. C. and O. Vogt. *A.R.,* sulcus arcuatus (rectus); *C.,* sulcus centralis; *F.O.,* sulcus fronto-orbitalis; *I.P.,* sulcus intraparietalis; *O.,* sulcus orbitalis; *O.I.,* sulcus occipitalis inferior; *O.S.,* sulcus occipitalis superior; *P.,* sulcus intraprorealis; *P. C. S.,* sulcus precentralis superior; *P.O.,* sulcus parieto=occipitalis; *R.O.,* ramus opercularis; *S.,* sulcus pseudosylvius; *S.L.,* sulcus lunatus; *T.M.,* sulcus temporalis medius; *T.S.,* sulcus temporalis superior. b) A lateral view of the brain of Felis domestics. Note how the marginal and ectosylvian gyris loop around the crucite sulcus which is the homologue of the Rolandic fissure of primates. *C.R.,* sulcus cruciatus; *E.S.A.,* sulcus ectosylvius anterior; *E.S.P.,,* sulcus ectosylvius posterior; *L.,* sulcus lateralis; *P.S.,* sulcus pseudosylvius; *SS.A.,* sulcus suprasylvius anterior; *SS.P.,* sulcus suprasylvius posterior. From: Ariens Kappers, C. U., Huber, G. C., & Crosby, E. C. (1960). *The Comparative Anatomy of the Nervous System of Vertebrates, Including Man.* New York: Hafner Publishing.

ing. This suggests that apraxia is due to some sort of abnormality in perceptual processing.

Praxis and skills are achieved through perceptual learning. As detailed in Lecture 8 and 9, the systems of the limbic forebrain become involved whenever the consequences of behavior become relevant to subsequent behavior. Vernon Brooks (see 1986 for review) performed a series of experiments that show how Rolandic and limbic systems interact. These experiments are somewhat similar to those just described. Brooks trained monkeys

> to move a lever so that its representation (cursor) on a display screen was superimposed on that of a target area which stepped from one position to another. The animals were rewarded for *what* they did, which in this case meant moving the lever into the target area and then holding it there for at least one second until a reward had been given. . . . Rewards were given . . . even if the animal had moved initially in the wrong direction or had moved prematurely during the required hold time, provided the arm was returned to the target area and the trial was brought to a successful conclusion by the accumulation of hold times. (p. 23)

A new trial was begun when the hold time reached 3 seconds. Skill was revealed "by the ability to make accurately programmed 'continuous' movements instead of nonprogrammed, feedback-dependent, 'discontinuous' ones" (p. 32). Skilled movements could therefore be recognized by their single-peaked velocity profiles in electromyographic recordings. The processes that determine the skill "define optimal phase-plane trajectories by relating . . . isometric forces [loads] to their rates of change . . . in such a manner that acceleratory transients (jerks) are minimized" (p. 32)

When brain electrical potentials were recorded from the anterior cingulate gyrus of the limbic forebrain in this and similar tasks, changes were observed to follow inappropriate, nonrewarded behavior. These "error potentials" are surface positive waves occurring around 250 msec and are noted by Brooks as sharing the properties of the P300 waves recorded in humans to follow infrequent, attended events. The P300 waveforms have been identified to occur whenever a cognitive process is ready to be "updated" (Donchin 1981; Pribram & McGuinness, 1975). These waveforms are discussed in detail in Lecture 10.

When a plot is constructed of the relationship between learning what to do (i.e., praxis) and the skill with which it is done, a sharp inflection point is seen to occur just prior to reaching a 50% point in the ratio between appropriate and inappropriate behaviors (Fig. 6.12). This inflection point indicates the beginning of "insightful" behavior and it is at this point that the error potentials begin to appear in the brain electrical records obtained from the cingulate cortex. More on this in Lectures 9 and 10 in discussions of the functions of the hippocampal system of which the cingulate cortex is an integral part.

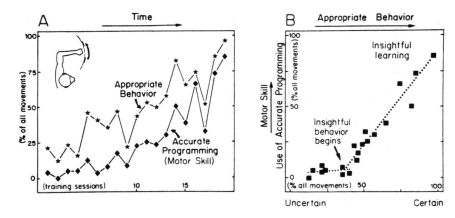

FIG. 6.12. Motor learning of the elbow movement task by monkeys has two successive phases. **A.** Learning *how* to move, i.e, motor skill (expressed as accurately programmed, continuous movements), develops roughly apace with learning *what* to do, i.e., insightful behavior (expressed as appropriate, task-related behavior plotted for all movements, i.e., pooled continuous and discontinuous flexions and extensions). **B.** Accurately programmed extensions (from pooled sample in A) are plotted against appropriate behavior (rather than time as in A). This reveals two phases of learning, the first leading towards the beginning of insightful behavior (interrupted vertical line) and the second insightful one leading towards certainty about appropriate behavior (abscissa) as well as towards final motor skill (ordinate). Lines of best fit show that skill rises linearly (R = 0.96) with growth of appropriate behavior. Data, but not graphs, from Brooks et al. (1983). A from Brooks (1984). From: Brooks, V. B. (1986). How does the Limbic System assist Motor Learning? A limbic comparator hypothesis. *Brain Behavior Evolution*, 29, 29–53.

THE CORPOREAL SELF AS REFERENCE FRAME

As described in lecture 5, the neural mechanisms that are involved in the construction of object-forms from images operate to extract invariances from sets of images by a process of convolving, correlating, and grouping. An object is experienced in an object space when the resultant of this process remains constant across movements of object-forms within a joint object-centered and occulocentric space.

Just as there are at least two frames (and their centers of symmetry) in vision (occulocentric and object-centered), so there are at least two frames in the somatic system: distal and proximal. The distal frame is composed by epaxial (e.g., hands, fingers), the proximal by axial (e.g., trunk) parts of the body. The representation of face is intermediate between distal and proximal frames. Distal parts are represented in the human cortex within and adjacent to the central (Rolandic) fissure; proximal representation occurs in the lateral premotor and inferior parietal cortex surrounding the central, Rolandic cortex (Woolsey, 1958). Damage to the Rolandic cortex impairs achievement-regulated skills, and the perception of object-forms (astereognosis).

As described in the previous sections, damage to the lateral premotor and inferior parietal cortex results in apraxias and neglect syndromes. These impairments can be considered to be due to a deficiency produced when invariants fail to be extracted as targets within a proximal frame. It is this frame and its center of symmetry that constitutes the corporeal self.

The corporeal self thus becomes defined as that which remains invariant across all targets, that is, all achievements. One can envisage a graduation of impairment ranging from apraxia to neglect. If this conception is correct, apraxias result from a failure in "centering" of the corporeal self: an awkwardness more pervasive than the impairment of skills.

What are the boundaries of this corporeal self, boundaries that determine the reference frame within which a skill can be excercised? In a series of studies (reviewed in 1975) Mountcastle and his colleagues showed that cells located within the confines of the intraparietal sulcus of monkeys respond specifically when an object of interest to the monkey appears within his reach. These responses occur independent of eye movement (Keys & Goldberg, 1989). Furthermore, not only are eye movements unnecessary for eliciting the responses from these cortical cells, reaching is unnecessary as well, that is, the responses are space-specific and movement independent. If the object appears beyond reach the cells "pay no attention" to it. Attention to the object within reach enhances their response (Mountcastle, Anderson & Motter, 1981). The system to which these cells belong can be thought of as determining the boundaries of the corporeal self, the boundaries of a joint visual-somatosensory action space for the organism.

A JOINT VISUOSOMATIC ACTION SPACE

Mountcastle (Motter, Steinmetz, Duffy, & Mountcastle, 1987) proposed that the visual input to these space-specific cells originates in another group of cells (to be discussed here) located in the posterior inferior parietal cortex (see also Mishkin, Ungerleider, & Macko, 1983). These particular cells in turn receive their input from cells within the parieto-occipital portion of the superior temporal sulcus, referred to as MT. Cells in MT and in the posterior inferior parietal cortex are unresponsive to somatosensory stimulation and show little selectivity for the orientation of gratings, for color or for the presence of objects within reach (Maunsell & Van Essen, 1983a,b,c). However, when the cortex of the posterior parietal region where these cells are located is resected in monkeys, difficulties ensue in locating objects in somatic (egocentric) space, that is, with respect to themselves (Brody & Pribram, 1978; Pohl, 1973; Pribram & Barry, 1956; Ungerleider & Mishkin, 1982; Wilson, 1975).

Mountcastle and his colleagues (Motter et al., 1987; Steinmetz et al., 1987) demonstrated that the cells in the posterior inferior parietal cortex show opponent directional selectivities produced by "large overlapping excitatory and inhibitory inputs that are symmetrically superimposed" to produce "inward" and "outward" directional sensitivities. The manner in which this can occur is summarized as follows:

> There is a model that accounts for our observations on opponent organization. Assume that each [Parietal Visual Neuron] PVN is related to large, superimposed, and almost completely overlapping inhibitory and excitatory [receptive fields] RFs, within which there is minimal local directionality. At the limit, these fields cover the entire visual field but have different spatial profiles of response intensity, illustrated by the double-Gaussian model in Figure 6.13 (Rodieck and Stone, 1965). It is well known that inhibitory synaptic events in cortical neurons are of much greater duration than are excitatory ones (Stephanis and Jasper, 1964; Creutzfeldt et al., 1974). Then, with reciprocal models for inward and outward

---

FIG. 6.13.   Impulse replicates (A), raw data histograms (B), and histograms of statistically significant responses (C) of a PVN activated by moving visual stimuli. The receptive field of the cell included most of the zone field tested (a 50° radius about the fixation point) and the point of fixation. The impulse replicates show the responses (each upstroke the instant of impulse discharge) during repeated trials with a 10° × 10° visual stimulus moving in each of 8 directions along the 4 meridians tested. Trials in the 8 directions were randomly sequenced. Stimuli were back projected upon a tangent screen at a 34 cm viewing distance and moving in the frontoparallel plane for a distance of 100° centered on the point of fixation. Stimulus speed, 60°/sec. *Vertical dashed lines* indicate stimulus onset; *small arrowheads,* the time at which stimuli crossed the fixation point. The radially oriented spatial histograms in 6 are separated by 20° in the center for clarity of display. Discharge frequencies during inwart halves of stimulus movements are shown by *hatching;* during out ward halves, by *solid shading.* Bin size is 52 msec and 3.125 °; calibration bar, 100 impulses/sec. The histograms in C show the bins in which discharge frequencies were significantly above control levels (T test, $p < 0.05$); bins with significant directionality are marked by *dots.* This neuron responded intensely to both stationary and moving stimuli in a small central zone at the point of fixation in which the directional preference of the neuron reversed. From: Motter, B. C., Steinmetz, M. A., Duffy, C. J., and Mountcastle, V. B. (1987). Functional properties of parietal visual neurons: Mechanisms of directionality along a single axis. *The Journal of Neuroscience, 7*(1), 154–176.

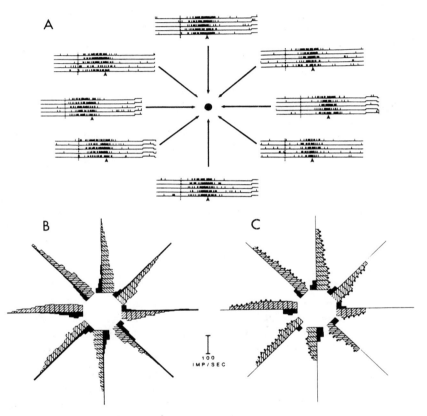

FIG. 6.13. (continued)

opponent organization of the directionalities of PVNs, our observations can be accounted for as follows (for the inward case). (pp. 173—174)

1. The strong inward directionality, arranged in an opponent fashion along single meridians, is produced by the long-range, feed-forward inhibition operating at different intensities in the 2 directions. This model is quite similar to that used by Heggelund (1981 a,b) in his studies of the receptive field organization of simple and complex cells in the cat striate cortex. The inhibition increments as stimuli move inwardly from the periphery towards the center of gaze, quenching the response to inward movement and preventing any response on the outward half of the axial movement. The size of the central zone of sparing and the question of whether it exists at all are accounted for by differences in the intensity profiles of the excitatory and inhibitory receptive fields for different PVNs.

2. The absence of a sharp axial selectivity and the centripetal directionality along all meridians are accounted for by the extension of the double-Gaussian model in 2 dimensions, where it is usually asymmetric. *A smooth, sinuosoidally distributed variation in response intensity along different axes consecutively in the circular dimension [results]. (Steinmetz, et al., 1987). (p. 174)*

These receptive field characteristics are thus best described by a sinusoidal function fitted in the "circular dimension." On the basis of this description Mountcastle and his colleagues constructed a linear (vector summation) model in which a matched population of cells "recognizes" the best flow fields generated by the stimulus. As noted in the previous lecture, the computations necessary to establish centers of symmetry in such flow fields are readily accomplished in the spectral domain:

An analysis of responses to motion along all the meridians tested revealed that they are accounted for with a high level of confidence by a sinusoidal function fitted in the circular dimension. This allowed us to calculate from the sinusoidal distribution the best or preferred meridional direction of stimulus motion for each PVN. PVNs are "broadly tuned" for direction, such that responses significantly greater than the average for all stimulus directions occur up to 45° on either side of the best direction (Fig. 6.14). We therefore sought to determine by analysis whether a more precise signal of the meridional direction of stimulus motion is coded in the pattern of discharge of the full population of PVNs activated by a given stimulus. (p. 188)

Precision was achieved by applying a population vector summation model to the data. The assumptions underlying the model have been detailed in Lectures 2 and 4 but are repeated in the present context to present the full picture of their application here:

The main assumption of the model in the present application is that the discharge of any single PVN, regardless of the direction of the stimulus activating it in any case, provides a signal of stimulus movement along the preferred axis of the cell. We

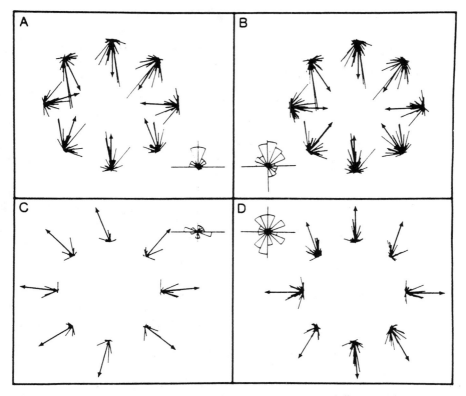

FIG. 6.14. Individual response vectors and the resulting population vectors (arrows) for the population of PVNs studies for each of the 8 directions of stimulus motion. *A,* Cells responding to inward motion only. *B,* All cells responding to inward motion. *C,* Cells responding to outward motion only. *D,* All cells responding to outward motion. *Insets* show the distributions of the preferred directions for each set analyzed. Length of maximum radius in insets *A–D* represents 12, 12, and 6 neurons, respectively. From: Steinmetz, M. A., Motter, B. C., Duffy, C. J., & Mountcastle, V. B. (1987). Functional properties of parietal vision neurons: Radial organization of directionalities within the visual field. *The Journal of Neuroscience, 7*(1), 177–191.

refer to this as the labeled line assumption. We then carried out a linear vector summation of the responses of all neurons in the population considered for each direction of stimulus motion tested.

The derived population vector responses differed on average by only 9.3° from actual direction of stimulus motion. This precise signal contrasts with the broad and relatively imprecise signal of the direction of stimulus movement provided by any single PVN of the population analyzed. It caused us to examine further the assumptions involved in the application of the model.

The first is the labeled line assumption described above. It appears to us to be inherently as likely as the ubiquitous modality specificity demonstrated repeatedly in the sensory systems of mammalian brains. The second assumption is that there exist neuronal mechanisms for recognizing labeled lines and for linear vector summation. No such mechanisms have, to our knowledge, been described, but their existence appears to us more plausible than the alternative, i.e., that summations of this kind are made by single neurons or even by small groups of neurons. It seems more likely that the flow-through of brain activity from inputs to outputs occurs by the interfacing of large neuronal populations, although little is presently known of the nature of those interfaces. . . .

We conclude that there is a more precise signal of the meridional direction of stimulus movement embedded in the population discharge of PVNs than exists in the discharge of any single member of the population. The vector summation model and analysis provide an exact description of this population signal, but whether the signal expressed as a vector can be detected and used by other neuronal populations remains to be established. (pp. 188–189)

Mountcastle conceives of these results in terms familiar to these lectures:

Linear motion of the head or rotation of the eye within the head results in a predictable motion of a static visual scene known as the "optic flow field" (Gibson 1966). Information derived from this optic flow is thought to be important for the perception of self-motion, for distinguishing self-motion from object motion, and for the visual guidance of locomotion. (p. 189)

These results are relevant to perception because processing in this distinct region of the parietal cortex establishes an action space in which self-motion is separated from object motion. This action space guides not only locomotion but other forms of self-motion such as those used in landing an airplane.

SUMMARY

The execution of actions is controlled by targets composed of images of achievement. Images of achievement are constructed by a two-part process: learning what to do and doing it skillfully. Skill is *defined* by a continuous movement toward a target. The velocity of this movement displays only a single maximum. Skill is *achieved* by an optimization procedure (learning what to do) that eliminates "errors", defined as movements that do not accord with the least action principle in perceptual processing. Reciprocal interrelations between the Rolandic somatic sensory-motor and limbic systems mediate error eliminations. (Other perceptual learning processes based on error elimination are described in the remaining lectures.)

Images of achievement center on the cortical representation of distal body parts such as hands and fingers. This representation in which errors have been eliminated, controls execution and is a function of the reciprocal interrelations between Rolandic sensory-motor and cerebellar systems.

Images of achievement develop within the context of a corporeal self: A reference frame composed of proximal, postural, and sensory (attitudinal) sets, developed by reciprocal interrelations between parietal/frontal peri Rolandic and basal ganglia systems. Damage to these systems produces apraxias and neglect syndromes. Interactions between these somatic and visual processes in the posterior parietal cortex composes an action space that separates self-motion from object motion. It is within this action space that the self achieves.

II COGNITIVE ASPECTS

Have I not erred in applying to historical thought, which is a study of living creatures, a scientific method of thought which has been devised for thinking about inanimate Nature? And have I not also erred further in treating the outcomes of encounters between persons as cases of the operation of cause and effect? The effect of a cause is inevitable, invariable and predictable. But the initiative that is taken by one or other of the live parties to an encounter is not a cause; it is a challenge. (Arnold Toynbee, A Study of History, Oxford University Press 1972, p. 97)

7

Comprehension: The Contributions of the Posterior Cerebral Convexity in Enhancing Processing Span

The question of "the span of consciousness" has often been asked and answered. . . . The number of things we may attend is altogether infinite, depending on the power of the individual intellect, on the form of the apprehension, and what the things are. When apprehended conceptually as a connected system, their number may be very large. (William James, Principles of Psychology, 1890/1950 p. 405)

INTRODUCTION

In this and the following lectures we depart from the sensory and motor-driven aspects of perception and embark on the cognitive aspects, the mind's eye of perceptual experience. Knowing does not always alter perceptions: We know the earth to be spherical, but perceive our residence to be established on flat land. In other respects, however, cognitions enter into perceptions in a top-down fashion: Recall that the perceptual act includes not only images and objects in their various perspectives, but as a rule, a categorical aspect as well. In fact, for the most part, the categorical aspect overrides the sensory perception which, though available, is ordinarily suppressed. A scene invokes colored surfaces or objects, but more especially the fact that these objects are sky, trees, and houses. This and the succeeding lecture are concerned with the brain systems involved in how we come to recognize trees as trees, houses as houses, and how in top-down fashion, the cognitive systems operate on the perceptual process.

Cognition injects into the perceptual process an input independent of direct, current sensory stimulation. The cognitive input is based on prior experience, genetically determined or learned. This input to perception originates in a variety of brain systems whose processes are to a considerable extent self-contained, that is, free of immediate receptor input. Receptor input acts as a challenge or trigger to, rather than as an integral part of, the process.

In turn, the cognitive systems act back onto the sensory systems and thus codetermine, with receptor input, the perceptual process. Critical is the hitherto neglected fact that these top-down cognitive operations *preprocess* the configural aspects of perception in a cascade of top-down processing stages arranged by virtue of an overlapping hierarchy of reciprocal connections.

Simulations of such cognitive systems have shown that an extra three-layered parallel-distributed processing network markedly enhances processing capability (see e.g., Sejnowski's 1981 Skeleton filer model). The extra network must be independent of receptor input but receptive of error signals. The loop from these "planning" systems to the middle layer acts back on the receptor layer by way of the reciprocal connectivity between receptor and middle layers.

In this lecture the evidence is reviewed regarding the role of the systems of the posterior cortical convexity in processing the cognitive aspects of perception. This evidence indicates, as William James noted in the quotation opening this lecture, "the power of the individual intellect, . . . the form of the apprehension and what things are" determine perceptual processing. Together, these factors enhance processing span, in other words, the number of percepts that can be processed in a given episode (the definition of episode is given in the succeeding lecture). In sum, these factors make percepts comprehensible. The ability to comprehend (grasp, hold together, take hold of—from the Latin *cum-prendere*) will be shown to be dependent on stimulus sampling (what things are), bias (the form of the apprehension), and the formation of prototypes (the power of the intellect).

The difference between comprehension and cognitive-free perception is most evident in reading. I can perceive the darkness of print against the white background. I can perceive the object-forms of letters on the page and their groupings. But when I read for comprehension these aspects of perception recede as I rapidly scan in a somewhat disordered fashion a line or even a paragraph at a time. Comprehension would be impossible if the light-dark shadings, object-forms, and groupings were not there to trigger the comprehension process, but the imperative produced by this higher order process transcends the perceptions resulting from earlier ones much as object-form perception transcends imaging.

Experiments designed to determine the role of the brain in organizing the cognitive aspects of perception have yielded several important insights that are detailed in the next four lectures. This lecture covers the brain process involved in comprehending, which entails sampling, biasing, and categorizing, processes that enrich perception and widen processing span. The subsequent lectures take up the processes serving a complementary function: how relevance to the organism of various perceptions, becomes anchored on some, rather than the full range of available sensations; processes that entail familiarization and innovation. The final lecture is concerned with perceiving when neither sensory input nor central process completely specify the percept. Much of what is contained in these four lectures is ordinarily subsumed under the headings memory, thought, emotion, motivation, and attention. What is covered here is the impact these processes have in shaping perception.

SOME HISTORY

The history of discovery of the neural systems involved in comprehending, in enriching perception, begins with observations made in the clinic. As noted in the previous lectures, patients with lesions outside the primary sensory-motor systems can develop neglect syndromes: When the lesions are in the parietal lobe, parts of the body fail to be perceived as belonging to the patient. When the lesions are in the temporal lobe and also involve the geniculostriate system, parts of the visual field can be neglected; that is, the patient can be shown to have a hemianopia of which he is unaware. When lesions are bilateral and do not involve the optic radiations images and objects may suddenly appear Lilliputian (micropsia) or magnified (macropsia). Other bizarre disturbances of vision occur; for instance, the entire visual scene temporarily turns upside-down only to right itself again in a few minutes.

The lesions producing these disturbances were often forward in the temporal lobe, far from the primary sensory-motor visual systems of the occipital lobe. It was assumed that all visual symptoms produced by such lesions were due to pressure on a part of the optic radiation that looped around the front of the temporal horn of the lateral ventricle. Much later, after the studies with primates described here had been accomplished, it was shown that this loop of fibers did not, in fact, exist.

The original primate experiments were undertaken, not only to investigate these and other clinically observed disturbances such as agnosia, the inability to identify objects (see e.g., the review by von Monakov, 1914), but also as part of a systematic experimental exploration of the effects (on behavior) of resection of various portions of the cerebral mantle. With respect to the temporal lobes, Sanger-Brown and Schaefer (1888) described an odd syndrome to follow the removal of both (left and right) temporal lobes of the cerebrum.

> A remarkable change is . . . manifested in the disposition of the Monkey. Prior to the operations he was very wild and even fierce, assaulting any person who teased him or tried to handle him. Now he voluntarily approaches all persons indifferently, allows himself to be handled, or even teased and slapped, without making any attempt at retaliation or endeavouring to escape. His memory and intelligence seem deficient. He gives evidence of hearing, seeing, and of the possession of his senses generally but it is clear that he no longer clearly understands the meaning of

sounds, sights, and other impressions that reach him. Every object with which he comes in contact, even those with which he was previously most familiar, appears strange and is investigated with curiosity. . . . And even after having examined an object in this way with the utmost care and deliberation, he will, on again coming across the same object accidentally even a few minutes afterwards, go through exactly the same process, as if he had entirely forgotten his previous experience. (p. 310–311)

These observations were essentially forgotten until inadvertently confirmed by Kluver and Bucy (1937), who did not know of the earlier work. In their experiments, the temporal lobes of the brain were removed in order to resect the hippocampus that lies buried in the medial surface of the lobe. The purpose of the hippocampal removal was to see whether the monkeys would still experience mescaline hallucinations as evidenced by their staring into space, swatting at nonexisting flying objects, and making other bizarre movements. The hallucinations remained, but the report of the dramatic effects of the resection now caught the imagination of the scientific community.

The temporal lobe of the brain is made up of a variety of structures all of which were removed in the radical surgical procedure of temporal lobectomy. In addition to the hippocampal cortex proper, mentioned earlier, its auxiliaries such as the entorhinal cortex were included in the resection. Furthermore, one of the basal ganglia, the amygdala, takes up the medial portion of the pole of the lobe. Finally, the convexity of the lobe is covered with the type of cortex (eugranular) found everywhere except in the specific sensory-motor areas. There is therefore no sharp boundary between this cortex and that covering the remainder of the posterior convexity of the brain.

SENSORY DISCRIMINATION

The obvious question was whether the constellation of effects of temporal lobe resection could be analyzed into components according to the anatomical subdivisions of the lobe. A good place to begin was the division between the cortex covering the convexity, the subject of this lecture, versus the amygdala and hippocampal formations on the medial portion of the lobe which are discussed in the next.

When the entire extent of the eugranular cortex of the posterior cerebral convexity of monkeys was resected bilaterally, and "sensory discrimination" tests were given in which cues had to be selected on the basis of reinforcing contingencies, clear cut effects were obtained (Blum, Chow, & Pribram, 1950). Subsequently the introduction of a "multiple dissociation technique" (Pribram, 1954) made it possible to divide this extent of cortex into specific regions associated with a particular sensory modality: a parietal region involved in somesthesis (Pribram & Barry, 1956; Wilson, 1957); a superior temporal region involved in audition (Dewson, Pribram, & Lynch, 1969; Weiskrantz & Mishkin, 1958); an anterior (polar) temporal region involved in gustation (Pribram & Bagshaw, 1953, Bagshaw & Pribram, 1953); and an inferior temporal region involved in vision (Blum, Chow & Pribram, 1950; Chow, 1951; Mishkin & Pribram, 1954).

These *multiple dissociations* (see Fig. 7.1) were obtained as follows: For each task deficit, the intercept was taken between (a) the sums of the extent of the resections that produced the deficit, and (b) the sum of the resections that failed to produce the deficit (reviewed by Pribram, 1954, 1982). The technique depends on

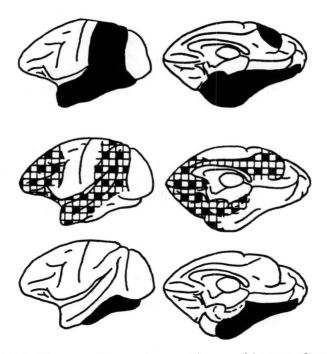

FIG. 7.1.   The upper diagrams represent the sum of the areas of resection of 15 subjects showing a decrement in the performance of a pre-operatively learned visual discrimination task. The middle diagrams represent the sums of the areas of resection of 25 subjects showing no such decrement. The lower diagrams represent the intercept of the area shown in black in the upper and that *not* checkerboarded in the middle diagram. This intersect represents the area invariably implicated in visual choice behavior by these experiments. From: Pribram, K. H. (1955). Neocortical Function in Behavior. Invited Address to the Eastern Psychological Association.

classifying the behavioral deficit produced by cortical resections into yes and no instances on the basis of some arbitrarily chosen criterion; then plotting on a brain map the total extent of tissue associated with each of the categories (a) resected: deficit; (b) resected: no deficit; and finally (c) finding the intercept of those two areas (essentially subtracting the sum of the no's from the sum of the yes's). This procedure is repeated for each type of behavior. The resulting map of localization of disturbances is then validated by making lesions restricted to the site determined by the intercept method and showing that the maximal behavioral deficit is obtained by the restricted lesion.

Once the neurobehavioral correlation has been established by the multiple dissociation technique, two additional experimental steps are undertaken. First, holding the lesion constant, a series of variations is made of the task on which performance was found defective. These experimental manipulations determine the limits over which the correlations among the brain-behavior disturbances hold and thus allow reasonable constructions of models of the psychological processes impaired by the various surgical procedures.

In addition, neuroanatomical and electrophysiological techniques are engaged to work out the relationships between the brain areas under examination and the rest of the nervous system. These experimental procedures allow the construction of reasonable models of the functions of the areas and of the mechanisms of impairment.

Much of the subsequent research devoted to understanding the nature of the involvement of the convexal cortex in sensory discrimination was performed in the visual mode—it is this research that is presented here.

For decades, a puzzling experimental result plagued understanding even these simple findings. Imagine that you disconnect a computer from its input systems and the computer continues to output the results of input processing as if nothing had happened. In the brain, such an effect was produced by radically disconnecting the inferotemporal cortex from all direct visual input without disturbing the visual-specific processing, even though this was completely disrupted by removal of the inferotemporal cortex.

Disconnections from visual cortical input were made by massive resections (see Fig. 7.2) of the peri- and prestriate cortex (Cardu, Ptito, Laporte, & Pribram, in prep.; Evarts, 1952; Pribram, Spinelli, & Reitz, 1969). Subcortical input from the thalamus was ruled out by large lesions in this structure (Mishkin, 1973). As the performance of the monkeys remained intact despite the disconnections, the possibility remained that either pathway could function in lieu of the other (Gross, 1973). However, even when both the cortical resection and the thalamic lesion were carrried out, (Ungerleider, Ganz, & Pribram, 1977) visual discrimination remained intact: that is, all of the monkeys were able to perform the tasks despite deep cuts into the optic radiations. (These radiations course just below the prestriate cortex—considerable degeneration of the lateral geniculate nucleus resulted producing scotomata and often long periods of blindness. In

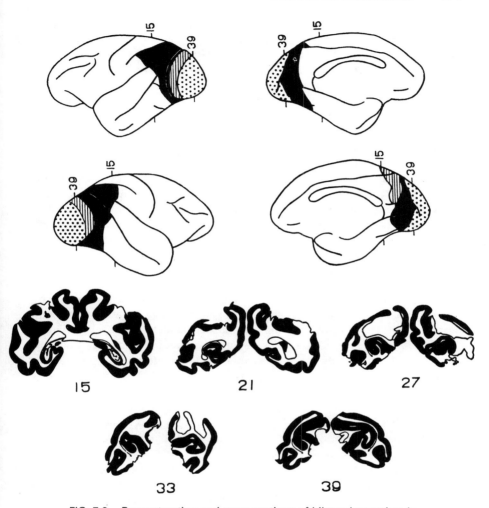

FIG. 7.2.   Reconstruction and cross sections of bilateral prestriate lesions after which monkey could still perform a visual discrimination (the numerals 3 vs. 8). In the reconstructions (not the cross sections) black indicates superficial lesions, stripes deep lesions, and dots intact visual cortex. From Pribram, Spinelli, and Reitz, 1969.

order to show that visual discrimination performance remains intact, it is important to suspend formal testing until the blindness due to this geniculostriate damage had been overcome. During recovery, monkeys were gradually trained to respond to peanuts suspended by a thread and dangled within reach of the monkey.)

The failure to impair visual discrimination performance by radical disconnection of the sensory input to the inferotemporal cortex demanded an alternative explanation for the visual deficit in discrimination produced by resections of the inferotemporal cortex. One proposed solution (Pribram, 1954) purports that the inferotemporal system stores the effects of previous experience and operates back onto the primary sensory-motor visual system.

The hypothesis was formulated that the effects on visual discrimination of resections of the inferotemporal cortex were due to such specific corticofugal, top-down, connections. To test this hypothesis, the existance of pathways from the inferotemporal cortex to the visual system had to be established. Tracts ending in the lateral geniculate nucleus were the obvious first choice, but silver stains failed to show any input from the inferotemporal cortex to thalamus except to the pulvinar, which is reciprocally connected to the inferotemporal cortex. Instead, the deeper layers of the superior colliculus and the pretectal region turned out to be the prime corticofugal targets (Graybiel, 1973; Whitlock & Nauta, 1956). These tectal and pretectal sites are the origins of systems that gate sensory input to the cerebral cortex via the reticular nucleus of the thalamus (Scheibel, Scheibel, & Davis, 1966). Specifically, for vision, these influences operate via the ventrolateral geniculate nucleus, a part of the thalamic reticular system.

Equally important, was the discovery of a heavy projection from the inferotemporal cortex to the putamen, a basal ganglion. This projection was demonstrated both by electrophysiological and anatomical techniques (Pribram, 1977; Reitz & Pribram, 1969). These connections can influence the visual system via a pathway: putamen to globus pallidus to the centromedian nucleus of the thalamus. The importance of such a pathway is supported by the fact that cross-hatching of the inferotemporal cortex results in no deficit in visual discrimination learning or performance, whereas lesions that undercut it have a profound effect (Pribram, Blehart, & Spinelli, 1966). Furthermore, not only undercutting this cortex but making lesions of the ventral putamen and adjacent structures has this effect (Buerger, Gross, & Rocha-Miranda, 1974).

Thus there appear to be at least two corticofugal pathways, one to the tectal region and another to the putamen. These pathways end on or near the output systems of the brain. It is the loop from these output systems to the primary sensory systems that mediates top-down influences on visual perception. Both tectum and putamen operate on the lateral geniculate nucleus of the thalamus via the central nuclei of the thalamus and the thalamic reticular gate (see Pribram, 1986b; Pribram & McGuinness, 1990 for review).

A HIERARCHY OF HETERARCHICAL PROCESSES

Whether one views the organization of perceptual processing as top-down or bottom-up, the central tenet of all information-processing theories is essentially the same: Overall, the perceptual systems are hierarchically organized. That some type of hierarchy exists is shown by the fact that resections of successive structures in a given sensory processing mode leave more and more of the sensory-guided behavior intact (Pribram, 1960). Hughlings Jackson (1882/ 1958), Henry Head (1920), and Carl von Monakov (1914), among others, made this point originally, and Alexander Romanovitch Luria (1973) emphasized it more recently. However, Luria, as opposed to Jackson, Head, and von Monakov, opted for a bottom-up organization of the hierarchy. Jackson, Head, and von Monikov provided evidence for major top-down components in each hierarchy. The top-down view is also much more in accord with the data already reviewed, upon which the model presented in these lectures is based.

Specifically the concept of hierarchy derives from the fact that excision of the eyes leaves the organism totally blind, whereas considerable residual vision remains after resections of the primary visual cortex (see Weiskrantz, 1986 Weiskrantz & Cowey, 1970; Weiskrantz, Warrington, Sanders, & Marshall, 1974). Resection of the peri- and prestriate systems leaves visual function still more intact. However, as noted in Lecture 5, this does not mean that vision is perfect: Size constancy is lost; the monkeys respond to retinal image size, ignoring the cues that ordinarily relate size to distance (Ungerleider, Ganz, & Pribram, 1977).

Resections of the cortex of the inferotemporal system also leave the organism with considerable visual skills. Only visual form and color discrimination (i.e., selections among stimulus patterns) are impaired (Blum, Chow, & Pribram, 1950; Chow, 1951; Mishkin & Pribram, 1954). The amount of deficit is related to the difficulty of the task as measured by the number of trials taken to learn it: Easy discriminations such as of color and three-dimensional objects are readily mastered, albeit always with some deficit in the number of learning or retention trials when compared with control performance.

In natural settings these visual deficits are hard to observe. Monkeys with inferotemporal lesions will track moving objects such as gnats and appear to respond normally to food, their conspecifics, and foreign intrusions (Pribram, 1984; Reynolds & Pribram, unpublished observations). Even in the laboratory, when discrimination among patterns is not involved, the monkeys can readily track changes in luminance (Ettlinger, 1959).

In summary, the deficit in visual discrimination following bilateral resections of the inferotemporal cortex becomes manifest only when selections among stimuli have to be made on the basis of a consistent reinforcement history. And, as noted, this deficit is not a global cognitive defect but is restricted to the visual modality: Recall that resections of other portions of the parieto-temporal-preoccipital convexity selectively impair somatosensory (Pribram & Barry, 1956; Wilson, 1957), gustatory (Pribram & Bagshaw, 1953), and auditory (Dewson, Pribram, & Lynch, 1969) discriminations.

THE NON-SENSORY ASPECT OF SENSORY
MODE SPECIFICITY

Within each sensory mode, the deficits following restricted resections of the posterior cortical convexity depend on a variety of factors. Some are sensory, for example, in vision, size, and luminance (Ettlinger, 1959; Mishkin & Hall, 1955). Other factors are situational, however, and have little to do with visual sensory input per se. As an example, a monkey with bilateral resection of the inferotemporal cortex can discriminate between an ashtray and a tobacco tin with only a marginal deficit when these are presented simultaneously. However, when the same cues are presented successively and he has to respond (to a right foodwell when an ashtray is presented halfway between two foodwells, and the left foodwell when the tobacco tray is presented) in the absence of the other cue, he fails miserably. The monkey shows that he is able to tell the difference between the two cues (in the simultaneous situation), but that he is unable to apply this ability to the somewhat harder successive task, even when trials of the simultaneous task are interspersed (Pribram & Mishkin, 1955).

The finding that the visual impairment following inferotemporal resections is not related merely to primary visual sensory factors alerts us to the fact that the essence of the deficit entails more than differentiating visual cues. Changes in the situation within which the sensory stimuli occur can impair performance. The monkeys with the lesions fail to comprehend or grasp the more difficult situation. More is involved than successive processing stages of abstraction from visual input: The fact that situational changes influence visual processing indicates that the processing "space" is critical in maintaining perceptual organization. Nevertheless, the fact that inferotemporal cortex resections produce a flattening of visual generalization gradients (Butter, Mishkin, & Rosvold, 1965), impairs luminance and visual size discrimination, and impairs discrimination only in the visual mode indicates that the impairment impinges critically on visual sensory processing and is not a global cognitive defect.

SENSORY DISCRIMINATION AS EFFICIENT
STIMULUS SAMPLING

The nature of the processing difficulty in sensory discrimination has been clarified in several experiments that used a powerful statistical technique. Basic to this technique is the fact that during sensory discrimination learning, responses to cues become segregated into separate domains. Appropriate performance depends on effective sampling from these separate domains.

In these experiments the ranges of cues sampled by monkeys with resections of the inferotemporal cortex were examined. In a "multiple object" experiment (Pribram, 1960) the monkeys were reinforced for choosing one of a number of objects. Once a particular object was consistently chosen, a novel object was added and reinforced instead. This procedure was continued, the number in the set increasing from 2 to 12. When the set of objects was small (up to 4) the monkeys with the cortical resection did as well as (or even better than) their controls but as the number of objects increased, all monkeys began to experience difficulty. However, performance of the lesioned monkeys was now considerably worse than that of the controls.

Using the statistical techniques developed in stimulus sampling theory, it was shown that the monkeys with resection of the inferotemporal cortex sampled fewer of the objects on any given series of trials (Fig. 7.3). This was due to the fact that the controls continued to sample previously reinforced objects while the lesioned monkeys sampled randomly. Random sampling improved performance when the object set was small, but when that set increased beyond four, the limitation was devastating to performance expecially as the control monkeys began to quickly ignore previously reinforced objects (Pribram, 1960). In this experiment the limitation on comprehension was due to a limited memory span but the following experiment indicates that the limitation is not restricted to memory.

In another experiment monkeys were taught to select one of two stick figures. Then one by one the sticks were removed (in random order) from the figures until they became more and more similar. Performance reaches chance level for the monkeys with the resections of inferotemporal cortex much more quickly than for controls irrespective of which of the sticks had been eliminated. It appeared that the monkeys with the cortical resection based their responses on fewer features, that is, they sampled fewer aspects of the cues, the orientation and

FIG. 7.3.   Graph of the average of the number of repetitive errors made in the multiple object experiment by each of the groups during search. Search trials are those anteceding the first "correct" response in a succession of trials, i.e., those anteceding the movement of the object (cue) under which a peanut has been placed. Note the difference between the location of the "hump" in the graph of the normal controls and in that of the posteriorly lesioned group (temporals). From: Pribram, K. H. (1959). On the Neurology of thinking. *Behavioral Science, 4*(4), 265–287.

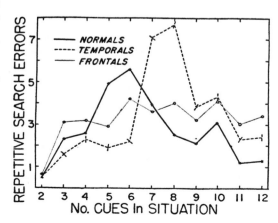

relative location of the sticks, than did the control monkeys (Butter, 1968). In short, the processing span, the number of cues determining the discrimination, became limited by the cortical resection.

Subsequently, Martha Wilson (Wilson, 1987; Wilson, & DeBauche, 1981) performed experiments to find out just what processing deficit was responsible for the restriction in span. She found that normal, not the lesioned monkeys, develop separate generalization curves for the length of each of a pair of lines on the basis of a sample length that established an "adaptation level." Her results confirmed previous demonstration that the generalization gradient (the steepness of the curve) to a single stimulus became flattened in monkeys with inferotemporal cortical resections (Butter, Mishkin, & Rosvold, 1965). Wilson however, was then able to directly relate the failure to sharpen generalization gradients to the failure in discrimination as tested in the experiments reviewed here: Her monkeys failed to develop an adaptation level against which other stimuli could be compared. The adaptation level is the weighted geometric mean of all of the "elements" to be sampled in the situation and is therefore cousin to "center of gravity" and center of symmetry computations. (Recall, for instance, the effect of illumination of various portions of a Mondrian on the perception of brightness or color described in Lecture 4.) In fact, a discrimination depends on the development of two such weighted means, which allows the specification of a distance between them—a higher order application of the distance-density function found so useful in image processing (Lecture 4 and also Shepard, 1987). According to the holonomic brain theory, the failure on the part of the monkeys with inferotemporal cortex resections to develop such weighted means indicates a failure to construct a metric within which stimuli can be processed, perceptions comprehended.

Restle (1978) tested the assumptions of a model similar to Wilson's on visual size illusions in normal human subjects. On the basis of his results, he proposed that the "elements" in adaptation level theory must be hierarchically organized cognitive structures. Simple set-theoretic sampling models fail to completely specify the results he obtained. Restle is not concerned with specifying the neurophysiology of such cognitive structures. But, according to the holonomic brain theory (see Appendix E), the lesioned monkeys fail to develop a *cognitive structure* because they fail to achieve optimization in *separate* domains; that is, they remain too far above the minimal uncertainty that describes sharp generalization gradients in each (reinforced) domain. Nonetheless, failure does not preclude attempts at processing because a 50% level of reward keeps the animal motivated. In the intact organism, however, processing ordinarily proceeds "efficiently", that is, with the aim to comprehend, i.e., to actively reduce the uncertainty that characterizes the set of alternatives—the definition given by John Dewey (1916) for "thinking." More evidence that the inferotemporal cortex is involved in comprehending follows in the next two sections: First, the association is established between the inferotemporal cortex and active uncertainty, then the evidence is presented for a dissociation between comprehension and behavior.

EFFICIENT STIMULUS SAMPLING AS SIGNAL ENHANCEMENT—BIAS

Another powerful statistical technique has been developed to aid in understanding performance in the face of active uncertainty. This set of methods, developed in decision theory, determines whether uncertainty results from difficulty in stimulus detection or whether it is due to a response bias resulting from failure of the outcome of the discrimination to provide a clear choice. Applying the statistical tools of the theory we found support for top-down processing in that resections of the inferotemporal cortex had essentially no effect on detection but markedly altered bias: In a situation in which one cue was reinforced 70% of the time and the other 30% of the time, the lesioned monkeys spent more trials than their controls examining stimuli with a history of low probability of reinforcement (Pribram, Spevack, Blower, & McGuinness, 1980).

This increase in examining poorly reinforced stimuli was confirmed by recording the eye movements of the monkeys. Those who failed visual discrimination tasks were shown to spend more time on the cues that had the history of low probability of reinforcement and returned more often to observe all cues than did their controls. (Bagshaw, Mackworth, & Pribram, 1972). At first, these results appeared paradoxical, because monkeys with amygdalectomy who showed no such difficulty in making visual discriminations scanned the cues so rapidly and rarely that it was difficult to quantify their eye movement responses when reading the eye camera films. It was as if the monkeys with the lesions were attempting to magnify what were for them weak signals in a background of noise (Mackworth & Bruner, 1970). An hypothesis that would explain this behavior suggests that the monkeys with resections of their inferotemporal cortex failed to comprehend what they were looking at; the monkeys kept searching the stimuli on successive trials as a possible aid to comprehension.

This continuing search appears to be caused by an inefficiency in processing: When the response-operator-characteristic (ROC) curves are plotted for the performance of the monkeys with resections of their inferotemporal cortex, their curves are shifted toward a lower signal/noise ratio than those of their control subjects (Pribram, Spevack, Blower, & McGuinness, 1980). The monkeys with the lesions appear to be unable to suppress responses "to irrelevant aspects of the environment" (p. 682). In a way as yet unknown, an intact inferotemporal cortex enhances signal in the presence of such noise.

To get a feel of this difficulty read the following *once* and note how many Fs there are in the passage:

Finished files are the result of years of scientific study combined with the experience of many years.

How many Fs did you notice? Three? There are actually more and it took me (just as if I were a monkey with the inferotemporal cortex removed) several scans before I "discovered" the remaining Fs. My bias to read for content rather than for function words made me miss those fs in the ofs. (Note that effective processing of the meaning of the paragraph was actually enhanced by the bias that made processing of Fs inefficient. The distinction between efficient and effective processing is taken up in greater detail in Lecture 10.)

BIAS IN THE DEVELOPMENT OF PROTOTYPES AND IN CATEGORIZING

When listening to sounds such as t and d or p and b we hear them distinctly as one or the other. This is so even when an intermediate form of the formants of these sounds is produced artificially by computers. There must be a brain process that categorizes the perception into "this or that." Almost always the categorical perception takes precedence over the perception of the object form or image per se indicating the pervasive strength of the top-down process.

Bateson (1964, 1972, 1976) performed a series of experiments describing the development of categorical perceptions. The process begins as with imprinting in chicks, which entails two-steps: If an animal has been raised in darkness, neither imprinting nor perceptual learning occurs. First the animal has to be exposed to an environment containing stimuli that can serve as a background. Only then does the imprinting stimulus take hold. In older animals (monkeys), discrimination learning was facilitated by first exposing them to such a background stimulus hung in their home cages.

This two-step process is effected as follows: Relationships among object-forms become composed into categories in a manner similar to that which describes the composition of object-forms from images. A central "figure" becomes framed as a target or prototype. Those figures falling outside the frame belong to a separate category (Rosch, 1975). Wilson's experiments with monkeys described earlier indicate that what is involved is a sharpening of generalization gradients within the frame of adaptation levels:

Within-category discrimination may be improved by the fact that extreme values on the continuum are more identifiable and hence more discriminable when they enter into stimulus pairs. This type of salience follows from adaptation-level theory as a consequence of the privileged status of stimuli that are the most distant from the indifference point and thus appear to be prototypical stimuli as described by Rosch (1973). Adaptation-level theory thus provides a conceptual bridge between categorical perception as studied in psychophysical research and studies of prototypes and exemplars. (Streitfeld & Wilson, 1986, p. 449)

Wilson's further experiments and those performed on humans (Grossman & Wilson, 1987) have shown that two types of categories can be distinguished: those that are image and object-form driven such as hue and shape and those that are comprehension-driven such as fruit and vegetables. In monkeys hemispheric specificity with respect to categorization has not been tested as yet; in humans, image and object-form-driven categorization is disrupted by right hemisphere lesions; left hemisphere lesions disrupt comprehension-driven categorization. Furthermore, category boundaries are disrupted by posterior not frontal lesions. Conversely, it is frontal lesions and not posterior ones that impair within category performance.

An example of a disturbance in object-form driven categorization is the report of a patient deprived of the capability to comprehend a basket (Warrington & McCarthy, 1983). This patient suffered a lesion in her right parietotemporal cortex. As a result she was unable to identify a basket when the basket was rotated from the ordinary horizontal position. She was still able to process the figure of the basket as an object-form and she could describe the various images making up that patterned figure (such as a curved protrusion, an oval opening), but in certain perspectives the combination of these images failed to cohere for her. Freud (1891/1953) coined the term *agnosia*, an inability to know, for such difficulties and Henry Head (1920) brought the term into English usage.

These results with respect to image and object-form driven categorization indicate that categorizing involves more than the inferotemporal system. Edelman (1987, 1989) has developed a comprehensive neural model of the categorizing process utilizing reciprocal re-entrant procedures based on reciprocal connectivity between forebrain systems. Mathematically these procedures act as editors where editing is based on the internal coherence of the process, i.e., its "interest". As noted, in the holonomic brain theory, object-forms are processed from iterations of images by a linear procedure that develops framed centers of symmetry. Edelman's reentrants process categories from iterations of object-forms in a non-linear, degenerative procedure: i.e., a prototypical group becomes selected from a remainder.

The inferotemporal system contributes to the categorizing process by the sharpening, on the basis of experience, of generalization gradients, setting up boundaries to domains within which cues become alternatives, that is, prototypical object-forms and images. These, then form the basis of comprehension driven categorization. (See Appendix E for a formal treatment of the development of prototypes.)

Comprehension driven categorization depends on comparison *between* prototypical object-forms and images. This can be accomplished by vector multiplication between domains. Models such as those of Edelman (1987, 1989),

Kohonen (1972), Anderson (1970; Anderson, Silverstein, Ritz, & Jones, 1977), and Pike (1984) have been devised to handle these stages of categorical processing. In such models, categorical learning proceeds by taking the outer product among vectors in separate matrices. To examine the possible role of the inferotemporal cortex in such models of comprehension driven categorizations, experiments were undertaken in which electrical activity was recorded from the various visual systems of monkeys. In the first set of such experiments the monkeys were trained to respond differentially to two categories, shape and color.

CENTRAL PROCESSING VS. BEHAVIOR

When electrical recordings are made simultaneously from the various visual systems during problem-solving behavior, it is possible to compare the activity of these systems in visual processing. For example, in one set of such experiments (Nuwer & Pribram, 1979; Rothblatt & Pribram, 1972) four cues were presented in brief exposures to monkeys who had been implanted with small bipolar macroelectrodes that recorded activity in a local population of cortical cells. The four cues were red and green squares and diamonds equated for extent of contour and luminance (Fig 7.4). Initially the monkeys were rewarded for selecting the color green in either shape: square or diamond. Once they had reached criterion performance of 90% correct, reinforcement was reversed to the red cue irrespective of its shape. Having mastered the "discrimination reversal," the monkeys were switched to the next task in which square was reinforced irrespective of its color and when this task was mastered the reinforcement was reversed so that now response to the diamond became correct irrespective of its color.

The various tasks were repeated until the monkeys were proficient in reversing and switching, taking fewer than 100 trials to achieve criterion performance (90% correct on 100 consecutive trials). At this point recordings of changes in the electrical brain activity were made from the striate cortex, from the prestriate cortex, and from the inferotemporal cortex. When analyzed, the recordings from the striate and prestriate cortices reflected the nature of the cues: green diamond, red square, green square, and red diamond each produced a consistent identifiable electrical pattern. By contrast, the recordings from the inferotemporal cortex did not show any differential activity that correlated with the cues presented. Instead the activity of the inferotemporal cortex was differential with respect to comprehension: the relevance of the cue in terms of whether the category color or form was being reinforced. This differential brain electrical activity did not emerge until the animal was well trained (Fig. 7.5).

In humans, using scalp recordings, Hudspeth (1990) performed experiments in which he demonstrated that scalp recorded event-related potential recordings from occipital placements can be analyzed much as in the monkey experiments. He demonstrated that separate factors for object-form and for color are indexed by vectors orthogonal to each other. He has now extended these studies to analyzing recordings from occipito-temporal lobe locations to determine whether in these recordings, differential responses (i.e., the vectors) are linked to comprehension: e.g., he has identified a vector representing "cat" irrespective of whether cat is presented verbally or pictorially. At the same time other vectors represent the verbal and pictorial modes of presentation, per se. These results indicate that there is available to the subject, the processing of "catness" as a separate dimension to be comprehended (Fig. 7.6).

Fuster & Jervey (1982), also using a technique similar to ours, found single neurons in the inferotemporal cortex that respond differentially to the categories color and object-form when and only when these dimensions had become relevant during a particular trial set (because of the reinforcing contingencies).

An interesting and unexpected finding in our monkey experiments was the fact that often the behavioral change made necessary by reversal and switching was accomplished before the change in the brain electrical recording became manifest. Thus the monkey would be responding appropriately to diamond, while his inferotemporal cortex still signalled the cue (red) that was correct before the switch.

We were at a loss for an explanation for this result until my collaborator (Marc Nuwer) called from England where he had gone to take a residency at the National Hospital, Queen's Square. He exclaimed, "I now know what was going on in our monkeys. It's just as when I cross a street here. I have learnt to think: don't look left, look right." It is as if the monkey were thinking "*not* red, diamond." The correct response was made as much on the basis of comprehending "not red" as on the basis of comprehending that diamond is correct.

The final experiment in this series was aimed at determining what input variables would initiate deliberate, thoughtful sampling. Recall that the receptive fields of neurons in the striate cortex are responsive to a variety of features; properties that describe sensory stimuli such as color, orientation, direction of movement, temporal, and spatial frequency. Recall also that according to the holonomic brain theory the configural aspects of sensory stimuli address these properties by the excitatory "weighting" of the probability amplitude that modulates the Fourier coefficients that represent these aspects. Furthermore, according to the reciprocity principle, such "weightings" can be initiated, as well, by central processes, that is, in a top-down fashion.

Shiffrin and Schneider (1977, 1984) performed experiments on humans that are relevant to determining the relative importance of the sensory vs the central components of this reciprocal process during discrimination. They distinguished between automatic and controlled processing, which in the holonomic brain theory translates into sensory vs centrally driven aspects of reciprocity. As these investigators used alphanumerical stimuli inappropriate for use with nonhuman primates we modified the task to reflect another, related, paradigm.

This paradigm was developed by Treisman (Treisman & Schmidt, 1982), who

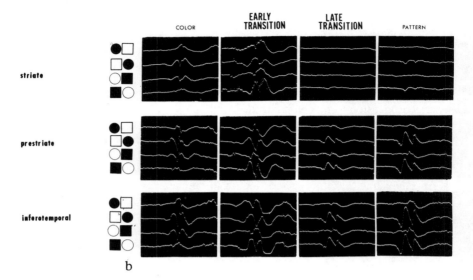

FIG. 7.4.   Results of an experiment demonstrating the functions of the inferotemporal cortex by behavioral electrophysiological techniques. The experiment is similar to the one described by Figs. 7-3 and 7-4. A monkey initiates a flashed stimulus display and responds by pressing either the right or left half of the display panel to receive a reward while electrical brain recordings are made on line with a small general purpose computer (PDP-8). In this experiment the flashed stimulus consisted of colored (red and green) stripes and circles. Reinforcing contingencies determined whether the monkeys were to attend and respond to the pattern (circle *vs* stripes) or color (red *vs* green) dimension of the stimulus. As in the earlier experiment stimulus, response, and reinforcement variables were found to be encoded in the primary visual cortex. In addition, this experiment showed that the association between stimulus dimension (pattern or color) and response occurs first in the inferotemporal cortex. This is presented in panel three of B where the electrophysiological data averaged from the time of response (forward for 250 msec and backward 250 msec from center of record) show clear differences in waveform depending on whether pattern or color is being reinforced. Note that this difference occurs despite the fact that the retinal image formed by the flashed stimulus is identical in the pattern and color problems. Once the monkeys have been overtrained this reinforcement produced attentional association between a stimulus dimension and response also becomes encoded in the primary visual cortex as is shown in a. From Rothblat, and Pribram, 1972.

182

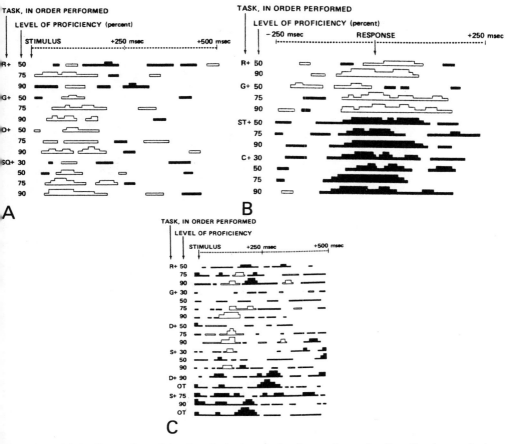

A

B

C

FIG. 7.5. (a) An illustration of the time-locked analysis of wave forms for the *stimulus-evoked* epoch. Statistically significant color-related (white bars) and pattern-related (dark bars) differences are shown. This example is taken from an electrode implanted in the striate cortex. It demonstrates *slide-related* variations since the differences found in the shapes of the wave form (especially at ± 125 msec) are consistently correlated over trials with the color arrangement on the slide-pair. (b) An illustration of the time-locked analysis of wave forms for the *response-evoked* epoch. Statistically significant color-related (white bars) or pattern-related (dark bars) differences are shown. This example is taken from an electrode implanted into the inferior temporal cortex. It shows *'task-related'* variations since there are consistently color-related (white bars) differences during color-reinforced tasks, and only pattern related (dark bars) differences during pattern-reinforced tasks. (c) Dimensional shift changes. This figure shows data taken during the stimulus-evoked epoch from one electrode implanted in the middle inferior temporal cortex. Of special interest are the data plotted between 50 and 200 msec post-stimulus. When the reinforcement contingencies were changed from a color dimension to a pattern dimension, after the seventh line on the graph, note that the wave form differences recorded still showed color-related difference (open bars) despite the fact that behaviorally the monkey was performing at a 90% criterion on the pattern problem. It was not until the second reversal of the pattern task that the recorded wave differences switched to being pattern-related (filled bars). R+, G+, D+, S+ are red-positive, green-positive, diamond-positive, and square-positive tasks.

183

A

VWP	
X	Y
0.000	0.999
0.464	0.772
0.984	0.173
0.731	-0.555
0.007	-1.000
-0.587	-0.742
-0.983	-0.176
-0.495	0.744
SUM R^2 = 91.8%	

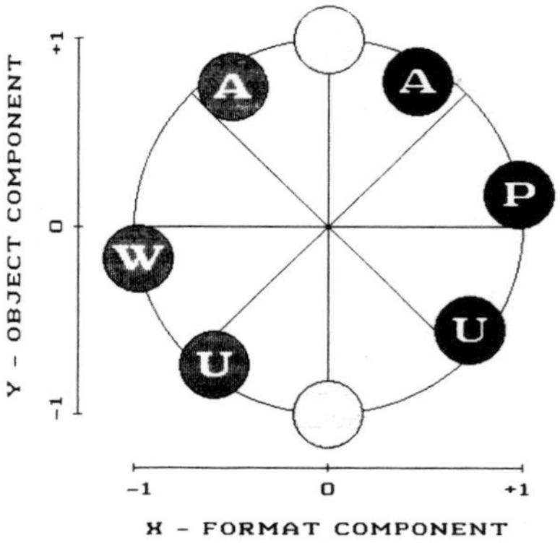

B

VFC	
X	Y
0.000	1.000
0.410	0.852
0.990	0.138
0.638	-0.710
0.000	-1.000
-0.588	-0.760
-0.991	-0.132
-0.474	0.796
SUM R^2 = 94.8%	

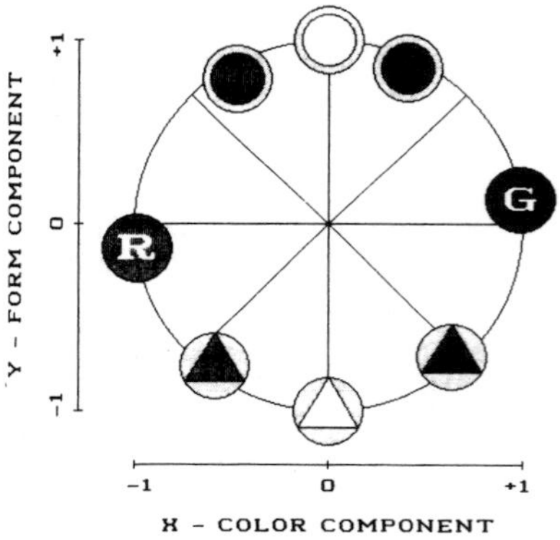

FIG. 7.6. Examples of the *orthogonal stimulus set* procedure de-signed by Hudspeth (1990). This procedure was used to demonstrate perceptual (a–VFC) and conceptual (b–VWP) categories in visual ERP waveshapes. a). (VFC) stimuli were composed of combined form (circles or trinagles) and color (green or red) attributes. b). (VWP) stimuli were composed of combined object (CAT or CUP) and format (Words or Pictures) attributes. In both cases, the polar (e.g., green or red) attributes were estimated from averages of the appropriate pairs of ERPs. Raw ERP difference-waveshapes for each bipolar attribute was identical, but 180° out of phase. The ERPs for each bipolar attribute were, however, uncorrelated and thus independent. ERP's for stimuli with combined attributes were composed of equal portions of two primary attributes. A varimax components analysis confirmed the ERP categories, as shown here. These studies show that it is possible to predict the precise attributes and categories for both perceptual and conceptual stimulus sets from ERP waveshapes.

184

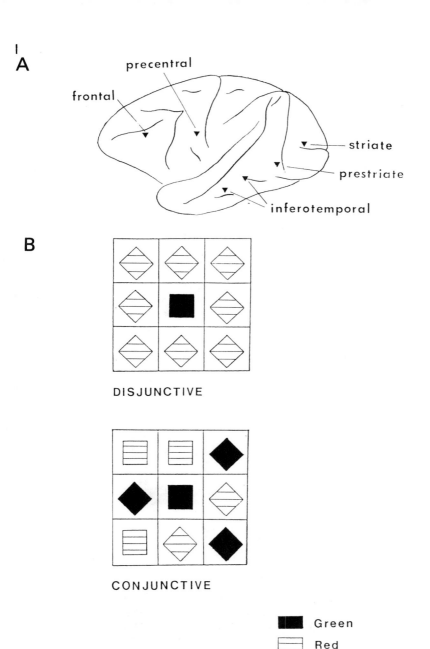

I
A

precentral

frontal

striate

prestriate

inferotemporal

B

DISJUNCTIVE

CONJUNCTIVE

■ Green

▭ Red

FIG. 7.7. a) Lateral view of macaque cerebral hemisphere, showing implant sites for transcortical electrodes. b) Examples of conjunctive and disjunctive arrays, with the target (green square) shown in the central position. From: Bolster, R. B., & Pribram, K. H. (in prep).

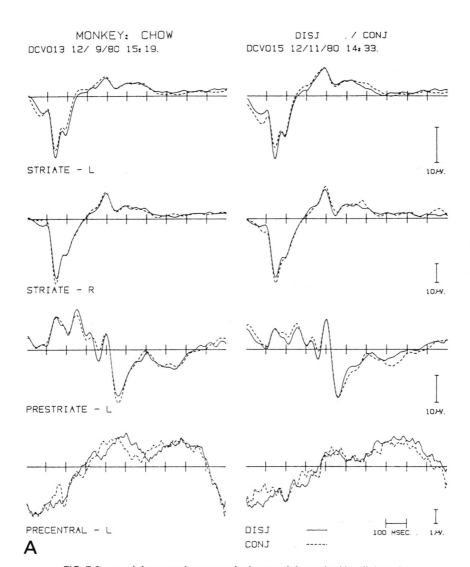

FIG. 7.8. a–c) Averaged transcortical potentials evoked by disjunctive and conjunctive arrays, "extrinsic electrode group (sites in projection cortex). Potentials are not sensitive to array type. Each EP represents an average of 54 trials from a single running day. Two consecutive running days are depicted, to demonstrate replicability of the EP waveform. d–f) Averaged transcortical potentials evoked by disjunctive and conjunctive arrays, "intrinsic" electrode group (sites in association cortex). Potentials are sensitive to array type. From: Bolster, R. B., & Pribram, K. H. (in prep). Conjunction–search in the monkey: Identification of colored form targets in briefly presented visual arrays.

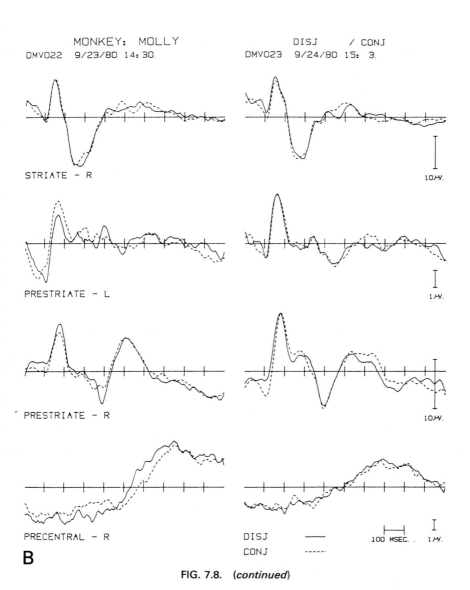

MONKEY: MOLLY
DMVO22 9/23/80 14: 30.

DISJ   / CONJ
DMVO23 9/24/80 15: 3.

STRIATE – R

10 µV.

PRESTRIATE – L

1 µV.

PRESTRIATE – R

10 µV.

PRECENTRAL – R

DISJ   ———
CONJ   ------

100 MSEC. .   1 µV.

B

FIG. 7.8. (*continued*)

187

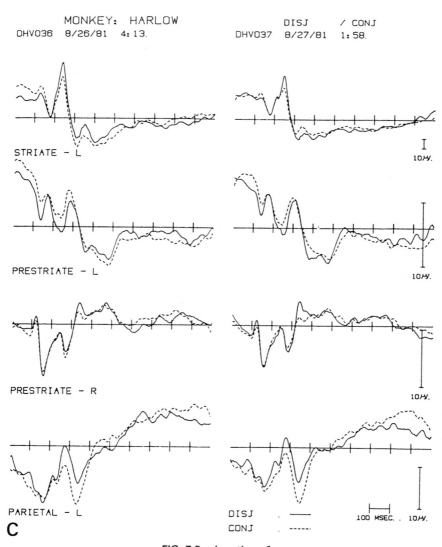

MONKEY: HARLOW
DHV036 8/26/81 4:13.

DISJ   / CONJ
DHV037 8/27/81 1:58.

STRIATE - L

10μV.

PRESTRIATE - L

10μV.

PRESTRIATE - R

10μV.

PARIETAL - L

C

DISJ _____
CONJ -------

100 MSEC. 10μV.

FIG. 7.8. (*continued*)

188

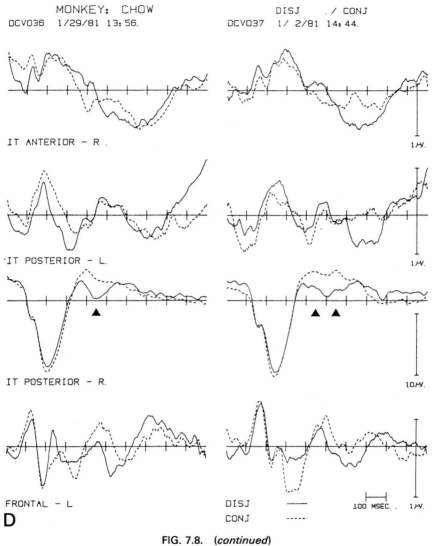

FIG. 7.8. (continued)

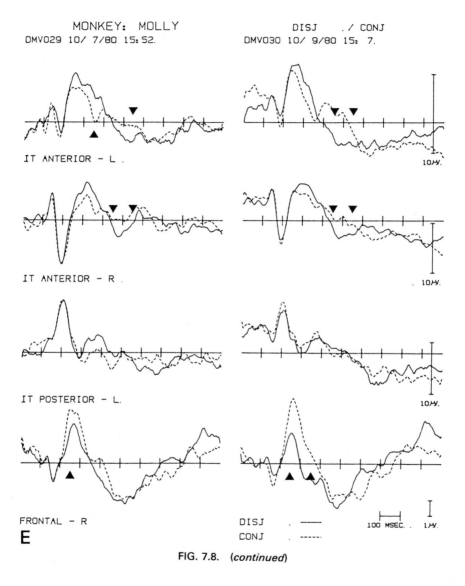

MONKEY: MOLLY
DMV029 10/ 7/80 15:52.

DISJ . / CONJ
DMV030 10/ 9/80 15: 7.

IT ANTERIOR - L .

IT ANTERIOR - R .

IT POSTERIOR - L.

FRONTAL - R

E

DISJ . ———
CONJ . ------

10μV.

10μV.

10μV.

100 MSEC. . 1μV.

FIG. 7.8.   (*continued*)

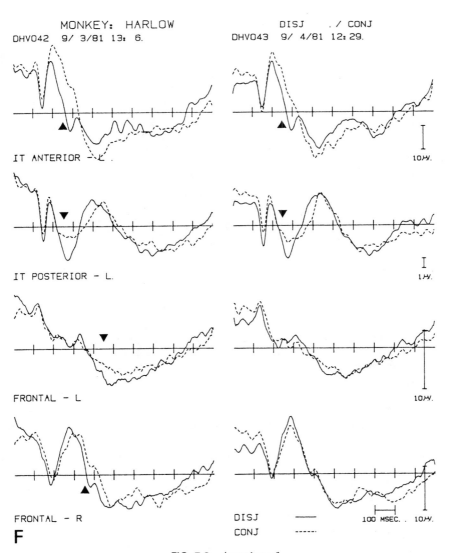

MONKEY: HARLOW   DISJ   . / CONJ
DHVO42 9/ 3/81 13: 6.   DHVO43 9/ 4/81 12: 29.

IT ANTERIOR - L .

IT POSTERIOR - L.

FRONTAL - L

FRONTAL - R

F

DISJ   ———
CONJ   ------

100 MSEC. . 10 µV.

10 µV.

1 µV.

10 µV.

FIG. 7.8. (*continued*)

191

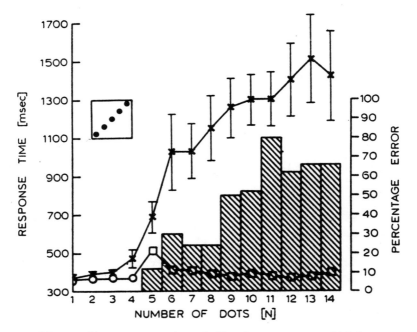

FIG. 7.9. Mean response times (left) and per cent errors (right) as a function of the number of dots, N. x indicates response/latency; □ indicates percent error. From: Campbell, F. W. (1985). How much of the information falling on the retina reaches the visual cortex and how much is stored in the visual memory. In C. Chagas, R. Gattass, & C. Gross (Eds.), *Pattern Recognition Mechanisms*, (pp. 83–95). Berlin: Springer-Verlag.

showed that, under certain conditions, illusory conjunctions among features can occur: for example, the orientation of a shadow is ascribed to its object. The occurrence of illusory conjunctions clearly speaks for top-down processing.

We, therefore, modified (Figs. 7.7 and 7.8) the Shiffrin-Schneider task to reflect the Treisman paradigm: We expected that whenever a discrimination depended solely on a single feature such as the color "green," processing time would be uninfluenced by the size of the feature set. This would be in accord with Shiffrin and Schneider's definition of *automatic processing*. When, however, discrimination depended on the occurrence of a conjunction of two (or more) features such as "green-diamond," processing time would be expected to increase monotonically as a function of the size of the feature set. This is what Shiffrin and Schneider called *controlled processing*. In normal monkeys these predictions were to a large extent verified (Bolster & Pribram, in prep.). For our hypothesis, the increased processing time should reflect the engagement of the inferotemporal system in the process.

Electrical brain recordings were made while the monkeys were performing the task. As expected, the records from the striate and prestriate cortex reflected only color and size of the stimulus set (which was varied). Also, in support of the hypothesis, recordings from the inferotemporal cortex differed between the conditions: (a) when the discrimination depended on only one feature (green), and (b) when the discrimination depended on the occurrence of a conjunction of two features (green-diamond). However, even when discrimination depended on only one feature and the feature set became larger than four, inferotemporal electrical activity (and response time) reflected controlled rather than automatic processing.

The number four was also found critical in the multiple object experiment reviewed earlier and even in a simpler task that consisted of determining whether the number of dots in a set of dots could be accurately discerned without error when tachistoscopically presented to humans. A distinct discontinuity can be observed as the dot set increased above 4. (Fig. 7.9, Campbell, 1985). These results indicate, as do those from the lesion experiments described earlier, that difficulty of task is the critical parameter (Mishkin, 1966; Pribram, 1984). Nonetheless, the conjoining of even two features poses a significant load on processing, demanding more careful scrutiny of the sample set and therefore the participation of the inferotemporal visual system.

CENTRAL SELECTIVITIES

More specific evidence regarding a model of comprehension driven categorization came from microelectrode recordings made from single neurons in the inferotemporal cortex. Individual units have been found to respond best to hands or faces and even to familiar facial perspectives or highly textured surfaces (Perrett, Rolls, & Caan, 1982; Rolls, 1985; Schwartz, Desimone, Albright, & Gross, 1983). These neurons also respond to other stimuli but not nearly as vigorously. There is moreover, evidence that prolonged experience with the particular stimuli can modify this selectivity: A cell responded best to a *green* hand (and *green* low spatial frequency) after the monkey had been rewarded for responding to a set of green stripes (Pribram, unpublished result).

These experimental results do not in themselves tell much about how processing proceeds. More interesting from the processing point of view are results showing that the responsiveness to a hand can be understood in terms of ensembles of orientation specific tangent vectors that describe the outlines of a form (Gauthier, 1977; Persoon & Fu, 1977; Zahn & Roskies, 1972). The possibility that inferotemporal neurons code shape on the basis of such tangent vectors was tested by Gross, Desimone, Albright, and Schwartz (1985), who call these vectors Fourier Descriptors:

The method depends first on determining the boundary orientation function for the shape, that is, the orientation or tangent angle of the shape's boundary measured at regular intervals around the perimeter. Then, the boundary orientation function is expanded in a Fourier series. Each term in the Fourier expansion is associated with a particular frequency, amplitude and phase and is known as a Fourier Descriptor or FD. Any shape is fully described by its constituent set of FDs, and a set of only the low-frequency terms can often provide the "gestalt" of a shape. Furthermore, this method of describing shape is independent of both the position and size of the stimulus. Thus, the FDs are a powerful and efficient alphabet for representing and classifying shapes. The inverse transform of a single FD uniquely determines a plane closed boundary with a specific number of lobes (frequency), lobe indentation (amplitude) and orientation (phase). We refer to these shapes as "FD stimuli". (p. 190)

By systematically varying the frequency or amplitude of Fourier Descriptor stimuli, these investigators were able to test inferotemporal units with parametrically varying shapes and thereby to characterize shape selectivity. Using these stimuli they were able to show that about half of the receptive fields of inferotemporal neurons were selectively tuned to the Fourier Descriptor stimuli. The remaining cells either did not respond to any of the stimuli or responded about equally to all. Most important, the selectivity of these neurons remained invariant over changes in stimulus size (ranging from 50 deg^2 to 13 deg^2). Gross and colleagues noted:

The finding that some [inferotemporal] IT cells maintain their selectivity for FD stimuli of a particular frequency over changes in size, position and contrast cannot be easily explained in terms of selectivity for local features such as the position or orientation of an edge. These cells must have been sensitive, in some fashion, to the overall shape of the stimulus. [Further] . . . if IT cortex is coding shape using a mechanism similar to that of Fourier Descriptors, at least some cells should be sensitive to the amplitude of the FD stimuli. We studied the effect of amplitude by holding frequency constant and varying amplitude over five octaves. For more than half of these cells, the magnitude of response was a monotonic function of amplitude.

In any case, the present results support the hypothesis that shape is an important stimulus dimension processed by IT cortex. Just as striate cortex analyzes local boundary orientation, [recall Maffei's experiments reviewed in Lecture 4 which were interpreted to indicate that complex receptive fields encode shading and/or texture of surfaces while simple receptive fields encode contour] IT cortex may be involved in the analysis of global boundary orientation. However, it should be stressed that even if some IT neurons represent or code boundary curvature, this cannot be the exclusive function of IT cortex. Some IT cells are selective for color, for texture, for spatial frequency, for three-dimensionality and for such complex stimuli such as faces. These stimulus dimensions are not readily described only in terms of boundary curvature. Selectivity for boundary curvature appears to be

FIG. 7.10. Examples of FD stimuli varying in frequency (2–64 cycles/perimeter) and amplitude (0.8 and 1.6). The upper row is the "standard" set of stimuli. Unless indicated otherwise, white stimuli were presented on a dark background. From: Gross, C. G., Desimone, R., Albright, T. D., and Schwartz, E. L. (1985). Inferior Temporal Cortex and Pattern Recognition. In: C. Chagas, R. Gattass, & C. Gross (Eds.), *Pattern Recognition Mechanisms*, (pp. 179–201). Berlin: Springer-Verlag.

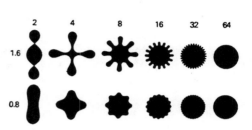

neither a characteristic of all IT cells nor the exclusive response property of many. (p. 192)

In another series of studies, Barry Richmond and Lance Optican (Optican & Richmond, 1987; Richmond & Optican, 1987; Richmond, Optican, Podell, & Spitzer, 1987) evoked responses from single neurons in the inferotemporal cortex by brief exposure (400 msec) to 64 two-dimensional patterns differing in their number of horizontal and vertical stripes. The stimuli thus ranged from a large blank square to a checkerboard composed of 8 x 8 small black-and-white striped squares filling the large square. The first 300 msec. of evoked spike trains in response to the stimulus were analyzed and showed that much of the information differentiating one train from another was contained in the first three components of the evoked histogram of the spike train intervals. A correlation was then found between the Walshe transforms (essentially digitized Fourier transforms) that described the stimuli and the temporal distribution of spikes within the information-carrying components.

On the basis of these results, Richmond and Optican formulated a multiplex-filter hypothesis of neural information transmission. Different stimulus properties are encoded in different temporal distributions in the first 300 msec. of the spike train evoked in a single neuron. This information is clearly retrievable in the short term when components of the neural electric response can be identified as in these experiments and in event-related brain potential recordings made with macroelectrodes and from the scalp in humans.

Richmond (personal communication) notes, therefore, that it takes several neurons to transmit information about any single feature. This conclusion is consonant with the data obtained for parietal lobe neurons by Mountcastle as described in the previous lecture. The receptive fields of these neurons constitute an ensemble—however, the ensemble is not made up of detectors each of which responds only to a single feature. Rather, selectivities are distributed among receptive fields much as they are in distributed processing simulations.

When the results of these experiments are placed into the context of the results of the experiments reviewed earlier, the role of the inferotemporal cortex in visual processing can be understood as follows: The neurons of the inferotemporal cortex display receptive fields responsive to a variety of stimulus dimensions. Many, though not all, of these dimensions such as shape, are of a higher order than those found to characterize receptive field properties in striate, peri- and prestriate cortices. Higher order means that the stimulus dimension can be analyzed into components, the lower order dimensions.

At the same time, the lower order dimensions are separately represented. Given the top-down nature of the process served by the inferotemporal system, the representation of both higher and lower order dimensions indicates that both images and object-forms can be addressed by the system.

The evidence reviewed indicates further that processing by the inferotemporal cortex is experience-dependent. Though some receptive field responsivities such as those for faces and hands may be built in, most are developed through learning. Thus processing span is enhanced through an increased memory store: that is, the number of stimulus dimensions that can be activated as a consequence of learning.

Activation of a stimulus dimension is ordinarily termed attending. Enhanced processing span implies an enhanced attention span, in other words, controlled rather than automatic processing.

CONCLUSION

The results of these experiments can be summarized as follows:

1. When discrimination among object-forms occurs processing involves sensory-mode specific brain systems that are anatomically distinct from the primary sensory-motor systems.

2. Primary sensory-motor systems are extrinsically connected; that is, they have dense reciprocal connections with sensory receptors and muscle effectors. Imaging and object-form perception devolve on the functioning of these systems.

   By contrast, the associated nonprimary sensory mode specific systems are mainly connected intrinsically, that is, they have dense reciprocal connections with the primary system with which they are associated. Because they are not directly connected to a sensory input, the intrinsically connected systems are triggered by sensory input to operate primarily in a top-down fashion on the primary perceptual process.

3. The evidence obtained for the visual (reviewed here) and auditory modes (see e.g., Dewson, 1966; Dewson, Nobel & Pribram, 1966) shows that the operations of the intrinsic sensory-specific systems enhance processing span. When these systems are intact, a greater number of features is attended (controlled rather than automatic processing). In part, this enhanced span is due to prior experience with these features, that is, memory.

4. These systems operate by separating stimulus patterns such as object forms into distinct domains by progressively sharpening the generalization gradient of each feature perceived. In object-form vision this accomplishes a metric (with "distances" between gradients) within which sets of orientation-specific tangent vectors can process contours in the spectral domain. This metric is subject to modification and sharpening through learning.

5. One aspect of these discoveries is best portrayed in the language of memory research although it applies equally to perception. This aspect concerns the fact that there are two modes of operation that characterized brain function: (a) a heterarchical parallel- *distributed* process that occurs at each level of a neural system, and (b) a *localized* hierarchy of relationships between levels of the system.

   The appeal of holographic theory is its emphasis on parallel-distributed processing, that is, nonlocality in storage and in processing. The holonomic brain theory also emphasizes heterarchical parallel-distributed processing. In the current lecture, on the other hand, emphasis has been on localized brain systems that operate hierarchically back on to those distributed processing events. By this means, as well as by movement, the "dismembered," distributed processing "core" located in the primary sensory-motor systems becomes "re-membered."

6. The critical functions of the receptive fields of each of the hierarchically operating systems are in turn distributed. Occasionally nodes of this distributed network respond best to integrated patterns such as "hands" and "faces." This accounts for the recording of "grandfather" cells.

7. Processing thus involves the interplay between separate systems each different from the other in its organization. Each system is localized in space and its operations can be located in time. The operations, however, proceed non-locally in phase space: probability amplitude modulated frequencies provide the currency of the calculation. Our well-worn friend, the piano is composed in this manner. The keyboard and strings are organized into octaves, spatially arranged. The strings vibrate, each at a certain bandwidth of frequency. When the instrument is a player piano a tape punched with holes provides additional (top-down) input to the system. Each hole addresses a particular key and the related string that produces a

particular frequency of sound. Think of each line of holes in the player tape as the equivalent of the receptive field of a cell in the inferotemporal cortex; think of each individual hole as an active synapse and a row of holes as representing a tangent vector. This vector addresses its counterpart, a frequency tuned neuron in the primary visual system. The better the arrangement and the finer the grain of correspondence between vectors (rows of holes) and frequency tuned neurons (strings), the greater the possible variety and complexity of the resulting perception.

8

Familiarization and Valuation: The Contributions of the Amygdala System to the Demarcation of an Episode

The idea that study of the brain and other biological subjects is useful for philosophy has been resisted more strongly in relation to questions of value than in any other aspect of human thinking and behavior. Nevertheless there are insistant reasons for further consideration of the process of valuing. Recent studies have shown that the achievement of satisfaction of various sorts of need is accomplished by activity in specific parts of the brain. (J. Z. Young, Philosophy and the Brain, *1987, p. 173, Oxford University Press)*

INTRODUCTION

Sometimes our perceptions are ambient, enhancing span by freely sampling sensory input and categorizing it. But for the most part our perceptions become directed by our interests. Interests are frequently initiated by imbalances in neurochemical states such as those leading to eating or sexual behavior. As often, however, we maintain interest in something that has become familiar and comfortable, especially when small changes in the familiar are brought about. The interests of gourmets, of connoisseurs of wine and of the arts, of readers of novels and of comic strips, of perusers of soap operas and of popular and classical music, and even the dedicated efforts of computer programmers, are determined by incremental changes in what has become familiar. In short, we are interested in perceptions relevant to our motives and memories. These interests are enhanced by incremental changes in our perceptions. In turn, what we perceive can be influenced by our interests. (Bruner, 1957; Hastorf & Knutson, 1954).

199

There is a close relationship between motive and memory. The previous lecture reviewed the role of reinforcing events in enhancing processing span. (A reinforcer is any sensory event that increases, a deterrent any sensory event that decreases, the probability of recurrence of behavior that becomes associated with it.) Reinforcers as used in animal experiments ordinarily address appetites (motives) and lead to changes in brain chemistry that, when subsequently activated, constitute memory. The effectiveness of such reinforcers is a function of deprivation as well as the schedules (programs) of presentation of the reinforcers.

The hedonic sensory processing that leads to reinforcement and deterrence is considerably different from the more familiar information processing discussed in the previous seven lectures. The current lecture describes distinct anatomical systems that connect receptors to distinct parts of the brain, brain systems involved in the process of reinforcement and deterrence. Studies of these brain systems, identified as protocritic, has provided insights into what makes a sensory event novel and interesting, relevant, reinforcing or deterrent. The next sections review some of the critical experimental results that led to these insights.

THE AMYGDALA SYSTEM

In order to analyze the complex of effects produced by total resection of the temporal lobe that were reviewed in the previous lecture, I devised surgical techniques to make possible restricted resections of the medially lying amygdala and hippocampus (Fig. 8.1 reviewed by Pribram 1954, 1958). When resections were restricted to the amygdala and adjacent pole of the temporal lobe, the marked taming of the monkeys, which had followed resection of the entire temporal lobe, was reproduced in its entirety (Pribram & Bagshaw, 1953). Once again, as in the case of resection of the posterior convexity of the lobe, it was then necessary to find out just what the resulting behavioral change signified.

First it was determined that not only were the monkeys tamed, but they also put everything in their mouths, gained weight, and increased their sexual behavior—all effects that had also followed the total temporal lobectomy. These changes in behavior were summarized under the rubric of the "four Fs": fighting, fleeing, feeding, and sex (Pribram, 1960).

Historically these apparently disparate behaviors were classified together as "instinct" (a term still used to describe the processes underlying such behaviors in the psychoanalytic literature). More recently this concept came into disfavor (see e.g., Beach, 1955) and ethologists substituted the category "species specific" behaviors for instinct because these behaviors can be shown to have a common genetic component. But this substitution loses much of the meaning of the older terminology: Human language is species-specific but not instinctive in the earlier sense. My preference is to retain the concept of instinct as descriptive of the four F's and that what these behaviors have in common is the fact that their

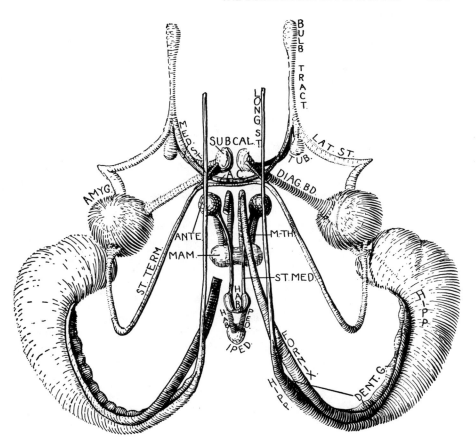

FIG. 8.1.   Reconstruction showing a few of the relationships between limbic (amygdala and hippocampus) and core (hypothalmic) structures. From Krieg, 1966.

patterns are shared by practically all species. What makes the study of geese and other birds so interesting is that we recognize our own behavior patterns in the descriptions provided by ethologists (see e.g., Lorenz, 1969). It is therefore *species-shared* behavior-patterns that are of interest in tracking the effects of amygdalectomy.

THE BOUNDARIES OF AN EPISODE

In our own work the apparently disparate behaviors that characterize the 4 Fs were shown by careful analysis to be influenced by a common process. It is worth summarizing the highlights of this analysis because identifying a common process operating on apparently disparate behaviors is a recurring problem in behavioral neuroscience as it is in behavioral genetics where it involves identifying genotypes from phenotypical behaviors. Qualitative and quantitative determinations were made in each of the four Fs with the following results.

In a social hierarchy fighting and fleeing were both diminished provided there was a sufficiently skillful antagonist (Fig. 8.2; Rosvold, Mirsky, & Pribram, 1954). As in the study reported by Sanger-Brown and Schaefer, when a monkey was returned to the social colony after amygdalectomy, he "voluntarily approaches all persons—and fellow monkeys indifferently." Also, having just interacted with his fellow monkey, and perhaps having been trounced, "he will go through the same process, as if he had entirely forgotten his previous experience."

This behavioral change was dramatically demonstrated by displaying a lighted match to such monkeys. They would invariably grab the match, put it into their mouth, dousing the flame, only to repeat the grab when the next lit match was presented. This behavior could be elicited for a hundred consecutive trials unless either the monkey or the experimenter became bored before the session was ended (Fulton, Pribram, Stevenson, & Wall, 1949).

The increases in feeding and sexual behavior that follow amygdalectomy were also shown to be due to a failure in stopping. For instance, as reported by Sanger-Brown and Schaefer, monkeys with such resections appear to be indiscriminate in what they pick up, put in their mouths, and swallow. But when tests were performed and a record was kept of the order in which the food and nonfood objects were chosen, it turned out that the order of preference was undisturbed by the brain operation; only now the monkeys would continue to pick up additional objects beyond those that they had chosen first (Wilson, 1959). In fact amygdalectomized animals may be a bit slow to start eating but continue eating far past the point when their controls stop eating (Fuller, Rosvold, & Pribram, 1957).

The fact that amygdalectomy impairs the stop—the satiety—mechanism,

---

FIG. 8.2.   A: dominance hierarchy of a colony of eight preadolescent male rhesus monkeys before any surgical intervention. B: same as A after bilateral amygdalectomy had been performed on Dave. Note his drop to the bottom of the hierarchy. C: same as A and B, except that both Dave and Zeke have received bilateral amygdalectomies. D: final social hierarchy after Dave, Zeke, and Riva have all had bilateral amygdalectomies. Note that Riva fails to fall in the hierarchy. Minimal differences in extent of locus of the resections do not correlate with differences in the behavioral results. The disparity has been shown in subsequent experiments to be due to Herby's nonaggressive "personality" in the second position of the hierarchy. From Pribram, 1962.

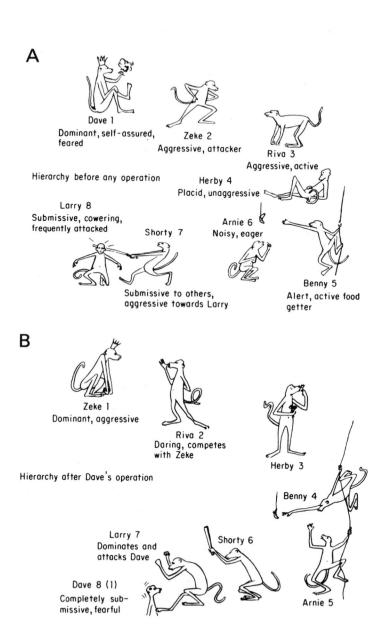

A

Dave 1
Dominant, self-assured, feared

Zeke 2
Aggressive, attacker

Riva 3
Aggressive, active

Hierarchy before any operation

Herby 4
Placid, unaggressive

Larry 8
Submissive, cowering, frequently attacked

Arnie 6
Noisy, eager

Shorty 7
Submissive to others, aggressive towards Larry

Benny 5
Alert, active food getter

B

Zeke 1
Dominant, aggressive

Riva 2
Daring, competes with Zeke

Herby 3

Hierarchy after Dave's operation

Benny 4

Larry 7
Dominates and attacks Dave

Shorty 6

Dave 8 (1)
Completely sub-missive, fearful

Arnie 5

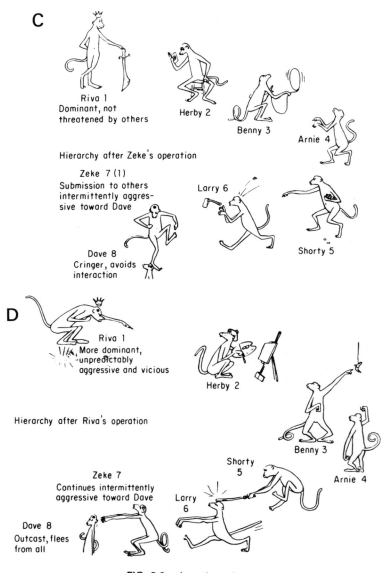

C

Riva 1
Dominant, not
threatened by others

Herby 2

Benny 3

Arnie 4

Hierarchy after Zeke's operation

Zeke 7 (1)
Submission to others
intermittently aggres-
sive toward Dave

Larry 6

Dave 8
Cringer, avoids
interaction

Shorty 5

D

Riva 1
More dominant,
unpredictably
aggressive and vicious

Herby 2

Hierarchy after Riva's operation

Benny 3

Arnie 4

Shorty
5

Zeke 7
Continues intermittently
aggressive toward Dave

Larry
6

Dave 8
Outcast, flees
from all

FIG. 8.2. (*continued*)

might suggest that amgydalectomized monkeys are hungrier or have greater appetite. This is not so, however. When deprived of food for from 24 to 72 hours, amygdalectomized monkeys do not eat more rapidly than they did before deprivation whereas, of course, their control subjects do (Weiskrantz, 1956).

After amygdalectomy the effectiveness of food as a reward is diminished. Ordinarily a change in the amount of reward given, changes its effectiveness. After amygdalectomy, changes in amount have much less effect than they do when control subjects are used (Schwartzbaum, 1960).

These disturbances in feeding after amygdalectomy were shown to be due to connections with the satiety mechanism centered in the ventromedial region of the hypothalamus. For instance, a precise relationship was established between the amount of carbachol injected into the amygdala and amount of feeding (or drinking) once the process had been initiated (Russel, Singer, Flanagan, Stone, & Russell, 1968). Injections into the ventromedial hypothalamic region simply terminate feeding.

Modulation of a stop process was also shown responsible for changes in fighting behavior. Fall in a dominance hierarchy after amygdalectomy was, when it occurred, related to the amount of aggressive interaction between the dominant and submissive animals of the group. After amygdalectomy such interactions were overly prolonged leading to a reorganization of the dominance hierarchy. It was as if the amygdalectomized monkeys approached each interaction as novel. Prior experience, which modulated the behavior of the control subjects, seemed to have little influence after amygdalectomy. This finding characterizes many of the experimental results to be described shortly.

Analyses of the effects of amygdalectomy and electrical stimulations of the amygdala on avoidance (fleeing) behavior brought a similar conclusion (Fig. 8.3). Escape behavior is unaffected and sensitivity to shock is not diminished (Bagshaw & Pribram, 1968). Nor is there a change in generalization gradient to aversive stimulation (Hearst & Pribram, 1964a, 1964b). What appears to be affected primarily is the memory aspect of avoidance—the expectation based on familiarity with the situation that aversive stimulation will occur. Such expectations are ordinarily referred to as fears that direct and constrain perception.

The theme recurs when the effects of amygdalectomy on sexual behavior are analyzed. The hypersexuality produced by the resections is found to be due to an increased territory and range of situations over which the behavior is manifest: Ordinarily cats perceive unfamiliar territory as inappropriate for such behavior (see Pribram 1960, for review).

The importance of the amygdala in more generally determining the bounding of an episode is attested by the results of another set of experiments. Kesner and DiMattia (1987) presented a series of cues to animals to allow them to become familiar and then paired the initial, intermediate, and final cues of the series with novel cues in a discrimination. When similar tasks are administered to humans, they recall the initial and final cues of the series more readily then they recall the

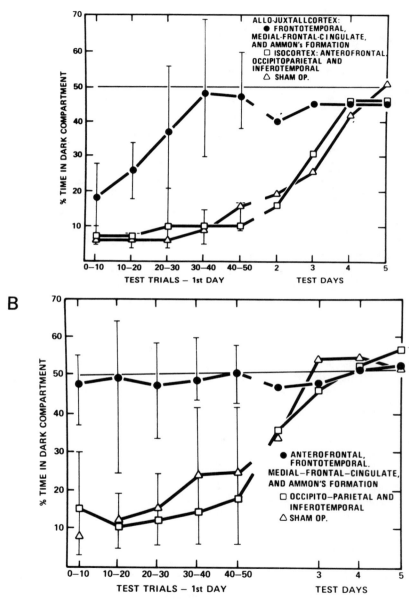

FIG. 8.3. a) Comparison of the effects of resections of the frontolimbic and posterior cerebral convexity on the acquisition of conditioned avoidance. b) Comparison of the effects of resections of the fronto-limbic and posterior cerebral convexity on the extinction of conditioned avoidance.

206

intermediate ones. This is termed the primacy and recency effect. Unoperated monkeys showed both effects in Kessler's experiments. However, after amygalectomy, monkeys failed to show either a recency or primacy effect. If the series is taken to be an episode, the effects of amygdalectomy can be considered to impair the demarkation of an episode. As described in the final lecture, after resections of the far frontal cortex, ordering within an episode becomes deficient.

A DISTURBANCE OF PERCEPTION

The finding that the amygdala is involved in a process that ordinarily operates to stop ongoing behavior also led to a series of studies on its role in the orienting reaction. Orienting not only stops ongoing behavior but directs perception to the orienting stimulus. A series of studies showed that only the visceroautonomic components of orienting were affected by amygdalectomy and that habituation of the behavioral components of orienting is dependent on the occurrence of these visceroautonomic responses.

Two related processes are involved in these effects: Amygdalectomy affects a particular dimension of perceptual experience and this dimension is critical to the process of familiarization.

To begin, an experiment was undertaken to determine whether the marked taming observed to follow amygdalectomy is due to the fact that the resection impairs the perception of the threat of a stimulus or whether the observed change is due to an impaired ability or inclination to respond to the perceived threat. The so-called split brain is the ideal preparation to determine whether the observed change is sensory or motor. In this preparation the hemispheres are severed from one another by sectioning the corpus callosum and anterior commissure (the large tracts connecting the two cerebral hemispheres) and the optic chiasm is cut so the visual input from each eye will go only to the hemisphere on the side of that eye.

When monkeys whose brains had been split in this fashion were given an amygdalectomy on one side only, and then examined with one eye occluded with an opaque contact lens, their responses were specific according to the side being tested. When the unoccluded eye was on the side of the amygdalectomy the monkey was tame; when the unoccluded eye was on the unoperated side, the monkey behaved normally fearful, avoiding all potentially threatening objects such as snakes and humans (Barrett, 1969; Doty & Nagrao, 1973).

Interestingly, when touched, the monkeys retreated from the tactile stimulation irrespective of the side stimulated; tactile stimuli are conveyed to both sides of the brain and no attempt had been made to isolate the tactile input to each hemisphere. Even after bilateral amygdalectomy, the threshold for initiating escape behavior by tactile stimuli remained unchanged (Bagshaw & Pribram, 1968). Furthermore, another set of experiments along the same lines showed that generalization remains unchanged after amygdalectomy (Hearst & Pribram, 1964a, 1964b). By contrast, amydgalectomy markedly altered avoidance of the stimulus when a signal indicated that this to-be-avoided stimulus would appear in 4 seconds (Pribram & Weiskrantz, 1957).

Two conclusions can be drawn from these experiments: (a) The change in behavior that follows amygdalectomy has to do with how the monkeys perceive stimuli and not with a change in the monkeys' somatic motor processing apparatus; and (b) the perceptual process involved has nothing to do with sensing or categorizing (threshold and generalization gradients remain unchanged) but with some other memory-based perceptual process.

EQUI-VALENCE: THE EVALUATION OF PERCEPTIONS

The nature of this other process became evident during the following experiments. When monkeys are trained to select the larger of two circles and then tested to see whether they will select the larger of two squares, unoperated controls select the larger of the squares with no hesitation. After amygdalectomy, transferring the selection to the new pair is severely impaired: Larger is no longer perceived as an independent dimension common to the pair of circles and the pair of squares (Bagshaw & Pribram, 1968). This change in perception is not due to any change in the monkeys' ability to discriminate between cues or between reinforcing events: generalization gradients remain unaltered by amygdalectomy in both a food reinforcement and a footshock deterrence procedure (Hearst & Pribram, 1964a, 1964b). The effect of resection is that larger fails to be perceived as equi-valent, of equal value for the purposes at hand.

This disruption of valuation was demonstrated in another similar experiment. In this experiment the monkeys were trained to select the lighter of two grey square panels embedded in a medium grey background. On test trials, panels of different shades of grey were substituted but the monkeys were still to choose the lighter shade. Control monkeys did just this. The amygdalectomized monkeys, however, hesitated and then selected either of the new panels on a random basis. They perceived the situation as novel, which it was, but failed to perceive it on the basis of the history of reinforcement that placed a value on the relation "lighter of two shades." It is this relation that made the original and substitute panels equivalent (Schwartzbaum & Pribram, 1960).

PROTOCRITIC PROCESSING:
A HEDONIC COMFORT-DISCOMFORT DIMENSION

The answer to the question "what process underlies the valuation (appraisal) of a perception," was gained by considering and pursuing what seems to be a most

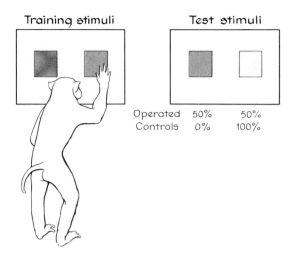

FIG. 8.4. Diagram of experiment testing transfer of training. Monkeys learned to choose the lighter of two panels (left figure), then were given test trials (right figure) in which the formerly lighter was now the darker of two panels, both of which concealed a reward. Normal monkeys continued to choose the lighter panel irrespective of its absolute luminance; amygdalectomized monkeys chose randomly indicating that they perceived the test trials as "novel" and not related to the training procedure.

extraordinary fact: Pain and temperature sensibility are coupled in a single pathway in the spinal cord (Fig. 8.5). (Considerable effort has gone into anaylzing the physiology of various submodalities of somatic sensory processes; see Kenshalo, 1968.) This coupling becomes evident when the spinothalamic tract of the cord is surgically severed in order to alleviate intractible pain or abnormal sensations accompanying a phantom limb. The temperature as well as the pain sense is abolished below the level of the transection. A similar effect is produced by the disease syringomyelia: A loss of pain and temperature sensibility ensues the interruption of fibers from the dorsal root of the cord (the channel for sensory input) across the midline to ascend in the spinothalamic tract. The disease consists of a degenerative enlargement of the spinal canal that occupies the center of the cord; the degeneration interrupts the pain and temperature fibers which cross in the midline.

What could be the common denominator uniting this odd couple? The answer to this question is not known, but a hint comes from the fact that in warm-blooded animals, keeping a constant temperature is basic to the entire metabolic process (Brobeck, 1963). When the basal temperature begins to fall, muscular contraction (activity), feeding, resting (slowing down respiration), and piloerection (ruffling the fur) prevent further temperature loss. When the basal tempera-

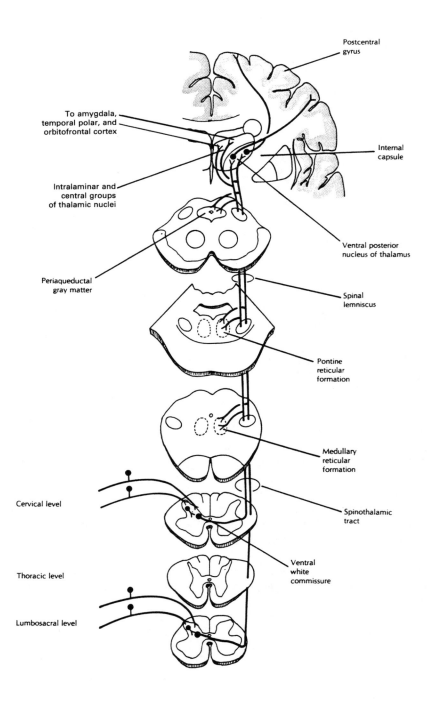

Postcentral
gyrus

To amygdala,
temporal polar, and
orbitofrontal cortex

Internal
capsule

Intralaminar and
central groups
of thalamic nuclei

Ventral posterior
nucleus of thalamus

Periaqueductal
gray matter

Spinal
lemniscus

Pontine
reticular
formation

Medullary
reticular
formation

Cervical level

Spinothalamic
tract

Thoracic level

Ventral
white
commissure

Lumbosacral level

ture rises, the organism pants, skin blood vessels dilate, sweating occurs, drinking ensues, and the organism may repair to a cooler place. These mechanisms operate to keep the organism within a metabolic comfort range.

Comfort-discomfort appears to be the dimension that characterizes the odd couple: the answer to the question "what process underlies valuation" is that temperature-pain sensibility makes an associated sensory input desirable or undesirable.

On this basis, the hypothesis was formulated (Pribram, 1960) that perhaps the comfort-discomfort dimension might also be responsible for the fact that resections of the amygdala affects all of the four Fs. Effects on fleeing and fighting would be due to interference with the pain-discomfort pole of the dimension; effects on feeding and sex would be due to interference with the temperature-comfort pole.

The effects of amygdalectomy on the pain-discomfort pole of this couplet have been reviewed earlier in this lecture. The fact that sexual processes have something to do with comfort can be readily appreciated; how, is somewhat more problematical: the connection with temperature sensibility appears to depend on its effect on the metabolic processes of warm blooded animals. There is, furthermore, the well-known connection between sexual attraction and olfaction and, in a theory attributed to Faraday, between olfaction and temperature (Pfaffman, 1951): Faraday proposed that the nose forms an infrared—heat—chamber and that odors depend on selective radiation through a monomolecular stereochemical film of oderant absorbed on the olfactory receptor surface (See also Beck & Miles, 1947).

To test the hypothesis that temperature as well as pain is processed by the forebrain systems of which the amygdala is a critical part, electrodes were implanted in the amygdala and in the pathways leading from it. Electrodes were also implanted in control sites such as various portions of the parietal cortex, where major portions of the sensory tracts from skin and muscle receptors terminate. The monkeys were trained on a temperature discrimination task using a visual task as a control. Electrical stimulation of the amygdala and related structures, but not of the parietal cortex, produced a marked disruption of performance on the temperature task leaving performance on the visual task intact (Chin, Pribram, Drake, & Greene, 1976).

The distinction between the type of sensory input that reaches the cortex of the posterior cerebral convexity, including that of the parietal lobe, and that reaching

---

FIG. 8.5. The spinothalamic system for pain, temperature, and touch. Adapted from: Barr, M. L. & Kiernan, J. A. (1983). *The Human Nervous System: An Anatomical Viewpoint*, Fourth Edition. Philadelphia, PA: Harper & Row.

the amygdala and associated limbic cortical formations can best be understood in terms of earlier observations on the functions of a fine fiber system of peripheral nerves. These nerves serve what in neurology is called "slow pain" because its conduction time is long compared to that which conveys the sharp effects of pin prick, touch, and pressure. Experiments performed by severing a peripheral nerve and describing the sensory experience as the nerve regenerates were performed by Henry Head (1920) early in the century. Initially, all the fibers of the regenerating nerve are of the same size, but as time goes on some of the fibers become larger while others remain small. For each sensory (and motor) nerve a specific fiber size spectrum develops, a spectrum that depends on the particular location innervated (Quilliam, 1956; Thomas, 1956). While the fibers are all the same size, stimulation of the innervated area produces a diffuse unpleasant sensation that is hard to locate and accurately describe. Normal sensibility is restored with the reconstitution of the normal fiber size spectrum. Head (1920) labelled the abnormal nonlocalizable sensation protopathic because it is primitive and pathological. He called the normal sensation epicritic because it displays what neurologists refer to as local sign: an experience critically located in space and time.

Those aspects of the somatic sensory process, which are epicritic, are relayed to the parietal portion of the cortex of the posterior cerebral convexity. The termination of the pathways of those aspects of somatic sensation that do not show local sign were until recently unknown. In the past 3 decades, anatomical studies have traced multisynaptic pain pathways to the amygdala and related limbic cortical structures (e.g., Morin, Schwartz, & O'Leary, 1951). This fact plus the results of the temperature discrimination experiments described earlier make it likely that those aspects of sensation that do not display "local sign" involve the amygdala and related limbic cortex. The effects of the electrical stimulation and resection of the amygdala interfered with discrimination of these dimensions of pain and of temperature: Because there is no pathological sensibility involved, I use the term *protocritic* rather than protopathic to describe these non-epicritic aspects of somatic sensation which characterize the comfort-discomfort dimension.

In humans, the protocritic dimension of experience is measured by administering tolerance techniques such as those described by McGuinness (1972; McGuinness & Cox, 1977). In these procedures the subject is asked to turn up a sensory stimulus such as a light or tone until its intensity reaches the upper limit of tolerance. Tolerance level is found to vary independently of threshold, which is determined by asking the subject when a sensory stimulus becomes perceptible.

In summary the brain systems involved in somatic sensibility are divided into two major divisions: (a) an epicritic system based on touch and pressure which transmits local sign, that is, the sensation can be critically localized in time and space; and (b) a protocritic system based on pain and temperature sensibility which processes a nonlocalizable hedonic dimension of the experience.

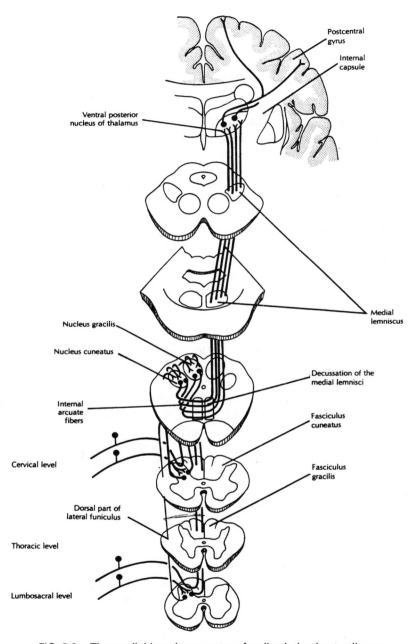

FIG. 8.6.   The medial lemniscus system for discriminative tactile sensation. From: Barr, M. L., & Kiernan, J. A. (1983). *The human nervous system: An anatomical viewpoint* (4th ed.). Philadelphia, PA: Harper & Row.

In the spinal cord the pathways for the protocritic experiences of pain and temperature appear to be inseparable. In the brainstem and thalamus the sites from which pain (deterrents) can be elicited are also intermingled to some extent with those that are involved in producing reinforcement: the repeated pressing of a panel in order to receive or to stop electrical brain stimulation (Olds & Milner, 1954, Olds, 1955). Furthermore, low frequency (10–20 Hertz) stimulation in these sites produces analgesia (Liebeskind et al., 1973, 1974), and when such stimulations are made in humans, sensations of cooling accompany the analgesia (Richardson & Akil, 1974).

The forebrain termination of the protocritic pathways is the amygdala and related limbic cortex. The forebrain termination of the epicritic system is the parietal portion of the cortex of the cerebral convexity.

The two distinct sets of brain systems, an epicritic and a protocritic, both operate on the perceptual process: The epicritic systems of the cerebral convexity serve comprehension by defining category boundaries, categorical alternatives, which enhances processing span; the protocritic limbic systems constrain processing within category boundaries on the basis of value, that is relevance to the organism.

FAMILIARIZATION AS CONSOLIDATION OF MEMORY, DEPENDENT ON PROTOCRITIC PROCESSING

A percept becomes relevant only when it is pertinent, germane to something familiar. In this section the evidence is reviewed to show that behavioral habituation serves as an indicator of familiarity and that habituation occurs as a result of visceroautonomic activity. What is oriented to, the novel, depends on prior experience. However, as will be detailed, the prior experience must either have been repetitiously experienced or to have induced a visceroautonomic reaction to become familiar.

It is, of course, clear from the host of other studies relating brain and behavior reviewed earlier, that not all memory storage processes critically depend on the occurrence of visceroautonomic responses. The learning of motor skills, perceptual categorizing, rote memorization, and so forth are examples where the memory storage mechanism operates on the basis of simple repetition. Still, it is equally clear that there are occasions when memory storage is dependent on a "booster" that places a value on the experience. It is this booster process in which the amygdala is involved (Pribram, Douglas, & Pribram, 1969).

Familiarity is a feeling regarding a valued experience. In the clinic, patients who have a lesion in the region of the amygdala (and the adjacent horn of the hippocampus) describe experiences that are called "jamais vu" and "deja vu"— the patient will enter a place such as his living room and experience a "jamais vu," a feeling of "never having seen," of complete unfamiliarity. Others will come into a place they have never been and feel that they have "already seen," are already, "deja," completely familiar with it.

In the laboratory, familiarity has been shown to be related to reinforcement history. Monkeys were trained to select one of two cues on the basis of a 70% reinforcement schedule: that is, selection of one cue was rewarded on 70% of the trials; selection of the other cue was rewarded on 30% of the trials. Then the cue that had been most rewarded was paired with a novel cue. Control monkeys selected the previously rewarded cue. Monkeys who had their amygdalas removed selected the novel cue. Familiarization by virtue of previous reinforcing experience had little effect on monkeys who lacked the amygdala (Douglas & Pribram, 1966). These monkeys were performing in a "jamais vu mode."

An extensive series of experiments was then undertaken to discover what might be the physiological basis for this deficiency in the familiarization process. The problem was found to center on the fact that ordinarily a novel or a reinforcing event produces a visceroautonomic reaction: A galvanic skin response due to a slight increase in sweating, a brief increase in heart rate, a change in respiratory rate, are some of the readily measurable effects. After amygdalectomy the visceroautonomic reactions to novel or reinforcing events fail to occur (Bagshaw & Benzies, 1968; Bagshaw & Coppock, 1968; Bagshaw, Kimble, & Pribram, 1965; Kimble, Bagshaw, & Pribram, 1965; Koepke & Pribram, 1967a; Koepke & Pribram, 1967b; Pribram, Reitz, McNeil, & Spevack, 1979).

These visceroautonomic responses are, in fact, elicited by electrical excitation of the amygdala and the related limbic cortex of the medial portions of the frontal lobe, anterior insula, and temporal pole (Kaada, Pribram, & Epstein, 1949; reviewed by Pribram, 1961a). Changes in blood pressure, heart and respiratory rate, gut and pupillary responses, as well as gross eye, head, and body responses are elicited. An entire mediobasal, essentially visceroautonomic, motor system involving the anterior portions of the limbic forebrain has been delineated (Fig. 8.7). As in the case of the classical precentral somatic motor system discussed in Lecture 6, the mediobasal process operates by way of a circuit that alters the peripheral receptors from which signals for perceptual processing originate. These signals are conveyed by the B fiber system of visceral afferents (see, Prechtl & Powley 1990).

The relationship between visceroautonomic responsivity and familiarization was firmly established in the experiments (described earlier) in which control subjects rapidly habituated both visceroautonomic and behavioral responses to novel stimuli (within 3 to 10 trials) while monkeys with their amygdalas resected failed to show any visceroautonomic effects. These monkeys failed to habituate their behavioral responses, showing the visceroautonomic responses to be necessary to rapid habituation: Visceroautonomic activity serves to boost the memory process.

In another series of experiments, McGaugh (reviewed by McGaugh & Hertz, 1972) showed that amygdalectomy impaired memory consolidation in rats. In a

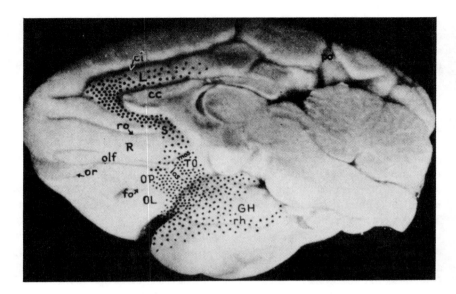

FIG. 8.7.   View of the mediobasal motor cortex (indicated by stippling) in monkey. Abbreviations: *cc*, corpus callosum; *ci*. cingulate sulcus; *fc*, fronto-orbital sulcus; *GH*, hippocampal gyrus; *IN*, insula; *L*, cingulate gyrus; *los*, lateral olfactory stria; *mos*, medial olfactory stria; *OL*, lateral orbital gyrus; *olf*, olfactory tract; *OP*, posterior orbital gyrus; *or*, orbital sulcus; *po*, parieto-occipital fissure; *R*, gyrus rectus; *rh*, rhinal fissure; *ro*, rostral sulcus; *S*, subcallosal gyrus; *TO*, olfactory tubercle. (From Kaada, 1951). From: Pribram, K. H. (1961). Limbic System. In D. E. Sheer (Ed.), *Electrical Stimulation of the Brain*, (pp. 311–320). Houston, TX; University of Texas Press.

task in which control rats remember not to jump into a mildly electrified grid having once done so, amygdalectomized rats jumped readily. Furthermore, it was shown that the amygdalectomy impaired adrenal visceroautonomic activity elicited by the behavioral task in normal subjects. Memory becomes consolidated when there is an event that arouses visceroautonomic activity. Behavioral habituation, familiarization, is thus likely due to the consolidation of memory of events experienced in a visceroautonomically arousing situation.

Habituation is fragile. The process is readily disrupted by head injury or distraction. Some of the factors governing distractibility such as pro- and retroactive interference are well known. Amygdalectomy and resections of forebrain systems related to the amygdala have been shown to increase susceptibility to distraction (Douglas & Pribram, 1969; Grueninger & Pribram, 1969). More on this shortly in the section on episodic processing.

In summary, the familiarization process is initiated and terminated by a stop to prior ongoing processing, an interrupt that begins and ends an episode. The episode is thus a demarcated period of stability within which the protocritic attributes of stimuli are processed. This allows valuation of the perception in terms of its relevance to the organism.

TOWARD A MODEL OF EPISODIC PROCESSSING

Whenever values are to be assigned to a process in a quantitative fashion, two attributes must be present: a reference and a unit of incrementation (Von Neumann & Morgenstern, 1953; Pribram, 1960, Sommerhoff, 1974). For instance, if we wish to describe the amount of heat in terms of temperature, we need a reference such as that provided by phase changes of water (the freezing and boiling points at appropriate atmospheric pressure), and also a unit of incrementation such as the degree Celsius that divides the range between the freezing and boiling points into 100 equal units (centigrades). For the model of episodic processing proposed here, an episode within which equivalence is achieved by familiarization can serve as the reference. The reference is demarcated by a destabilizing interrupt of prior ongoing processing (an orienting reaction) and ends with the next interrupt, which initiates a different processing episode. As reviewed, there is considerable evidence that the amygdala system is integral to this type of processing.

An episode is thus marked by the achievement of a temporary stability. Temporary stability is characterized by an inner shape, the structure of redundancy, of a processing holoscape. The holoscape of isovalent contours connecting equi-valent polarizations in the network of postsynaptic microprocesses is unique to the episode. Thus, when one is hungry, one notices restaurant signs by virtue of processing described by one particular contour map of the holoscape; when one needs to mail a letter, mailboxes are attended by virtue of processing described by another such contour map (Zeigarnik, 1972).

As the same distal stimulus situation may be involved, the difference in emphasis is due to the operation of the "mind's eye," a difference produced by the episode currently "motivating" the perceptual process (see e.g., Bruner & Postman, 1949; Hastorf & Kuntson, 1954). Despite considerable controversy regarding the experiments, the results produced the "new look" in perception in the 1950s.

Recall the experiment described earlier in which the same four cues were shown to monkeys but where, in different episodes, color or form were reinforced. Recall also that in these experiments, brain electrical activity reflected the previously reinforced cue (the effects of which were still "occupying" the monkey's brain and possibly his thoughts) while his behavior was correctly reflecting current reinforcing contingencies. These findings demonstrated the existence of operations independent of expressed behavior. Furthermore, these experiments showed that the cortex of the temporal lobe and not the primary sensory systems are critical to this operation. Posner (1973) showed how such "mind's eye" effects can be obtained in humans even in the absence of eye movement.

In terms of the holonomic brain theory, the holoscape of contours describing isovalent junctional polarizations would appear considerably different under the condition "mail a letter" from that mapped under the condition "hungry." Different configurations of values would display different hills and valleys on the polarization contour map. A simpler example would be attending to the color or form of a scene as in our monkey experiment. The pattern of isovalent contours produced by receptive fields responding to color and the pattern responding to form would be different, much as when one asks all those in a classroom to briefly raise their hands if they are wearing a red sweater and then asking those who are wearing glasses to raise their hands.

Thus, with regard to the units of incrementation (values given to polarizations of junctions in the dendritic microprocess) these units must describe the "distances" between domains of isovalent contours in each holoscape. The distance between domains is set in terms of the distances between the minimum uncertainty attainable in the entire processing space of domains.

In such a process, what characterizes familiarization? In the intact organism habituation of the visceroautonomic components of an orienting reaction occurs within 3 to 10 repetitions of the orienting stimulus. The orienting, distracting stimulus has perturbed a stable organization of redundancies (an organization, of context, of a processing space of domains, sometimes referred to as an apperceptive mass), which rapidly restabilizes. Originally, we thought these stabilities described states of equilibrium (Piaget, 1970; Pribram, 1958, 1969). The advent of Prigogine's descriptions of stabilities far from equilibrium offered a much richer model: Perturbations of equilibrium states could only lead to a return to equilibrium; perturbations of states far from equilibrium would lead to the potential for achieving novel states of temporary stability (McGuinness, Pribram, & Pirnazar, 1990; Appendix F).

The results of the experiments performed in my laboratory, which delineated the effects of amygdalectomy and resections made in related systems, can therefore be conceived as deficiencies in processing the temporary stabilities that define an episode (Pribram 1969, 1980a; Pribram, Reitz, McNeil, & Spevack 1979). The deficiency was shown to be related to an inability to properly process the structure of redundancy (Pribram 1969, 1987a; Pribram, Lim, Poppen & Bagshaw, 1966; Pribram & Tubbs, 1967. For a formal treatment of the structures of redundancy as "context" see Appendix C).

The thermodynamic considerations put forward by Prigogine (1980) regarding stabilities far from equilibrium are intriguing: Stabilities far from equilibrium are attractive; they operate as *attractors* toward which the process tends. Thus the episode, characterized by its temporary stability far from equilibrium, can act as an attractor during learning—in experimental psychology terms, it values the act by means of a reinforcing process. In the holonomic brain theory, this process is mediated by the protocritic (pain and temperature) system.

Often the neuropsychological system is actually operating close to equilibrium and perturbation is handled by a return to equilibrium: the distraction of an orienting reaction is either ignored or incorporated into the ongoing process through repetition and familiarization. However if the perturbation is great, a reaction we ordinarily call emotionally upsetting can result in turbulance and a new stability has to be achieved. When, as in the holonomic brain theory, the process is conceived to be composed of continuous functions, for example, as manifolds described by the Lie algebra, vortices can develop in the turbulent systems. Thus, an often realized possibility is to be "hung up" in the turbulance. But, because this is a state far from equilibrium, one can deliberately seek alternate constraints in order to change the state.

In his book *Design for a Brain* (1960), Ashby described an interesting and powerful method for dealing with turbulence, a method which leads to "catastrophic" restabilizations ("step functions"). In his computational model, stability was achieved by adding to the computation, numbers taken from a list of random numbers. Randomicity provides maximum variance, the widest spread of possible consequences (Miller, 1956). In a system with such a probability distribution there is also maximum possibility (potentiality) for new organizations to develop. As in Prigogine's model one cannot predict just how the system will restabilize because of the randomness injected into the turbulent system.

Ashby's and Prigogine's models have many things in common with the more recently developed thermodynamic models. Effective processing is achieved by a heuristic in which the addition of noise is important to preclude premature closure onto an overriding attractor.

However, as described in the final lecture, in intact organisms there is an alternative processing mode that leads to innovation which does not involve a catastrophic reaction. This mode utilizes equivocation, the sum of noise and redundancy. To achieve novel recombinations, the options provided by the "mind's eye" must be exercised. This is accomplished by selectively attending the variety of possibilities in a scene or, alternatively, through "envisioning" by virtue of memories of previous scenes as Beethoven did in composing while deaf. These options are provided by redundancies (formally described in Appendix D) that enhance effective processing of context and therefore constitute "structured" entropy (Gatlin, 1972; Shannon & Weaver, 1949). The isovalent contour maps of the holoscape describe the neural nature of this entropic structure.

Hinton and Sejnowski (1986) have developed a "hill climbing routine" that moves an element in a stepwise manner over such a contoured terrain. Processing proceeds perpendicular to the contours. In their model, "climbing" is actually down the mountain and is accomplished by random steps to the bottom of the mountain, when the "elasticity" of the process contracts the "line of climb" into the shortest path. This "moment of truth" may well describe the attainment of familiarity, the consolidation of an episode in memory (McGaugh, 1966; McGaugh & Hertz, 1972).

Hinton and Sejnowski's model can be usefully modified with respect to the data reviewed in this and the previous lecture. The process can be described as a matter of sharpening generalization gradients until separation between domains is achieved. The "moment of truth" is when the separation occurs. Hill "climbing" is replaced by a stepwise "steepening" of each gradient - by actually changing the shape of each hill, the generalization gradient, until each domain is clearly distinguished and specified.

In Summary: Perturbation, internally or externally generated, produces an orienting reaction which interrupts ongoing behavior and demarcates an episode. As the orienting reaction habituates, the weightings (values) of polarizations of the junctional microprocess become (re)structured on the basis of protocritic processing. Temporary stability characterizes the new structure which acts as a reinforcing attractor for the duration of the episode i.e., until dishabituation (another orienting reaction) occurs. The next two lectures describe how habituation leads to extinction and how an extinguished experience becomes reactivated i.e., made relevant. Innovating depends on such reactivation and is enhanced not only by adding randomness to the process, but also by adding structured variety produced by prior experience.

9

Irrelevance and Innovation: The Contributions of the Hippocampus and Limbic Forebrain to the Processing of Context

INTRODUCTION

What happens to sensory stimuli that have become habituated? Do they fail to influence perception and behavior? Many observations and experiments indicate that habituated sensory events, called *S delta* in operant behaviorism and *negative instances* in mathematical psychology, continue to shape the course of learning and, in general, to act as a contextual guide behavior.

In the process of achieving sensory discriminations, behavior toward the nonreinforced aspects of situation becomes extinguished in steps (see e.g., review by Pribram, 1986) as these aspects become habituated. Should the situation change, as when another aspect is reinforced (as in the experiments reviewed in the previous lecture), these cues are again noticed (spontaneous recovery). In fact they have been influential throughout the procedure serving as context, the "ground" within which a "figural" content becomes processed. The previous lecture has been concerned with the processing of content into context; the following experimental results concern the processing—and reprocessing—of context per se.

Whenever a situation changes, an orienting reaction occurs, previously habituated perceptions become dishabituated (Sokolov, 1963). The orienting reaction signals the perception of novelty, the perceived change in the situation. Perceived change can be generated internally—as when an organism becomes hungry. In such instances, "novel" perceptions—restaurant signs begin to populate the landscape—make relevant what had become irrelevant. Effort is expended, attention is "paid," and the familiar is experienced innovatively.

There is a great deal of confusion regarding the perception of novelty. In scientific circles, much of this confusion stems from the confounding of novelty with information. Shannon and Weaver (1949) introduced measures on information in terms of bits that reduced the amount of uncertainty in communication. Berlyne (1969) and others then suggested that bits of information and novelty were equivalently arousing, calling them collative variables. However, as will be detailed shortly, novelty in the sense used here, neither increases nor reduces the amount of uncertainty; rather it is due to a rearrangement of what is familiar. The skill in writing a novel resides not in providing information in the sense of reducing the amount of uncertainty in communication. Rather, the skill lies in portraying the familiar in novel ways, that is in new combinations. If the structure of a novel depended on increasing the amounts of information, *Reader's Digest* would not be in business. Nor is there a reduction in the amount of communicable uncertainty involved in the composition or production of a great piece of music. It is the arrangement and rearrangement of a theme that challenges composer and conductor; the manner in which to structure repetition: "Repetition, ah, there's the rub," exclaimed Leonard Bernstein in his comparison of musical composition to natural language (1976).

A definitive experiment that draws the distinction between novelty and measures of information (in Shannon's sense) was performed by Smets (1973). Smets used some of the same indicators of arousal as those used in our monkey experiments. He presented human subjects with a panel upon which he flashed displays, equated for difficulty in discrimination, differing either in the number of alternatives (bits) or in the arrangement of alternatives (orientations of lines) of a pattern. *Very little visceroautonomic activity was induced by varying the number of alternatives; by contrast the changes in arrangement evoked pronounced reactions.*

THE HIPPOCAMPAL SYSTEM

Innovation depends on an initial step, a process by which the familiar drops into background as current events produce orienting and habituation. But the earlier events remain available for renewed processing should demand arise. The floor, walls, and doors of a classroom are familiar objects; we are not aware of them. We walk through the door when class is over, failing to notice what we are perceiving while engaged in a discussion following the lecture. But, should an earthquake rearrange things, we become instantly aware of swaying floor and walls and head deliberately for the safety provided by the door's frame.

In the laboratory the process of familiarization is called *extinction*, and is demonstrated by a discrimination reversal procedure. Monkeys are trained to select one of two cues by consistently rewarding only one of the cues. After criterion performance (90% or better on 100 consecutive trials) is reached, the reward is shifted to the other cue. Ordinarily monkeys, after a few trials, stop selecting the now nonrewarded cue and proceed to select the now rewarded one.

The shift in behavior accelerates as the reversal is repeated. Response to the currently nonrewarded cue has been extinguished, but is rapidly reinstated once the situation demands it (Douglas & Pribram, 1969).

Hippocampectomy (i.e., removal of the entire hippocampal gyrus: hippocampus, and its surrounding subiculum and entorhinal cortex) radically alters this course of behavioral events. The hippocampus, a phylogenetically ancient cortex, is the other major anatomical structure lying within the medial portion of the temporal lobe. However, extinction (conceived as an extension of habituation) of the response to the now nonreinforced cue remains intact after hippocampectomy. And, not only do the hippocampectomized monkeys show normal *extinction*, the slope of *acquisition* of the currently appropriate response does not differ from that of the control monkeys.

What does occur is a long series of trials, which intervene between extinction and acquisition, during which the monkeys select cues at random. They receive a reward approximately 50% of the time, which is sufficient to keep them working (Pribram, Douglas & Pribram, 1969). There is no obvious event that pulls them out of this "period of stationarity"; quite suddenly the hippocampectomized monkeys resume the acquisition of more rewarding behavior. What goes on during the period of stationarity and what prolongs this period for monkeys who have had their hippocampal gyrus resected?

Explanation must rely on inference as there are currently no techniques for directly assessing what goes on during the period of stationarity. It is clear, however, that innovative rearrangement of the association between cue and reward must occurr and that this rearrangement must be perceived before it can be acted upon. Rearranging must be processed efficiently and appears to take effort (Pribram & McGuinness, 1975; Pribram, 1986b).

COGNITIVE EFFORT: EFFICIENCY IN PROCESSING NOVELTY

Removal of the hippocampal gyrus has also been shown to reduce the efficiency with which recombinations of analyzable stimulus attributes are processed. In an experiment in which we used a modified decision theory procedure, hippocampectomized monkeys were shown to be inordinately biased toward caution as compared with their controls (Spevack & Pribram, 1973). Recall that this result is the opposite from that obtained following resections of the inferotemporal cortex. Novelty entails risk and demands processing effort.

In the experiment in which we paired a novel cue with a cue that had previously been reinforced, monkeys with resections of the hippocampal gyrus performed as well as controls when the pairing was made with the cue that had been reinforced 70% of the trials during the training procedure. However, when the novel cue was paired with the cue that had been reinforced only 30% of the time, the monkeys with resections of the hippocampal gyrus chose the novel cue more often than did control monkeys. The processing of the previously less relevant cue had been inefficient when compared with that of controls (Douglas & Pribram, 1966). It can be important on a subsequent occasion to have processed not only what arouses interest, but also what is more generally experienced (latently learned).

The results of an additional experiment support the conclusion that, in the absence of a hippocampal gyrus, processing of the nonreinforced aspects of a situation becomes inefficient and that ordinarily such processing demands effort (in psychiatry this has been termed "listening with the third ear"). In one experiment monkeys had to choose a consistently rewarded cue from a set of nonrewarded cues. The number of nonrewarded cues influenced the performance of control monkeys, but not the performance of monkeys who had their hippocampus resected (Douglas, Barrett, Pribram & Cerney, 1969).

The findings are the same in rats. Gerbrandt & Ivy (1987), used X-irradiation technique to selectively kill hippocampal dentate granule cells still in the process of cell division in the first few days after a rat is born. Then, when the animals were adults, and tested in a standard radial-maze, using a radial maze they were found as were the controls, to systematically shift from arm to arm to find each of the 8 onetime food rewards on the 8 maze arms without repeating any choices. After each rat had cleaned out all the maze rewards, they were allowed to do what they wanted for another 15 minutes. At this point, since all reward arms had been visited, repeated visits to the reward depleted maze arms would start occurring. The findings were striking. Normal rats stopped visiting arms within 1 or 2 visits after they had cleaned out the maze. X-irradiated rats went on "forever".

The most critical evidence that the hippocampus is ordinarily involved in processing the nonreinforced rather than the reinforced aspects of a situation comes from an experiment in which we recorded electrical activity from the hippocampus while monkeys were performing discrimination tasks. In a go/no-go situation, the electrical activity (specifically, the amount of theta rhythm) was distinctly different during the go and no-go trials. When the cues were then presented simultaneously and the monkey had to select the consistently reinforced cue, we were greatly surprised to find that the hippocampal electrical activity was identical to that recorded on the no-go trials of the previous task (Crowne, Konow, Drake & Pribram, 1972). Again, as in the case of the electrical activity recorded from the inferotemporal cortex in the experiment described earlier, it is as if these systems were processing "don't look there" rather than "look-here."

The finding that hippocampal cells are involved in processing currently nonreinforced aspects of a situation provides a plausible explanation of Thompson's (Berger, Berry, & Thompson, 1986) results in classical "delayed" (4 sec) eyelid conditioning. Even before the behavioral indicator of conditioning appears, the distribution of hippocampal unit activity begins to form a pattern which is subsequently mirrored by the response pattern of the nictitating membrane. In my laboratory, Bagshaw and Copock (1968), using the galvanic skin response (GSR) found that over the initial conditioning trials, responses first became distributed away from the UCS, the unconditional response upon which they had been focused. As conditioning proceeded the shift continued until the responses more or less coincided with the appearance of the CS, the conditional stimulus. (This distribution and refocussing does not occur in amygdalectomized monkeys).

In classical conditioning the CS can be considered analogous to the unreinforced stimulus in the simultaneous discrimination. According to the data just reviewed, by virtue of operations performed by the amygdala system, the activity of hippocampal cells becomes distributed towards the CS, the unreinforced conditional stimulus. Once this has happened, the hippocampal pattern serves as a template or context within which the behavioral response is determined.

All of these situations have in common the fact that first the organism is responding to or has learnt to respond to a particular stimulus configuration which constitutes a figure, the content within a context. When the organism must shift responses to a novel figure, a novel content, *the original stimulus becomes a part of ground, context*. These shifts are not limited to instrumental responding. The effects are also observed when eye movements (observing responses) are recorded (Bagshaw, Mackworth, & Pribram, 1970a, 1970b, 1972).

Responding to context entails the risk of distraction and processing overload. Signal detection theory has developed techniques to measure perceptual risk, the bias with which an organism approaches a situation. As noted, using these techniques both inferotemporal and hippocampal resections were shown to shift bias, albeit in opposite directions (Pribram, Spevack, Blower, & McGuinness, 1980; Spevack & Pribram, 1973). Hippocampal resections shift bias toward caution; inferotemporal damage shifts bias toward risk.

Other investigators (see reviews of Amsel, 1986; Gray, 1982a, 1982b), using rats, have also demonstrated that hippocampectomy influences behavior in situations in which nonreinforcement plays an important role, especially when the now nonreinforced cues had been previously reinforced (frustrative nonreward). These authors note that the first step in discrimination learning is to anticipate reinforcement for responding (to either cue) and then to differentiate their responses to reinforced and nonreinforced cues. According to the results of our primate studies reviewed earlier, the amygdala is essentially involved in both of these initial steps. Hippocampectomy does not interfere with these primary aspects of learning (as example: go/no-go alternation, also called patterned alternation, remains intact after resections of the hippocampal formation in both monkeys and rats). By contrast, when a previously reinforced cue becomes "context", that is, the unreinforced element in a discrimination, hippocampectomized monkeys and rats fail to respond to changes in the number or position of these cues.

Taken together, the effects of amygdalectomy and hippocampectomy produce an organism deficient in composing a context (a containing text, a texture) within which events are made relevant. At times, such processing entails expending effort to efficiently recombine familiar and thus currently ignored events into contextual configurations perceived as novel.

RELEVANCE, DISTRACTION, AND THE LIMBIC FOREBRAIN

A patient (H. M., see Milner, 1959) with a bilateral resection of both his amygdala and hippocampus dramatically demonstrated these effects on familiarizing and innovating. When interviewed this patient appears normal, he answers questions readily, and adequately solve adequately the problems presented to him. The patient can accurately remember anything that happened before surgery had been performed on his brain. Furthermore, he can perform perceptual and motor skills that, through repetitive practice, he has learned since surgery. In fact, he shows no evidence of forgetting in any of these tasks. This is no different from what is found when monkeys with hippocampal resections are tested in this fashion. In one experiment, we trained monkeys on a visual discrimination, used them for other purposes, and then examined their retention 2 years later. Unoperated controls performed the first 100 trials at 80%–85% correct. Hippocampectomyized monkeys performed above 90% (92%–96%).

During an interview, however, once interrupted and distracted the patient fails to recall that the interrogation had taken place and even that he has ever seen the interrogator. In order to perform a daily task such as grocery shopping, he must carry a list (a common procedure for all of us but we are not totally lost as to what to do should we lose our list). In a procedure characterized by many interruptions, the patient failed to remember the contents of what he had experienced. "However, when the . . . procedure was modified in a manner that required [him] to focus on novelty, HM's . . . performance was above chance. These data suggest that HM's performance may reflect a heightened response on his part to the novel stimuli that [for him act as] distractors" (Freed, Corkin, & Cohen, 1987 p. 470).

As described in the previous lecture, familiarization and innovation occur within a processing space that defines an episode. Episodes provide the context within which perceptions are valued. Context (processing space) and content (stimuli sampled) interact in a reciprocal fashion. The nature of this interaction has been determined by using another set of tasks that have been called one trial learning or *trial unique tasks* (Mishkin, 1973; Nissen, 1951). Resections of the various anatomical structures that compose the limbic forebrain and its related frontal cortex and basal ganglia disrupt performance of these tasks while resections of the cortex of the posterior cerebral convexity do not. (Conversely, as reviewed in Lecture 7, resections of the cortex of the posterior cerebral convexity disrupt simple *sensory discrimination performances* dependent on stimulus sampling, whereas resections of the structures composing the frontolimbic forebrain do not.)

There are two basic forms of trial unique tasks, and there are also variations on these forms and combinations. The basic tasks are *delayed response* and *delayed alternation*. In the delayed response task a reward is hidden within sight of the monkey, an opaque screen is lowered and then raised after a period of 5 to 15 (or more) seconds, and the monkey is then allowed to find the reward. In the delayed alternation procedure rewards are hidden behind the opaque screen in two sites identical in appearance. The screen is raised and the monkey is allowed to find the reward. The screen is lowered for a period of 5 to 15 seconds and then raised, once more allowing the monkey to find the remaining reward. In order to find the reward on this trial, the monkey must adopt a win-shift strategy, that is, he must shift his response to the site other than the one in which he found the reward on the previous trial. For subsequent trials the reward is alternately hidden in the two locations while the screen is down.

Using the delayed response procedure, it was found that the distraction produced by the interference of the screen was the factor critically responsible for the disruption produced by resections of structures within the frontolimbic forebrain. When the delay was produced by darkening the test chamber instead of by lowering and raising a screen, monkeys with frontolimbic resections performed as well as their controls (Malmo, 1942; Pribram, 1961b; Pribram, Plotkin, Anderson, & Leong, 1977).

The difficulty produced by resections within the frontolimbic forebrain on the delayed alternation task has also been shown to be due to interference: when the delay between trials was equal irrespective of which location was baited, monkeys with frontolimbic resections failed the task; when the delay between trials was made unequal (e.g., 5 seconds when the left location was baited, 15 seconds when the right location contained the reward), monkeys with such resections performed as well as their controls (Pribram & Tubbs, 1967; Pribram, Plotkin, Anderson & Leong, 1977). It is well known that similarity is a powerful determinant of both pro- and retroactive interference. More on this in Lecture 10.

The delayed alternation task has two forms: a go-right, go-left, and a go/no-go version. These versions have been used to explore possible functional differences in various anatomical subdivisions of the frontolimbic forebrain (see Pribram, 1986b; 1987a for review). For example, hippocampectomy produces a deficit in the spatial (go-right, go-left) alternation task but not in the go/no-go version, nor, for that matter, in spatial, classical (go-right, go-left) delayed response. The studies by Kesner and diMattia (1987) on primacy and recency described in the previous lecture aid in understanding these hitherto unexplained results of hippocampectomy. In their studies hippocampectomy was shown to eliminate the primacy effect. Perhaps spatial alternation is more dependent on primacy while go/no go alternation and spatial delayed response in which trials are more clearly separated, are more dependent on recency. The fact that spatial cues are especially potent distractors (Douglas & Pribram, 1969) makes it plausible that primacy is more readily disrupted in tasks depending on successively alternating responses in two spatially very similar situations. As described earlier, hippocampal recordings indicate that in spatial tasks, the hippocampal theta rhythm reflects the no-go aspect of the task: thus extinction of the earlier (more primary) cue in the sequence of responding becomes the cue for the next response in the sequence.

A modification of the delayed response task, called the *indirect form* or the *delayed matching from sample* procedure, has also proved useful because it minimizes the spatial aspect critical to performance of the classical task. It has been further modified into a hybrid with delayed alternation. This hybrid is the *delayed nonmatching from sample* procedure. In both of these modifications the monkey is shown a cue, a screen is lowered for some seconds, and when it is raised the monkey confronts two cues, one of which is the previously sample shown. In the match from sample procedure, selecting the sample is rewarded, in the nonmatch from sample, selection of the novel cue is rewarded.

These modifications of the delay procedures also contain elements of sensory discrimination tasks. They have, therefore, proved useful in analyzing the functional relationships between the limbic and convexal portions of the temporal lobe of the brain. Just as the limbic part of the lobe is divided into amygdala and hippocampal formation, so is the convexal cortex of the temporal lobe divided into an anterior (polar) and a posterior part, which are functionally distinct (Fig. 9.1; Iwai & Mishkin, 1968; Pribram & Bagshaw, 1953; Pribram & MacLean, 1953). When objects are used in the nonmatching from sample procedure, resections of the anterior portion of the convexal cortex and of the amygdala produce severe deficits in performance, whereas resections of the posterior part of the inferotemporal cortex and of the hippocampal formation do not (Spiegler & Mishkin, 1981).

Mishkin interpreted these results to indicate that the anterior inferotemporal cortex and amygdala are involved in object-reward associations, which is consonant with the results of the series of experiments on the amygdala described earlier. As noted in Lecture 7, resections of the posterior portions of the inferotemporal cortex produce deficits best interpreted as a difficulty in stimulus sampling, for a number of reasons. First, in contrast to the effects of anterior inferior temporal lobe resections, the deficit in match and nonmatch to sample tasks is proportional to the difficulty of the task (see Mishkin, 1966 and Pribram, 1984 for review). In addition, as described earlier, when the monkeys had to choose one object out of a set of objects, stimulus sampling theory accounted quantitatively for differences in performance of the monkeys with the resections and their controls.

There are however indications that still another factor is involved in sampling,

Afferent connections   **Efferent connections**

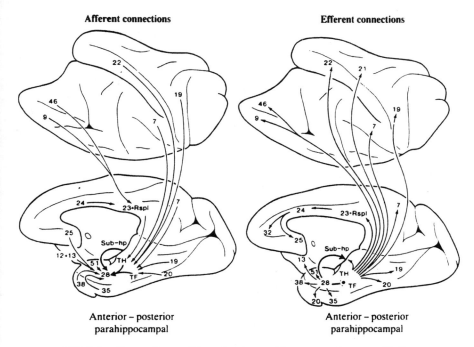

Anterior – posterior   Anterior – posterior
parahippocampal   parahippocampal

FIG. 9.1.   Connections of the primate parahippocampal gyrus with the neocortex (from Van Hoese, 1982). A medial view of the macaque brain is shown below, and a lateral view is shown inverted above. The hippocampus receives its inputs via the parahippocampal gyrus, areas TF and TH, and the entorhinal cortex, area 28. The return projections to the neocortex (shown on the right) pass through the same areas. (The hippocampus is behind area 28 in the diagram.) Cortical areas 19, 20 and 21 are visual processing areas, 22 is auditory processing cortex, 7 is somatosensory processing cortex, and 9, 46, 12 and 13 are frontal cortical processing areas. From: Rolls, E. (1989). The Representation and Storage of Information in Neuronal Networks in the Primate Cerebral Cortex and Hippocampus. In R. Dubrin, C. Miall, and G. Mitchison (Eds.), *The Computing Neuron* (pp. 125–159). Wokingham, England: Addison-Wesley.

a factor dependent on the functions of the hippocampal formation. Sampling, as shown in the Wilson study described in the previous lecture, proceeds as follows: Generalization gradients sharpen and this sharpening involves the setting of a baseline, an adaptation level. Once a baseline has been set, the nonreinforced aspects of the stimulus array must be gated (filtered) out, sharpening the focus on the reinforced aspect. In stimulus sampling theory this is accomplished one element at a time—and monkeys have been shown to learn visual discriminations in just this fashion (Blehart, 1966; Pribram, 1984). But, as described earlier, hippocampal resections have been shown to interfere with the monkeys' processing of these nonreinforced components of a situation, a result in many respects similar to that obtained after inferotemporal cortical resections in the multiple object study. Based on these results, an hypothesis can be formulated to the effect that it is likely that relevance (from the Latin *relevare*, to lift up), is often due to perceiving these nonreinforced, filtered events "in a new light." This hypothesis is basic to the model discussed in the last section of this lecture.

To summarize these results and their interpretation: Four distinct but interrelated processes are involved in perceiving an object as relevant. Each of these processes has been related to the functions of a separate system whose forebrain component lies in the temporal lobe of the brain. 1. The cortex of the posterior convexity of the lobe is involved in stimulus sampling. 2. The role of the amygdala of the medial portion of the lobe is to provide context by furnishing a familiar base. 3. Associations between objects and visceroautonomically arousing, reinforcing events are mediated by the cortex of the anterior (polar) convexity of the lobe. 4. The hippocampal formation furnishes the opportunity for perceiving novelty in processing the non-reinforced aspects of the situation.

The following relationships between these processes have been established. When novelty is experienced, sampling increases. In the absence of sampling, selection depends solely on object-reinforcement associations, which leads to stereotypy. In the absence of such associations, processing depends solely on the processing of novelty, which, as was shown by the eye movement and other experiments, can lead to much irrelevant exploration.

THE NEUROPHYSIOLOGY OF RELEVANCE

In his *Principles of Psychology* (1950), William James noted that values "color" perceptions giving them relevance. Relevance can be effected, he stated, either by operating through a separate brain system, or by utilizing the same pathways as those that organize perception. As we know now, both of James' possibilities are realized. The neuropsychological research reviewed in these lectures indicates that the limbic formations of the medial portion of the temporal lobe— amgdala and hippocampus—are critically involved in valuing perceptions. Valuation was shown to "relevate" percepts by way of inputs that deter or reinforce behavior. These inputs are routed to the limbic forebrain via a **separate set** of protocritic systems based on pain and temperature sensibility. In turn the limbic forebrain, including both amygdala and hippocampus are reciprocally connected with hypothalamic and mesencephalic brain stem nuclei. Corticopetal fibers from these nuclei exert widespread influence on the remainder of the forebrain (see Bloom, Lazerson, & Hofstadter, 1985 for review) and are therefore ideally situated to influence the same systems that process the sensory driven aspects of perception.

The hippocampal circuitry entailed in processing relevance involves three layers (much as in simulated PDP neural networks): the granule cell layer of the fascia dentata; the pyramidal cells of layer CA3; and those of layer CA1 (see Fig. 9.2). The granule layer receives an input from the upper layers of the entorhinal cortex which, in turn, is connected with temporal isocortical areas such as the inferotemporal. The signals from the granule layer inform layer CA3 and from there to layer CA1. One of the outputs of this layer is back to the deeper layers of the entorhinal cortex, thus completing the circuit.

Within this circuit, a "wipout" occurs due to basket cell activity in the layer. This wipeout occurs every few milliseconds—not just in the presence of input but even in its absence. Andersen (1975), points out that

A remarkable finding of all investigators using intracellular recording in the hippo-campal formation is the ubiquitous hyperpolarization associated with inhibition of

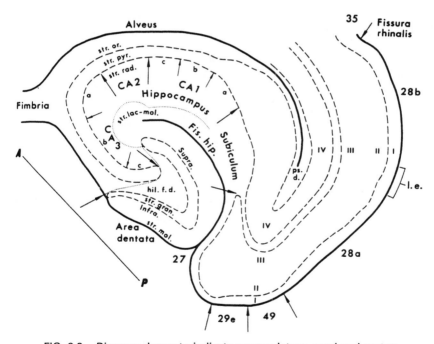

FIG. 9.2.   Diagram drawn to indicate nomenclature, areal and sector boundaries (long arrows), and subsector boundaries (short arrows). l.e., Transition zone between subareas 28b and 28a; ps.d., psalterium dorsale. From: Angevine, J. B., Jr. (1975). Development of the Hippo-campal Region. In R. L. Isaacson and K. H. Pribram, (Eds.), *The Hippo-campus Volume I: Structure and Development* (pp. 61–94). New York: Plenum.

cell discharge which follows excitation of the cell from all afferent sources studies so far . . . . This inhibition has a slightly longer latency than that of the excitation . . . and can be recorded as a baseline even with excitation (p. 430).

These inhibitory phenomena are reminiscent of those described in Lecture 6 for the cerebellum, whose architecture is also of a rather simple nature relative to the complexities of isocortex. However—and this is a second fact of interest—there are also differences in function. Despite the immediate inhibition produced by the hippocampal basket cells, Vinogradova (1975) has found (using extracellular recordings in the unanesthetized preparation) long-lasting changes (lasting several seconds) in the firing patterns of hippocampal neurons after afferent stimulation. Over half of these changes are in the direction of inhibition, but 40% of the cells show long-lasting excitation.

> How can we reconcile these two apparently contradictory findings—the intracellularly recorded inhibition and the extracellular recording of long-lasting inhibitory and excitatory changes? Although quantitative data are not available, it is plausible that the basket cell hyperpolarization builds slowly over successive inputs to the granular cell layer of the dentate gyrus. This could account for the progressive decrementing (habituation) of both the inhibitory and excitatory outputs recorded extracellularly. In the cerebellum the inhibitory reaction is immediate and overwhelming. It quickly wipes the "slate" clean between successive inputs. In the hippocampus hyperpolarization builds more slowly, necessitating a succession of inputs before output becomes blocked. Andersen's observations of a prolonged baseline of hyperpolarization are consonant with this view (Pribram and Isaacson, 1975, pp. 430–431).

These data suggest that the hippocampal circuitry serves as a buffer in which successive inputs are stored leading to extinction (output becomes blocked) unless there is a significant change in these inputs. Recall that these inputs include the protocritic aspects of sensory stimulation. Significant changes in such inputs produce two additional types of electrical activity that have been recorded from this circuitry. One type is a fluctuating polarization produced by a pair of generators of postsynaptic dendritic activity in the granular and CA1 layers at a frequency of 6–8 Hz. The generators are closely coupled and approximately phase reversed with respect to one another (see review by Winson, 1975). This theta type electrical activity is especially prominent during rapid-eye-movement sleep, and waking exploratory movement.

The other type of activity is irregular and related to either appetitive or approach-consumate behavior. Many cells "increase their rate of firing when the animal encounters a change in a previously explored environment. This increase in firing [is concommittant with behavioral orienting (or dishabituation) and results, for example,] from the presence of a novel object or the absence of a familiar one, and would lead to renewed exploration." (O'Keefe, 1986,

p. 82) Rats and monkeys are able to perform routine appetitive-approach-consumatory behaviors after hippocampal removals. Hippocampal activity reflects the "effort" entailed in "reviewing" or refreshing otherwise "irrelevant" situations.

O'Keefe and Nadel (1978) have proposed that hippocampal function reflects the construction of "cognitive maps" of previously explored and currently irrelevant environments. They emphasize that many hippocampal cells increase their activity when the organism encounters a change in a previously explored and therefore familiar *place*. Much of the evidence obtained by O'Keefe and Nadel and the evidence reviewed by them concerns the dorsal hippocampus. The input to the dorsal hippocampus is derived from the adjacent somatic sensory-motor areas of the cortex—thus *somatic* space, place, plays a major role in their findings. In the cat changes in familiar *visual* space produces a greater share of the responses produced in hippocampal cells.

In primates including humans, the dorsal hippocampus becomes vestigial. Visual and auditory signals to the remaining ventral hippocampus become the overwhelmingly significant inputs. Place remains important, but now more as a context for processing than as content. After bilateral resections of the hippocampal gyri, monkeys fail "spatial" delayed alternation tasks but not the go/no-go variants (Mishkin, 1954). This had led to an emphasis on the importance of place in processing delay tasks. However, as noted earlier, spatial delayed response performance remains intact after hippocampectomy. On the basis of the findings in other experiments that showed spatial cues to be potent distractors, and hippocampectomy to interfere with the primacy effect, the spatial deficit when it occurs can be interpreted to mean that after hippocampectomy there is sufficient interference between the highly similar (right-left) place cues in spatial alternation to prohibit the construction of a stable context within which the trial unique task can be properly performed.

TOWARD A MODEL OF INNOVATION

In order that sensory input become context, it must be available for processing. The form of availability is often referred to as a "representation" of that input. Landfield (1976) and O'Keffe, (an originator and strong proponent of the "cognitive map" interpretation of hippocampal function, 1986) note that the evidence precludes that such a map or representation of the environment can in any way be geometrically isomorphic with the environment represented. In keeping with the tenets of the holonomic brain theory, they suggest that the representation is of a holographic nature.

Attempts to gain an idea of the way in which an environment is represented in the hippocampus strongly suggest the absence of any topographic isomorphism between the map and the environment. For example, cells recorded next to each other in the CA1 pyramidal layer are as likely to have their major fields in different parts of the environment as in neighbouring parts. Furthermore, it appears that a small cluster of neighbouring pyramidal cells would map, albeit crudely, the entire environment. This observation, taken together with the ease that many experimenters have had in finding place cells with arbitrarily located electrodes in the hippocampus, suggests that each environment is represented many times over in the hippocampus, in a manner similar to a holographic plate. In both representation systems the effect of increasing the area of the storage which is activated is to increase the definition of the representation.

A second major similarity between the way in which information can be stored on a holographic plate and the way environments can be represented in the hippocampus is that the same hippocampal cells can participate in the representation of several environments (O'Keefe & Conway, 1978; Kubie & Ranck, 1983). In the Kubie and Ranck study the same place cell was recorded from the hippocampus of female rats in three different environments: an 8-arm radial maze, in which the animal was trained to retrieve pellets from each of the 8 arms without returning to a previously visited arm; an operant chamber, in which the animal was trained on a DRL 20 schedule; and a home box, where the female built a nest for herself and a litter of suckling pups. Each of the 28 non-theta cells had a place field in at least one of the environments, and 12 had a field in all three environments. The elevated radial arm maze enjoyed the greatest representation of cells with place fields (23 of 28), in contrast to the enclosed home box (17 of 28), and the operant chamber (15 of 28). There was no systematic relationship amongst the fields of the same neurone in the different environments. One can conclude that each hippocampal place cell can enter into the representation of a large number of environments, and conversely, that the representation of any given environment is dependent on the activity of a reasonably large group of place neurones.

The third major similarlity between the holographic recording technique and the construction of environmental maps in the hippocampus is the use of interference patterns between sinusoidal waves to determine the pattern of activity in the recording substrate (see Landfield, 1976). In optical holography this is done by splitting a beam of monochromatic light into two, reflecting one beam off the scence to be encoded and then interacting the two beams at the plane of the substrate. In the hippocampus something similar might be happening. . . . The beams are formed by the activity in the fibres projecting to the hippocampus from the medial septal nucleus (MS) and the nucleus of the diagonal band of Broca (DBB).

Pioneering work by Petsche, Stumpf and their colleagues (Stumpf, 1965) showed that the function of the MS and DBB nuclei was to translate the amount of activity ascending from various brainstem nuclei into a frequency modulated code. Neurons in the MS/DBB complex fire in bursts, with a burst frequency which varies from 4–12 Hz. Increases in the strength of brainstem stimulation produce increases in the frequency of the bursts but not necessarily in the number of spikes withing each burst (Petsche, Gogolak and van Zweiten, 1965). It is now widely accepted that this bursting activity in the MS/DBB is responsible for the synchronization of the hippocampal theta rhythm (O'Keefe, 1986, pp. 82–84).

The manner in which such a holographic-like process can operate was described by Pribram and Isaacson (1975) as follows:

> At the input layer (dentate and CA3), complex spike mechanisms are, according to Ranck's data, concerned with appetitive behaviors; at the ouput layer (CA1), they are concerned with "consummatory," "match-mismatch" processes. Ranck suggests that this difference results from a convergence at CA1 of (1) fibers from CA3 cells that are generally responsive in all appetitive situations with (2) fibers from other cells of CA3 that are active only when reinforcement occurs after an appropriate response. Neither appetitive nor consummatory behavior takes place when gross τ activity is being recorded. Attentional (search) and intentional (nonhabitual "voluntary" motor) processes are correlated with the generation of τ rhythms. In general, these processes involve reorganization of current brain states. Since τ rhythms are also found during REM sleep, there is a suggestion that reorganization can also occur during sleep (Winson, 1975).
>
> Pribram (1971) has distinguished the organization of appetitive-consummatory and other well-ingrained habitual behaviors which depend on the basal ganglia (and the nigrostriatal system) from attention-intentional behaviors which depend on the hippocampal and cerebellar circuits for their controlling operations. Isaacson (1974) emphasized the same distinction by attributing instinctive and well-trained behaviors to the basal ganglia and associated brain stem systems. Appetitive-consummatory and habitual behaviors are regulated primarily by closed-loop, homeostatic, feedback mechanisms. Attentional and intentional behaviors are characterized by parallel processing, open-loop, feedforward control systems. Habituation can be conceived as a change from an "or" gate state (in which responses of complex spike cells are activated by any of a variety of inputs occurring at different times) to an "and" gate state (in which a response depends on the convergent action of inputs). Essentially this means that in the presence of τ cell inhibitory activity, the complex spike channels are kep independent of each other. The system is maximally sensitive. Input systems can therefore act in parallel.
>
> The suggestion emerges that the hippocampus functions to determine whether appetitive-consummatory processes should proceed in their habitual manner or whether novel, unfamiliar inputs have occurred which must be attended to. If they have occurred, behavior must become intentional—i.e., programmed to evaluate new conditions. In such cases, attention must be given to a variety of novel inputs which do not directly relate to familiar appetitive-consummatory processes.
>
> The hippocampus can be conceived to compute in fast time—i.e., ahead of what occurs in real time—the likelihood that an appetitive-consummatory act can be carried to completion, given current environmental conditions. If that likelihood is high, the operation in the hippocampal desynchronized mode will continue, and the

hippocampus will be relatively insensitive to new input since it is operating in the "and" gate state. If the likelihood is low because of some novelty has been sensed, the activity of the hippocampus will be switched to the "or" gate mode, it will become sensitive to input, and attentional and intentional behavior will become manifest (Pribram and Isaacson, 1975, pp. 432–433).

O'Keefe comes to a somewhat similar conclusion:

> . . . The theta mechanism acts to "gate" the firing of cells in the hippocampus. Examination of the firing patterns of both the theta cells and the place cells shows that they exhibit considerable phase-locking to the EEG theta rhythm. The primary difference between the two classes of neurons is that the theta cells will fire in this pattern whenever the theta rhythm occurs, regardless of the animal's position in the environment. The place cell, on the other hand, will only become synchronized to the theta pattern when the animal is in the place field of that neurone.
>
> Ranck, Fox and their colleagues have been studying the relationship between hippocampal theta and the firing patterns of the two cell types in a careful systematic way. They find that all cell types in the hippocampus tend to fire at a particular phase of the theta cycle (although not necessarily the same phase), and that the excitability of these cells (the ease with which they can be activated by an afferent input) also varies with the theta cycle. The theta mechanism then, acts as a gate which defines the ponit in time during which an input to the cell can activate that cell (Fox, Wolfson, & Ranck, 1983).
>
> The second important piece of information about the theta mechanism stems from the work of Vanderwolf, Whishaw, Robinson and their colleagues. They have suggested that there are two different theta systems, which relate to different aspects of the animal's behaviour and which are sensitive to different drugs. The first theta occurs when an animal runs, swims, sniffs, rears, or otherwise explores its environment; the second theta occurs during the same behaviours and, in addition, in response to arousing or alerting stimuli in an animal such as the rabbit, but under less clearly defined circumstances in the rat. . . .
>
> If there are two independent theta mechanisms, and they each act as gates which determine the time period when afferents to a section of the hippocampus can activate the cells in that section, then the simultaneous operation of these two systems would act as a kind of logical AND gate, whose properties depended on the interactions between the two systems. Only when the two theta waves had the correct phase relationship would a particular set of afferents have preferential access to a particular cell. Following Landfield, I suggest that the direct non-movement theta input acts as a reference beam, while the indirect (via the entorhinal cortex) movement-related theta acts as a reflected beam, i.e. as a carrier signal, which has superimposed on it the amplitude and phase relations representing the sensory information in the entorhinal cortex (O'Keefe, 1986, pp. 84–86).

However, it is not necessary to conceive of the two theta rythms in terms of reference beams and "carriers" of information. A complex interference pattern can use any one of its inputs as a "reference" for the other(s) (Leith, 1976; Pribram, Nuwer, & Baron, 1974). What is entailed in this instance is the creation of a reference context. In the holoscape this context is formed by the coefficients of interference determined by the sinusoids of the two theta rythms modulated by the probability amplitudes of the activities of the complex spike cells. Computations depend on changing values or weights of these polarizations on the basis of mismatch signals. These result when the output layer generates something other than what the input layer is programmed to accept.

In PDP neural network simulations, computations were undertaken primarily to model the learning process. They are however, also relevant to modelling the cognitive aspects of perception because these aspects are largely due to learning. A computational model of brain processes that operate to value perceptions is therefore feasible.

When Hopfield (1982) described his network and Hinton and Sejnowski proposed the "Boltzmann" engine as a model of learning, the proposals immediately struck a responsive chord. As described, Pribram and McGuinness, 1975, had considered the functions of the hippocampus and related systems in terms of the concept of cognitive "effort," effort conceived as a measure of the degree of efficiency with which processing is proceeding (Fig. 9.3; McGuinness & Pri-

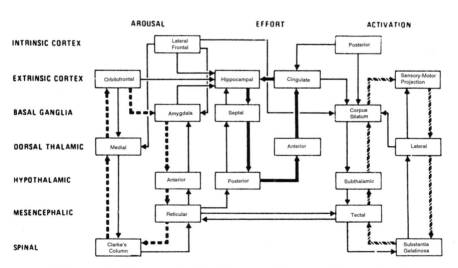

FIG. 9.3.   A highly oversimplified diagram of the connections involved in the arousal-familiarization (amygdala), activation-readiness (basal ganglia), and the effort (hippocampal) circuits.

bram, 1980; Pribram, 1986b; Pribram & McGuinness, 1975, 1990). The concept of efficiency is the basis of the second law of thermodynamics as formulated by Boltzmann (1886/1974). The thermodynamically based models should therefore, in some fashion, be able to formally describe the functions of the amygdala and hippocampus and related systems.

The potential for modelling is greatly enhanced by the modification of the Hopfield model proposed in the introductory lectures. The original model described energy minima as Hamiltonians. As noted, in our own work (Barrett, 1969) we also initially modelled brain functions in terms of Hamiltonians created by interference patterns: The cortex was conceived to be operating as an interferometer.

The current modification in terms of the holonomic brain theory deals with a Hilbert space of Gabor elementary functions, in which Hamiltonian operators are the vectors. Correlations are carried out by taking the inner products of the vectors. The Gabor functions are considered to be quanta of information, entropy minima, not energy (intensity) minima. In the brain, these functions describe channels, functional receptive field modules.

The Gabor channel is capacity-limited, and describes the minimum uncertainty, the minimum entropy with which a unit of information can be transmitted. The holonomic brain theory generalizes the Gabor relation to describe a multidimensional manifold. This manifold describes a competence of potential minima. Competence is entropic, its entropy defined (Lecture 2) as potential information. In keeping with the thermodynamic model, maximum efficiency (in its use as a communication engineering and processing concept) is attained not by pushing each Gabor relation to its unique minimum but by "innovatively" modifying the ensemble of Gabor relations until the ensemble computes with maximum efficiency. A likely possibility for doing this is altering bandwidth (see experiment by Caelli reported in Lecture 2). Appendix F is an initial attempt at providing the holonomic brain theory with a formal model of innovation.

10 Envisioning Proprieties and Priorities; Practical Inference: The Far Frontal Cortex as Executive Processor

Sensory experience presupposes . . . an order of experienced objects which precedes that experience and which cannot be contradicted by it, though it is itself due to other, earlier experience (Hayek, 1952, p. 172)

INTRODUCTION: AN EXECUTIVE PROCESSOR

This final lecture addresses the issue of an executive processor, a brain system that directs and allocates the resources of the rest of the brain. Whether concern centers on "mental faculties" (Gall & Spurtzheim, 1809/1969); "the society of mind" (Minsky, 1986); "the social brain" (Gazzaniga, 1985); or the systems analysis presented in these lectures, there are occasions that demand executive intervention. Ordinarily, input from sensory or internal receptors preempts allocation (for discussion see e.g., Miller, Galanter, & Pribram, 1960) by creating a "temporary dominant focus" of activation within one or another brain system (for review, see Pribram, 1971, pp. 78–80). However when input competition, incompleteness, or ambiguity place extra demands on the routine operations of allocation, envisioning proprieties and priorities, and practical inference become necessary. Proprieties must be evaluated, priorities must be ordered and practicalities assessed.

The anterior portions of the primate frontal lobe of the cerebral hemispheres (often called pre- or far frontal) are critical to such executive functions. With regard to perception, ambiguity, incompleteness, and competition among inputs present unique opportunities to study these frontal lobe executive processes. Often the perceiver is unaware that these processes are occurring—thus such terms as "unconscious inference" have been used to describe them (Helmholtz,

1909/1924; Rock, 1983). On other occasions, however, awareness accompanies processing and is experienced as envisioning probable or at least possible resolutions of the ambiguity, incompleteness, or competition (Cohen, 1959; Teuber, 1964; Ricci & Blundo, 1990).

ANATOMICAL CONSIDERATIONS

The far frontal cortex is surrounded by systems that, when electrically excited, produce movement and visceroautonomic effects. On the lateral surface of the frontal lobe lies the classical precentral motor cortex whose functions were discussed in Lecture 6. On the mediobasal surface of the lobe lie the more recently discovered "limbic" motor areas of the orbital, medial frontal and cingulate cortex (Kaada, Pribram, & Epstein, 1949; Pribram, 1961a). It is therefore likely that the functions of the far frontal cortex are, in some basic sense, related to these somatomotor and visceroautonomic effects.

At the same time, the far frontal cortex derives an input from the medial portion of the thalamus, the n. medialis dorsalis. This part of the diencephalon shares with those from anterior and midline nuclei (the origins of the input to the limbic cortex) an organization different from that of the projections from the ventrolateral group of nuclei to the cortex of the convexity of the hemisphere.

The thalamus is a three-dimensional structure, whereas the cortex is (from the standpoint of thalamic projections) essentially a two-dimensional sheet of cells. Thus, the projections from thalamus to cortex must "lose" one dimension. When one plots the precisely arranged "fan" of projections from each thalamic nucleus, one can readily determine which dimension is eliminated.

With regard to the projections from the anterior nuclear group and the n. medialis dorsalis, the anterior-posterior dimension is eliminated. An anterior-posterior file of cells in the thalamus projects to a single locus of cortex. Thus, for example, one finds degeneration of such an extended row of thalamic cells ranging from the most anterior to the most posterior portion of the n. medialis dorsalis after a resection limited to the frontal pole (Pribram, Chow & Semmes, 1953).

With regard to the ventrolateral group of nuclei, the situation is entirely different. Here the anterior-posterior dimension is clearly maintained: The front part of a nucleus projects to the forward parts of the cerebral convexity; as one proceeds back in the thalamus the projections reach the more posterior portions of the cortex, curving around into the temporal lobe when the projections of the pulvinar are reached. On the other hand, a file of cells extending, more or less, dorsoventrally (but angled somewhat laterally from its medial edge) projects to a single locus on the cortex (Chow & Pribram, 1956).

This distinction between the anterior and medial nuclei, on the one hand, and the ventrolateral group of nuclei, on the other, is supported by the fact that the

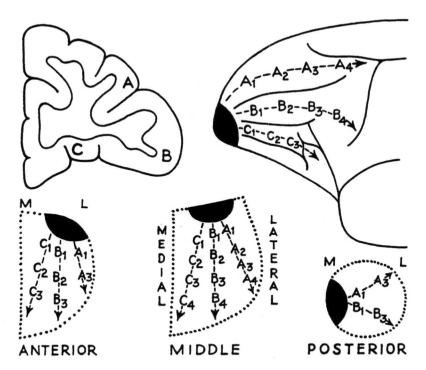

FIG. 10.1.   Diagrammatic representation of the nuclear origin and cortical termination of the projections of the n. medialis dorsalis in monkey, demonstrating the axial arrangement from eccentric core to periphery in anterior, middle, and posterior sections of the nucleus and corresponding cortical axes extending caudally from the frontal pole. From: Pribram, K. H., Chow, R. L., & Semmes, J. (1953). Limit and Organization of the Cortical Projection from the Media Thalamic Nucleus in Monkey. *The Journal of Comparative Neurology, 98*(3), 433–448.

internal medullary lamina separates the two classes of nuclei. Clearly, therefore, we should seek commonality among the functions of the anterior, far frontal parts of the cortex and the limbic formations (Pribram, 1958a, 1958b).

The close anatomical relationship of the far frontal cortex to the limbic medial forebrain is also emphasized when comparative anatomical data are reviewed. In cats and other nonprimates, the gyrus proreus is the homologue of the far frontal cortex of primates. This gyrus receives its projection from the midline magnocellular portion of the n. medialis dorsalis. This projection covers a good share of the anterior portion of the medial frontal cortex; gyrus proreus on the lateral surface is limited to a narrow sliver. There appears to have been a rotation of the medial frontal cortex laterally (just as there appears to have occurred a rotation medially of the occipital cortex—especially between monkey and man) during the evolution of primates.

THE WHAT, WHEN, AND HOW OF PROCESSING

From these physiological and anatomical considerations it appears likely that the far frontal cortex is concerned with relating the motor functions of the limbic to those of the dorsolateral convexity. This relationship has been expressed by Deeke et al. (1985) in terms of the what, when, and how of action.

Deeke et al. (1985) concluded an extensive review of their own studies of the organization of the entire human frontal cortex as follows: The orbital cortex becomes involved when the question is what to do; the lateral frontal cortex becomes active when the question is how something is to be done and the dorsal portions of the lobe mediate when to do it. With regard to perceptual processing as discussed in these lectures, "what" translates into propriety; "how" into practicality and "when" into priority. But, as will be described shortly, envisioning what to do when also involves where.

On an anatomical basis, as well, the far frontal systems have been shown to comprise three major divisions (see Pribram 1987a, 1990 for review): One, an orbital, is derived from the same phylogenetic pool as, and is reciprocally connected with, the amygdala (and other parts of the basal ganglia such as the n. accumbens, which have been shown to be involved in limbic processing). As might be predicted from the role of the amygdala in familiarizing, in deja and jamais vu phenomena, this orbital system augments and enhances sensitivities based on episodic processing. As described later, the result is envisioning, on the basis of familiarity with a situation, whether it is appropriate for further processing and possible action.

The second, a dorsolateral system, is derived from the same root as, and has connections with, the hippocampal system which includes the limbic medial frontal-cingulate cortex. As might be expected from the involvement of the hippocampus in recombinant processing—- in innovation—- the dorsal far frontal system controls the ordering of priorities to ensure effective action. A distinction must here be made between efficient (hippocampal) and effective (dorsolateral frontal) processing.

The following example illustrates the fact that sometimes efficiency has to be sacrificed if actions are to be effective. Recently I was engaged in a major move of my home and laboratory. Each day I would plan the most efficient route to minimize energy expenditure in making the rounds from office to various banking institutions, real estate companies and post offices only to find delays in processing, interfering interruptions, or just plain mismanagement. In order to actualize priorities, appointments had to be reshuffled, efficiency scuttled, and extra energy expended. Shifting flexibly among priorities according to their demands proved exhausting at times. The burden of overload came from coping with the overabundance of varieties context, not of information to be processed as is often supposed. Information can be chunked and, as will be developed shortly, chunking markedly enhances the competence of information processing. What remains to be investigated is how to envision effective processing of conflicting, ambiguous, or an overabundant variety of contexts without unduly impairing efficiency.

The third, a ventrolaterally located system has strong reciprocal connections with the posterior cerebral convexity. It is this system that involves the far frontal cortex in a variety of sensory-motor modalities when sensory input from the consequences of action incompletely specifies the situation. In such situations practical inference becomes necessary.

KRONOS AND KAIROS: THE DECISIVE MOMENT

Processing proprieties, priorities, and practicalities involves the far frontal systems in processing covariance, which is the basis for structuring episodes. As is reviewed in this lecture, episodic processing entails the structuring of redundancy in terms of covariations among more or less regularly recurring events to establish a context within which further processing procedes.

By contrast, as noted in earlier lectures, the systems of the posterior cortical convexity were shown to be involved in processing invariants, which results in the perception of prototypical object-forms.

Processing covariance results in episodes within which place and time keeping poses considerable difficulty. Which present did you unwrap first last Christmas, the one from John or the one from Mary? And which did you pick from the right and which from the left of the tree?

Covariation has posed special difficulties with respect to an understanding of time. Our common conception of time, based on successions of prototypical object-forms in space-time, was called "Chronos" by the classical Greeks. However, they recognized another form of time, "Kairos," which concerns the experiencing of an appropriate moment, a moment that may be characterized by an event or by its timelessness. The subjective aspects of Kairos were described by Bergson (1922/1965) in terms of "duré"—a duration that is not readily measured in chronological time. In his doctoral dissertation, Ornstein reviewed his own and others' experiments on the *Experience of Duration* (which in its published version was changed by sales minded editors to *The Experience of Time*, 1969).

The cyclic, redundant nature of processing recurrent regularities provides an hypothesis for understanding the experience of Kairos: the time being right, the decisive moment. An event in an episode is delineated when correlations are established by coherences among cycles, that is, between the contexts within which the event occurs. The duration of the event and its relation to other events in the episode are determined by the duration of coherences and correlations.

A technique that has been successfully used to probe the event-structure of Kairos is to ask a subject to recall the serial position of an event (item) previously experienced. The next section describes the results of studies on serial position and the factors that control perception in terms of relative recency.

COVARIATION AND EPISODIC COHERENCE

In addition to its demarcation by successive orienting reactions, a defining attribute of an episode is that what is being processed coheres—processing must deal with covariation. However, covariation can lead to interference, thus resulting in the inability to order processing stages. Recall that primacy and recency effects were impaired with amygdala and hippocampal damage (Lecture 8). With far frontal damage, monkeys show impairment in processing the latter part of the middle of a series. This impairment is attributed to increased pro- and retroactive interference among items in the series (Malmo & Amsel, 1948).

The impairment is also shown by patients with damage to their frontal cortex. These patients fail to remember the place in a sequence in which an item occurs: The patients lose the ability to "temporally tag" events, that is, to place them within the episode. With such patients, Milner (1974, see also Petrides & Milner, 1982) performed a series of experiments demonstrating how the processing impairment affects the middle portions of an episode. In her studies, it is *relative recency*, the *serial position* of covarying experiences, that becomes muddled. Other patients with fronto-limbic damage are described by Kinsbourne and Wood (1975). In keeping with the proposals put forward in the remainder of this lecture, they interpret the impairment in processing serial position as due to a derangement of the context that structures an episode.

Fuster (1988) conceptualized this context-content relationship in terms of cross temporal contingencies. Relative recency, for instance, implies that a temporal context exists within which recencies can be relative to one another. However, as indicated by experimental results in which spatial context is manipulated, as in variants of object constancy tasks (Anderson et al., 1976) the context-content relationship can be spatiotemporal as well as temporotemporal. In fact, in other experiments (Brody & Pribram, 1978; Pribram, Spinelli, & Kamback, 1967) and in the later sections of this lecture, data are presented indicating far frontal involvement whenever perception (or behavior) is influenced by two or more distinct sets of covarying contingencies, even when both are spatial.

More generally, therefore, far frontal cortex becomes implicated whenever perception entails relating current contingencies to a context computed from prior relevant contingencies, that is, an episodic context. The computation of this covariation demands that cross temporal, spatiotemporal, and cross spatial contingencies be perceived. In classical and operant conditioning, the consequences of behavior are contiguous in time and place with the stimulus conditions that initiate the behavior. Contiguity determines the episode or the conditioning "trial." When contiguity is loosened, stimulation that intervenes between initiation and consequence has the potential to distract and thus to prevent the processing of covariation. Perception is perturbed and processing is destabilized. Perturbation is controlled only if a stable state, an established context, instructs and directs the process.

INTERFERENCE

It is from the effects of interference on the establishment of such a stable state that one is able to discern the powerful role of context in controlling trial unique, episodic processing. When the interfering effect of distractors is removed (e.g., by darkening the testing chamber) during trial unique tasks such as delayed response, monkeys with far frontal resections perform the task as well as their controls (Malmo, 1942; Pribram 1961b; Pribram, Plotkin, Anderson, & Leong, 1977). The effects of interference occur primarily during stimulus presentation or shortly thereafter, not during the delay period (Pribram, 1961b; Stamm, 1969). Interference therefore is with the organization of a perceptual context within which subsequent performance occurs.

A personal example illustrates what is involved. When I first tested chimpanzees on the delayed response task using long delays, I found myself unable to remember the moment when the screen was to be lifted—until I made the mental image: "Open it when the second hand reaches 40" (or 55" or wherever it would be when the appropriate time had elapsed). From then on I had no difficulty: Recourse to this simple form of envisioning had solved the problem. Monkeys and chimpanzees often use a similar technique in performing this task. Their job is place rather than time keeping (note, however, that I also changed my task to placekeeping—envisioning the location of the minute hand of the watch). The animals would tap the correct side of the testing box or turn somersaults in the correct direction for awhile at the beginning of the delay period and then do other things until the screen was lifted when they would perform correctly. It is the efficacy of envisioning, of constructing a coherent imaginative context, that defines the episode and minimizes interference from subsequent distraction.

Difficulty in establishing a controlling context is also seen in the multiple object experiment described in Lecture 8. In this experiment monkeys were asked to find one object where location was randomized over 12 possible positions under which a peanut had been hidden in a well. The number of objects increased from 2 to 12, a novel object being added whenever the monkey attained the criterion of 5 correct (rewarded) responses. Recall that the monkeys with bilateral resections of the inferotemporal cortex showed deficiencies in sampling the range of objects, a deficiency due to a failure to bias their choices against objects that had been rewarded in previous sessions. One of the control groups in this study had received bilateral resections of the far frontal cortex. This group of monkeys showed no abnormality in sampling (compared to an unoperated control group), but did show a retardation of reaching criterion performance once the correct object had been identified. These monkeys would often make 4 successive correct responses only to stray to another object (or several) before returning to the correct choice (Pribram, 1960). The reinforcing contingencies had been ineffective in establishing a context for controlling the behavior of the monkeys with far frontal cortex removals.

During performance of trial unique tasks the presence and absence of reinforcers (and deterrents) gives structure to the experiences that occur within familiar and potentially innovative episodes. Such structures form an instructional context within which input serves as content. (Pribram, 1963, 1971, 1980b). Instructions linguistically initiated in the case of humans, instructions initiated by scheduled reinforcers in the case of monkeys, are insufficiently processed into a controlling context (Pribram, 1961b) when the far frontal cortex becomes damaged.

In one experiment the hypothesis that frontal damage interferes with the contextual ordering of perceptual experience was tested directly: A failure of contextual control should account for the failure of monkeys with far frontal lesions to perform adequately in other "trial unique" tasks such as delayed alternation. Perhaps for a frontally damaged monkey the required alternation appears much as does mareseatoatsanddoeseatoats to us. Try these:

INMUDEELSARE
INCLAYNONEARE
INPINETARIS
INOAKNONEIS

Proper perceptual (as well as behavioral) performance depends on a guiding context. An ABABABABAB alternation may be near the limit of a normal monkey's ability to contextualize; and with damage to the far frontal cortex, beyond this ability. However, by providing them with a *cognitive prosthesis*, a substitute for the missing process, monkeys with resections of the far frontal cortex ought to be enabled to perform adequately. This substitute was provided by changing the ordinarily symmetric delay interval between trials (i.e., between A and B and between B and A) to unsymmetrical (i.e., 5 sec between A and B vs. 15 sec between B and A). This change, by introducing a contextual "time tag," resulted in immediate remediation of the difficulty: the lesioned monkeys performed as well as their controls (Pribram, Plotkin, Anderson, & Leong, 1977; Pribram & Tubbs, 1967; Rosenkilds, Rosvold, & Mishkin, 1981).

PROPRIETIES: UTILIZING CONTEXT

A series of patients illustrates the manner in which context can fail to be effective. After recovering from the acute effects of frontal lobe damage, a patient was picked up at the hospital by his wife. She had bought a new dress for the occasion. The patient did not recognize her as the person with whom he had lived these many years. Instead he claimed that his former wife had introduced him to this new lady and a totally new family—and despite his injury, they lived happily ever after. This syndrome of fractionated episodic processing is called *paramnesia* (Stuss & Picton, 1978).

Another patient, this one with an extensive gunshot injury to his frontal lobe, illustrates what occurs when disruption is less severe. This patient had been coming to Teuber's clinic at Bellevue Hospital in New York every Thursday for testing and rehabilitation. In mid-November, the patient was told not to come the following Thursday because it was Thanksgiving day and no one would be in the clinic. When Thanksgiving arrived the patient told himself while dressing, "Today is Thanksgiving, I was told not to go to the clinic, no one will be there". He kept telling himself this as he left the house, and as he walked all the way to the hospital. He knocked on the door of the clinic; no response. As he turned to go home he exclaimed "See, I told you no one would be there."

Another patient in a hospital in Moscow was given tests in which she had to execute a series of instructions: Put your right index finger on the tip of your nose, then on the lobe of your left ear, and finally touch your other index finger. The patient could ordinarily accomplish such a series once, but if she were asked to perform several different sequences, she would fail miserably, usually repeating one act over and over. At the same time she might exclaim, "Oh that's not right" (Luria, Pribram & Homskaya, 1964). When other patients with frontal lobe damage were tested, a distinction between being able to identify errors and to utilize them effectively became obvious (Konow & Pribram, 1970). A similar experience was reported after a frontal leukotomy by a patient studied by Freeman and Watts (1942). This patient remarked, "Now that I have done it, I can see that it was not the right thing to do, but beforehand I couldn't say whether or not it would be right." This occurred despite the fact that he had often experienced similar situations. The patient insightfully reported his difficulty in envisioning the propriety of what he was doing.

PRIORITIES: THE BEST OF WELL LAID PLANS

Envisioning proprieties often entails specifying intended achievements. Searle (1983) distinguished between prior intentions and intentions-in-action, a distinction similar to one made by Miller, Galanter, & Pribram, (1960) in terms of strategies and tactics. Searle based this distinction on the following fictitious tale:

A woman in the throes of an affair wishes to put out a contract to have her husband done away with. She finds a thug willing to carry out the dastardly act, but he needs to be shown the territory in which the action is to take place. The woman drives the thug to her husband's place of work and their house, but is flustered and upset: She is not acustomed to premeditated murder. Just as she turns the corner to the street her house is on, a pedestrian dashes across the road and is stricken by her car. He dies. It is her husband. Is the woman guilty of murder or manslaughter? Searle argued (and American courts would undoubtedly uphold him) that the woman is not guilty of murder because murder was not her intention-in-action (only her prior intention). Incidentally, legally both the woman's and the thug's motivations are also irrelevant: Her motivation was love and his the acquisition of money, which are both laudable motives in our culture (see Miller, Galanter, & Pribram, 1960).

Intentions-in-action implement images of achievement as discussed in Lecture 6. By contrast, the patients just described have great difficulty either in constructing or utilitizing prior intentions due to a lack of an effective context directing "what to do where and when," before a serially ordered action is undertaken.

Prior intentions serve as contexts within which to achieve. These contexts sketch out the intended achievement, much as military strategies sketch out a particular intended action. Tactics, intentions-in-action, are left to field commanders to carry out, subject to immediate contingencies. Prior intentions or strategies, are envisioned whenever processing within an episode becomes so demanding that action cannot begin. The next section deals with the way in which far frontal lobe function aids in meeting the challenge to order posed by such demands.

PRACTICALITIES: CONTEXT - CONTENT RELATIONSHIPS

The context provided by propriety and priority becomes composed by virtue of the consequences of actions (praxis). As described in Lecture 6, action is driven by the environmental load placed on the somatomotor system. Environmental load must be perceived and is, therefore, in turn driven by sensory input. It is the connections of the midportions (ventrolateral) of the far frontal cortex with the somatic and other sensory-motor systems that makes possible processing of the consequences of actions.

Included in such processing are acts such as looking to see (observing responses), listening to hear, touching to feel, sniffing to smell, and oral sampling to taste. Based on motor-sensory reciprocity, these are perceptual acts.

Whenever the consequences of such perceptual acts incompletely specify a percept, assessment of practicalities entails inference. "Practical" inference must be distinguished from inference based on formal logical procedure. Practical inference has, therefore, been called *unconscious inference* (Helmholtz, 1909/1924; Rock, 1983), although the perceiver may, on occasion, be aware of attentional and other factors involved. More on this momentarily.

Assessing practicalities devolves on a procedure in which prior consequences have established a context within which the current contents of perception are processed. In this section evidence is presented that separate brain systems have been identified to process context and content and how these systems interact.

Evidence for the role of the far frontal cortex in establishing relations between perceptual context and content comes from an analysis of event-related brain electrical potentials. As developed in the previous lecture, whenever an orienting reaction occurs, the orienting stimulus is processed in two separate systems: protocritic and epicritic. According to the theme to be developed here, protocritic processing provides a general episodic context, to which epicritic processing provides the content. The evidence comes from the finding that some event-related brain electrical potentials reflect episodic, protocritic, whereas others reflect spatiotemporal, epicritic processing.

Brain electrical potentials evoked by a sensory stimulus fluctuate around a baseline forming identifiable negative and positive components. The earliest components (within 50–100 msec depending on sense modality) reflect subcortical processing. Beginning a bit later and peaking at approximately 100 msec, a negative deflection occurs that is contingent on both the physical characteristics of the stimulus (e.g., those that make detection difficult) and whether or not the subject is paying attention to the stimulus (Hillyard, Squires, Baver, & Lindsay, 1971). In tasks in which such deflections are studied, to-be-attended stimuli are presented to one ear and other stimuli to the other ear; or, rare stimuli are presented within a sequence of frequent stimuli: the odd-ball task (Picton & Hillyard, 1974). When the difference between wave forms produced by attended and unattended stimuli is taken, a resultant (the N_d) reflects processing that entails entering the sensory input into the ongoing episode as defined by the task—the processing context. The amplitude of this resultant is proportional to the amount of mismatch (mismatch negativity) and therefore the amount of processing demand (Naatenen, 1982).

Though the amplitude of the negative component, which reaches its maximum at 100 msec in the auditory mode, is greatest when recorded from the vertex of the skull, the maximum amplitude of the difference-wave peaks somewhat later (at 200 usec) and is recorded far-frontally. On the basis of behavioral experiments in which the latency of the wave form is manipulated, Naatenen (1982, 1990) further identified two subcomponents of this mismatch negativity; an early phase that reflects the identification of the task-relevant stimulus, and a later phase that relfects further processing effort, such as sustained rehearsal to maintain an expectancy, a context within which the expected input will be processed.

A positive deflection ordinarily signals the resolution of each of these nega-

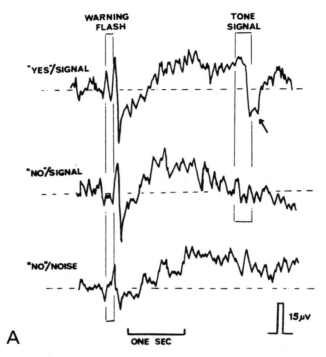

A

FIG. 10.2. a) Computer-averaged CNVs and evoked potentials from 10 trials of each type: In the top tracing, the CNV is large preceding a "hit," and the "P300" component (arrow) is large. At the center, the CNV is smaller preceding a "miss." Below, the CNV is large and sustained during correct "no" trials. b) Cortical-subcortical recording. Each trace is an average of 40 trials, and the epochs are simultaneous (negative up). FC = frontal cortical, SMC = sensory-motor cortical, PC = parietal cortical, and Trans = subcortical. c) Responses to four visual patterns. Four replications for each condition, N = 100 for each replication. Binocular stimulation (negative down). d) Suggested system of nomenclature applicable to the three types of AEP indicated. The total AEP is divided into six latency ranges with limits as indicated by the vertical lines. From: Dowchin, E. and Lindsley, D. B. (1969). *Average Evoked Potentials: Methods, Results and Evaluations.* Washington, DC: National Aeronautics and Space Administration.

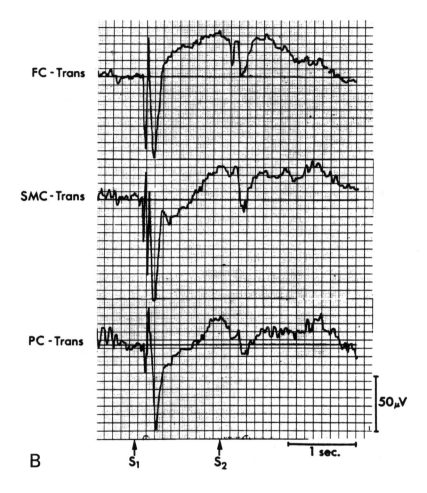

FC - Trans

SMC - Trans

PC - Trans

B

S₁

S₂

50 μV

1 sec.

FIG. 10.2.   (*continued*)

PATTERN

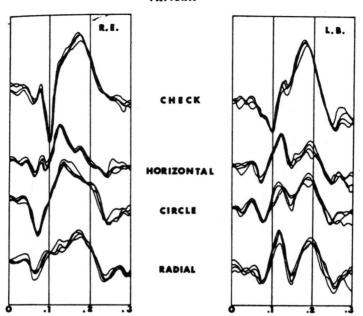

C

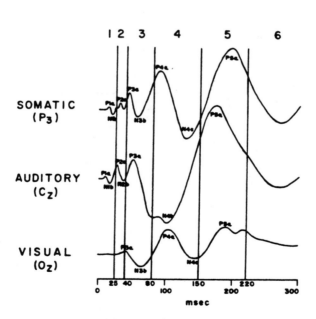

D

FIG. 10.2. (*continued*)

tivities. The positivities also show two components, a frontal (P_3a), which indicates the end of one and the initiation of a new episode. The other, a posterior (P_{3b}) indicates the necessity for updating expectancies. It is usually followed by further processing indexed by another negativity peaking at around 400 msec (the N400). Updating most likely operates by temporarily suppressing into background (extinguishing) all that is irrelevant to the process. These late components may well be related to the waveforms in monkeys who learn what to do by eliminating errors in the experiments performed by Brooks and colleagues (1969) reported in Lecture 6. (For a challenging review see articles by Verleger and by Donchin and Coles and subsequent commentaries in *Behavioral and Brain Sciences*, 1988)

Under somewhat different circumstances a more prolonged negativity can be recorded. This negativity also develops while an organism awaits an expected stimulus, and is called the contingent negative variation (CNV). This prolonged negativity also has a dual composition: (a) a modality specific "get ready" component, recorded locally over one or another region, and (b) a component recorded frontally that peaks around 400–800 msec during or after stimulus presentation (Donchin et al., 1973).

With regard to the modality specific components, Kornhuber, Deecke, the Langs and their collaborators (e.g., Kornhuber & Deecke, 1985; Lang, Lang, Kornhuber, Diekmann, & Kornhuber, 1988) showed that a negativity recorded over the dorsal pre-Rolandic region occurs just prior to the initiation of an action. This "motor readiness potential" can be clearly distinguished from the more generalized frontal negative variation, which is contingent on tasks that entail envisioning proprieties and priorities, and the operation of practical inference (Lang, Lang, Uhl, Kornhuber, Deecke, & Kornhuber, 1987). One such task is kin to matching from sample, the procedure used so successfully by Mishkin and his associates to analyse frontal and limbic functions in monkeys. In this task the subject is trained to respond differently when the matching stimulus is the same as, or when it is different from, the sample presented earlier in the trial. In the experiments with humans the negative brain electrical potential occurred in the parietal region during the intrastimulus interval indicating that attention was being paid; in the frontal region the potential occurred after the presentation of the second stimulus, especially when matching or mismatching could not have been predicted. The frontal potential, therefore, appears to reflect some postresponse processing of success or failure, an updating of the context within which the next trial will be tackled.

Another task that produced this negative potential in the frontal region (Lang et al., 1988a, 1988c) entailed learning a code similar to a Morse telegraphic code. Subjects were trained to identify the meaning of elementary signals and then had to infer the meaning of more complex signals. Again a dissociation between the production of posterior and frontal brain electrical activity was recorded, this time in desynchronization of the alpha rhythm. In the period preceding the presentation of the complex stimuli, the alpha rhythm is attenuated in the parietal region, whereas in frontal recordings alpha attenuation follows the presentation of the complex stimuli: presumably while the subject is processing this input and selecting a response. It is also during this period that the frontal negativity is recorded (Lang et al., 1988b, 1988d, 1988e). [In both these tasks it is especially the left frontal region that shows the negative shifts.]

These analyses in humans are congruent with the results of intracortical recordings made in monkeys (Donchin, Otto, Gerbrandt, & Pribram, 1973; Thatcher & John, 1977), which differentiated a far frontal generalized orienting response to a novel situation from a more localized response related to different specific aspects of a task. For example, the motor readiness potential was recorded just prior to a panel press required during the period while the monkey was awaiting the onset of a 2nd stimulus; a parietal negativity developed during the panel press per se. Only when the task was completely new or when the task was changed substantially, did the far frontal negative wave (described initially by Grey Walter, 1967) appear. This frontal component of the event-related brain electrical potential is, under most circumstances, highly correlated with the visceroautonomic responses of orienting (indicating dishabituation) described in the Lecture 8 (Bagshaw & Benzies, 1968; Lacey & Lacey, 1970).

The event-related brain electrical potential waveforms thus reflect various phases and aspects of perceptual processing. Much of what goes on is the active processing of what is currently relevant or irrelevant in the stimulus situation—the perceived relation between figure (content) and ground (context). As reviewed in the previous lecture such processing entails structuring and restructuring of context within an episode, which is the province of protocritic processing by the limbic forebrain, especially the hippocampal system. This type of processing is reflected in the negativity encompassing the peaks at 200 and 400 msec of the N_d and the related positivities (P_3) and in the late frontal component of the CNV.

The processing of figure, of the content of a stimulus situation, is reflected in the earlier components of event-related brain electrical potentials. As noted, experiments have shown that even these early components reflect prior and current experience, that what constitutes "figure" is in part determined by context. There is direct evidence that the first 100 msec of processing reflects changes produced by prior processing: Neurons in the primary (extrinsic) sensory systems are found responsive to both stimulus features and stimulus relevance, that is, reinforcement history (Bridgeman, 1982; Keys & Goldberg, 1989; Pribram, Spinelli, & Kamback, 1967). From these and surrounding systems, movement-related neurons have been identified such as those that respond when a movement is underway to a particular target, or even when a target is in a location within reach (Keys & Goldberg, 1989; Mountcastle et al., 1981). These movement-related neurons are those involved in the generation of object and action spaces as described in Lectures 5 and 6. (I have used the term spaces where in the older literature the term *proximal* or *local context* has often been used. Proximal contexts, spaces, are distinguished from more generalized contexts which are called episodic in the current lectures).

On the basis of these studies, the conclusion is warranted that the earliest components (within 100 msec) of the event-related brain electrical potentials reflect activity in the primary sensory systems and thus the content of perceptions; those components that are intermediate (100–200 msec) reflect activity in the surrounding sensory-associated systems. These components reflect movement-produced and attended selections among submodalities and features that determine the configuration spaces within which content becomes processed.

A most interesting fact was discovered when recordings were made in these sensory and sensory-associated systems in humans: The activity in the sensory-associated systems originates in the thalamocortical circuitry and is only then relayed to the brain stem (Velasco & Velasco, 1979; Velasco, Velasco, Machado, & Olvera, 1973). For vision the circuit is composed of a top-down pathway from prestriate and inferotemporal cortex to the deep layers of the superior colliculus of the tectum and to the pretectal region. The bottom-up portion of the circuit originates in the superior colliculus and pretectal region and connects to the reticular nucleus of the thalamus including the ventrolateral geniculate nucleus. The reticular nucleus of the thalamus acts as a gate to the remainder of the thalamus from which projections to the cortex arise—including the nuclei that project the sensory input to the cortex such as the dorsolateral geniculate nucleus for retinal input. The gate also operates on the thalamic projections that terminate in the prestriate and inferotemporal cortex thus completing the circuit. These data furnish further direct evidence for reciprocity—with an impressive top-down component—in processing as described in Lectures 5 and 6.

To summarize; two classes of interpenetrating processes have been identified by analyzing the waveforms of event-related brain electrical potentials. One class processes episodic context, the ground forming an episode within which perception becomes organized; another class processes content composed of perceptual figures and the spaces in which they occur. Contextual processes modify those responsive to content. Content itself is composed by selective processing: the "spaces" (including those that determine the corporeal self) within which perception becomes configured operate in a top-down fashion in reciprocally connected motor-sensory systems. The order in which these processes occur makes it likely that relating content to context depends on the operations that configure perceptual spaces. It is these operations that stabilize processing for the duration of an episode initiated and terminated by an orienting reaction. Stabilization proceeds throughout the later portions (the updating process) of the episode.

MODIFICATION OF PROCESSING COMPETENCE

In order for epicritic content to be influenced by protocritic context, that is, for envisioning proprieties and priorities and engaging the process of practical inference, the sensory channels must be flexible in their organization. Previous lectures (especially Lecture 4) presented some of the evidence regarding the nature of channel organization. The evidence from event-related brain electrical potentials indicates that episodic updating occurs, and thus calls into question the notion that processing capacity is inflexible. Additional evidence makes it unlikely that limitations in processing span are due to limitations imposed by some fixed channel capacity. Briefly, evidence runs as follows:

Two million input fibers converge onto 350 thousand output fibers. Sherrington (1911/1947) conceptualized a restriction on performance due to this convergence in his doctrine of a "limited final common path." However, Donald Broadbent (1974) showed that with regard to cognitive operations such as attention, limited span is not so much a function of the final common path as it is a function of the central processing mechanisms in the brain. Broadbent reviewed this aspect of his work in the 3rd Neurosciences Study Program (1974) and I devoted a whole section of this program to the topic under the title "How Is It That Sensing So Much We Can Do So Little."

The issue of limited span is usually discussed in terms of a fixed channel capacity. But as reviewed by Pribram and McGuinness (1975, 1982), a considerable volume of work has shown that the central processing span is not fixed. Thus Miller (1956), Garner (1962), and Simon (1974, 1986), among others, have clearly shown that information-processing span can be enhanced by reorganization such as that provided by "chunking." In fact, the limitations in processing can be overcome to such an extent that one is hard put to defining any "ultimate" limit.

These data and others have led to conceptualizing limitations in processing span as limitations in channel competence rather than in channel capacity (Pribram, 1986b; Pribram & McGuinness, 1975), a view also expressed by Maffei (1985). As described earlier, chunking has been shown, using the assymmetric delayed alternation procedure, to be influenced by resections of the far frontal cortex. In the current section, data are presented demonstrating that electrical excitation of the frontal cortex changes receptive field properties of neurons in the sensory channels of the primary visual cortex. These changes are directly related to the ability to parse or chunk the input. Thus the conception of a limited capacity depending on some fixed channel "exoskeleton" becomes untenable. An increase in processing capability, in competence (in the sense of a deep structure as developed by Chomsky, 1965), becomes possible by way of challenges to a flexible "endoskeleton" of the channel.

Processing competence can be computed as the reciprocal of equivocation (which in Shannon information measurement theory is the sum of redundancy and noise). Within this definition, effort was defined (Pribram, 1986b; Pribram & McGuinness, 1975) as representing the process of reducing equivocation in the channel. Kahneman (1973) defined attention as effort paid to allocate limited resources, the limitation due to a fixed and restricted channel capacity. By contrast, the concept of competence focuses on the fact that the structure of sensory channels can be perturbed and is flexible: Effort in response to challenge continually modifies span in the direction of more efficient and effective processing; when the organization of channels is altered, the allocation of perceptual resources changes.

Processing span is defined by the coherence among processing episodes and is sensitive to structuring as by chunking, a top-down cognitive process. The continuously updated channel structures are akin to narratives that become, with the accumulation of experience, fairly autonomous memory-based influences on processing span.

The particular experiments that demonstrate the neurophysiology of top-down processing, processing that implements changes in channel structure, were performed on the receptive field organization of single neurons in the lateral geniculate nucleus and the primary visual cortex of cats and monkeys (Lassonde, Ptito, & Pribram, 1981; Spinelli & Pribram, 1967). Receptive fields were mapped by displaying a small moving dot on a contrasting background. The location and motion of the dot were computer-controlled. Thus the computer could sum (in a matrix of bins representing the range over which the dot was moved) the number of impulses generated by the neuron whose receptive field was being mapped. This was done for each position of the dot because the computer "knew" where the dot was located.

The maps obtained for the lateral geniculate nucleus are shown in Figs. 10.3 and 10.4. The three-dimensional representation is usually called the Mexican hat function for obvious reasons. The brim of the hat represents the spontaneous background of impulse activity of the neuron. The crown of the hat represents the excitation of the cell by the dot of light shown to the animal when the cell is located at the center of the visual field. Where the crown meets the brim there is a depression indicating that the output of the cell has been inhibited.

The center-surround organization, first described at the optic nerve level by Kuffler (1953) is more clearly shown in Fig. 10.4 which is a cross section of the hat parallel to the brim. The inhibitory surround has been shown (e.g., Creutzfeldt, Kuhnt, & Benevento, 1974, for cortical cells) to be due to hyperpolarizing activity in a lateral network of "local circuit neurons" (Rakic, 1976), which do not generate nerve impulses.

It is this inhibitory surround that can be augmented or diminished by electrical excitation of other parts of the forebrain. Stimulation of the far frontal cortex or the head of the caudate nucleus diminishes the inhibitory surround, as indicated by F in Fig. 10.4; stimulation of the posterior intrinsic (association) cortex, specifically in this case, the inferotemporal portion of this cortex, or of another of the basal ganglia, the putamen, produces an augmentation of the inhibitory surround as indicated by IT in this figure.

The results for cortical neurons are somewhat more complex because their receptive fields are elongated. However, some of these receptive fields, classified as "simple" by Hubel and Wiesel (1959), demonstrate inhibitory flanks.

Others (classified as complex), although failing to show this type of internal organization, can nonetheless change their overall functionally active size. Despite these complexities the effects on visual cortical cell receptive fields of electrical excitation of far frontal cortex and caudate on the one hand, and of posterior cortex and putamen on the other, essentially parallel those obtained from the lateral geniculate nucleus.

Dendritic fields overlap to a considerable extent. Thus when the excitatory portion of the receptive fields become enlarged, the dendritic fields essentially merge into a more or less continuous functional field. By contrast, when the excitatory portion of the receptive fields shrinks, each neuron becomes functionally isolated from its neighbor.

This modifiability of the primary visual system in the direction of greater separation or greater confluence among channels was supported by testing the effects of the same electrical stimulations on the recovery cycles of the system as recorded with small macroelectrodes. Figure 10.5 graphs the effects obtained: Far frontal stimulations produce a slowing of recovery, whereas posterior stimulations result in a more rapid recovery as compared with an unstimulated baseline. Slow recovery indicates that the system is acting in unison; rapid recovery that the system is "multiplexed"—that its channels are separated and not encumbered by a more extensively interconnected system with consequent greater inertia.

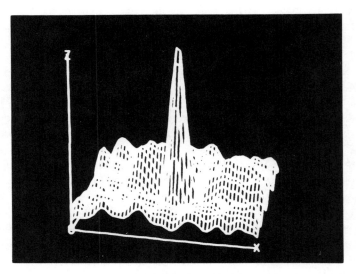

FIG. 10.3. Three dimensional (Mexican Hat) map of points on the retina at which a light spot produces responding in a particular lateral geniculate cell in the brain of the monkey.

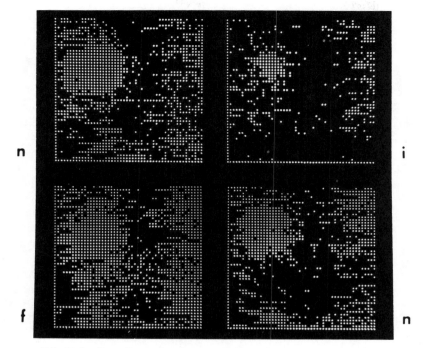

n

i

f

n

FIG. 10.4.   Two dimensional cross sections of the geniculate receptive field—two standard deviations above background activities (the brim of the hat). The effects of frontal stimulation are shown in f and those of the inferotemporal cortex are shown in i. Note the changes in the inhibitory surround n indicates control taken initially and two hours after initial baseline recordings.

ENVISIONING PROPRIETIES AND PRIORITIES: TOWARD A MODEL FOR PROCESSING SERIAL POSITION

The results of these experiments can be interpreted to indicate that far frontal brain stimulation drives the visual system towards a continuous mode of operation while posterior stimulation drives the system toward a discrete mode. A convolution-correlation model is therefore more appropriate when the focus of brain activity shifts toward the frontal lobes. A matrix model is more appropriate when the focus of brain activity lies more posteriorly. To test this interpretation we need to relate the known behavioral functions of the frontal and posterior portions of the brain to the known advantages of the two types of models.

Convolution-correlation mathematics have been used to model sensory-motor

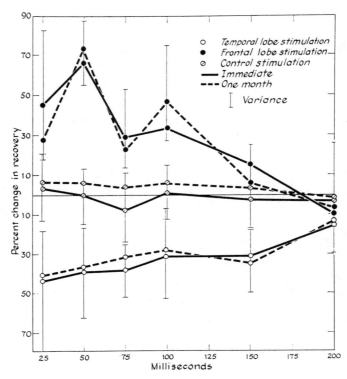

FIG. 10.5. The change in recovery of a response to the second of a pair of flashes compared with pre-stimulation. Control recordings were performed on the parietal cortex. Records were made immediately and after 1 month. Vertical bars represent variability of the records obtained in each group of four monkeys. From: Spinelli, D. N. & Pribram, K. H. (1967). Changes in Visual Recovery Functions and unit activity produced by frontal and temporal cortex stimulation. *Electroencephalography and Clinical Neurophysiology*, 143–149.

and perceptual-motor learning and skills. Thus Licklider (1951), Uttal (1975), and Reichardt (1978) developed temporal and spatial autocorrelation models to account for their results of experiments on perceptual performances. Cooper (1984) and Kohonen (1972, 1977) used a similar model to describe a variety of properties both perceptual and cognitive. Thus, for example, Cooper developed a model based on the effects of monocular deprivation on the responsiveness of neurons in the visual cortex and made successful predictions of outcomes of experiments inspired by the model. As reviewed earlier, our own efforts (Pribram & Carlton, 1986) have used this type of model to tease apart imaging as a function of convolving the various stages of processing in the primary visual system, from object perception, which depends on correlations among patterns in which centers of symmetry are determined by operations performed in the superior colliculus and the visuomotor system.

None of these perceptual and motor skills depend on functions that can be ascribed to the far frontal part of the brain. Nor are they related to the inferotemporal cortex and the posterior intrinsic "association" systems of which the inferotemporal cortex is a part. What is suggested by these successful models is that the convolution-correlation approach is the more appropriate for describing the configural aspects of perception leaving the matrix model as more appropriate for cognitive operations such as the formation of prototypes.

But certain aspects of cognitive processing are better described by a convolutional-correlational approach. These aspects entail episodic processing of protocritic inputs that place inordinate demands on ordering. The thesis to be presented proposes that such processing entails the computing of covariation by determining the inner products of sensory input vectors to establish a context, a processing episode. This is in contrast to the procedures involved in processing the configural aspects of perception: the formation of groups to process prototypical object forms.

Murdock (1979, 1982, 1983, 1985; Murdock & Lewandowsky, 1986) has reviewed the evidence that distinguishes convolution and matrix theories of associative memory. He pointed out that whereas the matrix model (as developed by Anderson, 1970, and Pike, 1984) has the advantage of simplicity in obtaining explicit expressions and to some extent in storage capacity, the convolution-correlation model is more powerful in other respects such as the handling of serial position effects, effects that entail far frontal lobe function.

The convolutional and matrix models differ in that in the convolutional model critical operations are performed on the inner products of its vectors, whereas in the matrix models such operations utilize the outer products of vectors. Murdock (1985) described the difference as follows:

> The basic issue seems to be as follows. I would suggest that an association can be represented as a convolution, information is stored in a common memory vector, and correlation is the retrieval operation. Pike would suggest that an association is the outer product of two vectors, information is stored in a memory matrix or set of matrices, and vector-matrix premultiplication and postmultiplication is the retrieval operation. (p. 132)

The convolutional approach "is not quite ready to be abandoned in favor of a matrix system" (Murdock, 1985, p. 132). But as processing prototypes characterizes the functions of systems of the posterior cerebral convexity (see e.g., Warrington & McCarthy, 1983) the matrix model also is not to be abandoned. This model is clearly viable in the hands of Anderson and his colleagues when applied to learning and performance of discrimination-type tasks (see Anderson, Silverstein, Ritz, & Jones, 1977 for review). Whenever categorical processes are involved, storage as outer products of vectors and retrieval by postmultiplication appears to be more appropriate than storage by association in a common vector produced by convolving inner products.

This line of reasoning leads to the suggestion that reference—that is, in humans, semantic—processing is best represented by a matrix model and that the convolution-correlation model be reserved for episodic processing (see Tulving, 1972, 1985 for review). It is therefore important to find out if indeed the convolution-correlation model more effectively models all aspects of episodic processing.

A central characteristic of episodic processing is its preservation of some sort of place keeping and time tagging: that is, in the perception of serial position within the total processing span. Murdock & Lewandowsky (1986) presented a detailed review of models constructed to account for serial position effects and the evidence upon which they are based. Interference, trace decay, distinctiveness, end- anchoring, dual trace (item and order), and organizational (chunking) factors were assigned critical roles in model building and the convolutional model efficiently handles them all.

How can such models developed to account for remembering serial position effects in the recall of lists of items be relevant to understanding how the brain processes episodic controls on perception? The key to understanding lies in the results of analysis of performance of the delayed-response task. Recall that in this task a reward or token is hidden in a particular location chosen from others similar in appearance while the animal is watching—a screen is then interposed between the location and the animal for a short (e.g., 5 seconds) period and then removed, allowing the animal to have access to the reward. After resection of the far frontal cortex, monkeys lose the ability to perform this task. Pro- and retroactive interference effects have been demonstrated to play a role in this impairment (Malmo, 1942; Pribram, 1958; Pribram, Plotkin, Anderson, & Leong, 1977; Stamm & Rosen, 1972; reviewed by Pribram, 1987a).

As noted, this impairment is almost entirely due to the fact that monkeys with such lesions fail to properly process the initial part of the trial, the hiding of the reward before the screen is interposed. It is the perceptual processing part of the task that is most susceptible to interference, not the memory trace of the initial perceptual experience. Furthermore, items that are identical produce interference in models dependent on trace decay; but as identical items do not interfere with recall of serial position, trace decay cannot account for difficulties experienced after far frontal lobe damage. When items are similiar, however, demands on ordering escalate as expected when the convolution-correlation model is used.

To summarize: The effects of (a) amygdalectomy on serial position, (b) the effects of hippocampectomy on primacy, and (c) the effects of far frontal lobe resections on intralist interference (relative recency) stem from inadequate perceptual processing at the time of initial exposure to the list of items, the establishment of an episode, the context that stabilizes further processing, and not to effects on the trace of the sensory input. We have all experienced a related phenomenon when we attempt to recite a poem or rehearse a melody: should we be interrupted or fail, for the moment, to be able to continue the recitation or rehearsal we often find it necessary to begin again at the beginning of the entire poem or piece, or at least at the beginning of a major section.

Murdock noted that convolutional and matrix models describe what must be processed but do not adress how processing proceeds. There is a class of models, however, that do describe "how" in terms of parallel-distributed processes. The next section reviews the evidence for, and describes extensions of, the convolutional model that indicates how processing procedes.

PRACTICAL INFERENCE: TOWARD A MODEL FOR PROCESSING COVARIANCES

Scientists interested in perception have been especially intrigued by illusions and pictures in which figures are to some extent hidden by the context in which they appear. Such interest exists because, as noted in Lecture 3, perception is ordinarily experienced as "direct"; the processes discussed in the lectures that comprise part 1 are difficult to study because, under normal circumstances, they are unavailable to conscious awareness. This is not so when the perceiver is challenged by an ambiguous input.

These perceptual ambiguities are the figural counterparts of the contextually covariant processes discussed so far in this lecture: injury to the far frontal cortex

FIG. 10.6. What's on a man's mind.

(and not the systems of the posterior cerebral convexity) dramatically influences the rate of reversal of such figures as Necker cubes, and faces/vases. When the injury is severe, reversals may not be experienced at all.

In hidden and reversible figures, ground and potential figures vie for dominance. Figure and ground must be separated out from the ambiguous sensory input. The rate of reversals in reversible figure experiments speeds as the perceiver becomes aware of both figures and this rate can be influenced to some degree by intending to reverse. Rock (1983) noted that reversals continue after each of the figures has been clearly perceived—indicating that the input continues to provide a processing challenge.

According to the holonomic brain theory, this challenge is met much as the other challenges to order that have been described here: centrally controlled changes are produced in the microprocesses occurring in the input channels. These changes can be conceived to operate much as does a zoom lens. When extended into the telephoto range, good separation between figure and ground occurs. A telephotograph has a very narrow depth of field and enhanced resolution. The same effect is obtained with a large surface hologram; by contrast, cutting such a surface into small areas reduces resolution but enhances depth of field. In the brain, large surface integration of a distributed process is achieved when the boundaries between overlapping receptive fields are attenuated, when the convolutional mode of processing is in force. The evidence presented here indicates that such a mode is placed in operation by virtue of the activities of the frontolimbic forebrain, activities which are produced in perception by the concentration of attention (see Pribram & McGuinness, 1991 for review).

Neurophysiologically an enhancement or reduction in integration is achieved by reducing or enhancing lateral inhibition. The separation between receptive fields can be varied. This variation becomes represented in the theory as variation in the extent of the sinusoidal component of the Gabor function. Recall that this extent is limited by a Gaussian envelope over the sinusoid. In the limit, therefore, lateral inhibition frames a span for the episode being processed: Complete merging of receptive fields provides one end of the limit as expressed in convolution theory, complete separation, as expressed in matrix theory, the other.

Smolensky (1986) has extended the convolutional model to cover inference. Smolensky's is a dynamical "harmony" theory in many respects similar to the holonomic brain theory pursued in these lectures. The transition from harmonic (such as Fourier) analysis to measures on the amount of information being processed is done in terms of electrical circuits (with two resistors in series) that compose a "knowledge atom" rather than in terms of Gabor elementary functions. However, the resultant measure on information is also statistical. Both theories aim at optimization in the neural circuitry—optimization in terms of measures on the efficiency of information processing rather than in terms of Hamiltonians per se (as in the initial formulation of the Boltzmann model and Hopfield network.)

Thus Smolensky (1986) stated that:

> The competence of the harmonium model (using Chomsky's meaning of the word) could be accurately described by symbolic inference procedures (e.g., productions) that operate on symbolic representations of the circuit equations. However, performance of the model (including its occasional errors) is achieved without interpreting symbolic rules. The answer is computed through a series of many mode updates, each of which is a microdecision based on formal numerical rules and numerical computations—- computed in parallel:—- When a given feature updates its value, its microdecision is based on the weighted sum of recommendations from all active areas. (p. 246)

In the holonomic brain theory the microdecisions are computed by way of the inner products composing vectors in a Hilbert space of Gabor elementary functions, that is, quanta of information.

Optimization is achieved in harmonium by simulated annealing, or, lowering the "computational temperature." This means that randomness of the initial state is "cooled" out: Inference is assumed to be stochastic. By this procedure a completely coherent interpretation can be constructed from an ambiguous input. Similarly, the harmonium model can answer ill-posed problems, those whose answers are replete with interference effects, just as it can answer well-posed problems: "There will be more than one state of highest harmony and the model will choose one of them. It does not stop dead due to insufficient information. Not 'any answer' will do [however]. Harmonium finds the best possible answers to ill posed problems on the basis of rules that have solved well posed problems" (p. 252).

One such ill-posed perceptual problem is the illusion called the *Aubert phenomenon*, a shift in the subjective vertical when a person's body is tilted in the dark. Mittelstaedt (1987) studied the shift of the subjective vertical with great care and has developed a processing model to account for this shift, a model in tune with both the harmony model and the holonomic brain theory. As such, the Mittelstaedt model serves as a precise illustration of this class of models for the resolution of ill-posed problems: When the ordinary context provided by an illuminated situation is absent, it is replaced by internally generated rules provided by previous established contexts.

Of special interest here is the fact that the Aubert phenomenon has been shown (Teuber & Mishkin, 1954) to be influenced by damage to the far frontal cortex. Thus, the model of top-down effects of the frontal influence on the dendritic microprocess of the sensory channel can be rendered with considerable precision.

Mittelstaedt found "that the apparent orientation of the visual world to the vertical and that of one's own body to the vertical result from two separate computations" (p. 65). The vertical of the visual world, is the resultant of a gravity vector produced by an input from the saccules of the inner ear, and an "idiotropic" vector. This idiotropic vector is not determined by the proprioceptive inputs that influence postural control and hence the orientation of the body to the vertical. What then might be the origin of the idiotropic vector?

Insight into the origin of the idiotropic vector comes from a study of the Aubert phenomenon. Aubert (1861) noted that an objectively vertical line of light in an otherwise dark room appeared tilted to 45° when observed with his body tilted to a 90° angle. When the room was lit so that he could see it with all its window frames, walls, and furniture, the line snapped into its true position. When the light was switched off again, the line slowly returned to its apparent—

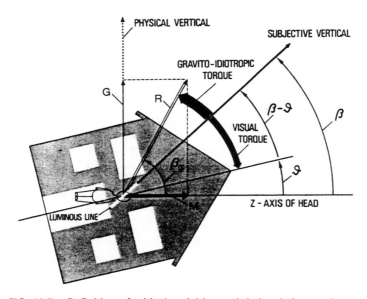

FIG. 10.7. Definition of critical variables and their relations to hypothetical determinants of the SV: 1. The "visual torque" which is supposed to be a function of $\beta-\theta$, the angle between the main axis of the tilted image and the luminous line when set subjectively vertical; 2> the "gravito-idiotropic torque" which is a function of $\beta-\beta_g$, the angle between the present SV and the direction it would have in the absence of visual cues. The latter function may be determined as $g = \sqrt{G^2 + M^2}$ $\sin \beta-\beta_g) = \sqrt{G^2 + M^2} \sin [\beta-\text{arccotan } (M/G)] = M \sin \beta - G \cos \beta$, with $G = 1$. All angles defined with respect to (long) Z-axis of head. From: Mittelstaedt, H. (1988). The Information Processing Structure of the Subjective Verticle. A Cybernetic Bridge between its Psychophysics and its Neurobiology. In H. Marko, G. Hauske, and A. Struppler (Eds.), *Processing Structures for Perception and Action,* (pp. 217–263). Weinheim: VCH Verlagsgesellschaft.

nonobjective—vertical position, that is, it was again seen as 45° rotated from objective verticality.

The frames provided by windows, walls, and so forth, influence to a variable degree the perception of the subjective vertical (see e.g., Stark & Bridgeman, 1983; Witkin & Asch, 1948). Mittelstaedt's experiments show that these frames and the idiotropic vector superimpose to form a new resultant. This resultant is computed by cross multiplication between "circular Fourier components selected from a central nervous system representation of the retinal pattern" and "a central nervous component generator, which is controlled by internal feedback" from the resultant of the cross multiplications.

Neurophysiologically, the extraction of the Fourier components is envisaged by Mittlestaedt to devolve on the orientation selective neurons of the primary visual cortex. "Let the output of all those [neurons] whose preferred orientation falls into the same sector be summed." If a field of parallel lines is used as a panorama, the output of each of the sectorial assemblies can be computed in terms of their Fourier coefficients. By introducing a weighting function, unequal cell densities within sectors and unequal mean amplitudes of the cells' tuning functions can readily be compensated.

In order for Mittelstaedt's model to work, before weighting, "a layer of polarity detectors would be required, that is, cells which peak just once within a full turn of the panorama." (Recall a similar and even more stringent requirement regarding rotation of the processing of Shepard figures in Lecture 7.) Such cells of course do exist: They are cells with receptive fields selective of directionality and orientation as well as the Fourier components specified by spatial and temporal frequency (Pribram, Lassonde, & Ptito, 1981; See review by DeValois & DeValois, 1988).

The fact that the Aubert phenomenon is dramatically altered in patients with frontal lesions (Teuber & Mishkin, 1954) indicates that the far frontal cortex is critically involved in computing the idiotropic vector. In fact, a reasonable speculation would hold that the idiotropic vector is supplied whenever the input from receptors is insufficient to completely specify perceptual context. In such cases, the perceptual system is challenged rather than determined. Percepts gradually drift (e.g., to new orientations) and appear to be no longer "directly" perceived. According to the Mittelstaedt model, in such cases the reciprocal feedback between cross multiplication of the Fourier components representing the sensory input with the central nervous system generator is largely determined by the output from that generator and to a lesser degree by sensory input.

In any generalization of the model to other situations in which the input is ambiguous, conflicting, or demanding of serial position effects, in other words, when the input poses problems that are poorly specified, the output from the central nervous system generator is critical. Due to the storage properties of the frontolimbic systems, the central generator becomes shaped by experience. The process "does not stop dead due to insufficient information." Rather, the process proceeds by constant interaction of the centrally generated component with the results of cross-multiplication of the input vectors, a process that attempts to specify prototypical objects and events. Interaction adds a centrally generated component to enrich each prototype within its boundaries. Inference makes use of this richness, the rules, structures of redundancy, that have been developed on the basis of experience where the input has more completely specified the product of cross multiplication and central generator. The total inference process thus leads to conceiving the best possible fit between prior experience and current input (Appendix G).

SUMMARY

This lecture has covered a host of phenomena dependent on the processing of covariance: Kaidos, the timeless decisive moment; envisioning proprieties and priorities, and inferring practicalities. The type of perceptual processing described in the first six lectures transforms the sensory input into a manageable "invariant," a reliable known spatiotemporal universe within which precise actions can be effected. By contrast, the type of processing covered in the current lecture utilizes input as a challenge to organizing a plausible perceptual future. This is accomplished by establishing coherences among episodes. Time and space become enfolded into cycles of covariance displaying only arbitrarily determined "befores" and "afters," primacies, and relative recencies. When stored, these cycles serve as internal, central generators in computations that involve ambiguous, incomplete, or conflicting sensory inputs. On the basis of these central generators, computations proceed "as if." The central generators thus provide the critical ingredient in the processes that underly narrative and creative imagination.

EPILOGUE

It sometimes appears that the resistance to accepting the evidence that cortical cells are responding to the two-dimensional Fourier components of stimuli [is due] to a general unease about positing that a complex mathematical operation similar to Fourier analysis might take place in a physiological structure like cortical cells. It is almost as if this evoked for some a specter of a little man sitting in a corner of the cell huddled over a calculator. Nothing of the sort is of course implied: the cells carry out their processing by summation and inhibition and other physiological interactions within their receptive fields. There is no more contradiction between a functional description of an ensemble of cortical cells as performing a spatial frequency analysis and their having receptive fields with certain physiological properties than there is between a functional description of some electronic component as being a multiplier and its being made up of transistors and resistors wired in a certain fashion. The one level functionally describes the process, the other states the mechanism. (DeValois & DeValois, 1988, p.288)

Looking back at the development of the holonomic theory of brain function as presented in these MacEachran lectures, I am constantly surprised by the following paradox: Giant strides appear to have been made in understanding figural perception during my research career. At the same time, the fundamental approaches that are of a sufficient magnitude to now constitute a paradigm shift were already accepted a century ago by Poincare, Helmholtz, and Lie (see Poincare, 1905a). Of course, real strides have been taken during the past 50 years: a multitude of experimental results have supported the earlier views and these views have been refined with the more sophisticated computational tools

269

now available. But perhaps the apparent magnitude of the strides is due to the fact that there has been an intermediate period wherein another, rather different, view of the perceptual process held sway: a view in which higher order perceptual complexities of form are synthesized from points and lines. The interim view contrasts sharply with the earlier one and to the lectures presented here. As developed in the holonomic brain theory, in vision (and to a considerable extent in somesthesis and audition) perceptions are derived from two sources: (a) a movement-initiated sensory input which drives the perception of object forms; (b) a set of top-down categorizing and evaluating procedures that are triggered by and preprocess the perception of these object-forms.

Perhaps the most interesting fact about the holonomic brain theory lies in the fact that it provides the neurobehavioral data needed to enliven the formalisms inherent in parallel-distributed processing. For vision, which depends on radiant energy, this parallel leads to a neurodynamics framed in terms identical to those used in the quantum theory of microphysics. But the formal parallel is not limited to vision: Gabor, upon whose work the holonomic brain theory is founded, developed a quantum psychophysics primarily for audition. His application stemmed from signal processing, which utilized an electromagnetic medium. Currently, his insights combined with those of Kolmogorov are leading the development of new mathematical computing principles almost identical to those presented in these lectures (Fatmi & Resconi, 1988).

This ubiquity of applications of the formalism of quantum mechanics has made it reasonable to attempt to model signal processing in the brain by the same formalism. The fact that such modelling could draw for support on so much evidence obtained with no knowledge of, or interest in, Gabor's contributions enhances the likelihood that the direction taken correctly reflects some important aspect of brain functioning.

The fact that the formalism describing the brain microprocess is identical with the formalism describing the physical microprocess allows two interpretations: (a) The neural microprocess is in fact based on relations among microphysical quantal events, and (b) that the laws describing quantum physics are applicable to certain macrophysical interactions when these attain some special characteristics.

Some directions experimental research might take have been provided by Margenau (1984), who bases his quantum formulations on tunnelling; by Edelman (1987), who defined the conditions under which group selection (and competition) can occur in neural networks—albeit not as yet in terms of a Hilbert space, and by Hameroff (1987), who suggested that the saltatory interactions among polarizations reflect holographic like constructions such as interfering soliton waves in the microtubules of the medium, possibly glia.

Collective nanosecond conformational states have been elegantly woven in a theory of *coherent* protein excitations by Professor Herbert Fröhlich who presently divides his time between Liverpool University and the Max Planck Institute in Stuttgart. Recognized as a major contributor to the modern theory of superconductivity, Fröhlich turned to the study of biology in the late 1960's and came to several profound conclusions. One is that changes in protein conformation in the nanosecond time scale are triggered by a charge redistribution such as a dipole oscillation within hydrophobic regions of proteins (Fröhlich, 1975). Another Fröhlich (1970) concept is that a set of proteins connected in a common voltage gradient field such as within a membrane or polymer electret such as the cytoskeleton would oscillate *coherently* at nanosecond periodicity if energy such as biochemical ATP were supplied. Fröhlich's model of coherency can explain long range cooperative effects by which proteins and nucleic acids in biological systems can communicate. A major component of Fröhlich's theory suggests that random supply of energy to a system of nonlinearly coupled dipoles can lead to coherent excitation of a single vibrational mode, provided the energy exceeds a critical threshold. Frequencies of the order of 10^9 to 10^{11} Hz are suggested by Fröhlich, who maintains that the single mode appears because all others are in thermal equilibrium. Far reaching biological consequences may be expected from such coherent excitations and long range cooperativity. (p. 181–182)

The possibility that the dendritic microprocess utilizes microphysical interactions must await the results of experimental investigation. I am, therefore, here as interested in exploring the possibility that the formulations necessary to account for quantum microorganization are also necessary to account for some aspects of macroorganization. These aspects are those commonly called information processing. Until the advent of content addressible parallel-distributed processing networks, information processing was conceived solely in terms of symbol processing. Symbol processing failed to achieve facility in pattern recognition. Whenever figural processing is critical, it appears that signals are better conceived in terms of Gaborlike elementary functions—*quanta rather than bits of information*. The full impact of this additional "dimensionality" with which to characterize information is still to be felt.

One locus of impact is certain to be in our understanding of the relations between mind and matter—or between mind and the sense organs and brain—the issue fundamental to these lectures. Elsewhere (Pribram, 1986) I have presented the case for holding the concepts comprising information, and therefore entropy and energy, ontologically neutral to the mind-brain duality. As repeatedly noted in these lectures, space-time and spectrum provide the dimensions within which information occurs. Whenever these dimensions become informed—rather than displaying their pre-formed potential (their entropy)—optimization, whether material or mental, in the form of the least action principle becomes possible.

Thus, one way of looking at the relationship between space-time and spectrum involves the least action principle, which mediates between two orders. On the one hand there are potential orders provided by an oscillation between change (measured as energy) and inertia (measured as momentum). On the other, are evolving space-time configurations. Information repeatedly actualizes potential into space-time configurations thus accounting for their evolution. One sort of evolving configuration is experienced by us as perceptual experience.

Another, and related possibility for understanding the mind/brain relationship devolves on superconductivity. Superconductivity, a special form of signal processing in macrophysical organizations, is one form of optimization. In his book on *What is Life* (1944), Schroedinger suggested that life is a manifestation of superconductivity at normal temperatures. As noted by Hameroff (1987) Fröhlich (1975) has carried this insight considerably further:

> According to Fröhlich, the biological effects [of coherent excitation and long range cooperativity] are not temperature effects. They show very sharp frequency resonances which indicates that localized absorption in very small spatial regions contributes to the biological actions.

> The sharp resonance of this sensitive window has a frequency width of about 2 x 10^8 Hz. The layer of ordered water and ions subjacent to membranes and cytoskeletal structures (the "Debye layer") absorbs in the region of 10^8 Hz. This suggests that the Debye layer is closely involved with the dynamic functional activities of the biostructures which they surround. Green and Triffet (1985) have modeled propagating waves and the potential for information transfer in dynamics of the Debye layer immediately beneath membranes and cytoskeletal proteins. They have hypothesized a holographic information medium due to the coherent vibrations in space and time of these biomolecules. The medium they consider is the ordered water and layers of calcium counter ions surrounding the high dipole moments in membranes and biomolecules. Thus they have developed a theory of ionic bioplasma in connection with nonlinear properties which relates to the existence of highly polar metastable states. The small scale and ordering would minimize friction in these activities. Fröhlich suggests the possibility of propagating waves due to the lack of frictional processes ("superconductivity") in the biomolecule itself as well as the layer of ordered water or Debye layer (Kuntz and Kauzmann, 1974). (p. 183)

Bohm (1986) has noted that quantum properties (e.g., quantum nonlocality) characterize superconductivity. If indeed the message in these lectures as developed formally in the appended mathematical treatises are in any sense correct, the superconductinglike informational properties of communication in certain forms of matter underlie and are coordinate with the informational aspects of mind.

Perceptual experiences may on occasion however, reflect the spectral energy/momentum potential more than they reflect space-time configurations. As described in lecture 10, one such occasion results when excitation in the frontolimbic formations greatly exceeds that in the posterior cerebral convexity. Frontolimbic excitation can be induced by internal neurochemical stimulation or by external methods such as concentrating on ambiguous (or otherwise meaning-less) stimuli provided by a mantra, for example. When the spectral dimension dominates the production of a perception, space and time become enfolded in the experienced episode. Time evolution ceases and spatial boundaries disappear. An infinity of envisioned covariations characterizes the episode. Therefore, the epi-sode is often referred to as spritual in the sense that, as a consequence of practiced inference, an effective union is envisioned between perceiver and per-ceived. The boundary between mind and matter, as all other boundaries, be-comes dissolved. More on this at a future occasion. Now, as appendeces, some initial attempts at formal implementations of aspects of the theory.

APPENDICES: *A THEORY OF NONLOCAL CORTICAL PROCESSING IN THE BRAIN*

Kunio Yasue
Mari Jibu
Research Institute for Informatics and Science
Notre Dame Seishin University, Japan

Karl H. Pribram
Center for Brain Research
and Informational Sciences
Radford University

There once was a planet called Solaris, far, far away from our universe and a long, long time before the creation of our universe. It was a planet of sea, but the sea manifested a systematized order in flow. The "sea" thought by its flow pattern . . . . . . (For further neurology of Solaris, see "SOLARIS" by Stanislaw Lem.)

Appendix A: *The Neurodynamics of Image Processing*

1. INTRODUCTION

The text of this volume claims that the mathematical formulations that have been developed for quantum mechanics and quantum field theory can go a long way toward describing neural processes due to the functional organization of the cerebral cortex. According to this formulation the computational power of the cortex results from cooperative saltatory interactions among polarizations occurring in dendritic networks. These interactions are seen responsible for influencing nerve cell output in an apparently nonlocal fashion. Before proceeding with an exposition of one mathematical formulation that has stemmed from this claim, it seems worthwhile to tell a little of the story of the development of *our* interaction. The story is indeed a manifestation of "nonlocality."

In the course of developing the ideas of neural holography and the holonomic brain theory at Stanford University in California, Karl Pribram realized that understanding the issues regarding the properties of "waves" versus "particles" in microphysics might shed some light on issues regarding the nature of the neural microprocess. He turned to his son, head of the physics department at Bates University in the state of Maine who explained the issues clearly and added that for a deeper understanding the works of David Bohm should be consulted.

Simultaneously, Bohm had heard of Pribram's work on the brain and had sent him an invitation to attend a conference in London. Bohm, in collaboration with the mathematician Basil Hiley, was developing alternative mathematical formulations of quantum mechanics and quantum field theory in order to cope with the issues of wave and particle duality and with the problems of nonlocality (e.g., Bohm & Hiley, 1971, 1973; Bohm, Hiley, & Stuart, 1975). Pribram also worked with Geoffry Chew and Henry Stapp of the physics department at the University of California at Berkeley and brought Bohm together with these investigators to clarify the mathematical descriptions of the "implicate-explicate" relationship which at first was thought to reflect the wave particle duality but turned out to be much more basic to an understanding of both microphysics and the neural microprocess. Lecture 2 of the Prolegomen formulates the results of these interactions.

Kunio Yasue had been inspired by David Bohm in the course of developing the probabilistic formulations of quantum mechanics and quantum field theory in Kyoto, Nagoya, and Geneva. Bohm's mathematical formulation of quantum mechanics had been incorporated into the realm of the probability theory by Edward Nelson (1967, 1984). Nelson's contributions provided an alternative probabilistic formulation of quantum mechanics and quantum field theory called stochastic mechanics and stochastic field theory, respectively. Kunio Yasue then demonstrated the application of a least action principle in this probabilistic formulation of quantum mechanics with the help of Jean-Claude Zambrini (Yasue, 1981a, 1981b; Zambrini, 1985, 1986a, 1986b, 1987). Meanwhile, Jean-Claude Zambrini discovered a rational mathematical theory of stochastic processes in Princeton with which Yasue's original idea of stochastic calculus of variations could be refined (Zambrini, 1986a, 1986b).

Coming back from Geneva to Tokyo, Yasue was looking for a proper field of research outside the quantum theory in which both probabilistic and variational ideas play important roles. Being settled in his home town, Okayama, he was innocent of Karl Pribram and his holonomic brain theory and of neuroscience. Mari Jibu, a young graduate student of Kei-ichi Hamano, a psychologist who had demonstrated α-wave generation in meditation, was courageous enough to ask Kunio Yasue about Pribram's idea of neural holography. Yasue saw immediately that a mathematical formulation in terms of variational and least action principles was relevant to understanding the neural microprocess: He asked himself, "Might not neural holography be a proper vehicle for probabilistic and variational ideas just as electron holography is in quantum theory?"

This is the story about how the collaboration of the present authors started. As will be described in the first appendix, a neural wave function akin to the Schrödinger wave equation is derived on the basis of a least action principle operating within a manifold representing the dendritic network. In the holonomic brain theory as developed here, this wave function describes the cooperative interactions among polarizations occuring in the dendritic network. The wave equation is then shown to be subject to a Fourier expansion, indicating that the polarizations can be represented by Fourier coefficients. In a very real sense, this derivation recapitulates in modern mathematical form, the historical development of these ideas from Euler, through Lagrange to Fourier and Schrödinger. In addition, the derivation can be considered one mathematical "proof" of Fourier's theorem (a proof that eluded its author and frustrated many further attempts).

This first appendix thus lays the ground for the subsequent appendices dealing with familiarization, the formation of prototypes, innovation, and inference.

2. FUNDAMENTAL OSCILLATIONS IN DENDRITIC NETWORKS

We begin by considering a dendritic network made up of horizontal dendritic membranes upon which perpendicular spines are superimposed. From the geometrical point of view, it is a complex spatial extent of surface. In the terminology of geometry, it is expressed as a multi-dimensional manifold. Mathematically therefore, we begin the description of the processes handled by this network by arbitrarily reducing its dimensionality to an idealized two-dimensional manifold and denote it by M. Any location on the dendritic network can be thought of as a point in the manifold M. Thus, each location can be distinguished by giving two real numbers, that is, two dimensional coordinates x^1 and x^2. The ordered set of coordinates $x = (x^1,x^2)$ represents a point in the manifold M and so a location on the dendritic membrane. From the physical point of view, in each location on the dendritic membrane, specified by the coordinate x, one finds biomolecules of high dipole moments and so a Debye layer of ionic bioplasma is formed immediately beneath the dendritic membrane. Therefore, we have a two-dimensional distribution of ionic bioplasma in the manifold M. Spatial and temporal distributions of ionic bioplasma on the dendritic membrane are in general not homogeneous. It is known that the biomolecules of high dipole moments oscillate periodically and are controlled by Ca^{2+} and ATP cyclic processes (Frölich 1970, 1975). Even though the induced membrane potential oscillation has a small amplitude, it can be considered as the basis of the cooperative activity by virtue of amplification by the dendrite cytoskeleton. In the current lectures, this activity is referred to as the neural microprocess which is the computational substrate of cortical function. As we will see in what follows, the dendritic network shows a systematized ordering controlled globally by the distribution of phase differences in the oscillations of these dendritic potentials. Gray and Singer (Singer, 1989; Gray & Singer, 1989; Gray, et al, 1989) have recorded direct experimental evidence of such oscillations and discussed in detail their significance for distributed non-local processing in the primary visual cortex.

First, we consider an extremely idealized case in which the oscillations of membrane potentials in every location of the dentritic network are perfectly synchronized. In this case, the membrane potentials manifest a harmonic oscillation with a uniform frequency everywhere. Let φ be the membrane potential in any location of the dendritic network in mV units. Since any location of the dendritic network can be specified by a point in the manifold M with coordinates $x = (x^1,x^2)$, the membrane potential φ becomes a real function $\varphi = \varphi(x,t)$ of coordinates x and time t. In the terminology of geometry, it is a scalar field on the manifold M. As the membrane potential φ is synchronized everywhere, it becomes in this case, only a function of t. The real function $\varphi(t)$ that describes this harmonic oscillation becomes

$$\varphi(t) = A \cos(\omega t + \alpha)$$

where A denotes the amplitude, ω is the angular frequency and α is the initial phase. Here, it is convenient to introduce a representative complex function

$$\theta(t) = e^{-i(\omega t + \alpha)}. \tag{1}$$

This is because only the phase patterns of the oscillations of membrane potentials are relevant in the overall control mechanism of dendritic microprocesses. We call $\theta(t)$ the synchronized fundamental oscillation of the dendritic network. In this extremely ideal case of synchronized harmonic oscillation, there are no ionic currents produced in the dendritic network. We interpret such a state of the dendritic microprocess as the stationary state because no signals (i.e., ionic currents) are operating in the dendritic network.

   To see the validity of this interpretation, we proceed next to a more realistic case, where the oscillations of the membrane potentials in each location of the dendritic network deviate from the idealized harmonic oscillation. The deviation is not uniform; the membrane potentials show oscillations with different phases in different locations. In the case of nonlinear oscillations, the scalar field φ representing the membrane potential differences, i.e., polarizations becomes a function of both space coordinates and time,

$$\varphi = \varphi\ (x,t).$$

Consequently, the representative complex function θ of the membrane polarization turns out to be of the form

$$\theta(x,t) = e^{iS(x,t)}. \tag{2}$$

Here S is a real function of coordinates x and time t and stands for the phase of oscillation. It contains detailed information about both spatial and temporal patterns of the oscillatory component of the membrane polarization. An ensemble of S's describes a dendritic holoscape made up of isophase contours of the membrane polarizations in the dendritic network. The phase function S describes how the density distribution of the ionic bioplasma evolves for each location within the dendritic network. For example, the gradient vector of S

$$k(x,t) = \nabla\ S(x,t)$$

$$= \left(\frac{\partial S(x,t)}{\partial x^1} , \frac{\partial S(x,t)}{\partial x^2} \right) \tag{3}$$

is nothing but the spatial frequency of the relations among (distances between) isophase contours in the point x at time t. The time derivative of S,

$$\omega(x,t) \;=\; -\,\frac{\partial S(x,t)}{\partial t}\,, \tag{4}$$

is the angular frequency of the contour in x at t. These spatial and angular frequencies characterize cooperativity among oscillations of the membrane potentials in the dendritic network.

Once the distribution of charge carriers in the ionic bioplasma evolves due to the distribution of dendritic isophase contours (2), the pattern of oscillations of the membrane potentials in each location changes. This is because the amount of charge carriers in each location affects the Ca^{2+} controlled ATP cyclic process and so the resulting oscillations of biomolecules of high dipole moments. Thus, the fundamental activity of the dendritic network is represented by a reciprocal feedback and feedforward control of the distribution of the dendritic ionic bioplasma due to the oscillating component of membrane polarizations. To summarize, let us recall the idealized case of synchronized oscillations (1). There, $S(x,t) = -(\omega t + \alpha)$ and we have a vanishing spatial frequency $k = 0$ and constant angular frequency ω. This highly cooperative oscillating network of membrane polarizations prohibits the flow of ions (i.e., charge carriers).

By contrast, under less idealized conditions, the charge carriers in the dendritic network evolve and distribute as a function of the local phase differences of the oscillating components of the membrane polarization. This less idealized general case describes a holoscape (2). The spatial frequency of the phase relations among the contours of the holoscape (3), guides the charge carriers in each location to change with an energy proportional to that frequency. In other words, the dendritic holoscape of contours (2) at any moment controls the further time evolution of charge carriers in the entire dendritic network. According to the theory presented here, this pattern of charge carriers (i.e., ionic bioplasma) in the dendritic network of primary sensory cortex processes sensory input. Thus, the dendritic holoscape (2) of this cortex can be regarded as coordinate with image processing.

3. NEURODYNAMICS

In this section, we make an elementary exposition of a mathematical framework regarding the reciprocal feedback and feedforward control mechanism of the distribution of dendritic ionic bioplasma and the fundamental oscillations of dendritic membrane polarizations. Again, we consider the geometric extent of the dendritic network as an idealized two dimensional compact manifold M. As we have seen in the preceding section, the complex function $\theta(x,t)$ given by Eq. (2) is a representative of the fundamental oscillations of membrane polarizations. It illustrates a system of isophase contours in the dendritic network, and controls the distribution of ionic bioplasma along the spatial frequency of the fundamental oscillations of dendritic membrane polarizations. Therefore, the complex function θ may be considered a control variable of the system.

Further, the changes in the distribution of the ionic bioplasma in the dendritic network are well described by the time evolution of a *density distribution* of ionic bioplasma at each point of the dendritic network M with coordinates x. We therefore choose the density distribution as a system variable. We denote this density distribution by $\rho(x,t)$. The dynamics of system and control variables, ρ and θ, in the dendritic network provide the key concepts for developing a formal neurodynamics; its mathematical formulation follows.

First, we consider the dynamics of the density distribution of ionic bioplasma in the dendritic network through the time evolution of the system variable ρ. The system variable ρ describes the evolution of the charge carriers in the Debye layer of ionic bioplasma immediately beneath the dendritic membrane. Namely, in each location x of the denditic network M, the density of ionic bioplasma $\rho(x,t)$ changes its value as time t passes because some locations become hyperpolarized, others depolarized.

Time evolution of the density distribution of ionic bioplasma may be well illustrated by a "flow" in the whole dendritic network. Flow in the ionic bioplasma in each location x at time t is described by a current velocity $v(x,t)$. For each t, it defines a vector field on the dendritic network M. As the current velocity v describes both direction and rate of change of ionic bioplasma, the density function ρ evolves according to the equation of continuity

$$\frac{\partial \rho}{\partial t} + \text{div}(\rho v) = 0. \tag{5}$$

Here, div denotes the computation of the divergence of a vector field on M. Thus, change in the density distribution of the ionic bioplasma characterizes the time evolution of system variables completely. The spatiotemporal pattern of the change in the ionic bioplasma over the whole network is assumed coordinate with initial perceptual processing by the brain.

Second, we consider the control mechanism operating on the ionic bioplasma. In neurodynamics, it is the relation among dendritic isophase contours θ that controls the system variable ρ via the maximum phase difference. Recall the spatial frequency of the relations among isophase contours given by the gradient vector of the phase function (3). It describes the phase difference of fundamental oscillations between neighboring locations. We assume in neurodynamics that the spatial frequency $k(x,t)$ of the relation among isophase contours $\theta(x,t)$ guides the density of the ionic bioplasma in each location x at time t to flow along it. In other words, the current velocity of change of the ionic bioplasma $v(x,t)$ is controlled in each location so as to be proportional to the spatial frequency vector $k(x,t)$. With an appropriate constant of proportionality $v > 0$, we have

$$v = \nu\, k$$

$$= \nu\, \nabla\, S. \tag{6}$$

It seems worthwhile to notice here that this type of control mechanism has been observed experimentally in the simple biological system of the amoeba. Such a control mechanism composed of phase differences may thus represent an essential ingredient in the development (ontogenesis) of biological systems. Here we incorporate it as the neurodynamics controlling the distribution of ionic bioplasma within the dendritic network.

Equations (5) and (6) yield one of the fundamental equations of neurodynamics

$$\frac{\partial \rho}{\partial t} = -\nu\, \text{div}(\rho\, \nabla\, S), \tag{7}$$

which describes how the system and control variables couple with each other.

However, to adequately describe the control mechanism of the dynamical system of ionic bioplasma, we need another fundamental equation. Since the system variable is the distribution density of the ionic bioplasma, we introduce a control process in terms of a least action principle. Namely, the variable θ controls, in each location of the dendritic network, the local amplitude of oscillation of membrane potentials so that the resulting global dynamics of the ionic bioplasma are governed by a least action principle.

Let us forget for the moment the existence of the control variable θ, and consider the global dynamics of the distribution of the density of the ionic bioplasma ρ. The total kinetic energy of the ionic bioplasma in the dendritic network is given by

$$\int_M \frac{1}{2}\, |v(x,t)|^2 \rho(x,t)dx, \tag{8}$$

where $|v|$ denotes the length of vector v and dx denotes the invariant surface element of the manifold M. The total static energy of the density distribution of the ionic bioplasma is of the form

$$\int_M V(\rho(x,t))\rho(x,t)dx, \tag{9}$$

where V is a certain given function describing the local static energy. The local static energy consists of extrinsic and intrinsic variables. The extrinsic local static energy represents a static energy of ionic bioplasma in each location x induced by the static interaction with the oligodendroglia and extracellular environment. This environment of the dendritic membrane in each location is composed of extracellular space or oligodendroglia. In a sense we may be allowed to think of the distribution of the density of the ionic bioplasma as occurring within constraints provided by the configuration of the extraneuronal space, especially the glia. Thus the local static energy does not depend on the distribution of the ionic bioplasma with density $\rho(x,t)$, but is constrained by a certain given function $U_{ex}(x)$. It may thus depend only remotely on the time parameter t, because the time scale of the change in the glia and interstitial chemical concentration is large compared with that of the evolution of the distribution density of the ionic bioplasma.

The intrinsic static energy of the ionic bioplasma is a kind of stress energy of the density distribution of bioplasma. Such a stress energy of the density distribution ρ may be given as a nonlinear function of ρ. A possible form of intrinsic static energy may be given by the "pressure"

$$U_{op}(\rho(x,t)) = \frac{v}{2} \left(\frac{1}{2} \frac{\nabla\rho(x,t)}{\rho(x,t)} \right)^2 \qquad (10)$$

which represents a stress energy due to differences in concentration of the local distribution of ionic bioplasma (Nagasawa, 1980; Nelson, 1967). Therefore, the total static energy of the ionic bioplasma in the dendritic network (9) becomes

$$\int_M (U_{ex} + U_{op})\, \rho dx. \qquad (11)$$

A dynamical quantity given by the difference between the total kinetic and static energies plays a central role in introducing the least action principle. It is called a Lagrangian of the system (of the density distribution of the ionic bioplasma) and defined to be

$$L = \int_M \left(\frac{1}{2} |v|^2 - U_{ex} - U_{op} \right) \rho dx. \qquad (12)$$

It determines the total time evolution of the density distribution of the ionic bioplasma through the following least action principle: the dynamics of the ionic bioplasma is described by a time evolution of the system variable ρ which makes the action integral

$$J = \int_a^b L\, dt$$

$$= \int_a^b \int_M \left(\frac{1}{2} |v|^2 - U_{ex} - U_{op} \right) \rho dx dt \qquad (13)$$

take its local minimum value.

The meaning of the least action principle may be understood with mathemati-

cal intuition. As the time passes, changes in the distribution of the ionic bioplasma evolve (due to the control represented by the isophase contour). Thus,
the system variable ρ manifests a systematized time evolution. Such a systematized time evolution of ρ differs from other virtual time evolutions at a point
that the action integral along the systematized time evolution is less than those
along other virtual ones. In this sense, the action integral (13) is the most
important quantity in neurodynamics which characterizes completely the global
dynamics of the distribution of ionic bioplasma in the dendritic network.

Now, let us recall that the systematized time evolution of the distribution of
the ionic bioplasma is achieved by the control represented by the isophase contours composing the holoscape. Therefore, in neurodynamics, we interpret the
least action principle with the action integral (13) representing the global control
of the distribution of the ionic bioplasma by the isophase contours. From the
point of view of the holonomic brain theory, the least action principle is therefore
nothing other than a control of the dendritic system by the patterns of isophase
contours.

4.   THE NEURAL WAVE EQUATION

We have proposed a least action principle in a neurodynamics of the density
distribution of the ionic bioplasma in the dendritic network. The system variable
ρ and the control variable θ manifest the system's time evolution as governed by
the least action principle (13) as well as the equation of continuity (7). Therefore,
we need to look for the functional forms of the system and control variables ρ and
θ which satisfy those principles and equations. They describe the interactions
among the ionic bioplasma and the fundamental oscillation of membrane polarizations in the dendritic network.

However, the least action principle in its original form of the action integral
(13) does not provide a direct functional relation between ρ and θ unlike the
equation of continuity (7). It is an indirect statement representing the time evolution of the system and control variables. From the practical point of view of
mathematical analysis, it would be better to obtain a direct functional relation
between ρ and θ from the least action principle. This would make the analysis of
the neurodynamics involved much easier. The least action principle as expressed
by the action integral (13) is a typical variational problem which at least formally
falls into a class described by the stochastic calculus of variations. (Blancher, et
al., 1987; Nelson, 1984; Yasue, 1981, 1981b; Zambrini, 1985, 1986a, 1986b,
1986b, 1987). It is of the same form as Lafferty's variational principle (Nelson,
1984). Here, we use the mathematical result of Lafferty's analysis.

The least action principle with respect to the action path integral is equivalent
to the following direct functional relations between system and control variables
ρ and θ.

$$-\frac{\partial S}{\partial t} = \frac{1}{2}|v|^2 + U_{ex} - U_{op} - \frac{v}{4}\Delta \log \rho. \tag{14}$$

Here $\Delta = \operatorname{div} \nabla$ is a second order partial differential operator called a Laplacian. Equation (14) is a conventional second order partial differential equation, though it is nonlinear in variables ρ and θ.

We have finally arrived at all the fundamental equations that characterize a neurodynamics in the form of differential equations (7) and (14). Notice that S is a phase function of the relations among dendritic isophase contours θ given by Eq. (2). The changes occuring in the density distribution of ionic bioplasma are related to S by Eq. (6). Therefore, the fundamental equations (7) and (14) become two coupled nonlinear partial differential equations for two unknown variables ρ and θ. Given the intial forms of distribution density ρ and relations among isophase contours θ at a certain initial time, say t = 0, Eqs. (7) and (14) determine completely the functional forms of ρ and θ for all times thereafter. The system and control variables thus determined, describe the systematized changes of the density distribution of the ionic bioplasma controlled by the oscillating membrane polarizations against the glial and extracellular static energy U_{ex}. These exchanges can be triggered by the discharge of neurotransmitters, neuroregulators, and neuromodulators by presynaptic activity, which dramatically changes U_{ex}.

The fundamental equations (7) and (14) are coupled nonlinear partial differential equations, and it is not easy to perform mathematical analyses with them. Therefore, it seems convenient to find a transformation with which to rewrite equations (7) and (14) into reduced forms. Let us introduce a complex-valued function $\psi = \psi(x,t)$ by

$$\psi = \sqrt{\rho}\, \theta$$
$$= \sqrt{\rho}\, e^{iS}. \tag{15}$$

This new dynamical variable contains information about both ionic bioplasma density distribution ρ and the relations among isophase contours θ. We call this a neural wave function characterizing the neurodynamic of the dendritic network. It is indeed a wave function because it is governed by a linear wave equation. Namely, the fundamental equations (7) and (14) for system and control variables ρ and θ can be converted into the following single linear partial differential equation for the new variable ψ by the transformation (15)

$$iv\frac{\partial \psi}{\partial t} = \left(-\frac{v^2}{2}\Delta + U_{ex}\right)\psi \tag{16}$$

Interestingly, *it is of the same form as the wave equation in quantum theory,* and will be called *a neural wave equation.* The systematized time evolution of system and of control variables of the dendritic network is well illustrated by the neural wave function ψ subject to the neural wave equation (16). In this sense, the equation describing the neural wave function is the single most fundamental in neurodynamics.

Because the neural wave equation (16) is linear, analysis of neurodynamics can be performed within the realm of conventional mathematical analysis. For example, the existence of solutions to the neural wave equation (16) for a wider class of external static potentials U_{ex} is known (Kato, 1964). The use of the neural wave equation in neurodynamics opens the possibility to represent the dendritic microprocess within a new mathematical framework.

It seems worthwhile to notice here that the formal similarity between neural and quantum processes has been pointed out both in physics and in neurology. In physics, Margenau (1984) has suggested that a process similar to electron tunnelling occurs in the neural microprocess. Hamerhoff (1987) has developed the theme that soliton waves occurring in microtubules could account for dendritic processing. And in the context of the current appendix, the formulations of Frölich (1975), Umezawa (Stuart et al., 1978; 1979), and Singer (Singer, 1989; Gray & Singer, 1989, Gray et.al., 1989) become especially relevant. Further as noted in Lectures 2 and 4 of this volume, Gabor developed a communication theory based on psychophysics that used the same formalisms as those used by Heisenberg in his descriptions of quantum microphysics. From the neurological standpoint, the holonomic brain theory is based on these proposals. Neurodynamics as developed in this appendix incorporates this formalism in a mathematical model in which the fundamental equation is of the same form as in the quantum theory.

5. TORUS AS AN IDEALIZED DENDRITIC ELEMENT

We have represented the spatial extent of the dendritic membrane network by a two dimensional manifold M. Because the dendritic network shows only finite extent, M becomes compact: The mathematical notion "compact" stands for the intuitive notion "finite." The dendritic network consists of many branches having mutual connections via chemical synapses, electric ephapses, and tight junctions. Therefore, the representative manifold M must necessarily be multiply connected. The simplest and most familiar example of such a two dimensional multiply connected manifold is a doughnut.

As the simplest model of a cross section of a dendritic membrane network, we consider a doughnut-like single loop. The processing element of a real dendritic network is, of course, much more complex (see e.g. end section of this Appendix). However, an essential aspect of neurodynamics may be well illustrated by this simplest model. The doughnut-like single loop can be represented by a manifold called a two dimensional torus. From the point of view of geometry, it is nothing but the surface of a doughnut. Topologicaly considered, the torus is a flat rectangle in which two facing edges are identified to be the same. In other words, the two dimensional torus is a flat rectangle with periodic boundary conditions at its edges.

Let us investigate the dendritic microprocesses in such a torus M by means of the neural wave equation (16). The neurodynamics of the density distribution of the ionic bioplasma represented by changes in the relations among isophase contours in M is illustrated by the time evolution of a neural wave function ψ subject to Eq. (16). Recall that the effect of an external environment on the dendritic network is described by the external static energy U_{ex}. As a consequence, the neural wave equation (16) can be decomposed into spatial and temporal parts,

$$\left(-\frac{v^2}{2} \Delta + U_{ex} \right) u(x) = \lambda\, u(x), \tag{17}$$

$$iv\, \frac{d}{dt} f(t) = \lambda\, f(t), \tag{18}$$

by assuming a specific form of the neural wave equation

$$\psi(x,t) = u(x)\, f(t). \tag{19}$$

Here, λ is the constant of separation. Equation (18) can be integrated immediately, obtaining

$$f(t) = \exp\left(-i\, \frac{\lambda}{v}\, t \right). \tag{20}$$

Equation (17) then becomes an eigen value problem, and the unknown constant λ is determined as an eigen value of the second order partial differential operator

$$-\frac{v^2}{2} \Delta + U_{ex}(x). \tag{21}$$

As the torus may be identified with a rectangle with periodic boundary conditions, the eigen value problem (17) is given in the rectangle with linear dimension $L > 0$. The periodic boundary conditions

$$u(0,x^2) = u(L,x^2), \tag{22}$$

$$u(x^1,0) = u(x^1,L), \tag{23}$$

are assumed for the solution u. Here, the positive constant L indicates the scale of spatial extent of the involved portion of the dentritic network.

Suppose that the external environment of the dendritic network M is very weak, and the external static energy U_{ex} can be considered very small. As an idealized approximation of the neurodynamics of such a situation, we can consider the neural wave equation (16) with vanishing U_{ex}. Then, Eq. (17) becomes

$$-\frac{v^2}{2}\,\Delta u(x) = \lambda\,u(x). \tag{24}$$

This eigen value equation with its periodic boundary conditions (22) and (23) can be solved for infinitely many values of λ,

$$\lambda = \frac{v^2}{2}\left(\frac{2\pi}{L}\right)^2 (n_1^2 + n_2^2) \tag{25}$$

where n_1 and n_2 are any integers. For each values of n_1 and n_2, $n = (n_1, n_2)$ may be considered as a two dimensional vector on the manifold M and Eq. (25) may be written as

$$\lambda = \frac{v^2}{2}\left(\frac{2\pi}{L}\right)^2 |n|^2$$

$$\equiv \lambda_n. \tag{26}$$

A solution of the eigen value equation (24) corresponding to the specific value of λ, say λ_n, is a plane wave function

$$u(x) = \left(\frac{1}{L}\right) \exp\left(i\,\frac{2\pi}{L}\,n\cdot x\right)$$

$$\equiv u_n(x), \tag{27}$$

where $n \cdot x = n_1 x^1 + n_2 x^2$ denotes the inner product of two vectors $n = (n_1, n_2)$ and $x = (x^1, x^2)$. By using Eq. (19) we find that the neural wave function

$$\psi_n(x,t) = \left(\frac{1}{L}\right) \exp\left\{\frac{i}{v}\left(\frac{2\pi}{L}\,v\cdot x - \lambda_n\,t\right)\right\} \tag{29}$$

solves the neural wave equation (16) with vanishing external static energy U_{ex}. It seems worthwhile to notice here that the neural function (29) describes the relations among isophase contours with a wave number vector n and a frequency λ_n/v. The wave number vector n is the spatial frequency (distance between or density distribution) of isophase contours.

As we have seen in the preceding sections, the neural wave function gives a complete description of neurodynamics through Eq. (15). There $\rho = |\psi|^2$ denotes the ionic bioplasma density distribution and $\theta = \psi/|\psi|$ denotes the changes of the relations among the isophase contours. Equation (29) yields

$$\rho = |\psi_n(x,t)|^2$$

$$= \left(\frac{1}{L}\right)^2 \tag{30}$$

and

$$\theta(x,t) = \exp\left\{\frac{i}{\nu}\left(\frac{2\pi}{L}\nu \cdot x - \lambda_n t\right)\right\}$$

$$\equiv \theta_n(x,t). \tag{31}$$

In neurodynamics, the ionic bioplasma flow in the dendritic network is driven by the phase differences among the isophase contours θ. The changes in relations among isophase contours (31) therefore describe a "flow" within the dendritic network M with current velocity (6) obtaining

$$\mathbf{v} = \frac{2\pi}{L}\nu. \tag{32}$$

This "flow" illustrates a typical collective flux in the density distribution of ionic bioplasma in the dendritic network which manifests a uniform flux of ionic bioplasma with a common velocity (32). Even though the polarization density distribution remains uniform as Eq. (30) shows, there may exist a constant flux in the density distribution of the ionic bioplasma. This situation seems analogous to hydrodynamics of an incompressible fluid.

6.   FOURIER DECOMPOSITION AND THE CYBERNETICS OF IMAGE PROCESSING

A more general solution of the neural wave equation (16) for vanishing external static energy U_{ex} can be obtained by assuming a linear superposition of the plane wave functions u_n's,

$$\psi(x,t) = \sum_n \alpha_n(t)\, u_n(x). \tag{33}$$

Substituting this expression into the neural wave equation (16), we obtain a system of decoupled ordinary differential equations,

$$i\nu \frac{d}{dt}\alpha_n(t) = \lambda_n\alpha_n(t). \tag{34}$$

This system can be integrated immediately and Eq. (33) becomes

$$\psi(x,t) = \sum_n \alpha_n\left(\frac{1}{L}\right) \exp\left\{\frac{i}{\nu}\left(\frac{2\pi}{L}\nu \cdot x - \lambda_n t\right)\right\}, \tag{35}$$

where α_n's are constants of integration. It is worthwhile to notice here that Eq. (35) is a Fourier series expansion of the neural wave function ψ.

Such a Fourier series expansion remains valid for nonvanishing U_{ex}. Substitution of Eq. (33) into the neural wave equation (16) yields a system of coupled ordinary differential equations

$$iv \frac{d}{dt} \alpha_n(t) = \lambda_n \alpha_n(t) + \sum_k U_{n-k} \, \alpha_n(t), \tag{36}$$

where U_p's are Fourier coefficients of the function $U_{ex}(x)$ such that

$$U_{ex}(x) = \sum_p U_p \left(\frac{1}{L}\right) \exp \left(i \frac{2\pi}{L} p \cdot x\right). \tag{37}$$

We see finally that the neural wave function describing the neurodynamics of the density distribution of the ionic bioplasma and, of the resulting oscillations of the membrane polarization is completely specified by the Fourier coefficients subject to Eq. (36). Once Fourier coefficients are obtained by solving Eq. (36), therefore, the patterns of flux of ionic bioplasma in the dendritic network M is specified.

Let us compute, for example, the ionic bioplasma density distribution ρ given by the neural wave equation ψ for nonvanishing static potential energy U_{ex}.

$$\rho(x,t) = |\psi(x,t)|^2$$

$$= \sum_n |\alpha_n(t)|^2 \left(\frac{1}{L}\right)^2$$

$$+ \sum_{n \neq k} \overline{\alpha_k(t)} \, \alpha_n(t) \left(\frac{1}{L}\right)^2 \exp \left\{i \frac{2\pi}{L} (n - k) \cdot x\right\}. \tag{38}$$

The second term in the right hand side of Eq. (38) shows the existence of a time-dependent interference pattern in the spatial density distribution of ionic bioplasma. In other words, the collective flux of ionic bioplasma in the dendritic network manifests a spatio-temporal interference pattern due to the Fourier series expansion and the external static energy U_{ex}. Given the effect of the external environment on the dendritic network M described by U_{ex}, the collective flux of density distribution of the ionic bioplasma in the dendritic network manifests a typical spatio-temporal interference pattern illustrated by the neural wave function ψ subject to the neural wave equation (16). Such a collective flux in the density of the ionic bioplasma represents the fundamental neural process considered to be coordinate with imaging.

As we have shown in Section 3 and 4, a neural wave function governed by the neural wave equation (16) describes the nonlocal control process of the distribution of ionic bioplasma in the dendritic network due to the globally tuned membrane potential oscillations. This nonlocal control mechanism generates a systematized order in the dendritic microprocesses.

In quantum mechanics, a wave function ψ governed by Schrödinger's wave equation describes both position and momentum of a quantum particle. The absolute square of the wave function $| \psi |^2$ is the probability distribution density of the position, and the gradient of the phase of ψ defines the momentum flux. In neurodynamics, the neural wave function ψ governed by the neural wave equation (16) describes the instantaneous state of isophase contours and the direction of its change is given by the density distribution $\rho = | \psi |^2$ and the gradient of the phase of ψ.

The instantaneous state of the holoscape of isophase contours described by the density distribution of the dendritic ionic bioplasma (i.e., the system variable) ρ is controlled globally by the distribution of phase differences (i.e., control variable) S. Such a global control process and the resulting order appear in many biological cooperative phenomena. For example, amoeba like cells show "image processing" activities in response to various stimuli by a control process similar to that described here. Thus, the global control system introduced in Section 2 as a model of the neurodynamics operating in the dendritic network may serve more generally as a type of "non-local cybernetics" essential for image processing activity in biology.

7.   SPIN AND THE CONFIGURATION OF THE DENDRITIC MICROPROCESS

The general form of the dendritic network is, of course, much more complex than the simple torus we have described in the preceding sections. As noted in Lecture 2, the dendritic polarizations and those of the dendritic spines form couplets that are perpendicular to each other. The actual form of the computational manifold M must be described as highly multiply connected and multidimensional. We have restricted our consideration only to polarization configurations occupying dendrites. Because of this simplification we could take only the spatial distribution pattern of the polarizations on the dendritic network manifold into account. There, the direction of polarization remains always perpendicular to the manifold of dendritic membranes, and it suffices to point out the translational coordinates of each polarization.

However, if we look into the detailed polarization configuration in both dendritic spines and dendrites, they interact with each other. As a result, we must also consider superposition of spine and dendrite polarization, that is, their vector sum. In this case, the direction of each polarization no longer remains fixed, that is, perpendicular to the dendritic membrane manifold. The vector sum of the spine polarization and the dendrite polarization provides a polarization vector at each location in the dendritic network, which indicates spatial direction. Therefore, the detailed polarization distribution pattern should contain not only the translational configuration in the dendritic network manifold but also the directional configuration of spherical rotation. Such a combination of translational and rotational degrees of freedom constitute a spin whose functions can be best illustrated by enlarging the configuration space of system variables from the dendritic network manifold M to the direct product space of M and the spherical rotation group manifold SO(3), that is M × SO(3). This processing space takes on special significance when invariences are extracted from the superposition of iterated sensory inputs. (See Appendix B.)

All the mathematical procedures developed in the preceding sections for neurodynamics on the dendritic network manifold M go on equally even for the enlarged configuration space M × SO (3) (Blanchard, Combe, & Zheng, 1987). Thus, we obtain a two component neural wave equation of the same form as the Pauli equation in quantum dynamics for spinning particles, just as we have obtained the neural wave equation of the same form as the Schrödinger equation. More of this in Appendix B.

Appendix B: *Symmetry, Invariance, and Group Theory In Object Perception*

1. INTRODUCTION

The variational approach taken in Appendix A makes certain assumptions that stabilize the variational integral; thus yielding the Euler-Lagrange equations of classical mechanics, the field equations of general relativity, and the foundation of contemporary quantum field theory. In the current appendix these assumptions are examined with regard to the brain processes coordinate with object-form perception. Mathematically, the Euler-Lagrange equations correspond to paths in configuration space. In perception these paths are defined by eye movements that change the relations between successive optical images within a reference frame constructed by these paths. Recall Poincaré's insightful statement that objects are relations. Mathematically, these relations are specified as groups. As we shall see, in mathematical group theory, relations within a transformation space are primary and are independent of particular inputs to that group. Thus, a group theoretical approach to perception associates with a particular perceptual relationship (an object-form), the mathematical group of transformations which conserves that relationship.

Basic to the development of the theory described here are the following assumptions. The evidence on which the assumptions are based are detailed in Part I of the lectures.

1. Optical images are formed by the optical system of the eye from the optic array, that is, the optic flow originating in the "layout" of the visual world as it is scanned by the moving eye. Optical images constitute an occulo-centric space.

295

2. Interactions of optical images are processed by the visual system in such a way that eye movements are controlled by relations among the iterated optical images.

3. These relations thus form an object centered space composed of invariants that circumscribe their own reference frames.

It is a fundamental result of the calculus of variations that it conserves a certain dynamical quantity (the invariant relationship). Such a conserved quantity provides symmetry (and therefore also a reference frame) in the neurodynamics of dendritic microprocesses, which is induced by iterations of optical images. In other words, the brain processes symmetries through the existence of a conserved quantity which remains invariant in the time evolution of the internal state of neurodynamics. Such a conserved quantity remains invariant even when the internal dynamical state of the dendritic system of ionic bioplasma density distributions producing membrane polarization oscillations evolves due to an imposed external static energy. It is in this sense, that symmetry properties in the iterations of optical images are to some extent generated by the dendritic microprocess: the conservation of the quantities that produce invariants is due to the very fact that the neurodynamics and therefore the eye movements that determine the optical images are governed by their action integral, through the least action principle.

More precisely, the symmetry property inherent in certain iterated optical images corresponds to the symmetry of the external static energy imposed on the dendritic network. Namely, the iterated optical images become integrated and mapped into the external static energy that manifests a symmetry property arising from the eye movement produced iterations. Thus, the Lagrangian describing the system of density distribution of the ionic bioplasma in the dendritic network naturally manifests the symmetry. The least action principle in neurodynamics asserts that such a Lagrangian ensures the existence of conserved quantitites that are kept invariant during the time evolution of the internal dynamical state of the microprocess. In other words, if there happens to be a quantity that is kept invariant or conserved in the neurodynamic time evolution of the dendritic microprocess, the symmetry property of the iterated optical image is maintained by way of eye movements that are guided by that symmetry.

In a series of papers, Carlton, in collaboration with Pribram and with Shepard developed a group theoretical formulation of invariance resulting from the motion of object forms (Carlton, 1989; Carlton & Shepard, 1988a, 1988b; Pribram & Carlton, 1986). These studies detail how psychologically experienced motion of object forms can be mapped into abstract representations describing the microstructure of neural activity in the visual systems. These representations are formulated in terms of a Hilbert space of Gabor elementary functions. The Gabor elementary function allowed Pribram and Carlton to introduce a concrete example describing the transformations occurring in the visual system.

However, other types of transformation (e.g., those in audition leading to the construction of phoneomes) different from those occurring in vision may not have this particular explicit form. We therefore will develop here a more general form of representation of the dynamics of dendritic microprocesses. This is because mathematically the explicit *solution* of the fundamental dynamical equation cannot always be obtained even though the explicit form of fundamental dynamics may be known. As will be described, knowing the explicit form of the dynamics does, however, allow the specification of that which is being processed (the conserved quantities).

We have shown in Appendix A that the least action principle in neurodynamics is equivalent to the neural wave equation. Passing to the geometrical formulation of the least action principle in the Hilbert space describing internal states (i.e., neural wave functions), the conserved quantity is, in the current appendix, shown to be transferred into an invariant subspace of the Hilbert space. We proceed then, to investigate the fundamental process constituting this subspace by means of the irreducible representation of the symmetry group and to show that this representation, in turn, determines the conserved quantity.

2. LEAST ACTION PRINCIPLE AND SYMMETRY

Before proceeding to neurodynamics, it may be of some interest to review here the principal role of the least action principle in the investigation of symmetry and the invariant property of dynamics of a physical system. The main source for this review is Abraham and Marsden (1978).

Let us consider a physical system with f degrees of freedom. The number f of the degrees of freedom may take any natural number. Time evolution of the physical system may be illustrated by considering the f degrees of freedom as functions of the time parameter t. Introducing appropriate physical units of the degrees of freedom, they become real valued functions of time, $q^1 = q^1(t)$, $q^2 = q^2(t), \ldots , q^f = q^f$ (t). The totality of these functions $\mathbf{q} = \mathbf{q}(t) = (q^1(t), q^2(t), \ldots , q^f(t))$ is the mathematical representative of the time evolution of the physical system. We call $\mathbf{q}$ the coordinate variable of the physical system. For example, if we consider the inter-continental flight of a Boeing 747 as a physical system, its coordinate variable may be $\mathbf{q} = (q^1, q^2, q^3)$, where q^1 denotes the latitude of the Boeing 747, q^2 the longitude, and q^3 the altitude. Of course, if you worry about your life insurance, you may consider a finer coordinate variable $\mathbf{q} = (q^1, q^2, q^3, q^4)$, where q^4 denotes the amount of fuel and the remaining variables are the same as above. Thus, the coordinate variable of the physical system may not be chosen uniquely. Certain degrees of freedom may be neglected so that the analysis of the physical system becomes much simpler.

We have seen that when we investigate the dynamics of the physical system, we first choose the coordinate variable. We can use any coordinate variable, but

it is convenient for further mathematical analysis to use that made of f independent functions of time. This is simply because the physical system with f degrees
of freedom can be always described by a proper coordinate variable made up of f
independent functions of time. We use such a proper coordinate variable of the
physical system in what follows.

Given the functional form of the coordinate variable $\mathbf{q} = \mathbf{q}(t)$, the dynamical
property of the physical system can be seen immediately in the time evolution $\mathbf{q}$
$= \mathbf{q}(t)$ as time t passes. If certain functional relations are found to hold for the
coordinate variable $\mathbf{q} = \mathbf{q}(t)$, they may describe dynamical laws of the physical
system. Among those dynamical laws, there may exist the most fundamental one
from which other ones can be derived functionally. It is called the fundamental
dynamical principle of the physical system. For a wider class of physical systems, the fundamental dynamical principle may take the following universal
form:

Time evolution of the physical system is described by the coordinate variable
$\mathbf{q} = \mathbf{q}(t)$, which minimizes the integral

$$J = \int_a^b L(\mathbf{q}(t),\dot{\mathbf{q}}(t),t)dt \tag{1}$$

taken between the initial time $t = a$ and the final time $t = b$, where L is a given func-
tion of the coordinate variable $\mathbf{q}(t)$, its time derivative $\dot{\mathbf{q}}(t) = \dfrac{d\mathbf{q}(t)}{dt}$ and time t.

It is called *the least action principle* or *the variational principle*. The integral
J is called the action integral or the action functional of the physical system. Its
integrand L is the most fundamental quantity that characterizes completely the
dynamics of the physical system, and it is called *the Lagrangian* of the physical
system. The least action principle may be thought of as the most fundamental
form of the dynamical law in physical science. Even if the physical system in
question manifests spatial extension and so the coordinate variable becomes a
field quantity $\phi = \phi(x,t)$ depending on both parameters x and t denoting the
spatial and temporal extension, the fundamental dynamical principle still maintains variational form:

Time evolution of the physical system with spatial extension is described by
the field variable $\phi = \phi(x,t)$ which minimizes the action integral

$$J = \int_a^b L\left(\phi,\nabla\phi, \frac{\partial\phi}{\partial t},t\right) dt, \tag{2}$$

where the Lagrangian is given by the spatial integral

$$L\left(\phi,\nabla\phi, \frac{\partial\phi}{\partial t},t\right) = \int \mathscr{L}\left(\phi(x,t),\nabla\phi(x,t), \frac{\partial\phi(x,t)}{\partial t},t\right) dx \tag{3}$$

The integrand $\mathscr{L}$ is a given function of the field variable $\phi(x,t)$, its gradient (i.e., spatial derivative) $\nabla\phi(x,t)$, its time derivative $\dfrac{\partial\phi}{\partial t}(x,t)$, and time t. It is charac-teristic to the physical system with spatial extension, and called the Lagrangian density. Recall that the least action principle in the neurodynamics of the system of the distribution of the ionic bioplasma and the fundamental membrane polariz-ation oscillation in the dendritic network takes this form. (See Appendix A)

The least action principle is the most fundamental dynamical law of the physical system because other dynamical laws may be derived from it. For example, the dynamical equation is derived from the action integral by means of a simple application of calculus of variations. The action integral J given by Eq. (1) leads to the dynamical equation

$$\frac{d}{dt}\left(\frac{\partial L}{\partial \dot{\mathbf{q}}(t)}\right) - \frac{\partial L}{\partial \mathbf{q}(t)} = 0, \tag{4}$$

whereas that given by Eq. (2) leads to

$$\frac{\partial}{\partial t}\left(\frac{\partial \mathscr{L}}{\partial \dfrac{\partial \phi}{\partial t}}\right) + \nabla\left(\frac{\partial \mathscr{L}}{\partial \nabla\phi}\right) - \frac{\partial \mathscr{L}}{\partial \phi} = 0. \tag{5}$$

Both dynamical equations (4) and (5) are called the Euler-Lagrange equations with respect to the action integrals (1) and (2), respectively, though the former is an ordinary differential equation for the coordinate variable $\mathbf{q} = \mathbf{q}(t)$ and the latter is a partial differential equation for the field variable $\phi = \phi(x,t)$.

The least action principle derives not only the dynamical equation but also many other dynamical laws of the physical system. Especially, it provides us with a systematic method to investigate a specific class of dynamical laws closely related to the symmetry of the physical system. Let us suppose that the time evolution of the physical system is described by the coordinate variable $\mathbf{q} = \mathbf{q}(t)$ subject to the least action principle with respect to the action integral (1). The Lagrangian L characterizes the dynamical property for the physical system com-pletely. In this sense, certain functional properties of the Lagrangian L may be understood to illustrate the corresponding dynamical properties of the physical system.

For the mathematical analysis it is convenient to think of the coordinate variable $\mathbf{q}(t)$ for each time t as a point in a certain representative space. Such a representative space is known to be a smooth manifold with the dimensionality equal to the number of degrees of freedom. It is frequently called the configura-tion space of the physical space, and denoted by Ω. Then, the instantaneous value $\mathbf{q}(t)$ of the coordinate variable corresponds to a point in the configuration space. In other words, every point in the configuration space Ω can be thought in principle to represent a possible instantaneous value (in vision, a Gabor elementary function) of the coordinate variable of the physical system. Let us consider now a group of one-to-one mappings from the configuration space Ω onto itself. Such a group is said to be a transformation group in Ω. Let $\{T_\alpha\}$ be a transformation group with index parameter α. For each value of α, the group element T_α is a one-to-one mapping from Ω onto Ω, that is, a transformation in Ω. The group property of the set of transformations $\{T_\alpha\}$ can be understood immediately because the transformations in a manifold are known to form a group with respect to the group multiplication given by the successive application of two transformations. A point, say q, in the configuration space Ω is mapped into a point, say r, in Ω by the transformation T_α. We write the image r of q as $T_\alpha\, q$.

Suppose we apply the transformation T_α in the configuration space of the physical system. Then, the coordinate variable of the physical system $q(t)$ is naturally mapped into $T\alpha\, q(t)$, and so its time derivative $\dot{q}(t)$ is mapped into $T_\alpha\, \dot{q}(t)$. The Lagrangian $L = L(q(t), \dot{q}(t), t)$ of the physical system becomes

$$L(T_\alpha q(t),\ T_\alpha \dot{q}(t), t).$$

It is most likely that the latter $L(T_\alpha q(t),\ T_\alpha \dot{q}(t), t)$ is different from the former $L(q(t), \dot{q}(t), t)$ due to the presence of the transformation T_α in the latter expression. However, it may happen that the Lagrangian of a specific physical system manifests accidentally the invariant property

$$L(T_\alpha q(t),\ T_\alpha \dot{q}(t), t) = L(q(t),\ \dot{q}(t), t)$$

for each element T_α of the transformation group $\{T_\alpha\}$. In this case, the Lagrangian L is said to be invariant under the transformation T_α, and the physical system characterized by the Lagrangian L is said to manifest symmetry under the transformation T_α.

It is worthwhile to notice here that the symmetry of the physical system can be stored or manifested in the time evolution of the coordinate variable. In other words, there exist several quantities which do not change their values in the time evolution as long as the symmetry of the physical system is kept. Such quantities provide us with proper representatives of the symmetry property of the physical system under the transformation group. They are called conserved quantities or invariants. We can represent the symmetry of the physical system by the invariant. Noether's theorem in the calculus of variations ensures the existence of such invariants. For example, an especially important class of dynamical laws called conservation laws such as the energy conservation law and the momentum conservation law are due to the invariant Lagrangian under certain transformation groups. More precisely, *the symmetry under the time translation is represented by the conserved energy, and that under the spatial translation by the conserved momentum.*

These considerations of symmetry and the invariance of the physical system can be extended immediately to the case of a physical system with spatial extension described by the field variable.

3. SYMMETRY AND INVARIANCE IN NEURODYNAMICS

We have seen in Appendix A that the dynamics of the system of density distribution of the ionic bioplasma distribution and fundamental membrane potential oscillation in the dendritic network can be illustrated as a physical system with two dimensional spatial extension. Dynamics of the system is described by the time evolution of the field variable ρ called the system variable. It stands for the density distribution of the ionic bioplasma in the dendritic network. There, the action integral

$$ J = \int_a^b \int_M \left(\frac{1}{2} |v|^2 - U_{ex} - U_{op} \right) \rho \, dxdt, \tag{6} $$

governs the dynamics, where v denotes the current velocity of the changes in density distributions of the ionic bioplasma subject to the equation of continuity

$$ \frac{\partial \rho}{\partial t} + \mathrm{div}(\rho v) = 0, \tag{7} $$

U_{ex} the extrinsic or external static energy, U_{op} the intrinsic static energy representing the stress energy of the ionic bioplasma distribution. The least action principle for the time evolution of the system variable ρ derives the fundamental dynamical equation

$$ -\frac{\partial S}{\partial t} = \frac{1}{2} |v|^2 + U_{ex} - U_{op} - \frac{v}{4} \Delta \log \rho, \tag{8} $$

where S denotes the phase of the control variable θ (i.e., the oscillating component of the membrane potential) which is related to the current velocity by

$$ v = v \nabla S, \tag{9} $$

with respect to the constant v. The fundamental dynamical equation (8) together with the equation of continuity (7) characterizes completely the neurodynamics of dendritic microprocesses. Due to the complicated functional form of the Lagrangian in terms of the system variable ρ, the fundamental dynamical equation (8) becomes nonlinear and seems to prevent us from further mathematical analysis. Not only the fundamental dynamical equation but also the conservation law suffers from the complicated functional form of the Lagrangian and it is not an easy task to find the symmetry property of the system that makes the

Lagrangian invariant under a certain transformation group. In other words, dynamics of the system of ionic bioplasma distribution ρ and fundamental polarization oscillation S is so sophisticated that the symmetry property of the system is hardly represented by the least action principle though the fundamental dynamical equations for the system and control variable ρ and S are barely derived from it.

The above difficulty may be understood to come from the choice of coordinate variables of the physical system directly related to the physical quantities such as the distribution density of the ionic bioplasma and the membrane potential. The least action principle is naturally concerned with dynamical variables with apparent physical meanings, because the Lagrangian would be chosen to have a concrete physical meaning of the difference between the kinetic energy and the static energy. This close relation of the action integral to physical quantitites makes it difficult to illustrate the symmetry property of the neurodynamics of dendritic microprocesses. For illustrating the symmetry or invariance property of the neurodynamics, we need to work with a coordinate variable which the group theoretical considerations of symmetry give intrinsically. Although such a coordinate variable may manifest less physical meaning and may not play as fundamental a role in the least action principle it must characterize the neurodynamics of the dendritic microprocesses completely in terms of symmetry and invariance. Therefore, it seems convenient to convert the fundamental dynamical equations (7) and (8) into other types of equations ready for the symmetry analysis in terms of this sort of abstract group theory. This becomes especially important if the neurodynamics of the dendritic microprocess is known to manifest a certain symmetry property induced by stimuli external to the system.

The most amenable form of the dynamical equation for this sort of group theoretical analysis is the eigen value problem for a linear equation. For example, the proper vibration of a building, the proper oscillation of molecules, and the sound resonance in a symphony hall are all described by eigen value problems for linear equations, and the group theoretical consideration of the symmetry property makes the analysis much easier. Fortunately, in neurodynamics of the system of ionic bioplasma distribution and fundamental membrane potential oscillation, the fundamental dynamical equations (7) and (8) can readily be converted into a linear equation, which turns out to be the eigen value problem. Let us introduce the new coordinate variable

$$\psi = \sqrt{\rho}\, e^{iS} \tag{9}$$

whose physical meaning is, at this juncture, difficult to understand. Then, the fundamental dynamical equations (7) and (8) can be converted into the linear partial differential equation

$$iv\, \frac{\partial \psi}{\partial t} = \left(-\frac{v^2}{2}\, \Delta + U_{ex} \right) \psi, \tag{10}$$

where Δ denotes the Laplacian operator. It is the neural wave equation of the dendritic microprocesses in which the symmetry property induced by the external stimuli appears.

4.   SYMMETRY GROUPS AND INTERNAL REPRESENTATIONS

As we have seen in the preceding section, the internal state of the fundamental process of neurodynamics in the dendritic network is given by the neural wave function $\psi(x,t) = \sqrt{\rho(x,t)}\theta(x,t) = \sqrt{\rho(x,t)}\exp\{iS(x,t)\}$, where $\rho(x,t)$ is the ionic bioplasma distribution density, $\theta(x,t)$ denotes the fundamental oscillation of the membrane potential, and $S(x,t)$ is the phase of the fundamental oscillation. The fundamental oscillation of the membrane potential $\theta(x,t)$ controls the distribution of the ionic bioplasma to drift along its spatial frequency $\nabla S(x,t)$ in the dendritic network. The fundamental process of neurodynamics is then illustrated by the time evolution of the neural wave function ψ. It is given by the neural wave equation (10). This is the fundamental equation of neurodynamics of dendritic microprocesses that describes the time evolution of the internal state of neurodynamics subject to the imposed external static energy U_{ex}.

It seems worthwhile to notice here that the external static energy U_{ex} imposed on the whole dendritic network manifests an integration of iterated external stimuli. Thus the external static energy U_{ex} has the role (in the neurodynamics of the dendritic microprocesses induced in the visual cortex) of representing the movement produced iterated optical images. The fundamental neural microprocess can be described directly by the Gabor transformation. This transformation necessarily preserves the symmetry property of movement produced iterations of optical images. In the more general case, the fundamental process of the dendritic microprocess is described only by the fundamental equation, that is, the neural wave equation (10), and the explicit form of the transformation of the external static energy U_{ex} to the neural wave function ψ is not known directly. Of course, the internal state of the neurodynamics of the dendritic microprocess represented by the neural wave function ψ is determined by the imposed external static energy U_{ex} with respect to the fundamental neural wave equation (10). The transformation of the external static energy U_{ex} to the internal state ψ is implicitly given by this equation so that whatever the symmetry property of the external static energy U_{ex} might be, it induces an equivalent symmetry in the internal state ψ. Therefore, with regard to the neurodynamics of dendritic microprocesses, we can refer to the symmetry property of the fundamental neural wave equation (10) whenever there is symmetry in U_{ex}.

What we are going to develop now is the reverse of the above procedure. We will show that the group representation of the symmetry property of the external static energy U_{ex} can be a consequence of the fundamental equation describing the neurodynamics of the system of density distribution of the ionic bioplasma and fundamental membrane potential oscillation in the dendritic network. Because we are mainly interested in the dynamical equation and not in the explicit form of its internal state (i.e., the neural wave function), it is more convenient to work with the abstract geometrical formulation of neurodynamics in the Hilbert space of neural wave functions that will be developed in this appendix.

The neural wave function $\psi(x,t)$ representing the internal state of neurodynamics is now considered as a normalized vector ψ_t in the Hilbert space $\mathcal{H}$ of square integrable functions. The neural wave equation (10) thus becomes a time evolution equation

$$iv \frac{d}{dt} \psi_t = K\psi_t, \tag{11}$$

with respect to the linear operator

$$K = -\frac{v^2}{2} \Delta + U_{ex}. \tag{12}$$

This linear operator K in the Hilbert space $\mathcal{H}$ is called the neural wave generator. Given the initial vector ψ_0 representing the initial internal state of neurodynamics at the initial time $t = 0$, the time evolution of the internal state of neurodynamics with respect to the imposed external static energy U_{ex} is given by the unitary flow.

$$\exp\left(-\frac{i}{v} Kt\right) \psi_0 \tag{13}$$

in the Hilbert space $\mathcal{H}$.

Suppose that a certain symmetry property characterizes the transformation group under a certain transformation of parameters of the process.

Let g_α be a transformation of such a parameter α. For example, g_α may be the Euclidean translation or rotation of an object form. Suppose that object form R is described as invariant under the group action of g_α. This invariant is first mapped and integrated into the external static energy U_{ex} imposed on the dendritic network M. Because it is the invariant representing the object-form R, we may write $U_{ex} = U_{ex}^R$. Let $U_{ex}^{R'} = U_{ex}^{g_\alpha R}$ be the imposed external static energy mapped from the object-form $R' = g_\alpha R$ transformed by the group action g_α. Because this object-form R is invariant under the group action g_α, we may conclude

$$R' = R \tag{14}$$

and so

$$U_{ex}^{R'} = U_{ex}^R. \tag{15}$$

In other words, the symmetry becomes represented by the invariance property of the external static energy U_{ex}. As the time evolution of the internal state of neurodynamics with respect to the imposed external static energy U_{ex} is given by the unitary flow (13), the symmetry is also represented in the time evolution of the internal state of neurodynamics of dendritic microprocesses. Recall that the external static energy U_{ex}, the neural wave generator $K = -\frac{v^2}{2}\Delta + U_{ex}$, and the unitary flow $\exp\left(-\frac{i}{v}Kt\right)$ are all kept invariant under the group action g_α. In other words, the group action g_α which makes the object-form invariant must also be represented in the Hilbert space $\mathcal{H}$ of internal states of neurodynamics in such a way that the representative of g_α leaves the neural generator K invariant.

Note that there exists a natural representation of the group action in the Hilbert space. Let $T(g_\alpha)$ be this natural representation of the group action g_α in the Hilbert space $\mathcal{H}$ of internal states or neural wave functions. We call it the internal representation of the symmetry group $\{g_\alpha\}$. There, $T(g_\alpha)$ denotes a linear operator in the Hilbert space $\mathcal{H}$. The group action g_α to the neural wave generator K is given by

$$T(g_\alpha)\, KT(g_\alpha)^{-1}, \tag{16}$$

where $T(g_\alpha)^{-1}$ denotes the inverse operator of $T(g_\alpha)$. The fact that the group action g_α leaves the neural wave generator K invariant means

$$T(g_\alpha)KT(g_\alpha)^{-1} = K, \tag{17}$$

and

$$T(g_\alpha)K = KT(g_\alpha). \tag{18}$$

Symmetry thus characterizes the invariant property of the fundamental dynamics of dendritic microprocesses which is represented mathematically by the fact that the neural generator commutes with the internal representation of the action of the symmetry group. The existence of such an internal representation of the symmetry group introduces the natural mathematical framework for the development of prototypes which will be described in Appendix F.

The neural wave generator K commuting with the internal representation of the symmetry group is known to be diagonalized by the vectors in $\mathcal{H}$ which are the basis of the irreducible representation of the symmetry group.

In summary, the time evolution of the neurodynamics of dendritic microprocesses can be well classified and investigated by means of the irreducible representation of the symmetry group within the realm of Hilbert space geometry. This generalizes and makes more explicit the motivation of Pribram and Carlton (1986) and Pribram (1990) in developing the holonomic brain theory of object-form perception.

Appendix C: The Definition of Context

1. INTRODUCTION

Given a processing formalism that describes the neural process coordinate with the perception of images (Appendix A) and object-forms (Appendix B), we turn to developing such a formalism for "context." In the lectures constituting Part I, the point was brought out that symmetry operations define their own immediate (local) context, their reference frames. Before objects and events can become further processed, however, a more comprehensive context must be developed, within which perceptions become familiar, innovative, categorized, or inferred. This appendix continues the development of the formalism utilizing eigenvectors in Hilbert space, (a formalism that was initiated in the preceding appendix), to delineate the conditions under which this system of eigenvectors forms a complete normalized orthogonal system—a CNOS, a processing context.

2. THE GEOMETRICS OF NEURODYNAMICS

With these goals in mind, let us look further at the abstract geometric formulation of neurodynamics starting from the neural wave function and equation. The neural wave function ψ is a complex-valued function of time t and position x in the dendritic network M. The dendritic network M is already thought of as a geometric object, that is, a two dimensional compact manifold. Then, it is immediately seen that the neural wave function ψ can also be thought of as a geometric object. It will fall into the class of well-known geometry of a Hilbert space.

For each instant t, the neural wave function is such a complex-valued function $\psi_t = \psi_t(x) = \psi(x,t)$ that the absolute square $|\psi_t|^2$ describes the ionic bioplasma density and so the integral

$$\int_M |\psi_t(x)|^2 dx \tag{1}$$

remains finite. Here, dx denotes the invariant volume element of the manifold M. We say in this case that ψ_t is square integrable on M for each t. Let us consider a set of all the square integrable complex-valued functions on the dendritic network M. We denote it by $L^2(M)$ or simply $\mathcal{H}$. From a mathematical point of view, this set of functions manifests a very intuitive geometric structure.

We suppose each element of $\mathcal{H}$ a vector. There, the constant multiplication $a\psi$ of a complex number a and a vector ψ is defined to be a vector in $\mathcal{H}$ corresponding to a function $a\psi = (a\psi) (x) = a\psi(x)$. The vector sum $\psi + \varphi$ of two vectors ψ and φ is defined to be a vector in $\mathcal{H}$ corresponding to a function $\psi + \varphi = (\psi + \varphi)$ $(x) = \psi (x) + \varphi (x)$.

Orthogonality of two vectors in $\mathcal{H}$ can be introduced by defining the inner product of two vectors. Inner product of any two vectors ψ and φ in $\mathcal{H}$ is denoted by $\langle \psi, \varphi \rangle$ and its value is given by the integral

$$\langle \psi, \varphi \rangle = \int_M \overline{\psi(x)}\ \varphi(x)dx, \tag{2}$$

where — means to take the complex conjugate. Then ψ and φ are said to be orthogonal with each other if their inner product vanishes, that is,

$$\langle \psi, \varphi \rangle = 0.$$

The inner product may be used to measure the length of a vector. Namely, the length of a vector ψ in $\mathcal{H}$ is given by a real number

$$\| \psi \| = \sqrt{\langle \psi, \psi \rangle},$$

which will be called a norm of ψ. This means that the inner product of ψ with itself becomes naturally a square of its length.

Having introduced the notions of vector calculus and norm (i.e., length), we can now measure the distance between two vectors in $\mathcal{H}$. Let ψ and φ be any two vectors in $\mathcal{H}$. Then the vector calculus claims their difference $\psi - \varphi$ to be another vector in $\mathcal{H}$. This vector $\psi - \varphi$ indeed represents a balance between ψ and φ. It is therefore natural to call the length $\|\psi - \varphi\|$ of this balance vector $\psi - \varphi$ a distance between two vectors ψ and φ. We denote it by $d(\psi, \varphi)$. The length of a vector is nothing else but a distance from it to a basis vector O. This basis vector O is called a zero vector, and stands for a unique vector in $\mathcal{H}$ with vanishing length. As a function on the dendritic network M, the zero vector O in $\mathcal{H}$ corresponds to a constant function with constant value equals to zero.

The totality of all the square inegrable complex-valued functions on M thus manifests a geometric structure in which vector calculus with inner products is allowed. Such a geometry is called a Hilbert space geometry in mathematics. It is in this sense that the set $\mathcal{H}$ may be called a Hilbert space.

3.   A SYSTEM OF EIGENVECTORS

The neural wave function $\psi_t = \psi_t(x) = \psi(x,t)$ for each instant t may be considered as a vector ψ_t in the Hilbert space of square integrable functions $\mathcal{H} = L^2(M)$. As time t passes, it evolves due to the neural wave equation (B10). In other words, the time-dependent vector ψ_t draws a curve in the Hilbert space $\mathcal{H}$. This curve may be denoted by $\{\psi_t \parallel 0 \leq t < \infty\}$.

We are thus working in a geometric framework of Hilbert space $\mathcal{H}$. It seems convenient therefore to rewrite the neural wave equation (B10) symbolically as an evolution equation in $\mathcal{H}$. First, let us see the right-hand side of Eq. (B10). The Laplacian is a second order linear partial differential operation, and multiplication by a given function U_{ex} is a linear operation. Therefore, we are allowed to think of the object

$$K = -\frac{v^2}{2}\Delta + U_{ex} \tag{3}$$

as a linear operator that transforms a vector ψ_t in the Hilbert space $\mathcal{H}$ to another vector $K\psi_t$ in $\mathcal{H}$. The term "linear" means that the operation by K to any vector preserves vector calculus. Namely, we have identities

$$K(\psi+\varphi) = K\psi + K\varphi)$$

where a is a constant, and ψ and φ are two vectrors in $\mathcal{H}$. We call this linear operator K a neural wave generator, and rewrite the neural wave equation (B10) as

$$iv\frac{d}{dt}\psi_t = K\,\psi_t. \tag{4}$$

In general, the neural wave equation (B10) defines an initial value problem. Given the initial neural wave function ψ_0, it determines the neural wave function ψ_t for all time after. Correspondingly, Eq. (4) may be understood to determine the vector ψ_t for all time after given the initial vector ψ_0 in $\mathcal{H}$.

Let $t > 0$ be a small time interval. Then

$$\psi_{\Delta t} - \psi_0 \simeq \frac{d}{dt}\psi_t\big|_{t=0}\,\Delta t,$$

and by Eq. (4) it claims

$$\psi_{\Delta t} \simeq \psi_0 - \frac{i}{\nu} K \psi_0 \Delta t$$

$$= \left(1 - \frac{i}{\nu} K \Delta t\right) \psi_0.$$

Successively, we have

$$\psi_{2\Delta t} \simeq \left(1 - \frac{i}{\nu} K \Delta t\right) \psi_{\Delta t}$$

$$\simeq \left(1 - \frac{i}{\nu} K \Delta t\right)^2 \psi_0,$$

$$\psi_{3\Delta t} \simeq \left(1 - \frac{i}{\nu} K \Delta t\right) \psi_{2\Delta t}$$

$$\simeq \left(1 - \frac{i}{\nu} K \Delta t\right)^3 \psi_0,$$

and so on. For arbitrary t, we have an identity

$$\psi_t = \psi_{Nt/N}$$

$$\simeq \left(1 - \frac{i}{\nu} K \frac{t}{N}\right)^N \psi_0$$

valid for any integer N. The approximative equality here becomes an exact equality as N passes to infinity. Namely, we obtain

$$\psi_t = \lim_{N \to 0} \left(1 - \frac{i}{\nu} K \frac{t}{N}\right)^N \psi_0.$$

This fact can be understood at least intuitively by the identity

$$\lim_{N \to \infty} \left(1 - \frac{i}{\nu} K \frac{t}{N}\right)^N$$

$$= \lim_{N \to \infty} \left\{\exp\left(-\frac{i}{\nu} K \frac{t}{N}\right)\right\}^N$$

$$= \lim_{N \to \infty} \exp\left(-\frac{i}{\nu} Kt\right)$$

$$= \exp\left(-\frac{i}{\nu} Kt\right).$$

This symbolic exponential function has the proper meaning of a linear operator acting on the Hilbert space $\mathcal{H}$. It is called a unitary operator since the transformed vector has the same norm (i.e., length) as the original one.

A solution of the evolution equation (4) can be found by applying the unitary operator $\exp\left(-\dfrac{i}{v}Kt\right)$ to the initial vector ψ_0 in $\mathcal{H}$. The curve $\{\psi_t | 0 \leqq t < \infty\}$ representing the time evolution of the neural wave function due to the neural wave equation (1) is given by

$$\left\{\exp\left(-\frac{i}{v}Kt\right)\psi_0 \middle| 0 \leqq t < \infty\right\}.$$

Although the neural wave equation (4) is considered as an initial value problem, it can be reduced to a time independent eigen value problem. We look for a special solution of Eq. (4) in a form

$$\psi_t = \varphi f(t),$$

where φ is a certain vector in the Hilbert space $\mathcal{H}$ and $f(t)$ is a complex-valued function of time t. Then, Eq. (4) can be separated into the following two equations

$$iv\,\frac{df(t)}{dt} = \lambda f(t), \tag{5}$$

$$K\varphi = \lambda\varphi. \tag{6}$$

The former is a simple linear differential equation that admits a special solution:

$$f(t) = e^{-i\lambda/vt},$$

where λ is a constant to be determined by equation (6). This constant plays a role of coupling the former and latter equations, and is called a constant of separation. Equation (6) is considered as a typical eigen value problem for the linear operator K in the Hilbert space $\mathcal{H}$. A vector φ in $\mathcal{H}$ is said to be a solution if there exists a certain constant λ with which it satisfies Eq. (6). The vector φ is called an eigen vector, and the constant λ is called an eigen value of the linear operator K. The linear operator

$$K = -\frac{v^2}{2}\Delta + U_{ex}$$

is known to admit infinitely many solutions of the eigenvalue problem (6) for a wider class of given function U_{ex} (Kato 1966).

Let $\{\varphi_n\}_{n=1}^{\infty}$ be the solutions of Eq. (6) with eigen values $\{\lambda_n\}_{n=1}^{\infty}$, namely, each vector φ_n in the Hilbert space $\mathcal{H}$ satisfies a linear equation

$$K\varphi_n = \lambda_n\varphi_n.$$

Without loss of generality, every eigenvector φ_n can be assumed normalized so that $\|\varphi_n\| = 1$. Even if this is not the case, each eigenvector φ_n may be normalized by dividing it by its norm. Suppose each eigenvalue λ_n differs from others. In this case, the eigenvalues of K are said to be nondegenerate. We assume this in what follows for keeping mathematical simplicity. Furthermore, the identity

$$
\begin{aligned}
\lambda_n \langle \varphi_m, \varphi_n \rangle &= \langle \varphi_m, K\varphi_n \rangle \\
&= \int_M \overline{\varphi_m(x)} \left(-\frac{v^2}{2} \Delta + U_{ex} \right) \varphi_n(x) dx \\
&= \int_M \overline{\left\{ \left(-\frac{v^2}{2} \Delta + U_{ex} \right) \varphi_m(x) \right\}} \varphi_n(x) dx \\
&= \langle K\varphi_m, \varphi_n \rangle \\
&= \lambda_m \langle \varphi_m, \varphi_n \rangle
\end{aligned}
$$

claims that

$$
\langle \varphi_m, \varphi_n \rangle = 0
$$

if $m \neq n$. This means that the system of eigenvectors $\{\varphi_n\}_{n=1}^{\infty}$ forms a *complete normalized orthogonal system (CNOS)* in the Hilbert space $\mathcal{H}$, and may be considered to define a specific coordinate basis of $\mathcal{H}$. In other words, any vector ψ in the Hilbert space $\mathcal{H}$ can be measured by the eigenvectors φ_n's of the neural wave generator K, obtaining

$$
\begin{aligned}
\psi &= \sum_{n=1}^{\infty} a_n \varphi_n \\
&= \sum_{n=1}^{\infty} \langle \varphi_n, \psi \rangle \varphi_n.
\end{aligned}
$$

Appendix D: Familiarization as Transfer Among Contexts

1. INTRODUCTION

Amygdalectomy was shown by some of the experiments described in Lecture 8 to impair transfer of training and in others to impair familiarization. In the current appendix the formalism in describing a CNOS, a context, will be shown to directly relate transfer and familiarization. This is accomplished by demonstrating that familiarization is due to transfer among contexts.

2. GENERALIZED FOURIER COEFFICIENTS

Recall that the neural wave function ψ_t for each instant t is a function on the dendritic network M belonging to the set $\mathcal{H}$. Therefore, the neural wave function can be considered as a vector in the Hilbert space $\mathcal{H}$. It draws a curve in $\mathcal{H}$ as the time t passes. The time evolution of a neural wave function thus illustrates the fundamental role of the dendritic network in perceptual processing. For developing such a geometric framework, we proceed further to the more detailed geometry of the Hilbert space $\mathcal{H}$.

Consider a set of infinitely many vectors in $\mathcal{H}$, and denote it by $\{\varphi_i\}_{i=1}^{\infty}$. Suppose that the length of each vector equals to unity, that is, $\| \varphi_i \| = 1$. Then the set $\{\varphi_i\}_{i=1}^{\infty}$ is said to be a normalized system of vectors in the Hilbert space $\mathcal{H}$. Suppose next that each two vectors φ_i and φ_j are orthogonal with each other, that is, $\langle \varphi_i, \varphi_j \rangle = 0$. In this case, we call the set $\{\varphi_i\}_{i=1}^{\infty}$ an orthogonal system of vectors in $\mathcal{H}$. Suppose that the set $\{\varphi_i\}_{i=i}^{\infty}$ is rich enough that a vector in $\mathcal{H}$ orthogonal to all the vectors φ_i's is necessarily a zero vector. Then, it is called a complete system of vectors in $\mathcal{H}$. It contains enough vectors pointing infinitely many different directions orthogonal with each other. In short, the Hilbert space $\mathcal{H}$ is an infinite dimensional Euclidean space in which the orthogonality relation is given by the inner product $\langle , \rangle$. Here, the complete normalized orthogonal system (CNOS) $\{\varphi_i\}_{i=1}^{\infty}$ described in the previous section, plays the role of basis for infinitely many coordinates. The vectors φ_i's form unit vectors spanning all the directions. Any vector in the Hilbert space $\mathcal{H}$ can be measured by coordinates in the CNOS. Namely, we have an identity

$$\psi = \sum_{i=1}^{\infty} a_i \, \varphi_i, \tag{1}$$

where a_i's are complex numbers given by the inner products

$$a_i = \langle \varphi_i, \psi \rangle, \; i = 1,2, \ldots \tag{2}$$

Those infinitely many constants a_i's components of the vector ψ along the basis vectors φ_i's. An ordered set of components $(a_1, a_2, a_3, \ldots)$ is a representative of the vector ψ within the realm of CNOS $\{\varphi_i\}_{i=1}^{\infty}$. We call it a coordinate representation of ψ in $\{\varphi_i\}_{i=1}^{\infty}$. Coming back to the original viewpoint of the vector ψ as a function $\psi = \psi(x)$ on the manifold M, the coordinate representation opens the possibility to consider a function by components along other well known functions forming a CNOS. Emphasizing this fact, we may rewrite Eqs. (1) and (2) as

$$\psi(x) = \sum_{i=1}^{\infty} a_i \varphi_i(x),$$

and

$$a_i = \int_M \overline{\varphi_i(x)} \, \psi(x) dx.$$

We have already seen a typical example of such a coordinate representation of function in the preceding appendix. Recall the simplest case of a dendritic network M in which M is identified with a two-dimensional torus. For all values of integers n_1 and n_2, plane wave functions

$$u_{n_1,n_2}(x^1,x^2) = \left(\frac{1}{L} \right) \exp \left\{ i \frac{2\pi}{L} \, (n_1 \, x^1 + n_2 x^2) \right\}$$

form a CNOS in the Hilbert space $\mathcal{H} = L^2(M)$. Then any neural wave function ψ can be expressed by a linear superposition of the plane wave functions, obtaining

$$\psi = \sum_{n_1,n_2=-\infty}^{\infty} a_{n_1,n_2} \, u_{n_1,n_2},$$

where a_{n_1,n_2}'s are Fourier coefficients given by the inner products

$$a_{n_1,n_2} = \langle u_{n_1,n_2}, \psi \rangle$$

$$= \frac{1}{L} \int_M \psi \exp \left\{ - i \frac{2\pi}{L} \, (n_1 x^1 + n_2 x^2) \right\} dx^1 dx^2.$$

The Fourier series expansion of the neural wave function ψ is thus nothing but a coordinate representation of ψ in a specific CNOS $\{u_{n_1,n_2}\}_{n_1,n_2=-\infty}^{\infty}$. Therefore, the coordinate representation (1) in a general CNOS $\{\varphi_i\}_{i=1}^{\infty}$ may be called a generalized Fourier series expansion of ψ. The inner products a_i's given by Eq. (2) are called generalized Fourier coefficients.

3. TRANSFER

Coming back to the general case of dendritic network M and the Hilbert space $\mathcal{H}$ $= L^2(M)$, there may exist many different CNOS's. This means that a vector ψ in $\mathcal{H}$ (representing a processed sensory input) may have many different coordinate representations. Let $\{\varphi_i\}_{i=1}^{\infty}$ and $\{\xi_j\}_{j=1}^{\infty}$ be two different CNOSs in the Hilbert space $\mathcal{H}$. Then the vector can be decomposed in both CNOSs $\{\varphi_i\}_{i=1}^{\infty}$ and $\{\xi_j\}_{j=1}^{\infty}$, obtaining

$$\psi = \sum_{i=1}^{\infty} \langle \psi, \varphi_i \rangle \, \varphi_i, \tag{3}$$

and

$$\psi = \sum_{j=1}^{\infty} \langle \psi, \xi_j \rangle \, \xi_j. \tag{4}$$

The same vector (i.e., neural wave function) ψ can be measured by coordinates ($\langle \psi, \varphi_1 \rangle$, $\langle \psi, \varphi_2 \rangle$, . . .) on the one hand, and ($\langle \psi, \xi_1 \rangle$, $\langle \psi, \xi_2 \rangle$, . . .) on the other. Each CNOS becomes an infinite dimensional orthogonal coordinate system to measure every vector in the Hilbert space $\mathcal{H}$. *The input has become familiarized.*

It is convenient here to introduce an intuitive notion of infinite dimensional column vector. If we measure the whole Hilbert space $\mathcal{H}$ by the CNOS $\{\varphi_i\}_{i=1}^{\infty}$, each vector ψ in $\mathcal{H}$ may be viewed as a column vector.

$$
\begin{pmatrix}
\langle \psi, \varphi_1 \rangle \\
\langle \psi, \varphi_2 \rangle \\
\langle \psi, \varphi_3 \rangle \\
\vdots \\
\vdots
\end{pmatrix}
\tag{5}
$$

We may equally measure the whole $\mathcal{H}$ by the other CNOS $\{\xi_j\}_{j=1}^{\infty}$, and in this case ψ can be seen as

$$
\begin{pmatrix}
\langle \psi, \xi_1 \rangle \\
\langle \psi, \xi_2 \rangle \\
\langle \psi, \xi_3 \rangle \\
\vdots \\
\vdots
\end{pmatrix}
\tag{6}
$$

Both column vectors represent the same vector ψ in the Hilbert space $\mathcal{H}$, and so they must be interconnected with each other. Let us decompose a basis vector ξ_j in the CNOS $\{\varphi_i\}_{i=1}^{\infty}$,

$$
\xi_j = \sum_{i=1}^{\infty} \langle \xi_j, \varphi_i \rangle \, \varphi_i.
$$

Then, we compute an inner product between ψ and ξ_j, obtaining

$$
\langle \psi, \xi_j \rangle = \sum_{i=1}^{\infty} \langle \xi_j, \varphi_i \rangle \langle \psi, \varphi_i \rangle.
\tag{7}
$$

This identity shows how the column vectors (5) and (6) are connected with each other. Equation (7) may be rewritten in an intuitive notion of matrix multiplication. Namely, we have an identity

$$
\begin{pmatrix}
\langle \psi, \xi_1 \rangle \\
\langle \psi, \xi_2 \rangle \\
\langle \psi, \xi_3 \rangle \\
\vdots
\end{pmatrix}
=
\begin{pmatrix}
\langle \xi_1, \varphi_1 \rangle \langle \xi_1, \varphi_1 \rangle \cdots \cdots \\
\langle \xi_2, \varphi_2 \rangle \langle \xi_2, \varphi_2 \rangle \cdots \cdots \\
\vdots \qquad \vdots
\end{pmatrix}
\begin{pmatrix}
\langle \psi, \varphi_1 \rangle \\
\langle \psi, \varphi_2 \rangle \\
\langle \psi, \varphi_3 \rangle \\
\vdots
\end{pmatrix}
\tag{8}
$$

There, an infinite dimensional matrix with the j–i component given by the inner product $\langle \xi_j, \varphi_i \rangle$ plays an important role. It will be called a *transfer* matrix from the CNOS $\{\varphi_i\}_{i=1}^{\infty}$ to the other CNOS $\{\xi_j\}_{j=1}^{\infty}$.

Appendix E: The Formation of Prototypes

1. INTRODUCTION

In Lecture 7 evidence was presented to show how, with consistent differential reinforcement, continuity in a sensory input could be broken into separate domains. Each domain resulted from a sharpened generalization gradient lifted above a background represented by familiarization, i.e. habituation to the sensory input—the adaptation level. In the previous appendices the adaptation level was shown to provide a context, which is described mathematically as a normalized orthogonal system (CNOS) in a Hilbert space. In the current appendix, separation of domains that are nonetheless related by their adaptation levels (CNOS's), is modeled in terms of the neurodynamics of mutually coupled dendritic networks.

2. PROCESSING DOMAINS

Recall that in Appendix C, we showed that the neurodynamics of a system of distribution densities of dendritic ionic bioplasma is based on fundamental oscillations of polarizations in the dendritic network. This neurodynamics was described by the neural wave equation

$$iv \frac{\partial \psi}{\partial t} = \left(-\frac{v^2}{2} \Delta + U_{ex} \right) \psi. \tag{1}$$

Here, ψ is a complex-valued function of position $x = (x^1, x^2)$ in the dendritic network M and time t, ν is a positive constant, Δ is the Laplacian of the manifold M, and U_{ex} is an external static excitation. The dendritic membrane network was identified with a two dimensional multiply connected compact manifold M. For each time t, the function $\psi (x,t)$ represents an instantaneous state of dendritic microprocesses in the dendritic network, and so it was called a neural wave equation.

From the physiological point of view, the function ψ describes on the one hand the ionic bioplasma distribution density ρ by its absolute square $|\psi|^2$, and on the other hand the fundamental membrane polarization oscillation by its phase $\psi / |\psi|$. The distribution function ρ describes the global flow pattern of the ionic bio-plasma. The phase factor $\theta = \psi / |\psi|$ represents the membrane potential oscillation which controls the polarization distribution globally. As was shown, in this sense, the neural wave function ψ has the role of mathematically representing both system and control variables operative in neurodynamics.

Proceeding with the investigation of mutually coupled dendritic networks described in the previous sections, we note that such networks provide a Hilbert space geometry basic to the formation of prototypes. Time-development of dendritic microprocesses in a dendritic network can be represented mathematically as a unitary flow in the state space (i. e., Hilbert space) $\mathcal{H}$ driven by the operator

$$T = e^{-i/\nu Kt}.$$

Any vector φ in $\mathcal{H}$ transforms to another one

$$e^{-i/\nu Kt} \varphi$$

by the unitary flow. A vector that remains unchanged except as a constant multiplication factor is said to be stable under the unitary flow. Thus, the states given by the eigenvectors $\{\psi_n\}_{n=1}^{\infty}$ of the neural wave generator K are stable under the unitary flow. In other words, they are stable fixed points of the unitary flow. In this sense, familiarization is due to a dendritic microprocess in the dendritic network which maintains its ionic bioplasma distribution pattern.

Keeping these facts in mind, a mathematical framework for the formation of separate domains based on the unitary flow T within a CNOS can be proposed. Domains are described by φ_n's. As the domains become stable under the unitary flow T, the process must attain invariance under the flow T. This can be realized mathematically only when the vectors refer to linear operators X's which commute with T, that is, XT = TX.

A linear operator X is a transformation law in the Hilbert space $\mathcal{H}$ which transforms a vector ψ in $\mathcal{H}$ into another one $X\psi$. It is linear in a sense that it keeps the vector calculus unchanged, that is,

$$X(\varphi + \psi) = X\varphi + X\psi,$$

$$X(a\varphi) = a(X\varphi)$$

for any vectors φ and ψ and any constant a.

3. PROTOTYPES

During this process any vector φ_n in the CNOS of the state space $\mathcal{H}$ becomes transformed into a vector $X\varphi_n$ which may as yet not specify a separate domain. However, it can become a separate domain, when and only when the linear operator X commutes with the unitary flow T. Therefore, the domains φ_n's must become identified consistently by refering to some linear operators X's which commute with the unitary flow T. Such a reference linear operator X may be understood as a mathematical representative of a certain group element. As indicated in Appendix B and by Pribram and Carlton (1986) and Carlton (1989), a three dimensional rotation group, a translation group, or more generally, a three dimensional Euclidean group are groups responsible for object-form perception. When the procedure of grouping is iterated around object-forms   made relevant through use and/or reinforcement, a prototypical group is formed by the group whose group element can be represented by the linear operator X_E which commutes with the unitary flow T. Domains φ_n's, become prototypical when such linear operators X_E's correspond to the internal representations of groups of object-forms (i.e., groups of groups).

    In order that object-forms compose groups, they must compose reference linear operator X. A subspace $\mathcal{B}$ of the state space $\mathcal{H}$ is said to be an invariant subspace of X if any vector φ in $\mathcal{B}$ is transformed by X into another one (i.e., $X\varphi$) still in $\mathcal{B}$. In other words, the transformation X leaves the subspace $\mathcal{B}$ unchanged. Suppose that an invariant subspace $\mathcal{B}$ contains a part of the domain $\{\varphi_n\}_{n=1}^{\infty}$, say $\{\varphi_{n(k)}\}_{k=1}^{\infty}$. In this way, the domains φ_n's are subdivided into two subspaces, that is, $\{\varphi_{n(k)}\}_{k=1}^{\infty}$ and the remainder. The invariant subspace of the reference linear operator defines a prototype. The more the reference linear operators, the prototypes, are referred to, the more invariant subspaces are introduced into the state space and its boundaries become defined.

Appendix F: Neurodynamics and Innovation

1. INTRODUCTION

An ensemble of CNOS becomes stabilized by virtue of the transfer functions entailed in familiarization. Under conditions in which probabilities play a minor role (such as the recurrent regularities that often characterize physiological states as, for example, those determining hunger and thirst) the stabilities define steady states at equilibrium. When, however, probabilities play a significant role, stabilities occur far from equilibrium and are thus subject to destabilizing influences. The current appendix discusses the manner in which such stabilizers far from equilibrium can become perturbed and how destabilization can provide the ground for innovation.

2. STABILITIES FAR FROM EQUILIBRIUM

To this end, let us consider a highly idealized dendritic network, which on the basis of familiarization has become stabilized and isolated electrochemically from other dendritic networks in the system. The dendritic microprocesses of the distribution of the density of the ionic bioplasma as it affects fundamental oscillations of membrane potentials in this isolated dendritic network M can be described by the neural wave equation (B10). We have seen that the neural wave equation (B10) may be written as Eq. (B11) within the realm of Hilbert space geometry. By reducing Eq. (B11) to a time-independent eigenvalue problem (C6), we have found infinitely many stationary solutions of the neural wave equation (B11). They are nothing but the eigenvectors $\{\varphi_n\}_{n=1}^{\infty}$ of the neural wave generator K. In other words, for each eigenvector φ_n and eigenvalue λ_n, a neural wave function

$$\psi(x,t) = \varphi_n(x)\, e^{-i\lambda_n/\nu t} \tag{1}$$

solves the neural wave equation (B10). As we have seen in the preceding Appendix, the absolute square of a neural wave function represents the density distribution of the ionic bioplasma that manifests the global dynamics of dendritic microprocesses. Thus, each eigenvector φ_n may be understood as a mathematical representative of the typical global dynamics of a dendritic microprocess given by a density distribution of the ionic bioplasma

$$\rho = |\varphi_n|^2 = |\varphi_n(x)|^2 \equiv \rho_n(x). \tag{2}$$

Those ionic bioplasma density distributions ρ_n's that do not change as the time t passes, manifest temporarily stationary dendritic microprocesses. This means that each eigenvector φ_n represents a set of stable dendritic microprocesses. The fundamental oscillations of dendritic membrane polarizations are synchronized within the dendritic network, and no effective currents of changes in the distribution of the density of the ionic bioplasma exist. In other words, the distribution of ionic bioplasma in the dendritic network is in a temporarily stable state during which no flow occurs. We call such a stable state of dynamics a stationary state of the dendritic network. The stationary state is stable in the sense that it remains unchanged as long as the dendritic network remains isolated. It is worthwhile to notice here that no other vectors in the Hilbert space different from the eigenvectors φ_n's can define the stable dendritic microprocesses.

As detailed in the previous appendix, the fact that the isolated dendritic network manifests selectively stable dendritic microprocesses represented by eigenvectors φ_n's provides us with the neuronal basis for familiarization. The isolated dendritic network reasonates only with selectively limited processes associated with the stationary states φ_n's. These tuned resonances are represented by the stationary "familiarized" states of the dendritic network,

$$\varphi_1, \varphi_2, \cdots\cdots, \varphi_n, \cdots\cdots.$$

Other types of resonance given by a vector φ different from the stationary states φ_n's cannot be realized, as they deform immediately into one of the stationary states by the dispersion effect.

The isolated dendritic network is capable of an infinite variety of stable dendritic microprocesses associated with the familiarized states φ_n's, because the neural wave equation (B10) admits infinitely many stationary solutions φ_n's.

3. WEAK INTERACTIONS AS POTENTIAL PERTURBATIONS

Each dendritic network of the system is, of course, actually not isolated but connected with other ones. To make the familiarization process of the dendritic network more realistic, we introduce weak dendritic interactions with other

networks. This induces multiple transitions between different states of familiarity. Existence of the weak dendritic interaction makes the lifetime of a stability
finite. Thus, the dendritic microprocess fluctuates among the temporarily stable
states φ_n's due to dendritic system weak interactions.

This fact may be well illustrated by means of perturbation theory. Suppose
that the dendritic network in question remains isolated until a certain instant, say
t_0, and a weak dendritic interaction is turned on at t_0. Time evolution of the
dendritic microprocesses is described by the neural wave equation (B11). However, the neural wave generator K in the right hand side has different forms
before and after the onset of a weak dendritic interaction. Let $U = U(t)$ be the
additional quasi static energy due to the weak dendritic interaction. The value of
U is relatively small compared with the external static energy U_{ex}. Then, the
neural wave equation (B11) has the form

$$iv \frac{d}{dt} \psi_t = K\psi_t \tag{3}$$

for $t < t_0$, and

$$iv \frac{d}{dt} \psi_t = (K + U(t)) \psi_t \tag{4}$$

for $t > t_0$. We call Eq. (3) a non-perturbed neural wave equation and Eq. (4) a
perturbed one. We consider onset of a weak dendritic interaction as a perturbation of the neural wave equation.

Suppose that the dendritic microprocess is in one of the isolated, familiarized
states, say φ_m, before the onset of perturbation. Then, Eq. (3) claims

$$\psi_t = \varphi_m e^{-i\lambda_m/vt}.$$

for $t < t_0$. This suggests that the perturbed neural wave equation (4) may be
solved with respect to the initial condition

$$\psi_{t_0} = \varphi_m e^{-\lambda_m/vt_0}.$$

The perturbed neural wave equation (4) may be solved by the following mathematical procedure.

Let ψ_t be the solution of Eq. (4). We introduce a time-dependent vector $\hat{\psi}$ in
the Hilbert space $\mathcal{H}$ by

$$\hat{\psi}_t = \exp\left(\frac{i}{v} Kt\right) \psi_t. \tag{5}$$

Then, it solves a reduced perturbed neural wave equation

$$iv \frac{d}{dt} \hat{\psi}_t = \hat{U}_t \hat{\psi}_t, \tag{6}$$

where

$$\hat{U}_t = \exp\left(\frac{i}{\nu} Kt\right) U(t) \exp\left(-\frac{i}{\nu} Kt\right) \tag{7}$$

is a time-dependent operator in $\mathcal{H}$. The initial condition for ψ_t yields the initial condition

$$\hat{\psi}_{t_0} = \varphi_m$$

for $\hat{\psi}_t$. Equation (6) can be solved immediately by the perturbation series

$$\hat{\psi}_t = \left[1 + \left(\frac{1}{i\nu}\right)\int_{t_0}^t \hat{U}_s ds + \left(\frac{1}{i\nu}\right)^2 \int_{t_0}^t \int_{t_0}^t \hat{U}_s ds\, \hat{U}_u du \right.$$
$$\left. + \cdots\cdots \right] \varphi_m. \tag{8}$$

Because the perturbation U is small, the perturbation series (8) can be well approximated by the first two terms, obtaining

$$\hat{\psi}_t = \left[1 + \left(\frac{1}{i\nu}\right)\int_{t_0}^t \hat{U}_s ds\right] \varphi_m. \tag{9}$$

Finally, Eqs. (5) and (9) give a first order approximation to the solution ψ_t of the perturbed neural wave equation (4),

$$\psi_t = \exp\left(-\frac{i}{\nu} Kt\right) \varphi_m$$

$$+ \exp\left(-\frac{i}{\nu} Kt\right)\left(\frac{1}{i\nu}\right)\int_{t_0}^t \hat{U}_s ds\, \varphi_m$$

$$= e^{-i/\nu \lambda_m t}\varphi_m$$

$$+ \exp\left(-\frac{i}{\nu} Kt\right)\left(\frac{1}{i\nu}\right)\int_{t_0}^t \hat{U}_s ds\, \varphi_m.$$

It is convenient to measure the vector ψ_t in the Hilbert space $\mathcal{H}$ by means of the specific CNOS $\{\varphi_n\}_{n=1}^\infty$ because the perturbation U is so small that ψ_t may not deviate much from the initial state φ_m. Let

$$\psi_t = \sum_{n=1}^\infty a_n \varphi_n$$

be the coordinate expansion of ψ_t in terms of the CNOS $\{\varphi_n\}_{n=1}^\infty$. Here, the coordinates a_n's are given by the inner product

$$a_n = \langle \varphi_m, \psi_t \rangle$$

$$= e^{-i/\nu\lambda_m t}\langle \varphi_n, \varphi_m \rangle$$

$$+ \left(\frac{1}{i\nu}\right)\int_{t_0}^t \langle e^{i/\nu\, Kt}\varphi_n, \hat{U}_s\, \varphi_m \rangle ds$$

$$= e^{-i/v\,\lambda_m t}\,\delta_{nm}$$

$$+ \left(\frac{1}{iv}\right) e^{-i/v\lambda_n t} \int_{t_0}^{t} \langle \varphi_n, e^{i/v\,Ks}\, U(s)e^{-i/v\,Ks}\,\varphi_m \rangle ds$$

$$= e^{-i/v\,\lambda_m t}\,\delta_{nm}$$

$$+ \left(\frac{1}{iv}\right) e^{-i/v\lambda_n t} \int_{t_0}^{t} e^{i/v\,(\lambda_n - \lambda_m)s} \langle \varphi_n, U(s)\varphi_m \rangle ds.$$

Namely, we have

$$a_n = \left(\frac{1}{iv}\right) e^{-i/v\lambda_n t} \int_{t_0}^{t} e^{i/v\,(\lambda_n - \lambda_m)s} \langle \varphi_n, U(s)\varphi_m \rangle ds$$

for $n \neq m$ and

$$a_m = \left(1 + \frac{1}{iv} \int_{t_0}^{t} \langle \varphi_m, U(s)\varphi_m \rangle ds \right) e^{-i/v\,\lambda_m t} .$$

Thus the onset of perturbation causes the change of coordinates from

$$\begin{pmatrix} 0 \\ 0 \\ \vdots \\ 0 \\ e^{-i/v\,\lambda_m t} \\ 0 \\ \vdots \\ 0 \end{pmatrix} \tag{10}$$

to

$$\begin{pmatrix} a_1 \\ a_2 \\ \vdots \\ a_m \\ \vdots \end{pmatrix} \tag{11}$$

In other words, the onset of perturbation forces the vector ψ_t to deviate from the initial stable, familiarized state φ_m so that it has nonvanishing components along other familiarized states φ_n's.

4. NOVEL ASSOCIATIONS

Here, we need a consistent interpretation of the dendritic microprocess associated with the vector ψ_t in $\mathcal{H}$, and coin a new mathematical formulation of association. When the vector ψ_t has the coordinate representation (10) with respect to the CNOS $\{\varphi_n\}_{n=1}^{\infty}$ the dendritic microprocess described by ψ_t remains identical with that of a specific state φ_m. If there is no perturbation, that dendritic network remains isolated and keeps the initial familiarized state φ_m. Perturbation modifies the vector ψ_t so that its coordinate representation becomes (11).

Let us compute the length of vector ψ_t in terms of the coordinates (11). As the states φ_n's form a CNOS in the Hilbert space, we have

$$\|\psi_t\|^2 = \sum_{n=1}^{\infty} |a_n|^2.$$

Before the onset of perturbation, $a_n = 0$ except for $n = m$, and this can be written as

$$\|\psi_t\|^2 = |a_n|^2$$
$$= |e^{-i/\nu \, \lambda_m t}|^2$$
$$= 1$$

After the onset, we have

$$\|\psi_t\|^2 = \left| 1 + \frac{1}{i\nu} \int_{t_0}^{t} \langle \varphi_m, U(s)\varphi_m \rangle ds \right|^2$$
$$+ \sum_{n \neq m}^{\infty} \left| \left(\frac{1}{i\nu}\right) \int_{t_0}^{t} e^{i/\nu(\lambda_n - \lambda_m)s} \langle \varphi_n, U(s)\varphi_m \rangle ds \right|^2.$$

It is worthwhile to notice here that the perturbation acts on the vector ψ_t so that it is no longer parallel to the eigen vector φ_m. It comes to point along many other independent directions of eigen vectors φ_n's. For any $t > t_0$ and $n \neq m$,

$$|a_n|^2 = \left(\frac{1}{\nu}\right)^2 \left| \int_{t_0}^{t} e^{i/\nu(\lambda_n - \lambda_m)s} \langle \varphi_n, U(s)\varphi_m \rangle ds \right|^2.$$

gives a relative proportion of the vector ψ_t to point along the n-th eigenvector φ_n. As the n-th eigenvector φ_n is a stable dendritic microprocess, the dendritic microprocess specified by the vector ψ_t realizes those of the other state φ_n's with relative proportion $|a_n|^2$. Thus, the perturbation causes the neural wave function ψ_t to represent typical dendritic microprocesses that resemble those of state φ_n's with relative proportion $|a_n|$'s. Such a neural wave function may represent a novel association in which the several independent states can be associated on the basis of frequencies given by their relative proportion.

Appendix G: Neurodynamics and Inference

1. INTRODUCTION

In this final appendix we apply the insights gained from Murdoch's, Smolenski's, and Mittlestaedt's models of the inference process to neurodynamics as developed in the holonomic brain theory. We have noted that external stimuli affect the internal states of dendritic microprocess so that the state vector satisfies the neural wave equation. Time evolution of the state vector is, then, given by a unitary flow in $\mathcal{H}$ generated by a unitary operator $\exp\left(-\frac{i}{\nu}Kt\right)$. For each external stimulus, the neural wave generator K is specified and so is the unitary operator. Then specific state vectors that are invariant under the unitary flow with generator K play important roles in representing stable states induced by various external stimuli. They can be called "memory" states and specified mathematically as eigen vectors of the operator K. The well-known mathematical fact that these eigen vectors form a CNOS in the Hilbert space $\mathcal{H}$ may provide us with a mechanism of *multiple* associations between the familiar and a novel perception.

2. BIAS

We consider the simplest case of a process made up of two dendritic networks, unit A and unit B. Unit A is directly connected to a certain sense organ via nerve fibers and synapses so that it receives a neural signal generated by the effect of the surroundings of the sense organ. As we have seen in the preceding sections,

327

the dendritic network manifests limited and temporarily stable dendritic micro-processes. They are represented by stationary neural wave functions, that is, stable states in the Hilbert space $\mathcal{H}$ of the unit A. Thus a stable stationary state of the unit A becomes perturbed by the neural stimulus from the sense organ. The perturbation, as we have seen, can trigger a reorganization of the previously stable state.

Suppose that the unit A is excited by a stimulus from a sense organ, causing the dendritic microprocesses of the unit A to resonate. This produces the station-ary state of the Hilbert space $\mathcal{H}_A$. If the unit A becomes isolated, it resonates in this fashion "forever." However, because unit A is connected not only with the sense organ but also with unit B, there is a possibility for mutual interaction. Existence of the influence from the unit B makes the lifetime of the resonating stationary state u_A of the unit A shorter.

When unit A is driven both by input from the sense organ and output from unit B, the output of the unit B plays the role of biasing unit A. The dendritic network of A then resonates to the output of the sense organ with a bias from B. Conse-quently, the state vector of the unit A becomes a stationary state u_A which is perturbed by the input from the sense organ as biased by the state of the unit B. In other words, the perception of the output of the sense organ depends on the process carried by a state vector u_B of the unit B.

Units A plus B can be considered as an isolated dendritic network as long as the sense organ does not send another input to unit A. This means that the state vectors u_A and u_B of the units A and B are kept unchanged until next series of inputs is generated by the sense organ. Therefore, the synaptic connections between the units A and B become especially tuned to this pair of state vectors u_A and u_B. We call this specific synaptic weighting between the units A and B a neural channel $u_A \otimes u_B$. This highly tuned neural channel $u_A \otimes u_B$ can remain effective even when the next series of inputs from the sense organ again perturbs the state vectors u_A, and u_B. This is the origin of inference. Once a temporary stability has become established by means of a neural channel $u_A \otimes u_B$, it now acts as the bias contributed by unit B. Thus, the next series of perturbations from the sense organ become biased by the channels established by preceding pertur-bations. This simple process based on the interaction between dendritic networks A and B provides us with an interesting mathematical model of a more realistic inference process.

Suppose we have a finite number of neural channels between the unit A and B of certain familiarization processes. We denote them by $(u_A{}^1 \otimes u_B{}^1)$, $(u_A{}^2 \otimes u_B{}^2)$, $\cdots$, $(u_A{}^M \otimes u_B{}^M)$ for $M > 0$, where $u_A{}^k$'s and $u_B{}^j$'s are stationary states of the units A and B, respectively. Each neural channel then composes a familiar perception. This strength of susceptibility of each neural channel represents the effectivity of the familiar. Thus, the totality of neural channels between the units A and B specifies the knowledge already obtained. In such a situation, if there happens to be the same input from the sense organ as one of the preceding ones, the bias output of the unit B through the corresponding channel, say $u_A{}^k \times u_B{}^j$, enforces the units A and B to resonate to the stationary states $u_A{}^k$ and $u_B{}^j$, respectively.

On the other hand, suppose we have a novel input from the sense organ. The neural channels representing previously experienced perceptions then heavily bias units A and B, and making them keenly sensitive to the stationary states $u_A{}^k$'s and $u_B{}^j$'s, respectively. We investigate this process from the point of view of the Hilbert space geometry.

First, we notice that the finite number of stationary states $\{u_A{}^k\}_{k=1}^M$ span a finite dimensional subspace of the Hilbert space $\mathcal{H}_A$. Similarly, $\{u_B{}^j\}_{j=1}^M$ span also a finite dimensional subspace of $\mathcal{H}_B$. We denote those subspaces by $\mathcal{M}_A$ and $\mathcal{M}_B$, respectively. Then, the state vector ψ_A in the Hilbert space $\mathcal{H}_A$ can be decomposed into a form

$$\psi_A = \sum_{i=1}^{\infty} \alpha_i u_A^i$$

$$= \sum_{i=1}^{M} \alpha_i u_A^i + \sum_{i=M+1}^{\infty} \alpha_i u_A^i$$

$$\equiv \psi_A' + \psi_A''.$$

Here, ψ_A' and ψ_A'' are components of the state vector ψ_A lying in and orthogonal to the finite dimensional subspace $\mathcal{M}_A$. The neural channels between the units A and B biases the unit A so that the component ψ_A' in $\mathcal{M}_A$ is easily accomplished but the other one ψ_A'' orthogonal to $\mathcal{M}_A$ is not. This is because of the absence of neural channels biasing the state vectors u_A^i,s for $i > M$.

Consequently, this inference process makes the system A and B resonate to the stationary states $\{u_A{}^K\}_{k=1}^M$ and $\{u_B{}^j\}_{j=1}^M$ with probability $\mid \alpha_k \mid^2$ for $k = 1,2,\cdots,M$. In other words, the temporary stability in the units A and B of the novel input from the sense organ becomes related to the finite number of stationary states which represent prior experiences. Such a relation to prior experience then drives the neural channel.

3. INFERENCE AS THE METHOD OF LEAST SQUARES

It seems surprising that the present mathematical model of the inference process realizes a mechanism of inference similar to that known as method of least-squares in probability theory. Notice that the state vector ψ_A' is the best estimate of the state vector ψ_A in a sense that ψ_A' is closest to ψ_A within the learned "knowledge" described by the finite dimensional subspace $\mathcal{M}_A$. In the terminology of statistical modelling, the finite dimensional subspace $\mathcal{M}_A$ is an estimation space and its orthogonal complement is an error space. The orthogonal projections ψ_A' of the state vector ψ_A onto the estimation space $\mathcal{M}_A$ is nothing but a least squares estimator.

Such an inference process takes place when a novel input from the sense organ modifies the state vector of the unit A. However, if this novel input continues for a longer period, the bias effect of the neural channels of the familiarized outputs becomes less dominant and a new neural channel will be made which reflects the orthogonal component ψ_A''. Then, this unfamiliar input from the sense organ comes to be stored in the new neural channel between the units A and B. The inference process thus has a procedure for enlarging the scope of inference.

References

Ackley, D. H., Hinton, G. E., & Sejnowski, T. J. (1985). A learning algorithm for Boltzmann Machines. *Cognitive Science, 9*(2), 147—169.

Albe-Fessard, D. (1957). Activities de projection et d'association du neocortex cerebral des mammiferes. *Extrait du Journal de Psychiolgie, 49*, 521–588.

Allport, F. H. (1955). *Theories of perception and the concept of structure.* New York: Wiley.

Amsel, A. (1986). Daniel Berlyne memorial lecture: Developmental psychobiology and behavior theory: Reciprocating influences. *Canadian Journal of Psychology, 40*(4), 311–342.

Andersen, P. (1975). Organization of hippocampal neurons and their interconnections. In R. L. Isaacson & K. H. Pribram (Eds.), *The Hippocampus, Volume 1: Structure and Development* (pp. 155–176). New York: Plenum.

Anderson, J. A. (1970). Two models for memory organisation using interactive traces. *Mathematical Biosciences, 8*, 137–160.

Anderson, J. A., Silverstein, J. W., Ritz, S. A., & Jones, R. S. (1977). Distinctive features, categorical perception, and probability learning: Some applications of a neural model. *Psychological Review, 84*, 413–447.

Anderson, R. M., Hunt, S. C., Vander Stoep, A. & Pribram, K. H. (1976). Object permanency and delayed response as spatial context in monkeys with frontal lesions. *Neuropsychologia, 14*, 481–490.

Andrews, B. W., & Pollen, D. A. (1979). Relationship between spatial frequency selectivity and receptive field profile of simple cells. *Journal of Physiology, 287*, 163–176.

Ashby, W. R. (1956). *An introduction to cybernetics.* London: Chapman & Hall.

Ashby, W. R. (1960). *Design for a brain: The origin of adaptive behaviour.* (2nd Ed.). New York: Wiley.

Asratyan, D. G., & Feldman, A. G. (1965). Functional tuning of the nervous system with control of movement or maintenance of a steady posture. Mechanographic analysis of the work of the joint on execution of a postural task. *Biophysics, 10*, 925–935.

Attick, J. J., & Redlich, A. N. (1990). Mathematical model of the simple cells in the visual cortex. *Biological Cybernetics*, (in press).

Attneave, F. (1954). Some informational aspects of visual perception. *Psychological Review, 61*, 183–193.

Attneave, F. (1968). Triangles as ambiguous figures. *American Journal of Psychology, 81*, 447–453.

Aubert, H. (1861). Uber eine scheinbare Drehung von Objekten bei Neigung des Kopfes nach rechts oder links. *Virchow's Archives, 20*, 381–393.

Bagshaw, M. H., & Benzies, S. (1968). Multiple measures of the orienting reaction and their dissociation after amygdalectomy in monkeys. *Experimental Neurology, 20*, 175–187.

Bagshaw, M. H., & Coppock, H. W. (1968). Galvanic skin response conditioning deficit in amygdalectomized monkeys. *Experimental Neurology, 20*, 188–196.

Bagshaw, M. H., Kimble, D. P., & Pribram, K. H. (1965). The GSR of monkeys during orienting and habituation and after ablation of the amygdala, hippocampus and inferotemporal cortex. *Neuropsychologia, 3*, 111–119.

Bagshaw, M. H., Mackworth, N. H., & Pribram, K. H. (1970a). Method for recording and analyzing visual fixations in the unrestrained monkey. *Perceptual and motor skills, 31*, 219—222.

Bagshaw, M. H., Mackworth, N. H., & Pribram, K. H. (1970b). The effect of inferotemporal cortex ablations on eye movements of monkeys during discrimination training. *International Journal of Neuroscience, 1*, 153—158.

Bagshaw, M. H., Mackworth, N. H., & Pribram, K. H. (1972). The effect of resections of the inferotemporal cortex or the amygdala on visual orienting and habituation. *Neuropsychologia, 10*, 153–162.

Bagshaw, M. H., & Pribram, K. H. (1953). Cortical organization in gustation (Macaca mulatta). *Journal of Neurophysiology, 16*, 499–508.

Bagshaw, M. H., & Pribram, K. H. (1968). Effect of amygdalectomy on stimulus threshold of the monkey. *Experimental Neurology, 20*, 197–202.

Barlow, H. B. (1972). Single units and sensation: A neuron doctrine for perceptual psychology? *Perception, 1*, 371–394.

Barrett, T. W. (1969a). The cortex as inferferometer: The transmission of amplitude, frequency, and phase in cortical structures. *Neuropsychologia, 7*, 135–148.

Barrett, T. W. (1969b). The cerebral cortex as a diffractive medium. *Mathematical Biosciences, 4*, 311–350.

Barrett, T. W. (1972). On vibrating strings and information theory. *Journal of Sound and Vibration, 20*(3), 407–412.

Barrett, T. W. (1973a). Uncertainty relations in interaural parameters of acoustical stimulation: An evoked potential study of the auditory cortex in the anesthesized cat. *Behavioral Biology, 8*(3), 299–323.

Barrett, T. W. (1973b). Structural information theory. *Journal of Acoustical Society of America, 54*(4), 1092—1098.

Barrett, T. W. (1973c). Comparing the efficiency of sensory systems: A biophysical approach. *Journal of Biological Physics, 1*(3), 175–192.

Bates, J. A. V. (1947). Some characteristics of human operator. In the proceedings at the convention on automatic regulars and servo-mechanisms. *Journal of Electrical Engineers, 94 part IIa*(2), 298—304.

Bateson, P. G. R. (1964). Changes in chick's responses to novel moving objects over the sensitive period for imprinting. *Animal Behavior, 12*, 479–489.

Bateson, P. G. R. (1972). Retardation of discrimination learning in monkeys and chicks previously exposed to both stimuli. *Nature, 237*(5351), 173–174.

Bateson, P. G. R. (1976). Psychology of knowing another side. *New Scientist, Jan.*, 166—167.

Beach, F. A. (1955). The descent of instinct. *Psychological Review, 62*, 401—410.

Beck, C. H., & Miles, W. R. (1947). Some theoretical and experimental relationships between infrared absorption and olfaction. *Science, 106*, 511–513.

Bekesey, G. von (1959). Synchronism of neural discharges and their demultiplication in pitch perception on the skin and in hearing. *Journal of Acoustical Society of America, 31*, 338–349.

Bekesey, G. von (1960). *Experiments in hearing.* New York: McGraw-Hill.

Bekesey, G. von (1967). *Sensory inhibition*. Princeton: Princeton University Press.

Bell, C. (1811). *Idea of a new anatomy of the brain submitted for the observation of his friends*. London: Strahan and Preston.

Berger, D., Pribram, K. H., Wild, H., & Bridges, C. (1990). An analysis of neural spike train distribution: Determinants of the response of visual cortex neurons to changes in orientation and spatial frequency. *Experimental Brain Research, 80,* 129–134.

Berger, T. W., Berry, S. D., & Thompson, R. F. (1986). Role of the hippocampus in classical conditioning of aversive and appetitive behaviors. In R. S. Isaacson & K. H. Pribram (Eds.), *The Hippocampus* (Vol. 4, pp. 203—240). New York, NY: Plenum.

Bergson, (1922/1965). Duration and simultaneity. Indianapolis: Bobbs-Merrill.

Berlyne, D. E. (1969). The development of the concept of attention in psychology. In C. R. Evans & T. B. Mulholland (Eds.), *Attention in neurophysiology*, (pp. 1–26). New York: Appleton-Century-Crofts.

Bernstein, L. (1976). *The unanswered question*. Cambridge, MA: Harvard University Press.

Bernstein, N. (1967). *The co-ordination and regulation of movements*. New York: Pergamon Press.

Bierre, P., Wild, H., Bridges, C., & Pribram, K. H. (in prep.) Does a single neural spike train encode specific sensory information?

Bishop, G. (1956). Natural history of the nerve impulse. *Physiological Review, 36,* 376–399.

Bizzi, E., Dev, P., Morasso, P., & Polit, A. (1978). Effect of load disturbance during centrally initiated movements. *Journal of Neurophysiology, 41,* 542–556.

Bizzi, E., Polit, A., & Morasso, P. (1976) Mechanisms underlying achievement of final head position. *Journal of Neurophysiology, 39,* 435–444.

Blakemore, C. (1974). Developmental factors in the formation of feature extracting neurons. In F. O. Schmitt & F. G. Worden (Eds.), *The neurosciences third study program*, (pp. 105–113). Cambridge, MA: MIT Press.

Blanchard, Ph., Combe, Ph. & Zheng, W. (1987). Mathematical and physical aspects of stochastic mechanics. In *Lecture notes in physics*, New York: Springer-Verlag.

Blehart, S. R. (1966). Pattern discrimination learning with Rhesus monkeys. *Psychological Reports, 19,* 311–324.

Bloom, F. E., Lazerson, A., & Hofstadter, L. (1985). *Brain, mind and behavior*. New York: W. H. Freeman.

Blum, H. (1967). A new model of global brain function. *Perspectives in Biology and Medicine, 10*(3), 381–406.

Blum, H. (1973). Biological shape and visual science (Part I). *Journal of Theoretical Biology, 38,* 205–287.

Blum, H. (1974). A geometry for biology. *Annals of the New York Academy of Sciences, 231,* 19–30.

Blum, J. S., Chow, K. L., & Pribram, K. H. (1950). A behavioral analysis of the organization of the parieto-temporo-preoccipital cortex. *Journal of Comparitive Neurology 13,* 127–135.

Bohm, D. J. (1971–1973). Quantum theory as an indication of a new order in physics. *Foundations of Physics, Part A, 1*(4), 354–381.

Bohm, D. J. (1986). A new theory of the relationship of mind and matter. *Journal of the American Society for Physical Research, 80,* 113–135.

Bohm, D. J., & Hiley, B. J. (1975). On the intuitive understanding of non-locality as implied by quantum theory. *Foundation of Physics, 5,* 93–109.

Bohm, D., Hiley, B. J., & Stuart, A. E. G. (1970). On a new mode of description in physics. *International Journal of theoretical Physics, 3*(3), 171–183.

Bolster, R. B., Hendricks, S. E., & Pribram, K. H. (in prep.) Conjunction - search in the monkey: Identification of colored form targets in briefly presented visual arrays.

Bolster, R. B., Ruff, R. M., Cutcomb, S. D., Harrington, M. J. & Pribram, K. H. (in prep.) Event related potential distribution in monkeys during automatic and controlled processing of colored form targets.

Boltzmann, (1897/1974). *Theoretical physics and philosophical problems.* Boston, MA: Reidel. (Translated to English by Paul Foulkes).

Bracewell, R. N. (1965). *The Fourier transform and its applications.* New York: McGraw-Hill.

Bracewell, R. N. (1989). The fourier transform. *Scientific American*, 86–95.

Bremer, F. (1944). L'activité 'spontané' des centres nerveuses. *Bulletin of Academics of royal Medicine Belgique, 9,* 148–173.

Bridgeman, B. (1982). Multiplexing in single cells of the alert monkey's visual cortex during brightness discrimination. *Neuropsychologia, 20*(1), 33–42.

Brillouin, L. (1962). *Science and information theory.* New York: Academic Press.

Broadbent, D. E. (1974). Divisions of function and integration. *Neurosciences Study Program III.* New York: MIT Press.

Broadbent, D. E. (1977). The hidden preattentive process. *American Psychologist, 32*(2), 109–118.

Brobeck, J. R. (1963). Review and synthesis. In M. A. B. Brazier (Ed.), *Brain and Behavior* (Vol. 2, pp. 389–409). Washington, DC: American Institute of Biological Sciences.

Broca, P. P. (1863). Localisation des founctions cerebrales. *Bulletin of Social Anthropology Paris, 4,* 200–202.

Brody, B. A., & Pribram, K. H. (1978). The role of frontal and parietal cortex in cognitive processing: Tests of spatial and sequence functions. *Brain, 101,* 607–633.

Brooks, V. B. (1981). The nervous system. *Handbook of Physiology, 2.* Bethesda, MD: American Physiological Society.

Brooks, V. B. (1986). How does the limbic system assist motor learning? A limbic comparator hypothesis. *Brain and Behavioral Evolution, 29,* 29–53.

Brooks, V. B., Horvath, F., Atkin, A., Kozlovskaya, I., & Uno, M. (1969). Reversible changes in voluntary movement during cooling of sub-cerebellar nucleus. *Federation Proceedings, 28,* 396.

Bruner, J. S. (1957). Neural mechanisms in perception. *Psychological Review, 64,* 340–358.

Bruner, J. S., & Postman, L. (1949). On the perception of incongruity: A paradigm. *Journal of Personality, 18,* 206–223.

Brunswick, E. (1966). *The psychology of Egon Brunswick.* K. R. Hammond, (Ed.). New York: Holt, Rinehart & Winston.

Buerger, A. A., Gross, C. G., & Rocha-Miranda, C. E. (1974) Effects of ventral putamen lesions on discrimination learning by monkeys. *Journal of Comparative and Physiological Psychology, 86,* 440–446.

Bullock, T. H. (1945). Problems in the comparative study of brain waves. *Yale Journal of Biology and Medicine, 17,* 657–679.

Bullock, T. H. (1947). Problems in invertebrate electrophysiology. *Physiology Review, 27,* 643–664.

Bullock, T. H. (1957). Neuronal integrative mechanisms. In B. T. Scheer (Ed.) *Recent Advances in Invertebrate Physiology.* Eugene, Oregon: University of Oregon Press.

Bullock, T. H. (1981). Spikeless neurones: where do we go from here? In B. M. H. Bush & A. Roberts, (Eds.) *Neurones without impulses* (pp. 269–284). Cambridge: Cambridge University Press.

Bundesen, C., & Larsen, A. (1975). Visual transformation of size. *Journal of Experimental Psychology: Human perception and performance, 1,* 214–220.

Bunge, M. (1980). *The mind-body problem.* Oxford, Eng.: Pergamon Press.

Burgess, A. E., Wagner, R. F., Jennings, R. J., & Barlow, H. B. (1981). Efficiency of human visual signal discrimination. *Science, 214,* 93–94.

Burr, D. C., Ross, J., & Morrone, M. C. (1986). *Proceedings of the Royal Society of London, B227,* 249–265.

Butter, C. M. (1968). The effect of discrimination training on pattern equivalence in monkeys with inferotemporal and lateral striate lesions. *Neuropsychologia, 6,* 27–40.

Butter, C. M., Mishkin, M., & Rosvold, H. E. (1965). Stimulus generalization in monkeys with inferotemporal and lateral occipital lesions. In D. J. Mustofsky (Ed.), *Stimulus Generalization* (pp. 119–133). Stanford, CA: Stanford University Press.

Caelli, T. (1984). On the specification of coding principles for visual image processing. In P. C. Dodwell & T. Caelli (Eds.), *Figural synthesis*, (pp. 153–184). Hillsdale, NJ: Lawrence Erlbarum Associates.

Caelli. T., Hoffman, W. C., & Lindman, H. (1978a). Apparent motion: Self-excited oscillations induced by retarded neuronal flaws. In E. L. J. Leeuwenberg & H. F. J. M. Buffart (Eds.), *Formal theories of visual perception*, (pp. 103–116). New York: Wiley.

Caelli, T., Hoffman W. C., & Lindman, H. (1978b). Subjective Lorentz transformations and the perception of motion. *Journal of the Optical Society of America, 68*, 402–411.

Caelli, T., & Hubner, M. (1983). On the efficient two-dimensional energy coding characteristics of spatial vision. *Vision Research, 23*(10), 1053–1055 .

Caelli, T., & Julez, B. (1979). Psychophysical evidence for global feature processing in visual texture discrimination. *Journal of the Optical Society of America, 69*, 675–678.

Caelli, T., & Moraglia, G. (1985). On the detection of Gabor signals and discrimination of Gabor textures. *Vision Research, 25*(5), 671–684.

Campbell, F. W. (1974). The transmission of spatial information through the visual system. In F. O. Schmitt & F. G. Worden (Eds.), *The Neurosciences Third Study Program* (pp. 95–103). Cambridge, MA: MIT Press.

Campbell, F. W. (1985). How much of the information falling on the retina reaches the visual cortex and how much is stored in the visual memory? In C. Chagas, R. Gattass & C. Gross (Eds.), *Pattern recognition mechanisms*. (pp. 83–96). Berlin: Springer-Verlag.

Campbell, F. W., & Blakemore, C. (1969). On the existence of neurons in the human visual system selectively sensitive to the orientation and size of retinal images. *Journal of Physiology, 203*, 237–260.

Campbell, F. W., & Robson, J. G. (1968). Application of Fourier analysis to the visibility of gratings. *Journal of Physiology, 197*, 551—566.

Cardu, B., Ptito, M., LaPorte, F., & Pribram, K. H. (in prep.) The effects of lesions of the prestriate cortex of monkeys on visual discrimination performance.

Carlton, E. H. (1988). Connection between internal representation of rigid transformation and cortical activity paths. *Biological Cybernetics, 59*, 419–429.

Carlton, E. H., & Shepard, R. N. (In press). Psychologically simple motions as geodesic paths: I. Asymmetric objects. *Journal of Mathematical Psychology*.

Carlton, E. H., & Shepard, R. N. (In press). Psychologically simple motions as geodesic paths: II. Symmetric objects. *Journal of Mathematical Psychology*.

Carlton, E. H., & Shepard, R. N. (in prep.). A geometrical basis for preferred motions of objects in space.

Cassirer, E. (1944). The concept of group and the theory of perception. *Philosophy and Phenomenological Research, 5*, 1–15.

Cavanaugh, P. (1975). Two classes of holographic processes realizable in the neural realm. In T. Storer & D. Winter (Eds.), *Formal aspects of cognitive processes* (pp. 14–40). Berlin: Springer-Verlag.

Cavanaugh, P. (1976). Holographic and trace strength models of rehearsal effects in the item recognition task. *Memory and cognition, 4*, 186–199.

Cavanaugh, P. (1984). Image transforms in the visual system. In P. C. Dodwell & T. M. Caelli, (Eds.), *Figural Synthesis*. Hillsdale, NJ: Lawrence Erlbaum Associates, 185–218.

Cavanaugh, P. (1985). Local log polar frequency analysis in the striate cortex as a basis for size and orientation invariance. In D. Rose & V. G. Dobson (Eds.), *Models of the visual cortex* (pp. 85–95). New York: Wiley.

Cayley, A. (1845). On certain results relating to quaternions. *Philosophical Magazine, 26*, 141–145.

Cherry, C. (1978). *On human communication*. Cambridge, MA: MIT Press.

Chin, J. H., Pribram, K. H., Drake, K. & Greene, L. O., Jr. (1976). Disruption of temperature discrimination during limbic forebrain stimulation in monkeys. *Neuropsychologia, 14*, 293–310.

Chomsky, N. (1965). *Aspects of the theory of syntax*. Cambridge, MA: MIT Press.

Chow, K. L. (1951). Effects of partial extirpations of the posterior association cortex on visually mediated behavior. *Comparative Psychology Monographs, 20*, 187–217.

Chow, K. L. (1961). Anatomical and electrographical analysis of temporal neocortex in relation to visual discrimination learning in monkeys. In J. F. Delafresyne, A. Fesard, & J. Konorski (Eds.), *Brain mechanisms and learning* (pp 375–392). Oxford: Blackwell Scientific Publications.

Chow, K. L. (1970). Integrative functions of the thalamocortical visual system of cat. In K. H. Pribram & D. Broadbent (Eds.), *Biology of memory* (pp. 273–292). New York: Academic Press.

Chow, K. L., & Pribram, K. H. (1956). Cortical projection of the thalamic ventrolateral nuclear group in monkeys. *J. Comp. Neurol., 104*, 37–75.

Clifford, W. K. (1882). Preliminary sketch of biquaternions. *Mathematical Papers*. London.

Cohen, L. (1959). Perception of reversible figures after brain injury. *Archives of Neurological Psychology, 81,*765–775.

Cooper, L. N. (1984). Neuron learning to network organization. In M. S. Berger (Ed.), *J. C. Maxwell, The Sesquicentennial Symposium* (pp. 41–90). Amsterdam: Elsevier North Holland.

Coss, R. G., & Perkel, D. H. (1985). The function of dendritic spines: A review of theoretical issues. *Behav. Neural Biol., 44*, 151–185.

Craik, F. I. M. (1989). On the making of episodes. In H. L. Roediger, III & F. I. M. Craik (Eds.), *Varieties of Memory and Consciousness: Essays in Honour of Endel Tulving* (pp. 43–57). Hillsdale, NJ: Lawrence Erlbaum Associates.

Creutzfeldt, O. D., Kuhnt, U. & Benevento, L. A. (1974). An intracellular analysis of visual cortical neurons to moving stimuli: Responses in a cooperative neuronal network. *Experimental Brain Research., 21*, 251–272.

Crick, F. H. C., & Asanuma, C. (1986). Certain aspects of the anatomy and physiology of the cerebral cortex. In J. L. McClelland & D. E. Rumelhart (Eds.), *Parallel distributed processing: Explorations in the microstructure of cognition, Vol. II: Psychological and biological models*. Cambridge, MA: MIT Press.

Crowne, D. P., Konow, A., Drake, K. J., & Pribram, K. H. (1972). Hippocampal electrical activity in the monkey during delayed alternation problems. *Journal of Electroencephalography and Clinical Neurophysiology, 33*, 567–577.

Cutting, J. E. (1985). Gibson, representation, and belief. *Contemporary Psychology, 30*, 186–188.

Cutting, J. E. (1986). *Perception with an eye for motion*. Cambridge, MA: MIT Press.

Daintith, J. (1981). *The Facts on File Dictionary of Physics*. New York: Facts on File.

Daugman, J. G. (1980). Two dimensional spatial analysis of cortical receptive field profiles. *Vision Research, 20*, 847–856.

Daugman, J. G. (1984). Spatial vision channels in the Fourier plan. *Vision Research, 24*, 891–910.

Daugman, J. G. (1985). Representational issues and local filter models of two-dimensional spatial visual encoding. In D. Rose & V. G. Dobson (Eds.), *Models of the Visual Cortex*, (pp. 96–107). New York: Wiley.

Daugman, J. G. (1988a). Complete discrete 2-D Gabor transforms by neural networks for image analysis and compression. *IEEE Transactions on Acoustics, Speech and Signal Processing, 36*(7), 1169–1179.

Daugman, J. G. (1990). An information-theoretic view of analog representation in striate cortex. In E. Schwartz (Ed.), *Computational neuroscience*. Cambridge, MA: MIT Press.

Deecke, L., Kornhuber, H. H., Long, M., & Schreiber, H. (1985). Timing function of the frontal cortex in sequential motor and learning tasks. *Human Neurobiology, 4*, 143–154.

Desimone, R., Schein, S. J., & Albright, T. D. (1985). Form, color, and motion analysis in prestriate cortex of the macaque. In C. Chagas, R. Gattass, & C. Gross (Eds.), *Pattern Recognition Mechanisms* (pp. 165–201). Berlin: Springer-Verlag.

Deutsch, J. A., & Deutsch, D. (1963). Attention: some theoretical considerations. *Psychological Review, 70,* 80–90.

DeValois, R. L. (1982). Address to American Psychological Association.

DeValois, R. L., Albrecht, D. G., & Thorell, L. G. (1978). Cortical cells: bar and edge detectors, or spatial frequency filters? In S. J. Cool & E. L. Smith (Eds.), *Frontiers in visual science* (pp. 544–556). New York: Springer-Verlag.

DeValois, R. L., & DeValois, K. K. (1980). Spatial vision. *Annual Review of Psychology, 31,* 309—341.

DeValois, R. L., & DeValois, K. K. (1988). *Spatial vision* (Oxford psychology series No. 14). New York: Oxford University Press.

DeValois, R. L., DeValois, K. K., & Yund, E. W. (1979). Responses of striate cortex cells to grating and checkerboard patterns. *Journal of Physiology, 291,* 483–505.

Dewey, J. (1916). *Essays in experimental logic.* Chicago, IL: University of Chicago Press.

Dewson, J. H., III (1966). Complex auditory discrimination and lesions of temporal cortex in the monkey. *Journal of the Acoustical Society of America, 39,* 1259.

Dewson, J. H., III (1968). Efferent olivocochlear bundle: some relationships to stimulus discrimination in noise. *Journal of Neurophysiology, 31,* 122–130.

Dewson, J. H., III, Nobel, K. W., & Pribram, K. H. (1966). Corticofugal influences at cochlear nucleus of the cat: Some effects of ablation of insulotemporal cortex. *Brain Research, 2,* 151–159.

Dewson, J. H. III, Pribram, K. H., & Lynch, J. (1969). Effects of ablations of temporal cortex upon speech sound discrimination in the monkey. *Experimental Neurology, 24,* 579–591.

Dirac, P. A. M. (1930). *The principles of quantum mechanics.* Oxford: Oxford University Press.

Dirac, P. A. M. (1951). Is there an aether? *Nature, 168,* 906.

Ditchburn, R. W., & Ginsborg, B. L. (1952). Vision with a stabilized retinal image. *Nature, 170,* 36.

Dodwell, P. C. (1984). Local and global factors in figural synthesis. In P. C. Dodwell & T. Caelli (Eds.), *Figural synthesis* (pp. 219–248). Hillsdale, NJ: Lawrence Erlbaum Associates.

Dodwell, P. C., & Caelli, T. (1984). *Figural synthesis.* Hillsdale, NJ: Lawrence Erlbaum Associates.

Donchin, E. (1981). Surprise!—- Surprise? *Psychophysiology, 18,* 493—513.

Donchin, E., & Coles, G. H. (1988). Is the P300 component a manifestation of context updating? *Behavior and Brain Sciences, 11,* 357–374.

Donchin, E., Otto, D. A., Gerbrandt, L. K., & Pribram, K. H. (1973). While a monkey waits. In K. H. Pribram & A. R. Luria (Eds.), *Psychophysiology of the frontal lobes* (pp. 125–138). New York: Academic Press.

Doty, R. W., & Nagrao, N. (1973). Forebrain commissures and vision. In R. Jung (Ed.), *Handbook of sensory physiology* (Vol. 7/3B, pp. 543–582). Berlin: Springer-Verlag.

Douglas, R. J., Barrett, T. W., Pribram, K. H., & Cerny, M. C. (1969). Limbic lesions and error reduction. *Journal of Comparative and Physiological Psychology, 68,* 437–441.

Douglas, R. J., & Pribram, K. H. (1966). Learning and limbic lesions. *Neuropsychologia, 4,* 197–220.

Douglas, R. J., & Pribram, K. H. (1969). Distraction and habituation in monkeys with limbic lesions. *Journal of Comparative and Physiological Psychology, 69,* 473–480.

Dowling, J. E. (1967). Site of visual adaptation. *Science, 155,* 273.

Dowling, J. E., & Boycott, B. B. (1965). Neural connections of the retina: Fine structures of the inner plexiform layer. *Quantitative Biology, 30,* 393–402.

Eason, R. G. (1981). Visual evoked potential correlates of early neural filtering during selective attention. *Bulletin of the Psychonomic Society, 18,* 203–206.

Eason, R. G., Flowers, L., & Oakley, M. (1983). Differentiation of retinal and nonretinal contributions to averaged responses obtained with electrodes placed near the eyes. *Behavioral Research Methods and Instruments, 15,* 13–21.

Eason, R. G., Harter, M. R., & White, C. T. (1969). Effects of attention and arousal on visually evoked cortical potentials and reaction time in man. *Physiology and Behavior, 4,* 283–289.

Eason, R. G., Oakley, M., & Flowers, L. (1983). Central neural influences on the human retina during selective attention. *Physiological Psychology, 11*(1), 18–28.

Eccles, J. C. (1986). Do mental events cause neural events analogously to the probability fields of quantum mechanics? *Proceedings of the Royal Society of London, 277*, 411–428.

Eccles, J. C., Ito, M., & Szentagothai, J. (1967). *The cerebellum as a neuronal machine.* New York: Springer-Verlag.

Edelman, G. (1987). *Neural Darwinism: The theory of neuronal group selection.* New York: Basic Books.

Edelman, G. (1989). *The Remembered Present.* NY: Basic Books.

Enroth-Cugell, C., & Robson, J. G. (1966). The contrast sensitivity of retinal ganglion cells of the cat. *Journal of Physiology, 198*, 517–552.

Epstein, W. (1987). Contrasting conceptions of perception and action. In B. Bridgeman, D. A. Owens, W. L. Shebilske, & P. Wolff (Eds.), *Sensorymotor interactions in space perception and action* (pp. 103–115). North Holland: Elvesier.

Ettlinger, G. (1959). Visual discrimination following successive temporal ablations in monkeys. *Brain, 82*, 232–250.

Evarts, E. V. (1952). Effect of ablation of prestriate cortex on auditory-visual association in monkey. *Journal of Neurophysiology, 15*, 191–200.

Evarts, E. V. (1966). Pyramidal tract activity associated with a conditioned hand movement in the monkey. *Journal of Neurophysiology, 29*, 1011–1027.

Evarts, E. V. (1967). Representation of movements and muscles by pyramidal tract neurons of the precentral motor coertex. In M. D. Yahr & D. P. Purpura (Eds.), *Neurophysiological basis of normal and abnormal motor activities* (pp. 215–254). Hewlett, NY: Raven.

Evarts, E. V. (1968). Relation of pyramidal tract activity to force exerted during voluntary movement. *Journal of Neurophysiology, 31*, 14–27.

Evarts, E. V. (1969). Activity of pyramidal tract neurons during postural fixation. *Journal of Neurophysiology, 32*, 375–385.

Fatmi, H. A., & Resconi, G. (1988). A new computing principle. *Il Nuovo Cimento, 101B*(2), 239–242.

Ferrier, D. (1886/1978). *The functions of the brain.* New York: Putnam. Reprinted in D. Robinson (Ed.), *Significant contributions to the history of psychology, Vol. III, Series E.*

Festinger, L., Burnham, C. A., Ono, H., & Bamber, D. (1967). Efference and the conscious experience. *Journal of Experimental Psychology, 74*, 1–36.

Feynman, R. P., Leighton, R. B., & Sands, M. (1963). *The Feynman lectures on physics.* Reading, MA: Addison-Wesley.

Feynman, R. P. (1985) *QED.* Princeton, NJ: Princeton University Press.

Flanagan, J. L. (1972). *Speech analysis, synthesis and perception* (2nd ed.), Berlin: Springer-Verlag.

Flechsig, P. (1896). *Gehirn und Seele,* (2nd ed.). Leipzig: Verlag Velt & Co.

Flechsig, P. (1900). *Les centres de projection et d'association du cerveau humain.* XIII Congres International de Medicine. France: Paris, 115–121.

Field, D. J. & Tolhurst, D. J. (1986). *Proceedings of the Royal Society London, B228*, 379–400.

Flourens, P. (1846/1978). *Phrenology examined.* (C. L. Meigs, Trans.). Philadelphia, PA: Hogan & Thompson. Reprinted in D. Robinson (Ed.), *Significant contributions to the history of psychology, Vol. II, Series E.*

Fodor, J. A. (1980). Methodological solipsism as a research strategy for cognitive psychology. *Behavioral and Brain Sciences, 3*, 63–110.

Foerster, O. (1926). Sensible corticale Felder. In O. Bumke, and O. Foerster (Eds.), *Handbuch der Neurologie* (pg. 358). Berlin: J. Springer.

Foster, D. H. (1975). Visual apparent motion of some preferred paths in the rotation group SO(3). *Biological Cybernetics, 18*, 81–89.

Foster, D. H. (1978). Visual apparent motion and the calculus of variations. In E. L. J. Leeuwenberg & H. F. J. M. Buffart (Eds.), *Formal theories of visual perception* (pp. 67–82). New York: Wiley.

Fowler, C. A., & Turvey, M. T. (1978). Skill acquisition: An event approach with special reference to searching for the optimum of a function of several variables. In G. E. Stelmach (Ed.), *Information processing in motor control and learning* (pp. 1–40). New York: Academic Press.

Fowler, C. A., & Turvey, M. T. (1982). Observational perspective and descriptive level in perceiving and acting. In W. B. Weimer & D. B. Palermo (Eds.), *Cognition and the symbolic processes* (pp. 1–19). Hillsdale, NJ: Lawrence Erlbaum Associates.

Fox, S. E., Wolfson, S. and Ranck, J. B. (1983). Investigating the mechanisms of hippocampal theta rhythms: approaches and progress. In W. Seifert (Ed.), *Neurobiology of the Hippocampus*, (pp. 303–319). New York: Academic Press.

Freed, D. M., Corkin, S., & Cohen N. J. (1987). Forgetting in H. M.: A second look. *Neuropsychologia, 25*(3), 461–471.

Freeman, W. (in prep.). Oscillatory potentials. In D. E. Sheer & K. H. Pribram (Eds.), *Attention, cognitive and brain processes and clinical applications*. New York: Academic Press.

Freeman, W., & Watts, J. W. (1942). *Psychosurgery*. Springfield, IL: Charles C. Thomas.

Freud, S. (1891/1953). *On aphasia*. New York, NY: International Universities Press.

Freud, S. (1895/1966). *Project for a scientific psychology*. (Standard Ed., Vol. 1, pp. 281—397). London: Hogarth.

Freyd, J. J. (1987). Dynamic mental representation. *Psychological Review, 94*, 427–438.

Fröhlich, H. (1968). Long range coherence and energy storage in biological systems. *International Journal of Quantum Chemistry, 2*, 641–649.

Fröhlich, H. (1970). Long range coherence and the actions of enzymes. *Nature, 228*, 1093.

Fröhlich, H. (1975). The extraordinary dielectric properties of biological materials and the action of enzymes. *Proceedings of National Academy of Science, USA, 72*(11), 4211–4215.

Fröhlich, H. (1983). Evidence for coherent excitation in biological systems. *International Journal of Quantum Chemistry, 23*, 1589–1595.

Fröhlich, H. (1986). Coherent excitation in active biological systems. In F. Gutman & H. Keyzer (Eds.), *Modern Bioelectrochemistry* (pp. 241–261). New York: Plenum.

Fuller, J. L., Rosvold, H. E., & Pribram, K. H. (1957). The effect of affective and cognitive behavior in the dog of lesions of the pyriform-amygdala- hippocampal complex. *Journal of Comparative and Physiological Psychology, 50*, 89–96.

Fulton, J. F., Pribram, K. H., Stevenson, J. A. F., & Wall, P. (1949). Interrelations between orbital gyrus, insula, temporal tip and anterior cingulate gyrus. *Transactions of the American Neurological Association*, 175–179.

Fuster, J. M. (1988). *The prefrontal cortex*. Anatomy, Physiology and Neuropsychology of the frontal lobe (2nd ed.). New York: Raven.

Fuster, J. M., & Jervey, J. P. (1982). Neuronal firing in the inferotemporal cortex of the monkey in a visual memory task. Journal of Neuroscience, 2(3), 361–375.

Gabor, D. (1946). Theory of communication. *Journal of the Institute of Electrical Engineers, 93*, 429–441.

Gabor, D. (1948). A new microscopic principle. *Nature, 161*, 777–778.

Gabor, D. (1968). Improved holographic model of temporal recall. *Nature, 217*, 1288–1289.

Gall, F. J., & Spurtzheim, G. (1809/1969). Research on the nervous system in general and on that of the brain in particular. In K. H. Pribram (Ed.), *Brain and Behavior*, (pp. 20–26). Middlesex: Penguin.

Ganz, L. (1971). Sensory deprivation and visual discrimination. In H. L. Teuber (Ed.), *Handbook of sensory physiology, 8*, (pp.). New York: Springer-Verlag.

Garcia-Rill, E., & Skinner, R. D. (1988). Modulation of rhythmic function in the posterior midbrain. *Neurosciences, 27*, 639–654.

Garner, W. R. (1962). *Uncertainty and structure as psychological concepts*. New York: Wiley.

Garner, W. R. (1974). *The processing of information and structure*. Hillsdale, NJ: Lawrence Erlbaum Associates.

Gatlin, L. (1972). *Information theory and the living system*. New York, NY: Columbia University Press.

Gauthier, R. F. (1977). *Metrics and models in form perception*. Unpublished doctoral dissertation, Dept. of Psychology, Stanford University.

Gazzaniga, M. S. (1985). *The social brain: Discovering the network of the mind*. New York: Basic Books.

Geldard, F. A. (1975). *Sensory saltation, metastability in the perceptual world*. Hillsdale, NJ: Lawrence Erlbaum Associates.

Gerbrandt, L. K., & Ivy, G. O.(1987). Effects of dentate granule cell depletion in rats: Failure to recall more than one event at the same place. In: P. Ellen and C. Thinus-Blanc (Eds.), *Cognitive processes and spatial orientation in animal and man: Volume II. Neurophysiology and Developmental Aspects*, (pp. 106–115). Boston, MA: Martinus Nijhoff Publishers.

Gerstein, G. L., & Mandelbrot, B. (1964). Random walk models for the spike activity of a single neuron. *Biophysical Journal, 4*, 41–68.

Gibson, C. (1981). *The Facts on File Dictionary of Mathematics*. New York: Facts on File.

Gibson, J. J. (1966). *The senses considered as perceptual systems*. Boston: Houghton Mifflin.

Gibson, J. J. (1977). On the analysis of change in the optic array in contemporary research in visual space and motion perception. *Scandinavian Journal of Psychology, 18*(3), 161–163.

Gibson, J. J. (1979). *The ecological approach to visual perception*. Boston: Houghton Mifflin.

Gibson, J. J., & Gibson, E. J. (1955). Perceptual learning: Differentiation or enrichment. *Psychological Review, 62*, 32–41.

Ginsburg, A. (1971). *Psychological correlates of a model of the human visual system*. Master's thesis, Air Force Institute of Technology.

Ginsburg, A., (1978). *Visual information processing based on spatial filters constrained by biological data*. Publication of the Aerospace Medical Research Laboratory, Wright-Patterson Air Force Base, Ohio.

Glezer, V. D. (1985). Spatial and spatial frequency characteristics of receptive fields of the visual cortex and piecewise Fourier analysis. In D. Rose & V. G. Dobson (Eds.) *Models of the visual cortex* (pp. 265–272). New York: Wiley.

Glezer, V. D., Ivanoff, V. A., & Tscherbach, T. A. (1973). Investigation of complex and hypercomplex receptive fields of visual cortex of the cat as spatial frequency filters. *Vision Research, 13*, 1875–1904.

Goldberg, G. (1985). Supplementary motor area: Review and hypotheses. *Behavioral and Brain Sciences, 8*, 567–588.

Goldscheider, A. (1906). Uber die materiellen veranderungen bei der assoziationsbildung. *Neurologische Zentralblatt., 25*, 146.

Gray, C. M., & Singer, W. (1989). Stimulus-specific neuronal oscillations in orientation of cat visual cortex. *Proceedings of the National Academy of Science, USA, 86*, 1698–1702).

Gray, C. M., König, P., Engel, A. K., & Singer, W. (1989). Oscillatory responses in cat visual cortex exhibit inter-columnar synchronization which reflects global stimulus properties. *Nature, 338*(6213), 334–337.

Gray, J. A. (1970). Sodium amobarbital, the hippocampal theta rhythm and the partial reinforcement extinction effect. *Psychological Review, 77*, 465–480.

Gray, J. A. (1972). Effects of septal driving of the hippocampal theta rhythm on resistance to extinction. *Physiology and Behavior, 8*, 481–490.

Gray, J. A. (1982a). *The neuropsychology of anxiety*. Oxford, Eng.: Oxford University Press.

Gray, J. A. (1982b). Precis of the neuropsychology of anxiety: An enquiry into the functions of the septo-hippocampal system. *Behavioral and brain sciences, 5*, 469–484.

Graybiel, A. M. (1974). Studies on the anatomical organization of posterior association cortex. *The Neurosciences, 3*, 205–214.

Green, H. S. & Triffet, T. (1985). Extracellular fields within the cortex. *Journal of Theoretical Biology, 115*(1), 43–64.

Grillner, S. (1974). Locomotions in vertebrates: Central mechanisms and reflex interactions. *Physiology Review, 55*, 274–304.

Grillner, S. (1981). Control of locomotion in bipeds, tetrapods, and fish. In V. B. Brooks (Ed.), *Handbook of physiology - the nervous system II* (pp. 1199–1236). Baltimore: Waverly Press.

Grillner, S. (1985). Neurobiological bases of rhythmic motor acts in vertebrates. *Science, 228*, 143—149.

Gross, C. G. (1973). Inferotemporal cortex and vision. In E. Stellar & J. M. Sprague (Eds.), *Progress in physiological psychology,* (Vol. 5, pp. 77–124). New York: Academic Press.

Gross, C., Desimone, R., Albright, T. D. & Schwartz, E. L. (1985). Inferior temporal cortex and pattern recognition. In C. Chagas, R. Gattas, & C. Gross (Eds.), *Pattern recognition mechanisms* (pp. 179–202). Berlin: Springer-Verlag.

Grossman, M., & Wilson, M. (1987). Stimulus categorization by brain injured patients. *Brain and Cognition, 6*, 55–71.

Grueninger, W. E., & Pribram, K. H. (1969). Effects of spatial and nonspatial distractors on performance latency of monkeys with frontal lesions. *Journal of Comparitive and Physiological Psychology, 68*, 203–209.

Hameroff, S. R. (1987). *Ultimate computing: Biomolecular consciousness and nanotechnology.* Amsterdam: North Holland Press.

Hamilton, W. R. (1844). On quaternions; or on a new system of imaginaries in algebra. *Philosophical Magazine, 25*, 10–13.

Hamilton, W. R. (1853). *Lectures on quaternions.* Dublin: Hodges & Smith.

Hammond, P. (1972). Spatial organization of receptive fields of LGN neurons. *Journal of Physiology, 222*, 53–54.

Hart, E. (1976). (ALOPEX) Visual perception: A dynamic theory. *Biological Cybernetics, 22*, 169—180.

Harth, E., Unnikrishnan, P., & Pandya, A. S. (1987). The inversion of sensory processing by feedback pathways: Model of visual cognitive functions. *Science, 237*, 184–187.

Hartley, R. V. L., (1928). Transmission of information. *Bell System Tech. J., 7*, 535.

Hastorf, A. H., & Knutson, A. L. (1954). Motivation, perception and attitude change. *Psychol. Rev., 56*, 88–97.

Hatfield, G., & Epstein, W. (1985). The status of the minimum principle in the theoretical analysis of visual perception. *Psychological Bulletin, 97*, 115–186.

Hayek, F. A. (1952). *The sensory order.* Chicago, IL: University of Chicago Press.

Head, H. (1920). *Studies in neurology,* (2 Vols.). London: Oxford University Press.

Hearst, E., & Pribram, K. H. (1964a). Facilitation of avoidance behavior by unavoidable shocks in normal and amygdalectomized monkeys. *Psychogical Reports, 14*, 39–42.

Hearst, E., & Pribram, K. H. (1964b). Appetitive and aversive generalization gradients in amygdalectomized monkeys. *Journal of Comparative and Physiological Psychology, 58*, 296–298.

Hebb, D. O. (1949/1961). *The organization of behavior, a neuropsychological theory.* New York: Wiley.

Hecht, S. (1934). In C. Murchison (Ed.), *Handbook of general experimental psychology* (pp. 704–828). Worcester, MA: Clark University Press.

Hecht, E., & Zajac, A. (1974). *Optics.* Menlo Park, CA: Addison-Wesley.

Heckenmueller, E. G. (1968). Stabilization of the retinal image: A revision of method, effects and theory. In R. N. Haber (Ed.), *Contemporary theory and research in visual perception* (pp. 280–294). New York: Holt, Rinehart & Winston.

Heggelund, P. (1981a). Receptive field organization of simple cells in cat striate cortex. *Experimental Brain Research, 42*, 89–98.

Heggelund, P. (1981b). Receptive field organization of complex cells in cat striate cortex. *Experimental Brain Research, 42*, 99–107.

Heilman, K. M., & Valenstein, E. (1972). Frontal lobe neglect. *Neurology, 28*, 229–232.

Heilman, K. M., & Valenstein, E. (1979). Introduction in Heilman & Valenstein (Eds.), *Clinical Neuropsychology* (pp. 3–16). New York: Oxford University Press.

Held, R. (1968). Action contingent development of vision in neonatal animals. In D. P. Kimble (Ed.), *Experience and capacity* (pp. 31–111). New York: New York Academy of Sciences.

Helmholtz, H. von (1863/1877). *Lehre von den Tonempfindungen*. Braunschweig: Vieweg. Translated to English on *The Sensations of Tone*, reprinted 1954. New York: Dover.

Helmholtz, H. von (1909/1924). *Handbook of physiological optics,* (3rd ed., J. P. C. Southall, Trans.) Rochester, NY: Optical Society of America.

Henry, G. H. (1977). Receptive field classes of cells in the striate cortex of the cat. *Brain Research, 133*, 1–28.

Henry, G. H., & Bishop, P. O. (1971). Simple cells of the striate cortex. In W. D. Neff (Ed.), *Contributions to sensory physiology*. New York: Academic Press.

Hering, E. (1964). *Outlines of a theory of the light sense* (L. Hurvich & D. Jameson, Trans.). Cambridge, MA: Harvard University Press. (Original work published 1878)

Hillyard, S. A., Squires, K. C., Baver, J. W., & Lindsay, P. H. (1971). Evoked potential correlates of auditory signal detection. *Science, 172*, 1357–1360.

Hinton, G. E. (1979). Imagery without arrays. *Behavior and Brain Science, 2*, 555–556.

Hinton, G. E., & Anderson, J. A. (1989). *Parallel models of associative memory*. Hillsdale, NJ: Lawrence Erlbaum Associates

Hinton, G. E., McClelland, J. L., & Rumelhart, D. E. (1986). Distributed representations. In D. E. Rumelhart & J. L. McClelland (Eds.), *Parallel distributed processing: Explorations in the microstructure of cognition. Vol. 1: Foundations*. Cambridge, MA: MIT Press.

Hinton, G. E., & Sejnowski, T. J. (1986). Learning and relearning in Boltzmann machines in parallel distributed processing. In D. E. Rumelhart & J. L. McClelland (Eds.), *Parallel distributed processing: Explorations in the microstructure of cognition. Vol. 1: Foundations*. Cambridge, MA: MIT Press.

Hirsch, H. V. B., & Spinelli, D. N. (1970). Visual experience modified distribution of horizontally and vertically oriented receptive fields in cats. *Science, 168*, 869–871.

Hochberg, J. (1984). Form perception: experience and explanations. In P. C. Dodwell & T. Caelli (Eds.), *Figural Synthesis,* (pp. 1–30). Hillsdale, NJ: Lawrence Erlbaum Associates.

Hoffer, J. A. (1982). Central control and reflex regulation of mechanical impedence: The basis for a unified motor-control scheme. *The Behavioral and Brain Sciences, 5*, 548–549.

Hoffman, K. P., & Stone, J. (1971). Conduction of velocity of afferents to cat visual cortex: a correlation with cortical receptive field properties. *Brain Research, 32*, 460–466.

Hoffman, W. C. (1966). The Lie algebra of visual perception. *Journal of Mathematical Psychology, 3*, 65–98.

Hoffman, W. C. (1978). The Lie transformation group approach to visual neuropsychology. In E. L. J. Leeuwenberg & H. F. J. M. Buffart (Eds.), *Formal theories of visual perception* (pp. 27–66). New York: Wiley.

Hoffman, W. C. (1984). Figural synthesis by vectorfields: Geometric neuropsychology. In P. C. Dodwell & T. Caelli (Eds.), *Figural synthesis* (pp. 249–282). Hillsdale, NJ: Lawrence Erlbaum Associates.

Hopfield, J. J. (1982). Neural networks and physical systems with emergent collective computational abilities. *PNAS, 79*, 2554–2558.

Hosford, H. L. (1977). *Binaural waveform coding in the inferior colliculus of the cat: Single unit responses to simple and complex stimuli*. Unpublished doctoral thesis, Stanford University.

Houk, J. C., & Henneman, E. (1967). Responses of golgi tendon organs to the active contractions of the soleus muscle of the cat. *Journal of Neurophysiology, 30*, 466–481.

Houk, J. C., & Rymer, W. Z. (1981). Neural control of muscle length and tension. In V. B. Brooks (Ed.), *Motor control*. Bethesda, MD: American Physiological Society Handbook of Physiology.

Hubel, D. H., & Livingstone, M. (1981). Regions of poor orientation tuning coincide with patches of cytochrome oxidase staining in monkey strite cortex. *Neuroscience Abstracts, 7*, 357.

Hubel, D. H., & Wiesel, T. N. (1959). Receptive fields of single neurons in the cat's striate cortex. *Journal of Physiology, 148*, 574–591.

Hubel, D. N., & Wiesel, T. N. (1962). Receptive fields, binocular interaction and functional architecture in the cat's visual cortex. *Journal of Physiology, 160*, 106–154.

Hubel, D. N., & Wiesel, T. N. (1968). Receptive fields and functional architecture of monkey striate cortex. *Journal of Physiology, 195*, 215–243.

Hubel, D. N., & Wiesel, T. N. (1977). Ferrier Lecture: Functional architecture of Macaque monkey visual cortex. *Proceedings of the Royal Academy of London, 198*, 1–59.

Hudspeth, W. J. (1989a). Human cortical transfer functions for form-color classification. In preparation.

Hudspeth, W. J. (1989b). Human cortical transfer functions for object-concept classifications. In preparation.

Hudspeth, W. J., & Pribram, K. H. (1990). Stages of brain and cognitive maturation. *Journal of Educational Psychology, 82*(4), 881–884.

Hudspeth, W. J., & Pribram, K. H. (1991). Stages of neuropsychological maturation. Manuscript submitted for publication to *International Journal of Psychophysiology*.

Hurlbert, A., & Poggio, T. (1988). Synthesizing a color algorithm from examples. Science, 239, 482–485.

Hurvich, L., & Jameson, D. (1957). An opponent-process theory of color vision. *Psychological Review, 64*, 384–404.

Hyden, H. (1969). Biocheical aspects of learning and memory. In K. H. Pribram (Ed.), *On the Biology of Learning* (pp. 95–125). New York: Harcourt, Brace & World.

Ickes, B. P. (1970). A new method for performing digital control system attitude computations using quaternions. *AIAA Journal, 8*, 13–17.

Isaacson, R. L. (1974). *The limbic system*. New York: Plenum.

Iwai, E., & Mishkin, M. (1968). Two visual foci in the temporal lobe of monkeys. In N. Yoshii & N. A. Buchwald (Eds.), *Neuropsychological basis of learning and behavior* (pp. 1–11). Osaka, Japan: Osaka University Press.

Jackson, J. H. (1882/1958). On some implications of dissolution of the nervous sytem. In J. Taylor (Ed.), *Selected writings of John Hughlings Jackson* (Vol.2, pp. 29–44). London: Hodder and Stoughton.

James, W. (1950). *Principles of psychology*. (Vol. 1 and 2). New York: Dover Publications, Inc.

Jami, L., & Petit, J. (1976). Heterogeneity of motor neurons activating single Golgi tendon organs in cat leg muscles. *Experimental Brain Research, 24*, 485–493.

Johansson, G. (1978). About the geometry underlying spontaneous visual decoding of the optical message. In E. L. J. Leeuwenberg & H. F. J. M. Buffart (Eds.), *Formal theories of visual perception* (pp. 265–276). New York: Wiley.

Johansson, G., von Hofsten, C., & Jansson, G. (1980). Event perception. *Annual Review of Psychology, 31*, 27–66.

John, E. R. (1977). *Functional Neuroscience, Vol II: Neurometrics: Clinical Applications of Quantitative Neurophysiology*. Hillsdale, NJ: Lawrence Erlbaum Associates.

Jones, L. A. (1988). Motor illusions: What do they reveal about proprioception? *Psychological Bulletin, 103*(1), 72–86.

Julez, B. (1971). *Foundations of Cyclopean Perception. Chicago, IL: The University of Chicago Press*.

Julez, B., & Pennington, K. S. (1965). Equidistributed information mapping: An analogy to holograms and memory. Journal of the Optical Society of America, 55, 605.

Jung, R. (1961). Neuronal integration in the visual cortex and its significance for visual information. In W. A. Rosenblith (Ed.), *Sensory communication* (pp. 627–674) New York: Wiley.

Kaada, B. R. (1951). Somato-motor, Autonomic and electrocorticographic responses to electrical
stimulation of rhinencephalic and other stuctures in primates, cat & dog. *Acta Physiologica
Scandinavica, 23,* 83.

Kaada, B. R., Pribram, K. H., & Epstein, J. A. (1949). Respiratory and vascular responses in
monkeys from temporal pole, insular, orbital surface and cingulate gyrus. *Journal of Neurophysiology, 12,* 347–356.

Kabrisky, M. (1966). *A proposed model for visual information processing in the human brain.*
Urbana, IL: University of Illinois Press.

Kahneman, D. (1973). *Attention and Effort.* Englewood Cliffs, NJ: Prentice-Hall.

Kant, E. (1965). *Critique of pure reason.* (N. Kemp Smith, Trans.). New York: MacMillan.

Kato, T. (1966). *Perturbation theory for linear operators.* New York: Springer-Verlag.

Kaufman, L., & Richards, W. (1969). Spontaneous fixation tendencies for visual forms. *Perception
and Psychophysics, 5,* 85–88.

Kelly, D. H. (1983). Spatiotemporal variation of chromatic and achromatic contrast thresholds.
Journal of the Optical Society of America, 73, 742.

Kelso, J. A. S., & Saltzman, E. L. (1982). Motor control: Which themes do we orchestrate? *The
Behavioral and Brain Sciences, 5*(4), 554–557.

Kenshalo, D. R. (1968). *The skin senses.* Springfield, MA: Charles C. Thomas.

Kesner, R. P., & DiMattia, B. V. (1987). Neurobiology of an attribute model of memory. In A. N.
Epstein & A. Morrison (Eds.), *Progress in psychobiology and physiological psychology.* (Vol.
12, pp. 207–277). New York: Academic Press.

Keys, W. & Goldberg, M. E. (in prep.). Unit potentials. In D. E. Sheer & K. H. Pribram (Eds.),
Attention: Cognition, brain function and clinical application. New York: Academic Press.

Kimble, D. P. (1965). *The anatomy of memory.* Palo Alto, CA: Science & Behavior Books.

Kimble, D. P., Bagshaw, M. H., & Pribram, K. H. (1965). The GSR of monkeys during orienting
and habituation after selective partial ablations of cingulate and frontal cortex. *Neuropsychologia,
3,* 121–128.

Kimble, G. A. (1967). *Foundations of conditioning and learning.* New York: Appleton-Century-
Crofts.

Kinsbourne, M., & Wood, F. (1975). Short term memory and pathological forgetting. In. J. A.
Deutsch (Ed.), *Short term memory.* New York: Academic Press.

Klein, F. (1893). A comparative review of recent researches in geometry. *Bulletin of the New York
Mathematical Society, 2,* 215–249.

Kluver, H., & Bucy, P. C. (1937). "Psychic blindness" and other symptoms following bilateral
temporal lobectomy in Rhesus monkeys. *American Journal of Physiology, 119,* 352–353.

Koenderink, J. J. (1989). *The brain as a geometry engine.* Presentation at the Conference on
Domains of Mental Functioning: Attempts at a Synthesis. Bielefeld, West Germany.

Koepke, J. E., & Pribram, K. H. (1967a). Habituation of the vasconstriction response as a function
of stimulus duration and anxiety. *Journal of Comparative and Physiological Psychology, 64,*
502–504.

Koepke, J. E., & Pribram, K. H. (1967b). Effect of food reward on the maintenance of sucking
behavior during infancy. *Proceeding of 75th Annual Convention, APA,* 111–112.

Kohler, I. (1964). Psychological issues. In G. Kleine (Ed.), *The formation and transformation of the
perceptual world.* New York: International Universities Press.

Kohler, W., & Held, R. (1949). The cortical correlate of pattern vision. *Science, 110,* 414–
419.

Kohonen, T. (1972). Correlation matrix memories. *IEEE Transactions: Computers, 21,* 353–359.

Kohonen, T. (1977). *Associative memory: A system theoretic approach.* Berlin: Springer-Verlag.

Kohonen, T., & Oja, E. (1987). Technical comments, in *Science, 235,* 1227.

Konow, A., & Pribram, K. H. (1970). Error recognition and utilization produced by injury to the frontal cortex in man. *Neuropsychologia, 8,* 489–491.

Kornhuber, H. H. (1974). Cerebral cortex, cerebellum, and basal ganglia: An introduction to their motor functions. In F. O. Schmitt & F. G. Worden (Eds.), *The Neurosciences III* (pp. 267–280). Cambridge, MA: MIT Press.

Kornhuber, H. H., & Deecke, L. (1985). The starting function of SMA. *Behavioral and Brain Sciences, 8,* 591–592.

Kosslyn, S. M. (1980). *Image and mind.* Cambridge, MA: Harvard University Press.

Krieg, W. J. S. (1966). *Functional Neuroanatomy.* Brain Books.

Kronauer, R. E., & Zeevi, Y. Y. (1985). Reorganization and diversification of signals in vision. IEEE Trans. Systems, Man and Cybernetics, 15(1), 91–101.

Kruger, L., & Porter, P. (1958). A behavioral study of the functions of the rolandic cortex in the monkey. *Journal of Comparative Neurology, 109,* 439–469.

Krumhansl, C. L. (1978). Concerning the applicability of geometric models to similarity data: The interrelationship between similarity and spatial density. *Psychological Review, 85,* 445–463.

Kubie, J. L. & Ranck, J. B. (1983). Sensory-behavioural correlates in individual hippocampus neurones in three situations: space and context. In W. Seifert (Ed.), *Neurobiology of the Hippocampus,* (pp. 433–447). London: Academic Press.

Kuffler, S. W. (1953). Discharge patterns and functional organization of mammalian retina. *Journal of Neurophysiology, 16,* 37–69.

Kuffler, S. W., & Nicholls, J. G. (1976). *From neuron to brain.* Sunderland, MA: Sinauer Associates.

Kuhn, T. (1962). *The structure of scientific revolutions.* Chicago, IL: University of Chicago Press.

Kulikowski, J. J., Marcelja, S., & Bishop, P. O. (1982). Theory of spatial position and spatial frequency relations in the receptive fields of simple cells in the visual cortex. *Biological Cybernetics, 43,* 187–198.

Kuntz, L. D. & Kauzmann, W. (1974). In: *Advances in Protein Chemistry* (pp. 239–345). New York: Academic Press.

Kupfmuller, K. (1924). Uber Einschwingvorgange in Wellenfiltern, *Elektronische Nachrideten-Tech, 1,* 141.

Lacey, J. I., & Lacey, B. C. (1970). Some autonomic central nervous system interrelationships. In P. Black (Ed.), *Physiological correlates of emotion* (pp. 205–227). New York: Academic Press.

Lackner, J. R. (1988). Some proprioceptive influences on the perceptual representation of body shape and orientation. *Brain, 111,* 281–297.

LaMotte, R. H., & Mountcastle, V. B. (1979). Disorders in somesthesis following lesions of parietal lobe. *Journal of Neurology, 42*(2), 400–419.

Land, E. H. (1986). An alternative technique for the computation of the designator in the retinex theory of color vision. *Proceedings of the National Academy of Science, 83,* 3078–3080.

Landfield, P. W. (1976). Synchronous EEG rhythms: their nature and their possible functions in memory, information transmission and behaviour. In E. H. Gispen (Ed.) *Molecular and Functional Neurobiology.* Amsterdam: Elsevier.

Lang, M., Lang, W., Uhl, F., Kornhuber, A., Deecke, L. & Kornhuber, H. H. (1987). Slow negative potential shifts indicating verbal cognitive learning in a concept formation task. *Human Neurobiology, 6,* 183–190.

Lang, W., Lang, M., Kornhuber, A., Diekmann, V., & Kornhuber, H. H. (1988a). Event related EEG-spectra in a concept formation task. *Human Neurobiology, 6,* 295–301.

Lang, W., Lang, M., Podreka, I., Steiner, M., Uhl, F., Suess, E., Muller, Ch., & Deecke, L. (1988b). DC-potential shifts and regional cerebral blood flow reveal frontal cortex involvement in human visuomotor learning. *Experimental Brain Research, 71,* 353–364.

Lang, W., Lang, M., Uhl, F., Kornhuber, A., Deecke, L., & Kornhuber, H. H. (1988c) Left frontal lobe in verbal associative learning: A slow potential study. *Experimental Brain Research, 70,* 99–108.

Lang, W., Lang, M., Uhl, F., Koska, Ch., Kornhuber, A., & Deecke, L. (1988d) Negative cortical DC shifts preceding and accompanying simultaneous and sequential finger movements. *Experimental Brain Research, 71*, 579–587.

Lang, W., Zilch, O., Koska, Ch., Lindinger, G., & Deecke, L. (1988e) Negative cortical DC shifts preceding and accompanying simple and complex sequential movements. *Experimental Brain Research, 200*, 1–6.

Lashley, K. S. (1929). Brain mechanisms and intelligence. Chicago, IL: University of Chicago Press.

Lashley, K. S. (1942). The problem of cerebral organization in vision. In *Biological Symposia, Vol. VII, Visual Mechanisms* (pp. 301–322). Lancaster: Jaques Cattell Press.

Lashley, K. S. (1951). The problem of serial order in behavior. In Jeffries (Ed.), *Cerebral mechanisms in behavior, the Hixon Symposium* (pp. 112–146). New York: Wiley.

Lashley, K. S., Chow, K. L., & Semmes, J. (1951). An examination of the electrical field theory of cerebral integration. *Psychological Review, 58*, 123–136.

Lassonde, M. C., Ptito, M., & Pribram, K. H. (1981). Intracerebral influences on the microstructure of visual cortex. *Experimental Brain Research, 43*, 131–144.

Lehky, S. R., & Sejnowdki, T. J. (1990). Neural network model of visual cortex for determining surface curvature from images of shaded surfaces. *Proceedings of the Royal Society of London, B240*, 251–278.

Leith, E. N. (1976). White-light holograms. *Scientific American, 235*(4), 80.

Leyton, M. (1986a). A theory of information structure: I. General principles. *Journal of Mathematical Psychology, 30*, 103–160.

Leyton, M. (1986b). A theory of information structure: II. A theory of perceptual organization. *Journal of Mathematical Psychology, 30*, 257–305.

Leyton, M. (1986c). Principles of information structure common to six levels of the human cognitive system. *Information Sciences, 38*, 1–120.

Leyton, M. (1988). A process-grammar for shape. *Artificial Intelligence, 34*, 213–247.

Liberman, A. M., Cooper, F. S., Shankweiler, D. P., & Studdert-Kennedy, M. (1969). Perception of the speech code. In K. H. Pribram (Ed.), *Brain and behavior, Vol. IV: Adaptation* (pp. 105–148). Harmondsworth, Middlesex, Eng.: Penguin.

Licklider, J. C. R. (1951). Basic correlates of the auditory stimulus. In S. S. Stevens (Ed.), *Handbook of experimental psychology* (pp. 985–1039). New York: Wiley.

Liebeskind, J. C., Guilbaud, G., Besson, J. M., & Oliveras, J. L. (1973). Analgesia from electrical stimulation of the periaqueductal gray matter in the cat: Behavioral observations and inhibitory effects on spinal cord interneurons. *Brain Research, 50*, 441–446.

Liebeskind, J. C., Mayer, D. J., & Akil, H. (1974). Central mechanisms of pain inhibition: Studies of analgesia from focal brain stimulation. In J. J. Bonica (Ed.), *Advances in neurology, Vol. 4, Pain*. New York: Raven.

Linsker, R. (1987) Development of feature-analyzing cells and their columnar organization in a layered self-adaptive network. In R. Cotterill (Ed.), *Computer simulation in brain science*. Cambridge, MA: Cambridge University Press.

Livingstone, M. S., & Hubel, D. H. (1984). Anatomy and physiology of a color system in the primte visual cortex. *Journal of Neuroscience, 4*, 309–356.

Livingstone, M. S., & Hubel, D. H. (1988). Segregation of form, color, movement and depth: Anatomy, physiology and perception. *Science, 240*, 740–749.

Loeb, J. (1907). *Comparative physiology of the brain and comparative psychology*. New York: Putman.

Lorenz, K. (1969). Innate bases of learning. In K. H. Pribram (Ed.), *On the biology of learning* (pp. 13–94). New York: Harcourt Brace & World.

Luria, A. R. (1973). *The working brain*. London, Eng.: Penguin.

Luria, A. R., Pribram, K. H., & Homskaya, E. D. (1964). An experimental analysis of the behavioral disturbance produced by a left frontal arachnoidal endothelloma (meningioma). *Neuropsychologia, 2,* 257–280.

MacKay, D. M. (1969). *Information mechanism and meaning.* Cambridge, MA: MIT Press.

Mackworth, N. H., & Bruner, J. S. (1970). How adults and children search and recognize pictures. *Human Development, 13,* 149–177.

Mackworth, N. H., & Otto, D. A. (1970). Habituation of the visual orienting response in young children. *Perception and psychophysics, 7*(3), 173–178.

MacLean, P. D. (1990). *The Triune Brain in Evolution: Role in Paleocerebral Functions.* New York: Plenum Press.

Maffei, L. (1985). Complex cells control simple cells. In D. Rose & V. G. Dobson (Eds.), *Models of the visual cortex* (pp. 334–340). New York: Wiley.

Maffei, L., & Fiorentini, A. (1973). The visual cortex as a spatial frequency analyzer. *Vision Research, 13,* 1255–1267.

Magendie, F. (1822). Experiences sur les fonctions des racines des nerfs rachidiens. *Journal of Physiological Experience, 2,* 276–279.

Malis, L. I., Pribram, K. H., & Kruger, L. (1953). Action potentials in "motor" cortex evoked by peripheral nerve stimulation. *Journal of Neurophysiology, 16,* 161–167.

Malmo, R. B. (1942). Interference factors in delayed response in monkeys after removal of frontal lobes. *Journal of Neurophysiology, 5,* 295–308.

Malmo, R. B., & Amsel, A. (1948). Anxiety-produced interference in serial rote learning with observations on rote learning after partial frontal lobectomy. *JEP, Vol. 38,* 440–454.

Mandelbrot, B. B. (1977). *Fractals: Form, chance and dimension.* San Francisco, CA: W. H. Freeman.

Marcelja, S. (1980). Mathematical description of the responses of simple cortical cells. *Journal of the Optical Society of America, 70,* 1297–1300.

Margenau, H. (1984). *The miracle of existance.* Woodbridge, CT: Oxbow Press.

Marr, D. (1982). *Vision: A computational investigation into the human representation and processing of visual information.* San Francisco, CA: W. H. Freeman.

Marrocco, R. T. (1986). The neurobiology of perception. In J. E. LeDoux & W. Hirst (Eds.), *Mind and brain: Dialogues in cognitive neuroscience* (pp. 33- 79). Cambridge, Eng.: Cambridge University Press.

Matthews, P. B. C. (1964). Muscle spindles and their motor control. *Physiological Review, 44,* 219–288.

Matthews, P. B. C. (1981). Muscle spindles: Their messages and their Fusimotor Supply. In V. B. Brooks (Ed.), *Handbook of physiology.* Bethesda, MD: American Physiological Society.

Maturana, H. R. (1969). The neurophysiology of cognition. In P. Garvin (Ed.), *Cognition: A multiple view.* New York: Spartan Books.

Maturana, H. R., Lettvin, J. Y., McCullough, W. S., & Pitts, W. H. (1960). Anatomy and physiology of vision in the frog (Rana pipiens). *Journal of General Physiology, 43*(6), 129–175.

Maunsell, J. H. R., & Van Essen, D. C. (1983a). Funtional properties of neurons in middle temporal visual area of the Macaque monkey. I. Selectivity for stimulus direction, speed, and orientation. *Journal of Neurophysiology, 49,* 1127–1147.

Maunsell, J. H. R., & Van Essen, D. C. (1983b). Functional properties of neurons in middle temporal visual area of the Macaque monkey. II. Binocular interactions and sensitivity to binocular disparity. *Journal of Neurophysiology, 49,* 1148–1167.

Maunsell, J. H. R., & Van Essen, D. C. (1983c). The connections of the middle temporal visual area (MT) and their relationship to a cortical hierarchy in the Macaque monkey. *Journal of Neuroscience, 3*(12), 2563–2586.

Maxwell, G. (1976). Scientific results and the mind-brain issue: Some afterthoughts. In G. G. Globus, G. Maxwell, & I. Savodnik (Eds.), *Consciousness and the brain: A scientific and philosophical inquiry* (pp. 329–358). New York: Plenum.

McCulloch, C. (1965). *Embodiments of Mind*. Cambridge, MA: MIT Press.

McCullough, W. S., & Pitts, W. (1943). Logical calculus of the ideas immanent in nervous activity. *Bulletin of Mathematical Biophysics, 5*, 115–133.

McGaugh, J. L. (1966). Time-dependent processes in memory storage. *Science, 153*, 1351–1358.

McGaugh, J. L., & Hertz, M. L. (1972). *Memory consolidation*. San Francisco, CA: Albion Press.

McGuinness, D. (1972). Hearing: Individual differences in perceiving. *Perception, 1*, 465–473.

McGuinness, D., & Cox, R. J. (1977). The effect of chronic anxiety level upon self control of heart rate. *Biological Psychology, 5*, 7–14.

McGuinness, D., & Pribram, K. H. (1980). The neuropsychology of attention: Emotional and motivational controls. In M. C. Wittrock (Ed.), *The brain and psychology* (pp. 95–139). New York: Academic Press.

McGuinness, D., Pribram, K. H., & Pirnazar, M. (1988). Upstaging the stage model. In C. N. Alexander & E. Langer (Eds.), *Beyond formal operations: Alternative endpoints to human development*. Oxford: Oxford University Press.

Miller, A. I. (1984). *Imagery in Scientific Thought*. Boston, MA: Birkhauser Boston.

Miller, G. A. (1956). The magical number seven, plus or minus two, or some limits on our capacity for processing information. *Psychological Review, 63*, 81–97.

Miller, G. A., Galanter, E. H., & Pribram, K. H. (1960). *Plans and the structure of behavior*. New York: Holt, Rinehart & Winston.

Milner, B. (1959). The memory defect in bilateral hippocampal lesions. *Psychiatric Research Reports, 11*, 43–52.

Milner, B. (1974). Hemispheric specialization: Scope and limits. *The Neurosciences, 4*, 75–89.

Minsky, M. (1986). *Society of mind*. New York: Simon & Schuster.

Mishkin, M. (1954). Visual discrimination performance following partial ablations of the temporal lobe: II. Ventral surface vs. hippocampus. *Journal of Comparative and Physiological Psychology, 47*, 187–193.

Mishkin, M. (1966). Visual mechanisms beyond the striate cortex. In R. W. Russell (Ed.), *Frontiers in physiological psychology* (pp. 93–119). New York: Academic Press.

Mishkin, M. (1973). Cortical visual areas and their interaction. In A. G. Karczmar & J. C. Eccles (eds.), *The brain and human behavior* (pp. 187–208). Berlin: Springer-Verlag.

Mishkin, M., & Hall, M. (1955). Discriminations along a size continuum following ablation of the inferior temporal convexity in monkeys. *Journal of Comparative and Physiological Psychology, 48*, 97–101.

Mishkin, M., & Pribram, K. H. (1954). Visual discrimination performance following partial ablations of the temporal lobe: I. Ventral vs. lateral. *Journal of Comparative and Physiological Psychology, 47*, 14–20.

Mishkin, M., & Ungerleider, L. G. (1982). Contribution of striate inputs to the visuospatial functions of parieto-preoccipital cortex in monkeys. *Behavioral and Brain Research, 6*, 57–77.

Mishkin, M., Ungerleider, L. G., & Macko, K. A. (1983). Object vision and spatial vision: Two cortical pathways. *Trends in Neuroscience, 6*, 414–417.

Misner, C. W., Thorne, K. S., & Wheeler, J. A. (1973). *Gravitation*. San Francisco, CA: W. H. Freeman.

Mittelstaedt, H. (1987). The subjective vertical as a function of visual and extraretinal cues. *Acta Psychologica, 63*, 63–85.

Monakov, C. von (1914). *Die Lokalisation im Grosshien und der Abbau der Funktion Durch Korticale Herde*. Wiesbaden: J. F. Bergmann.

Morin, F., Schwartz, H. G., & O'Leary, J. L. (1951). Experimental study of the spinothalamic and related tracts. *Acta Psychiatry et Neurologica Scandinavia XXVI, 3 and 4*.

Morrone, C. M., Burr, D. C., & Maffei, L. (1982) Functional implications of cross- orientation inhibition of cortical visual cells. I. Neurophysiological evidence. *Proceedings of the Royal Society of London, B., 216*, 335–354.

Motter, B. C., Steinmetz, M. A., Duffy, C. J., & Mountcastle, V. B. (1987). Functional properties of parietal visual neurons: mechanisms of directionality along a single axis. *Journal of Neuroscience, 7,* 154–176.

Mountcastle, V. B. (1957). Modality and topographic properties of single neurons of cat's somatic sensory cortex. *Journal of Neurophysiology, 20,* 408–434.

Mountcastle, V. B., Anderson, R. A., & Motter, B. C. (1981). The influence of attentive fixation upon the excitability of the light-sensitive neurons of the posterior parietal cortex. *Journal of Neuroscience, 1,* 1218–1235.

Mountcastle, V. B., Lynch, J. C., Georgopoulos, A., Sakata, H. & Acuna, C. (1975). Posterior parietal association cortex of the monkey: Command functions for operations within extrapersonal space. *Journal of Neurophysiology, 38,* 871–908.

Mountcastle, V. B., Talbot, W. H., Sakata, H., & Hyvarinen, J. (1969). Cortical neuronal mechanisms in flutter-vibration studies in unanesthetized monkeys. Neuronal periodicity and frequency discrimination. *Journal of Neurophysiology, 32,* 452–484.

Movshon, J. A., Thompson, I. D., & Tolhurst, D. J. (1978a). Spatial summation in the receptive fields of simple cells in the cat's striate cortex. *Journal of Physiology, 283,* 53–77.

Movshon, J. A., Thompson, I. D., & Tolhurst, D. J. (1978b). Receptive field organization of complex cells in the cat's striate cortex. *Journal of Physiology, 283,* 79–99.

Movshon, J. A., Thompson, I. D., & Tolhurst, D. J. (1978c). Spatial and temporal contrast sensitivity of neurons in areas 17 and 18 of the cat's visual cortex. *Journal of Physiology, 283,* 101–120.

Moyer, R. S. (1970). On the possibility of localizing visual memory. Doctoral dissertation, Stanford University.

Munk, H. (1881). Uber die Functionen der grosshirurinde. Hiershwald: Berlin.

Murdock, B. B., Jr. (1979). Convolution and correlation in perception and memory. In L. G. Nilsson, (Ed.), *Perspectives on memory research* (pp. 105–119). Hillsdale, NJ: Lawrence Erlbaum Associates.

Murdock, B. B. (1982). A theory for the storage and retrieval of item and associative information. *Psychological Review, 89,* 609–626.

Murdock, B. B. (1983). A distributed memory model for serial-order information. *Psychological Review, 90,* 316–338.

Murdock, B. B. (1985). Convolution and matrix systems: A reply to Pike. *Psychological Review, 92,* 130–132.

Murdock, B. B., & Lewandowsky, S. (1986). Chaining, one hundred years later. In F. Klix & H. Hagendorf (Eds.), *Human memory and cognitive capatilities: Mechanisms and performances* (pp. 79–96). Holland: Elsevier.

Naatenen, R. (1982). Processing negativity. *Psychological Bulletin, 92*(3), 605–640.

Naatenen, R. (1990). The role of attention in auditory information processing as revealed by event-related potentials and other brain measures of cognitive function. *Behavioral and Brain Sciences, 13,* 201–288.

Nagasawa, M. (1980). Segregation of a population in an environment. *Journal of Mathematical Biology, 9,* 213.

Nelson, E. (1967). *Dynamical theories of Brownian motions.* Princeton, NJ: Princeton University Press.

Nelson, E. (1984). *Quantum fluctuations.* Princeton, NJ: Princeton University Press.

Nissen, W. H. (1951). Phylogenetic comparison. In S. S. Stevens (Ed.), *Handbook of experimental psychology* (pp. 347–386). New York: Wiley.

Norman, D. A. (1964). A comparison of data obtained with different false-alarm rates. *Psychogical Review, 71,* 243–246.

Nuwer, M. R., & Pribram, K. H. (1979). Role of the inferotemporal cortex in visual selective attention. *Journal of Electroencepholography & Clinical Neurophysiology, 46,* 389–400.

Nyquist, H. (1924). Certain factors affecting telegraph speed. *Bell System Technical Journal, 3,* 324.

Ohm, G. S. (1843). Uber die definition des tones, nebst daran geknupfter theorie der sirene und ahnlicher tonbildener vorrichtungen. *Annals of Physikalische Chemie, 59*, 513–565.

O'Keefe, J. (1986). Is consciousness the gateway to the hippocampal cognitive map? A speculative essay on the neural basis of mind. *Brain and Mind*, 59–98.

O'Keefe, J. & Conway, D. H. (1978). Hippocampal place units in the freely moving rat: why they fire where they fire. *Experimental Brain Research 31*, 573–590.

O'Keefe, J. & Nadel, L. (1978). *The Hippocampus as a Cognitive Map.* Oxford: Clarendon Press.

Olds, J. (1955). Physiological mechanisms of reward. In R. R. Jones (Ed.), *Nebraska Symposium on Motivation* (pp. 73–138). Lincoln, NB: University of Nebraska Press.

Olds, J., & Milner, P. (1954). Positive reinforcement produced by electrical stimulation of septal area and other regions of rat brain. *Journal of Comparative and Physiological Psychology, 47*, 419–427.

Optican, L. M., & Richmond, B. J. (1987). Temporal encoding of two-dimensional patterns by single units in primate inferior temporal cortex. III. Information theoretic analysis. *Journal of Neurophysiology, 57*(1), 162–178.

Ornstein, R. E. (1969). *On the experience of time.* Hammondsworth, Eng.: Penguin Education.

Oshins, E. (1984). A quantum approach to psychology: Spinors, rotations, and non-selecting ambiguity—Part I: Quantum logic representations of psychology. In D. McGoveran (Ed.), *Discrete approaches to natural philosophy (Proceedings of the 1st Annual Western Regional meeting of the Alternative Natural Philosophy Association).* Boulder Creek, CA: Alternative Natural Philosophy Association.

Oshins, E., & McGoveran, D. (1980). . . . Thoughts about logic about thoughts . . . The question "schizophrenia". In B. H. Banathy (Ed.), *Systems science and society (Proceedings of the 24th annual North American Meeting of the Society for General Systems Research)*, (pp. 505–514). Louisville, KY: Society for General Systems Research.

Palmer, S. E. (1982). Symmetry, transformation, and the structure of perceptual systems. In J. Bech (Ed.), *Representation, and organization in perception* (pp. 95–144). Hillsdale, NJ: Lawrence Erlbaum Associates.

Palmer, S. E. (1983). The psychology of perceptual organization: A transformational approach. In J. Beck, B. Hype & A. Rosenfeld (Eds.), *Human Machine Vision* (pp. 269–339). New York: Academic Press.

Palmer, S. E. (1988). Reference frames in the perception of shape and orientation. In B . Shepp & S. Ballesteros (Eds.), *Object perception: Structure and process.* Hillsdale, NJ: Lawrence Erlbaum Associates.

Papert, S. (1965). Introduction. In W. S. McCulloch (Ed.), *Embodiments of mind* (pp. XIII - XX). Cambridge, MA: MIT Press.

Partridge, L. D. (1982). How was movement controlled before Newton. *The Behavioral and Brain Sciences, 5*(4), 561.

Peele, T. L. (1944). Acute and chronic parietal lobe ablations in monkeys. *Journal of Neurophysiology, 7*, 269–286.

Pellionisz, A., & Llinas, R. (1979). Brain modeling by tensor network theory in computer simulation. The cerebellum: distributed processor for predictive coordination. *Neuroscience, 14*, 323–348.

Penfield, W., & Boldrey, E. (1937). Somatic motor sensory representation in the cerebral cortex of man as studied by electrical stimulation. *Brain, 60*, 389–443.

Perez, J. C. (1988a). *De Nouvelles Voies Vers L'Intelligence Artificielle.* Paris: Masson.

Perez, J. C. (1988b). *La memoire holographique fractale.* IBM Publication #9067.

Perkel, D. H. (1982–1983). Functional role of dendritic spikes. *Journal of Physiology Paris, 78*, 695–699.

Perkel, D. H., & Perkel, D. J. (1985). Dendritic spines - role of active membrane in modulating synaptic efficacy. *Brain Research, 525*, 331–335.

Perrett, D. I., Rolls, R. T., & Caan, W. (1982). Visual neurons responsive to faces in the monkey inferotemporal cortex. *Experimental Brain Research, 47*, 329–342.

Persoon, E., & Fu, K. S. (1977). Shape discrimination using Fourier descriptors. *IEEE Transactions on systems, man, and cybernetics*, 170–179.

Peterhans, E., & von der Heydt, R. (1989). Mechanisms of contour perception in monkey visual cortex. II. Contours bridging gaps. *Journal of Neuroscience, 9*, 1749–1763.

Petrides, M., & Milner, B. (1982). Defecits on subject-ordered tasks after frontal-and temporal-lobe lesions in man. *Neuropsychologia, 20*, 249–262.

Petsche, H., Gogolak, G. & van Zweiten, P. A. (1965). Rhythmicity of septal cell discharges at various levels of reticular excitation. *Electroencephalography and Clinical Neurophysiology, 19*, 25–33.

Pettigrew, J. D. (1974). The effect of visual experience on the development of stimulus specificity by kitten cortical neurons. *Journal of Physiology, 237*, 49–74.

Pfaffmann, C. (1951). Taste and smell. In S. S. Stevens (Ed.), *Handbook of experimental psychology*, (pp. 1143–1171). New York: Wiley.

Phelps, R. W. (1973). The effect of spatial and temporal interactions on the responses of single units in the cat's visual cortex. *International Journal of Neuroscience, 6*, 97–107.

Phelps, R. W. (1974). Effects of interactions of two moving lines on single unit responses in the cat's visual cortex. *Vision Research, 14*, 1371–1375.

Phillips, C. G. (1965). Changing concepts of the precentral motor area. In J. C. Eccles (Ed.), *Brain and conscious experience* (pp. 389–421). New York: Springer-Verlag.

Piaget, J. (1970). *Structuralism*. New York: Basic Books.

Picton & Hillyard, (1974)

Pike, R. (1984). Comparison of convolution and matrix distributed memory systems for associative recall and recognition. *Psychogical Review, 91*, 281–294.

Pitts, W., & McCullogh, W. S. (1947). How we know universals. The perception of auditory and visual forms. *Bulletin of Mathematical Biophysics, 9*, 127.

Poggio, G. F., & Fisher, B. (1977). Binocular interaction and depth sensitivity of striate and prestriate cortical neurons of the behaving monkey. *Journal of Neurophysiology, 40*, 1392–1405.

Poggio, T. & Torre, V. (1980). A new approach to synaptic interactions. In H. Palm (Ed.), *Approaches to complex systems* (pp.). Berlin: Springer-Verlag.

Poggio, T., Torre, V., & Koch, C. (1985). Computational vision and regularization theory. *Nature, 317*, 314–319.

Pohl, W. G. (1973). Dissociation of spatial and discrimination deficits following frontal and parietal lesions in monkeys. *Journal of Comparative and Physiological Psychology, 82*, 227–239.

Poincare, H. (1905a). *The value of science*. (Reprinted 1958, G. Halsted, Trans.). New York: Dover.

Poincare, H. (1905b). *Science and hypothesis*. (Reprinted 1952). New York: Dover.

Pollen, D. A., & Feldon, S. E. (1979) Spatial periodicities of periodic complex cells in the visual cortex cluster at one-half octave intervals. *Investigations in Opthalmology and Visual Science,*

Pollen, D. A., Lee, J. R., & Taylor, J. H. (1971). How does the striate cortex begin reconstruction of the visual world? *Science, 173*, 74–77.

Pollen, D. A., & Ronner, S. E. (1980). Spatial computation performed by simple and complex cells in the cat visual cortex. *Experimental Brain Research, 41*, A14–15.

Pollen D. A., & Taylor, J. H. (1974). The striate cortex and the spatial analysis of visual space. In F. O. Schmitt & F. G. Worden (Eds.), *The Neurosciences Third Study Program* (pp. 239–247). Cambridge, MA: The MIT Press.

Popper, K. R. (1962). *Conjectures and refutations*. London: Routledge & Kegan Paul.

Posner, M. I. (1973). Coordination of internal codes. In W. G. Chase (Ed.), *Visual information processing* (pp. 35–73). New York: Academic Press.

Posner, M. I. (1987). *Chronometric explorations of mind*. Hillsdale, NJ: Lawrence Erlbaum Associates.

Prechtl, J. C., & Powley, T. L. (1990). B-Afferents: A fundamental division of the nervous system mediating homeostasis? *Behavioral and Brain Sciences, 13,* 289–331.

Pribram, K. H. (1954). Toward a science of neuropsychology (method and data). In R. A. Patton (Ed.), *Current trends in psychology and the behavioral sciences* (pp. 115–142). Pittsburg, PA: University of Pittsburg Press.

Pribram, K. H. (1954/1969). Toward a science of neuropsychology (method and data). In K. H. Pribram (Ed.), *Brain and Behavior, Vol. 2, Perception and Action* (pp. 266–287). London, Eng.: Penguin.

Pribram, K. H. (1958a). Comparative neurology and the evolution of behavior. In G. G. Simpson (Ed.), *Evolution and behavior* (pp. 140–164). New Haven, CT: Yale University Press.

Pribram, K. H. (1958b). Neocortical functions in behavior. In H. F. Harlow & C. N. Woolsey (Eds.), *Biological and biochemical bases of behavior* (pp. 151–172). Madison, WI: University of Wisconsin Press.

Pribram, K. H. (1960). The intrinsic systems of the forebrain. In J. Field, H. W. Magoun, & V. E. Hall (Eds.), *Handbook on physiology, neurophysiology II* (pp. 1323–1344). Washington, DC: American Physiological Society.

Pribram, K. H. (1961a). Limbic system. In D. E. Sheer (Ed.), *Electrical stimulation of the brain* (pp. 563–574). Austin, TX: University of Texas Press.

Pribram, K. H. (1961b). A further experimental analysis of the behavioral deficit that follows injury to the primate frontal cortex. *Experimental Neurology, 3,* 432–466.

Pribram, K. H. (1963). Reinforcement revisited: A structural view. In M. Jones (Ed.), *Nebraska symposium on motivation* (pp. 113–159). Lincoln, NB: University of Nebraska Press.

Pribram, K. H. (1966). Some dimensions of remembering: Steps toward a neuropsychological model of memory. In J. Gaito (Ed.), *Macromolecules and behavior* (pp. 165–187). New York, NY: Academic Press.

Pribram, K. H. (1969). The neurobehavioral analysis of limbic forebrain mechanisms: Revision and progress report. In D. S. Lehrman, R. A. Hinde, & E. Shaw (Eds.), *Advances in the study of behavior* (pp. 297–332). New York: Academic Press.

Pribram, K. H. (1971). *Languages of the brain: Experimental paradoxes and principles in neuro-psychology.* Englewood Cliffs, NJ: Prentice-Hall.

Pribram, K. H. (1972). Review of "Chance and necessity" by J. Monod, in *Perspectives in Biology and Medicine.*

Pribram, K. H. (1973). The primate frontal cortex—executive of the brain. In K. H. Pribram & A. R. Luria (Eds.), *Psychophysiology of the frontal lobes* (pp. 293–314). New York: Academic Press.

Pribram, K. H. (1975). Toward a holonomic theory of perception. In S. Ertel, L. Kemmler , & M. Stadler (Eds.) *Gestalttheorie in der modern psychologie* (pp. 161–184). Koln: Erich Wengenroth.

Pribram, K. H. (1977). New dimensions in the functions of the basal ganglia. In D. Chagass, S. Gershon, & A. J. Friedhoff (Eds.), *Psychopathology and brain dysfunction* (pp. 77–95). New York: Raven Press.

Pribram, K. H. (1980a). The orienting reaction: Key to brain representational mechanisms. In H. D. Kimmel (Ed.), *The orienting reflex in humans* (pp. 3–20). Hillsdale, NJ: Lawrence Erlbaum Associates.

Pribram, K. H. (1980b). Cognition and performance: The relation to neural mechanisms of conse-quence, confidence and competence. In A. Routtenberg (Ed.), *Biology of reinforcement: Facets of brain stimulation reward* (pp. 11–36). New York: Academic Press.

Pribram, K. H. (1982a). Functional organization of the cerebral isocortex. In G. Schaltenbrand & A. E. Walker (Eds.), *Stereotaxy in the human brain* (pp. 306–328. Stuttgart, Germany: Verlag.

Pribram, K. H. (1982b) Localization and distribution of function in the brain. In J. Orbach (Ed.), *Neuropsychology after Lashley* (pp. 273–296). New York: Lawrence Erlbaum Associates.

Pribram, K. H. (1982c). Brain and the ecology of mind. In W. S. Weimer & D. S. Palermo (Eds.),

Cognition and the Symbolic Process (pp. 361–381). Hillsdale, NJ: Lawrence Erlbaum Associates.

Pribram, K. H. (1984). Brain systems and cognitive learning processes. In H. L. Rothblat, T. G. Bever, & H. S. Terrace (Eds.), *Animal cognition* (pp. 627–656). Hillsdale, NJ: Lawrence Erlbaum Associates.

Pribram, K. H. (1986a). The cognitive revolution and mind/brain issues. *American Psychologist, 41*, 507–520.

Pribram, K. H. (1986b). The hippocampal system and recombinant processing. In R. Isaacson & K. H. Pribram (Eds.), *The hippocampus, Vol. 4* (pp. 329–370). New York: Plenum.

Pribram, K. H. (1987a). Subdivisions of the frontal cortex revisited. In E. Brown and E. Perecman (Eds.), *The frontal lobes revisited* (pp. 11–39). IRBN Press.

Pribram, K. H. (1987b). The implicate brain. In B. Hiley & F. David Peat (Eds.), *Quantum implications*. London: RKP.

Pribram, K. H. (1988). *The holonomic brain theory*, Lecture notes.

Pribram, K. H. (1990). The frontal cortex - A Luria/Pribram rapprochement. In E. Goldberg (Ed.), *Contemporary Neuropsychology and the Legacy of Luria*, (pp. 77–97). Hillsdale, NJ: Lawrence Erlbaum Associates.

Pribram, K. H., & Bagshaw, M. H. (1953). Further analysis of the temporal lobe syndrome utilizing frontotemporal ablations in monkeys. *Journal of Comparative Neurology, 99*, 347–375.

Pribram, K. H., & Barry, J. (1956). Further behavioral analysis of the parieto- temporo-preoccipital cortex. *Journal of Neurophysiology, 19*, 99–106.

Pribram, K. H., Blehart, S. R., & Spinelli, D. N. (1966). Effects on visual discrimination of crosshatching and undercutting the inferotemporal cortex of monkeys. *Journal of Comparative and Physiological Psychology, 62*, 358–364.

Pribram, K. H., & Carlton, E. H. (1986). Holonomic brain theory in imaging and object perception. *Acta Psychologica, 63*, 175–210.

Pribram, K. H., Chow, K. L., & Semmes, J. (1953). Limit and organization of the cortical projection from the medial thalamic nucleus in monkeys. *Journal of Comparative Neurology, 95*, 433–440.

Pribram, K. H., Douglas, R. J., & Pribram, B. J. (1969). The nature of nonlimbic learning. *Journal of Comparative and Physiological Psychology, 69*, 765–772.

Pribram, K. H.. & Isaacson, R. L. (1975). *The Hippocampus, Volume 2: Neurophysiology and Behavior*. New York: Plenum.

Pribram, K. H., Kruger, L., Robinson, F., & Berman, A. J. (1955–1956). The effects of precentral lesions on the behavior of monkeys. *Yale Journal of Biology & Medicine, 28*, 428–443.

Pribram, K. H., Lassonde, M. C., & Ptito, M. (1981). Classification of receptive field properties. *Experimental Brain Research, 43*, 119–130.

Pribram, K. H., Lim, H., Poppen, R., & Bagshaw, M. H. (1966). Limbic lesions and the temporal structure of redundancy. *Journal of Comparative and Physiological Psychology, 61*, 365–373.

Pribram, K. H., & MacLean, P. D. (1953). Neuronographic analysis of medial and basal cerebral cortex. II. *Journal of Neurophysiology, 16*, 324–340.

Pribram, K. H., & McGuinness, D. (1975). Arousal, activation and effort in the control of attention. *Psychological Review, 82*(2), 116–149.

Pribram, K. H., & McGuinness, D. (1982). Commentary on Jeffrey Gray's 'The neuropsychology of anxiety: An enquiry into the functions of the septohippocampal system'. *The Behavioral and Brain Sciences, 5*, 496–498.

Pribram, K. H., & McGuinness, D. (in prep.). Brain systems involved in attention and para-attentional processing. *New York Academy of Science*.

Pribram, K. H., & Mishkin, M. (1955). Simultaneous and successive visual discrimination by monkeys with inferotemporal lesions. *Journal of Comparative and Physiological Psychology, 48*, 198–202.

Pribram, K. H., Nuwer, M., & Baron, R. (1974). The holographic hypothesis of memory structure in brain function and perception. In R. C. Atkinson, D. H. Krantz, R. C. Luce, & P. Suppes (Eds.), *Contemporary Developments in Mathematical Psychology* (pp. 416–467). San Francisco, CA: W. H. Freeman.

Pribram, K. H., Plotkin, H. C., Anderson, R. M., & Leong, D. (1977). Information sources in the delayed alternation task for normal and "frontal" monkeys. *Neuropsychologia, 15*, 329–340.

Pribram, K. H., Reitz, S., McNeil, M., & Spevack, A. A. (1979). The effect of amygdalectomy on orienting and classical conditioning in monkeys. *Pavlovian Journal, 14*(4), 203–217.

Pribram, K. H., Sharafat, A., & Beekman, G. J. (1984). Frequency encoding in motor systems. In H. T. A. Whiting (Ed.), *Human motor actions—Bernstein reassessed* (pp. 121–156). North-Holland: Elsevier.

Pribram, K. H., Spevack, A. A., Blower, D., & McGuinness, D. (1980). A decisional analysis of the effects of inferotemporal lesions in the Rhesus monkey. *Journal of Comparative and Physiological Psychology, 94*, 675–690.

Pribram, K. H., Spinelli, D. N., & Kamback, M. C. (1967). Electrocortical correlates of stimulus response and reinforcement. *Science, 157*, 94–96.

Pribram, K. H., Spinelli, D. N., & Reitz, S. L. (1969). Effects of radical disconnexion of occipital and temporal cortex on visual behaviour of monkeys. *Brain, 92*, 94–96.

Pribram, K. H., & Tubbs, W. E. (1967). Short-term memory, parsing and the primate frontal cortex. *Science, 156*, 1765–1767.

Pribram, K. H., & Weiskrantz, L. (1957). A comparison of the effects of medial and lateral cerebral resections on conditioned avoidance behavior of monkeys. *Journal of Comparative and Physiological Psychology, 50*, 74–80.

Prigogine, I. (1980). *From Being to Becoming - Time and Complexity in the Physical Sciences.* San Francisco, CA: Freeman.

Prigogine, I., & Stengers, (1984) *Order out of chaos.* New York: Bantam Books.

Psaltis, D., Brady, D. Gu, X. G., and Lin, S. (1990). Holography in artificial neural networks. *Nature, 343,* 325–330.

Putnam, H. (1973). Reductionism and the nature of psychology. *Cognition, 2*, 131–146.

Pylishin, Z. W. (1983). A psychological approach. In M. Studdert-Kennedy (Ed.), *Psychobiology of language* (pp. 17–19). Cambridge, MA: MIT Press.

Quilliam, T. A. (1956). Some characteristics of myelinated fiber populations. *Journal of Anatomy, 90*, 172–187.

Rakic, P. (1976). *Local circuit neurons.* Cambridge, MA: MIT Press.

Rall, W., & Rinzel, J. (1973). Branch input resistance and steady attenuation for input to one branch of a dendritic neuron model. *Biophysics Journal, 13*, 648–688.

Ramoa, A. S., Shadlen, M., Skottun, B. C., & Freeman, R. D. (1986). A comparison of inhibition in orientation and spatial frequency selectivity of cat visual cortex. *Nature, 321*, 237–239.

Ranson, S. W., & Clark, S. L. (1959). *The Anatomy of the Nervous System.* Philadelphia, PA: Saunders.

Ratliff, F. (1965). *Mach bands.* San Francisco, CA: Holden Day.

Reichardt, W. E. (1978). Cybernetics of the insect optomotor response. In P. Buser (Ed.), *Cerebral correlates of conscious experience.* Amsterdam: North Holland.

Reitz, S. L., & Pribram, K. H. (1969). Some subcortical connections of the inferotemporal gyrus of monkey. *Experimental Neurology, 26*, 632–645.

Restle, F. (1978). Relativity and organization in visual size judgements. In E. L. J. Leeuwenberg & H. F. J. M. Buffart (Eds.), *Formal theories of visual perception* (pp. 247–263). New York: Wiley.

Ricci, C., & Blundo, C. (1990). Perception of ambiguous figures after focal brain lesions. *Neuropsychologia, 28*(11), 1163–1173.

Richards, W., & Kaufman, L. (1969). "Center-of-gravity" tendencies for fixations and flow patterns. *Perception and psychophysics, 5*(2), 81–84.

Richardson, D. E., & Akil, H. (1974). Chronic self-administration of brain stimulation for pain relief in human patients. *Proceedings of the American Association of Neurological Surgeons*, St. Louis, MO.

Richmond, B. J., & Optican, L. M. (1987). Temporal encoding of two-dimensional patterns by single units in primate inferior temporal cortex. II. Quantification of response waveform. *Journal of Neurophysiology, 57*(1), 147–161.

Richmond, B. J., Optican, L. M., Podell, M., & Spitzer, H. (1987). Temporal encoding of two-dimensional patterns by single units in primate inferior temporal cortex. I. Response characteristics. *Journal of Neurophysiology, 57*(1), 132–146.

Riggs, L. A., Ratliff, F., Cornsweet, J. C., & Cornsweet, T. N. (1953). The disappearance of steadily fixated test objects. *Journal of the Optical Society of America, 43*, 495–501.

Robson, J. G. (1975). Receptive fields: Neural representation of the spatial and intensive attributes of the visual image. In E. C. Carterette (Ed.), *Handbook of perception, Vol. V, Seeing* (pp. 81–116). New York: Academic Press.

Rock, I. (1975). *Introduction to perception*. New York: MacMillan.

Rock, I. (1983). *The logic of perception*. Cambridge, MA: MIT Press.

Rock, I., & Halper, F. (1969). Form perception without retinal image. *American Journal of Psychology, 82*, 425–440.

Rodieck, R. W. (1965). Quantitative analysis of cat retinal ganglion cell response to visual stimuli. *Vision Research, 5*, 279–301.

Rodieck, R. W., & Stone, J. (1965). Response of cat retinal ganglion cells to moving visual patterns. *Journal of Neurophysiology, 28*, 833–850.

Rolls, E. T. (1985). Neuronal activity in relation to the recognition of stimuli in the primate. In C. Chagas, A. Gattas, & C. Gross (Eds.), *Pattern recognition mechanisms* (pp. 203–213). Berlin: Springer-Verlag.

Rosch, E. (1973). On the internal structure of perceptual and semantic categories. In T. E. Moore (Ed.), *Cognition and the acquisition of language* (pp. 111–144). New York: Academic Press.

Rosch, E. (1975). Cognitive representation of semantic categories. *Journal of Experimental Psychology, 104*, 192–233.

Rosenkilde, C. E., Rosvold, H. E., & Mishkin, M. (1981). Time discrimination with positional responses after selective prefrontal lesions in monkeys. *Brain Research, 210*, 129–144.

Rosvold, H. E., Mirsky, A. F., & Pribram, K. H. (1954). Influence of amygdalectomy on social interaction in a monkey group. *Journal of Comparative and Physiological Psychology, 47*, 173–178.

Rothblat, L. & Pribram, K. H. (1972). Selective attention: Input filter or response selection? *Brain Research, 39*, 427–436.

Ruch, T. C. (1951). Motor systems. In S. S. Stevens (Ed.), *Handbook of experimental psychology* (pp. 154–208). New York: Wiley.

Rumelhart, D. E., McClelland, J. L., & the PDP Research Group. (1986). *Parallel distributed processing, Vol. I and II*. Cambridge, MA: MIT Press.

Russell, R. W., Singer, G., Flanagan, F., Stone, M. & Russell, J. W. (1968). Quantitative relations in amygdala modulation of drinking. *Physiology and Behavior, 3*, 871–875.

Sakitt, B. (1972). Counting every quantum. *Journal of Physiology, 223*, 131–150.

Sakitt, B., & Barlow, G. B. (1982). A model for the economic cortical encoding of the visual image. *Biological Cybernetics, 43*, 97–108.

Sanger-Brown, & Schaefer, E. A. (1888). An investigation into the functions of the occipital and temporal lobes of the monkey's brain. *Philosphical Transactions of the Royal Society of London, 179*, 303–327.

Scarr, S. (1978). Comments on psychology, genetics and social policy from an anti- reductionist. Paper presented at the conference: *Psychology and Society: Psychology Second Century, Enduring Issues*, Houston, TX: Holt, Rinehart & Winston.

Schade, O. H. (1956). Optical and photoelectric analog of the eye. *Journal of the Optical Society of America, 46*, 721–739.

Scheibel, M. E., Scheibel, A. B., & Davis, T. H. (1966). Patterns of organization in specific and nonspecific thalamic fields. In T. L. Frigyesi & E. Rinvik Eds.), *The thalamus* (pp. 131–156). New York: Columbia University Press.

Schiller, P. H., Finlay, B. L., & Volman, S. F. (1976). Quantitative studies of single- cell properties in monkey striate cortex. Spatiotemporal organization of receptive fields. *Journal of Neurophysiology, 39*, 1288–1319.

Schmidt, R. A. (1980). Past and future issues in motor programming. *Research Quarterly for Exercise and Sports, 51*, 122–140.

Schmidt, R. A., & McGowan, C. (1980). Terminal accuracy of unexpectedly loaded rapid movements: Evidence for a mass-spring mechanism in programming. *Journal of Motor Behavior, 12*, 149–161.

Schmitt, F. O., Dev, P., & Smith, B. H. (1976). Electronic processing of information by brain cells. *Science, 193*, 114–120.

Schroedinger, E. (1944). *What is life? Mind and matter.* Cambridge University Press.

Schwartz, E. L. (1977). Spatial mapping in the primate sensory projection: Analytic structure and relevance to perception. *Biological Cybernetics, 25*, 181–194.

Schwartz, E. L., Desimone, R., Albright, T. D., & Gross, C. G. (1983). Shape recognition and inferior temporal neurons. *Proceedings of the National Academy of Sciences, U.S., 80*, 5776–5778.

Schwartz, M. L. & Goldman-Rakic, P. S. (1984). Callosal and intrahemispheric connectivity of the prefrontal association cortex in rhesus monkey: relation between intraparietal and principal sulcal cortex. *Journal of Comparative Neurology, 226*, 403–420.

Schwartzbaum, J. S. (1960). Changes in reinforcing properties of stimuli following ablation of the amygdaloid complex in monkeys. *Journal of Comparative and Physiological Psychology, 53*, 388–396.

Schwartzbaum, J. S., & Pribram, K. H. (1960). The effects of amygdalectomy in monkeys on transposition along a brightness continuum. *Journal of Comparative and Physiological Psychology, 53*, 396–399.

Searle, J. R. (1983). *Intentionality: An essay on the philosophy of mind.* Cambridge, Eng.: Cambridge University Press.

Searle, J. R. (1984). *Minds, brains and science.* Cambridge, MA: Harvard University Press.

Sejnowski, T. J. (1976). On global properties of neuronal interaction. *Biological Cybernetics, 22*, 85–95.

Sejnowski, T. J., (1981). Skeleton filters in the brain. In G. E. Hinton and J. A. Anderson (Eds.), *Parallel Models of Associative Memory*, (pp. 189–212). Hillsdale, NJ: Lawrence Erlbaum Associates.

Sejnowski, T. J., & Lehky, S. R. (1987). *Neural Networks Models of Visual Processing.* Computational Neuroscience.

Shannon, C. E., & Weaver, W. (1949). *The mathematical theory of communications.* Urbana, IL: The University of Illinois Press.

Shapley, R. & Lennie, P. (1985). Spatial frequency analysis in the visual system. *American Review of Neuroscience, 8*, 547–583.

Shaw, R., Turvey, M. T., & Mace, W. (1982). Ecological psychology: The consequence of a committment to realism. In E. Weimer & D. S. Palermo (Eds.), *Cognition and the symbolic processes* (pp. 159–239). Hillsdale, NJ: Lawrence Erlbaum Associates.

Sheer, D. E., & Grandstaff, N. W. (1970). Computer analysis of electrical activity in the brain and its relations to behavior. In H. T. Wycis (Ed.), *Current research in neurosciences 10:/60 topical problems in psychiatry and neurology* Karger, NY:

Shepard, R. N. (1981). Psychophysical complementarity. In M. Kubovy & J. Pomerantz (Eds.), *Perceptual organization* (pp. 279–341). Hillsdale, NJ: Lawrence Erlbaum Associates.

Shepard, R. N. (1987b). Toward a universal law of generalization for psychological science. *Science, 237*, 1317–1323.

Shepard, R. N. (1988). The role of transformations in spatial cognition. In J. Stiles-David, M. Kritchevsdy, & U. Bellugi (Eds.), *Spatial cognition: Brain bases and development* (pp. 81–110). Hillsdale, NJ: Lawrence Erlbaum Associates.

Shepard, R. N., & Chipman, S. (1970). Second-order isomorphism of internal representations: Shapes of states. *Cognitive Psychology, 1*, 1–17.

Shepherd, G.M. (1990). The significance of real neuron architectures for neural network simulations. In E.L. Schwartz (Ed.), *Computational Neuroscience* (pp. 82-96). Cambridge, MA: MIT Press.

Shepherd, G. M. (1988). *Neurobiology* (2nd ed.). Oxford, Eng.: Oxford University Press.

Shepherd, G. M., Brayton, R. K., Miller, J. P., Segey, I., Rindsel, J., & Rall, W. (1985). Signal enhancement in distal cortical dendrites by means of interactions between active dendritic spines. *Proceedings of the National Academy of Science, 82*, 2192–2195.

Shepherd, G. M., & Greer, C. A. (1987). The dendritic spine: Adaptations of structure and function for different types of synaptic integration. In: R. Lassek (Ed.), *Intrinsic Determinants of Neuronal Form*. New York: Alan R. Liss.

Sherrington, C. (1911/1947) *The integrative action of the nervous sytsem*. New Haven, CT: Yale University Press.

Shiffrin, R. M. & Schneider, W. (1977). Controlled and automatic human information processing II. Perceptual learning, automatic attending and a general theory. *Psychological Review, 84*, 128–190.

Shiffrin, R. M. & Schneider, W. (1984). Automatic and controlled processing revisited. *Psychological Review, 91*, 269–276.

Shoemake, K. (1985). Animating rotation with quaternion curves. *Computer graphics, 19*, 245—254.

Simon, H. (1974). How big is a chunk? *Science, 183*, 482–488.

Simon, H. (1986). The parameters of human memory. In F. Klix & H. Hagendorf (Eds.), *Human memory and cognitive capabilities: Mechanisms and performances* (pp. 299–309). Holland: Elsevier.

Singer, W. (1989). Search for coherence: A basic principle of cortical self-organization. *Concepts in Neuroscience 1*(1), 1–25.

Skarada, C. A., & Freeman, W. J. (1987). How brains make chaos in order to make sense of the world. *Behavioral and Brain Sciences, 10*(2), 161–173.

Skinner, B. F. (1989). The origins of cognitive thought. *American Psychologist, 44*(1), 13–18.

Sloper, J. J. (1971). Dendro-dendritic synapses in the primate motor cortex. *Brain Research, 34*, 186–192.

Smets, G. (1973). *Aesthetic judgment and arousal*. Leuven, Belgium: Leuven University Press.

Smolensky, P. (1986). Information processing in dynamical systems: Foundations of harmony theory. In D. E. Rumelhart, J. L. McClelland, & the PDP Research Group (Eds.), *Parallel distributed processing: Explorations in the microstructure of cognition. Vol. 1: Foundations* (pp. 194–281). Cambridge, MA: MIT Press.

Sokolov, E. N. (1963). *Perception and the conditioned reflex*. New York: MacMillan Publishing.

Sokolov, E. E., & Izmailov, Ch. A. (1980). Spherical model of color and brightness descrimination. Presented at meeting on Mind and Brain, Blelefeld, Germany.

Sommerhoff, G. (1974). *Logic of the living brain*. New York: Wiley.

Sperling, G. (1984). A unified theory of attention and signal detection. In R. Parasuraman & D. R. Davies (Eds.), *Varieties of attention* (pp. 103–181). New York: Academic Press.

Sperry, R. W. (1947). Cerebral regulation of motor coordination in monkeys following multiple transection of sensorimotor cortex. *Journal of Neurophysiology, 10*, 275–294.

Sperry, R. W. (1980). Mind/brain interaction—Mentalism, yes—Dualism, no. *Neuroscience, 2*, 195–206.

Spevack, A., & Pribram, K. H. (1973). A decisional analysis of the effects of limbic lesions in monkeys. *Journal of Comparative and Physiological Psychology, 82*, 211–226.

Spiegler, B. J., & Mishkin, M. (1981). Evidence for the sequential participation of inferior temporal cortex and amygdala in the acquisition of stimulus-reward associations. *Behavioral Brain Research, 2*, 303–317.

Spinelli, D. N. (1966). Visual receptive fields in the cat's retina: Complications. *Science, 152*, 1768–1769.

Spinelli, D. N. (1970). O.C.C.A.M.: A computer model for a content addressable memory in the central nervous system. In K. H. Pribram & D. E. Broadbent (Eds.), *Biology of memory* (pp. 293–306). New York: Academic Press.

Spinelli, D. N., & Barrett, T. W. (1969). Visual receptive field organization of single units in the cat's visual cortex. *Experimental Neurology, 24*, 76–98.

Spinelli, D. N., & Pribram, K. H. (1967). Changes in visual recovery function and unit activity produced by frontal cortex stimulation. *Electroencepholography and Clinical Neurophysiology, 22*, 143–149.

Spinelli, D. N., Pribram, K. H., & Bridgeman, B. (1970). Visual receptive field organization of single units in the visual cortex of monkey. *International Journal of Neuroscience*, 67–74.

Spinelli, D. N., Pribram, K. H., & Weingarten, M. (1965). Centrifugal optic nerve responses evoked by auditory and somatic stimulation. *Experimental Neurology, 12*, 303–319.

Spinelli, D. N., Starr, A., & Barrett, T. (1968). Auditory specificity in unit recording from cat's visual cortex. *Experimental Neurology, 22*, 75–84.

Spinelli, D. N., & Weingarten, M. (1966). Afferent and efferent activity in single units of the cat's optic nerve. *Experimental Neurology, 3*, 347–361.

Stamm, J. S. (1969). Electrical stimulation of monkeys' prefrontal cortex during delayed response performance. *Journal of Comparative and Physiological Psychology, 67*, 535–546.

Stamm, J. S., & Pribram, K. H. (1961). Effects of epileptogenic lesions in inferotemporal cortex on learning and retention in monkeys. *Journal of Comparative and Physiological Psychology, 54*, 614–618.

Stamm, J. S., & Rosen, S. C. (1972). Cortical steady potential shifts and anodal polarization during delayed response performance. *Acta Neurobiologiae Experimentalis, 32*(2), 193–209.

Stark, L., & Bridgeman, B. (1983). Role of corollary discharge in space constancy. *Perception and Psychophysics, 34*(4), 371–380.

Stark, L., & Sherman, P. M. (1957). A servoanalytic study of consensual pupil reflex to light. *Journal of Neurophysiology, 20*, 17–26.

Steinmetz, M. A., Motter, B. C., Duffy, C. J., & Mountcastle, V. B. (1987). Functional properties of parietal visual neurons: radial organization of directionalities within the visual field. *Journal of Neuroscience, 7*, 177–191.

Stelmach, G. E., & Diggles, V. A. (1982). Motor equivalence and distributed control: Evidence for nonspecific muscle commands. *The Behavioral and Brain Sciences, 5*(4), 566–567.

Stent, G. (1973). A physiological mechanism for Hebb's postulate of learning. *Proceedings of the National Academy of Science, USA, 70*, 997–1001.

Stephanis, C. & Jasper, H. (1964). Intracellular microelectrode studies of antidromic responses in cortical pyramidal tract neurons. *Journal of Neurophysiology, 27*, 828–854.

Stone, J. (1983). *Parallel processing in the visual system.* New York: Plenum.

Stork, D. G., & Wilson, H. R. (1990). Do Gabor functions provide appropriate descriptions of visual cortical receptive fields? *Journal of the Optical Society of America.*

Stratton, G. (1896). Some preliminary experiments on vision without inversion of the retinal image. *Psychological Review, 3*, 611–617.

Stratton, G. (1897a). Upright vision and the retinal image. *Psychological Review, 4*, 182–187.

Stratton, G. (1897b). Vision without inversion of the retinal image. *Psychological Review, 4*, 341–360, 463–481.

Streitfeld, B., & Wilson, M. (1986). The ABC's of categorical perception. *Cognitive Psychology,* *18*, 432–451.

Stuart, C. I. J. M., Takahashi, Y., & Umezawa, H. (1978a). On the stability and non-local properties of memory. *Journal of Theoretical Biology, 71*, 605–618.

Stuart, C. I. J. M., Takahashi, Y., & Umezawa, H. (1978b). Mixed-system brain dynamics: Neural memory as a macroscopic ordered state. *Foundations of Physics, 9*, 301–327.

Stuart, D. G., Mosher, C. G., Gerlach, R. L., & Ranking, R. M. (1972). Mechanical arrangement and transducing properties of Golgi tendon organs. *Experimental Brain Research, 14*, 274–292.

Stumpf, C. (1965). Drug action on the electrical activity of the hippocampus. *International Review of Neurobiology, 8*, 77–138.

Stuss, D. T., & Picton, T. W. (1978). Neurophysiological correlates of human concept formation. *Behavioral Biology, 23*, 135–162.

Sutter, E. (1976). A revised conception of visual receptive fields based on pseudorandom spatio-temporal pattern stimuli. In P. Z. Marmarelis & G. D. McCann (Eds.), *Proceedings 1st Symposium on Testing and Identification of Nonlinear Systems* (pp. 353–365). Pasadena, CA: California Institute of Technology.

Svaetichin, G. (1967). Horizontal and amaercne cells of retina-properties and mechanisms of their control upon bipolar and ganglion cells. *Acta Cientienna U.S., 18*, 254.

Syrdal, A. K. (1985). Aspects of a model of the auditory representation of American English. *Communication, 4*, 121–135.

Szentagothai, J. (1985). Functional anatomy of the visual centers as cues for pattern recognition concepts. In D. Chagas, R. Gattass & C. Gross (Eds.), *Pattern recognition mechanisms* (pp. 39–52). Berlin: Springer-Verlag.

Taylor, C. A. (1978). *Images*. London: Wykeham Publications.

Teuber, H. L. (1964). The riddle of frontal lobe function in man. In J. M. Warren and K. Akert (Eds.), *The Frontal Granular Cortex and Behavior,* (pp. 410–444). New York: McGraw-Hill.

Teuber, H. L., & Mishkin, M. (1954). Judgment of visual and postural vertical after brain injury. *Journal of Psychology, 38*, 61–175.

Thatcher, R. W., & John, E. R. (1977). *Functional neuroscience, Vol. I.* Hillsdale, NJ: Lawrence Erlbaum Associates.

Thomas, P. K. (1956). Growth changes in the diameter of peripheral nerve fibers in fishes. *Journal of Anatomy, 90*, 5–14.

Thompson, R. F. (1986). The neurobiology of learning and memory. *Science, 233*, 941–947.

Tootell, R. B., Silverman, M. S., & DeValois, R. L. (1981). Spatial frequency columns in primary visual cortex. *Science, 214*, 813–815.

Toynbee, A. (1972). *A study of history.* Oxford: Oxford University Press.

Treisman, A. M. (1969). Strategies and models of selective attention. *Psychological Review, 76*, 282–299.

Treisman, A. M., & Schmidt, H. (1982). Illusary conjunctions in the perception of objects. *Cognitive Psychology, 14*, 107–141.

Tulving, E. (1972). Episodic and semantic memory. In E. Tulving & W. Donaldson (Eds.), *Organization of memory* (pp. 382–403). New York: Academic Press.

Tulving, E. (1985). On the classification problem in learning and memory. In L. G. Nilsson & T. Archer (Eds.), *Perspectives in learning and memory* (pp. 67–91). Hillsdale, NJ: Lawrence Erlbaum Associates.

Ullman, S. (1979). Against direct perception. *The Behavioral and Brain Sciences, 3*, 373–415.

Ungerleider, L., Ganz, L., & Pribram, K. H. (1977). Size constancy in Rhesus monkeys: Effects of pulvinar, prestriate and infero-temporal lesions. *Experimental Brain Research, 27*, 251–269.

Ungerleider, L., & Mishkin, M. (1982). Two cortical visual systems. In D. J. Ingle, R. J. W. Mansfield, and M. A. Goodale (Eds.), *The analysis of visual behavior* (pp. 459–586). Cambridge, MA: MIT Press.

Uttal, W. R. (1975). *An autocorrelation theory of form detection*. Hillsdale, NJ: Lawrence Erlbaum Associates.

Van Essen, D. C. (1979). Visual areas of the mammalian cerebral cortex. *Annual Review of Neuroscience, 2,* 227–263.

Van Essen, D. C., & Maunsell, J. H. R. (1983). Hierarchical organization and functional streams in the visual cortex. *Trends in Neuroscience, 6,* 370–375.

Van Heerden, P. J. (1963). A new method of storing and retrieving information. *Applied Optics, 2,* 387–392.

Varela, F. (1979). *Principles of biological autonomy*. New York: Elsevier/North-Holland.

Velasco, F., & Velasco, N. (1979). A reticulo-thalamic system mediating propriceptive attention and tremor in man. *Neurosurgery, 4,* 30–36.

Velasco, N., Velasco, F., Machado, J., & Olvera, A. (1973). Effects of novelty, habituation, attention, and distraction on the amplitudes of the various components of the somatic evoked responses. *International Journal of Neuroscience, 5,* 30–36.

Verleger, R. (1988). Event-related potentials and cognition: A critique of the context updating hypothesis and an alternative interpretation of P3. *Behavioral and Brain Sciences, 11,* 343–427.

Vinogradova, O. S. (1975). Functional organization of the limbic system in the process of registration of information: facts and hypotheses. In R. L. Isaacson & K. H. Pribram (Eds.), *The Hippocampus, Volume 2: Neurophysiology and Behavior* (pp. 3–69). New York: Plenum.

von der Heydt, R., & Peterhans, E. (1989). Mechanism of contour perception in monkey visual cortex. I. Lines of pattern discontinuity. *Journal of Neuroscience, 9,* 1731–1748.

Von Foerster, H. (1965). Memory without record. In D. P. Kimble (Ed.), *The anatomy of memory* (pp. 388–433). Palo Alto, CA: Science & Behavior Books.

Von Neumann, J., & Morgenstern, O. (1953). *Theory of games and economic behavior*. Princeton: Princeton University Press.

Wald, G. (1964). The receptors of human color vision. *Science, 145,* 1007–1017.

Walshe, F. M. R. (1948). *Critical studies in neurology*. Edinburgh, Scotland: E & S Livingstone.

Walter, W. Grey (1967). Electrical signs of association, expectancy and decision in the human brain. *Electroencephlography and Clinical Neurophysiology, 25,* 258–263.

Warrington, E. K., & McCarthy, R. (1983). Category specific access dysphasia. *Brain, 106,* 859–878.

Watson, A. B., & Ahumada, A. J., Jr. (1985). A model of human visual motion sensing. *Journal of the Optical Society of America, A2,* 322–342.

Wechsler, H. (1991). *Computational Vision*. New York: Academic Press.

Weimer, W. B., & Palermo, D. S. (1982). *Cognition and the Symbolic Process*. Hillsdale, NJ: Lawrence Erlbaum Associates.

Weiskrantz, L. (1956). Behavioral changes associated with ablation of the amygdaloid complex in monkeys. *Journal of Comparative and Physiological Psychology, 49,* 381–391.

Weiskrantz, L. (1986). *Blindsight: A case study and implications*. Oxford: Clarendon Press.

Weiskrantz, L., & Cowey, A. (1970). Filling in the scotoma: A study of residual vision after striate cortex lesions in monkeys. In E. Stellar & J. M. Sprague (Eds.), *Progress in physiological psychology*, (Vol. 3, pp. 237–260). New York: Academic Press.

Weiskrantz, L., & Mishkin, M. (1958). Effect of temporal and frontal cortical lesions on auditory discrimination in monkeys. *Brain, 81,* 406–414.

Weiskrantz, L, Warrington, E. K., Sanders, M. D., & Marshall, J. (1974). Visual capacity in the hemianopic field following a restricted occipital ablation. *Brain, 97*(4), 709—728.

Weisstein, N. (1980). The joy of Fourier analysis. In C. S. Harris (Ed.), *Visual coding and adaptability* (pp. 365–380). Hillsdale, NJ: Lawrence Erlbaum Associates.

Weisstein, N., & Harris, C. S. (1974). Visual detection of line segments: An object-superiority effect. *Science, 186,* 752–755.

Weisstein, N., & Harris, C. S. (1980). Masking and the unmasking of distributed representations in the visual system. In C. S. Harris (Ed.), *Visual coding and adaptability* (pp. 317–364). Hillsdale, NJ: Lawrence Erlbaum Associates.

Welt, C., Aschoff, J. D., Kameda, K., & Brooks, V. B. (1967). Intracortical organization of cat's motorsensory neurons. In M. D. Yahr & D. P. Purpura (Eds.), *Neurophysiological Basis of Normal and Abnormal Motor Activities* (pp. 255–294). Newlett, NY: Raven.

White, D. L., & White, C. T. (in prep.). Selective attention and discrimination in the peripheral visual field: Effect of experience.

Whitlock, D. G., & Nauta, W. J. (1956). Subcortical projections from the temporal neocortex in Macaca Mulatta. *Journal of Comparative Neurology, 106*, 183–212.

Wiesel, T. N., & Hubel, D. H. (1965a). Comparison of the effects of unilateral and bilateral eye closure on cortical unit responses in kittens. *Journal of Neurophysiology, 28*, 1029–1040.

Wiesel, T. N., & Hubel, D. H. (1965b). Extent of recovery from the effects of visual deprivation in kittens. *Journal of Neurophysiology, 28*, 1060–1072.

Wigner, E. P. (1939). On unitary representations of the inhomegeneous Lorentz group. *Annals of Mathematics, 40*, 149–204.

Wild, H. M., Butler, S. R., Carden, D., & Kulikowski, J. J. (1985). Primate cortical area V4 important for colour constancy but not wavelength discrimination. *Nature, 313*, 133–135.

Willshaw, D. (1981). Holography, associative memory and inductive generalization. In G. E. Hinton & J. A. Anderson (Eds.), *Parallel models of associative memory* (pp. 83–102). Hillsdale, NJ: Lawrence Erlbaum Associates.

Wilson, M. (1957). Effects of circumscribed cortical lesions upon somesthetic and visual discrimination in the monkey. *J. Comp. Physiol. Psychol., 50*, 630–635.

Wilson, W. H. (1959). The role of learning, perception and reward in monkey's choice of food. *Am. J. Psychol., 72*, 560–565.

Wilson, M. (1987). Brain mechanisms in categorical perception. In S. Harnad (Ed.), *Categorical perception* (pp. 387–417). New York: Cambridge University Press.

Wilson, M., & DeBauche, B. A. (1981). Inferotemporal cortex and categorical perception of visual stimuli by monkeys. *Neuropsychologia, 19*, 29–41.

Winson, J. (1975). The mode of hippocampal function. In R. L. Isaacson & K. H. Pribram (Eds.), *The Hippocampus, Volume 2: Neurophysiology and Behavior* (pp. 169–183). New York: Plenum.

Witkin, H. A., & Asch, S. E. (1948). Studies in space orientation: IV further experiments on perception of the upright with displaced visual fields. *Journal of Experimental Psychology, 38*, 762–782.

Woolsey, C. N. (1958). Organization of somatic sensory and motor areas of the cerebral cortex. In H. F. Harlow & C. N. Woolsey (Eds.), *Biological and biochemical bases of behavior* (pp. 63–81). Madison, WI: University of Wisconsin Press.

Woolsey, C. N., & Chang, T. H. (1948). Activation of the cerebral cortex by antidromic volleys in the pyramidal tract. *Research Publication of the Association of Nervous Mental Diseases, 27*, 146.

Yasue, K. (1981a). Quantum mechanics and stochastic control theory. *Journal of Mathematical Physics, 22*, 1010.

Yasue, K. (1981b). Stochastic calculus of variations. *Journal of Functional Analysis, 41*, 327.

Yevick, M. L. (1975). *Holographic or Fourier logic pattern recognition* (pp. 197–213). Oxford: Pergamon Press.

Young, J. Z. (1987). *Philosophy and the brain*. New York: Oxford University Press.

Zahn, C. T., & Roskies, R. Z. (1972). Fourier descriptors for plane closed curves. *IEEE Transactions on Computers, C–21*, 269–281.

Zambrini, J. C. (1985). Stochastic dynamics: A review of stochastic calculus of variations. *International Journal of Theoretical Physics, 24*, 277.

Zambrini, J. C. (1986a). Stochastic mechanics according to E. Schrodinger. *Physiological Review, 33*, 1532.

Zambrini, J. C. (1986b). Variational processes and stochastic versions of mechanism. *Journal of Mathematical Physics, 27*, 2307.

Zambrini, J. C. (1987). Euclidean quantum mechanics. *Physiological Review, 35*, 3631.

Zeevi, Y. Y., & Daugman, J. G. (1981). Some psychophysical aspects of visual processing of displayed information. *Proceedings of the Image II Conference*, Phoenix, AZ.

Zeigarnik, B. V. (1972). *Experimental abnormal psychology*. New York: Plenum.

Zeki, S. M. (1980). The representation of colours in the cerebral cortex. *Nature, 284*, 412–418.

Zeki, S. M. (1983a). Colour coding in the cerebral cortex: The reaction of cells in monkey visual cortex to wavelengths and colours. *Neuroscience, 9*, 741- 765.

Zeki, S. M. (1983b). Colour coding in the cerebral cortex: The responses of wavelength-selective and colour coded cells in monkey visual cortex to changes in wavelength composition. *Neuroscience, 9*, 767–781.

Glossary

This glossary is furnished as an aid to understanding the meaning of certain terms as they are used in these lectures. Most of the definitions are paraphrased from Webster's New International Dictionary, 3rd Edition; The Dictionary of Physics, by Daintith (1980); and The Dictionary of Mathematics by Gibson (1981).

Associativity: see Group.

Attractor: When the area in a phase space fails to be conserved, i.e., become dissipated, the point to which the area contracts is called an attractor. Attractors which have non integer dimensions (fractions) are called chaotic or strange attractors.

Axial Musculature: Large body musculature.

Bayes Theorem: A formulation expressing the probablility of an intersection of two or more sets (the elements common to them) as a product of the individual probablilities for each.

Boolian choice: A binary choice: for instance, the on or off of a switch.

Bottom-up: Description of relationships among components that are presumed to causally determine a higher level of description.

Brain (Neural) Systems: Anatomically and/or physiologically distinguishable parts of the central nervous system that have been shown to have a relation to selected aspects of behavior and experience.

Channel: A path or conduit in a multiple-path system for simultaneously and separately transmitting signals from more than one source.

Coefficient: A ratio that describes the efficient interaction between two factors (agents, quantities).

Commutivity: Denoting an operation that is independent of the order of combination.

Complementarity: The philosophical position that a phenomenon can be defined and/or understood only by recourse to polar and mutually exclusive observations and descriptions.

Complex Number: A number which is composed by the sum of two real numbers one of which is multiplied by the square root of minus one.

Coordinate Space: Space in the usual three (or four) dimensional geometric sense as opposed to various symbolic phase spaces.

Corticofugal: Connections that transmit signals away from the cortex.

Cross ratio: An anharmonic ratio; i.e., a ratio that cannot be expanded into a simple sine and cosine (Fourier) series.

Density: A measure of closeness in distribution.

Depolarization: When the potential difference measured across the membrane enclosing a neuron's cell body or a branch moves from its resting potential of about -60 to -70 mV towards zero it produces an excitatory polarization which may or may not be propagated along the membrane depending in part on the cross sectional size of the branch.

Detector: A mechanism which responds *uniquely* to a selcted input (a feature or property) such as radioactivity or a limited band width of frequency of electromagnetic energy.

Distribution: Apportionment. A description of an arrangement achieved through assignments, allotment, division or scatter of a quantity.

DOG: Acronym for the difference by algebraic subtraction between adjacent and overlapping Gaussian distributions.

Effective: The capability to accomplish a desired end.

Efficient: The least wasteful means of accomplishing a task or purpose.

Engram: A hypothesized protoplasmic change in neural tissue that accounts for the persistence of a specific memory.

Entropy: A measure of the efficiency with which a communication or computing process proceeds. The amount of initial uncertainty reflects the amount of entropy. Thus the greater the amount of certainty achieved the less the resultant entropy.

Epaxial Musculature: Fine muscles of the hand and feet.

Expansion: A quantity expressed as a sum of a series of terms.

Extrinsic Systems: Those forebrain systems which have direct input-output connections with peripheral receptors or effectors. Also called projection systems.

Feature: A constituent.

Fourier Descriptor: The tangent vector to the curvature of a figure at a radius reaching from a "center of gravity" or "center of symmetry" of the figure to its perimeter.

Fourier Series: A method of expanding a function by expressing it as an infinite series of periodic functions (sines and cosines). The frequencies of the sines and cosines are increased by a constant factor with each successive term.

Fourier Theorem: This theorem proposes that any configuration can be represented by (decomposed into) a series of regular wave forms differing in amplitude, frequency and the phase relations among them. The utility of the Fourier procedure depends on representing both the sine and cosine forms of each frequency and measuring the amplitude of their intersections (their quadriture) as discrete coefficients. The theorem states further that the original configuration can be completely restored from an infinite number of such coefficients. In practice satisfactory restoration can be completed in from 7 to 12 frequency components.

Fractals: Sets of phase spaces that are self-similar (i.e., invariant) across variations in scale. Strange attractors are examples of fractals.

Frame: The immediate local context that influences the perception of a sensory input. A Mondrian.

Frequency: The density of repetition of a periodic oscillation. This density can occur over space (spatial frequency) or over time (temporal frequency). Frequencies can be graphed in terms of their spectra, i.e., their distributions.

Function: Any procedure that relates one quantity or set of quantities to another quantity or set of quantities. The function can be regarded as a relationship between the elements of one set (the range) and those of another set (the domain). For each element of the first set there is a corresponding element of the second set into which it is mapped by the function.

Gaussian Distribution: A normal distribution, i.e., a distribution whose probability density function is bell shaped and symmetrical about a point on an axis representing a dimension.

Geodesic Path: The shortest route over a three dimensional surface. The great circle route taken by aircraft over the North Atlantic is an example of a geodesic.

Gradient Descent: As in hill climbing but supported by the gradient. See Search Strategies; Hill Climbing.

Group: A set that has the following properties:

1) **Closure** which describes a binary operation for which the elements of the set can be related in pairs giving results that are also members of the group.

2) **Identity** which describes an operation in which an element of a set combining with another element leaves it unchanged.

3) **Inversion** which describes the fact that for each element of the group there is another element—its inverse. Combining an element with its inverse produces the identity element.

4) **Associativity** which describes the fact that combinations of elements of the group can be commutative, i.e., independent of the order of combination.

Hamiltonian: According to the 1st Law of Thermodynamics, the law of conservation of energy, any physicochemical process tends to run in the direction of the least expenditure of energy, its Hamiltonian, before reaching equilibrium.

Harmonic analysis: The method of expanding a function by expressing it as an infinite trigonometric series of periodic functions (sines and cosines). The frequencies of the sines and cosines are increased by a constant factor (an increment in the frequency) with each successive term.

Hermitian: See Orthogonal functions.

Hilbert Space: A phase space in which the geometric coordinates are supplemented by dimensions representing spectral variables (frequency, probability amplitude, and phase).

Hill Climbing: As in the random walk, steps are taken but now with respect to a gradient against which energy or effort is expended. See Search Strategies; Random Walk.

Histogram: A graphical respresentation of a frequency (density) distribution by means of bars along an axis which represents the size of the intervals between occurrences (interval or interresponse histogram) and whose heights represent the numbers of such intervals.

Holography: A method for representing space-time configurations (images) by their spectral transformations. The initial configuration can be reconstructed from the representation by the inverse transform.

Holonomic: As used in these lectures, holonomic refers to representations in a Hilbert phase space defined by both spectral and space-time coordinates. Holonomic representations are considered to be constrained by dynamic processes (such as the least action principle) in distinction to structural representations which are more permanently constrained.

Hyperpolarization: When the potential difference measured across the membrane enclosing a neuron's cell body or branches moves in a negative direction beyond its -60 to -70 Mv resting potential it produces an inhibitory polarization.

Hyperspace: A space of more than three dimensions.

Identity: See Group.

Information: The pattern (internal form) of signals used in communication and computation. Information can be measured in terms of the potential for reduction in uncertainty posed by alternative patterns (Shannon and Weaver, 1949). When the alternatives per se are measured as Boolian (on-off) units the measures on information are made in BITS (BInary digiTS). When the alternatives are measured as ensembles of Gaborian (minima of uncertainty) units, measures are made in Logons or Quanta of Information.

Interference Patterns: Sets of discrete nodes produced by the algebraic summation (superposition) of waves passing through the same region.

Interneurons: Neurons that are intercalated between sensory and motor neurons.

Intrinsic Systems: Those forebrain systems which do not have direct input-ouput connections with peripheral receptors or effectors. Cortical parts are often called association areas but one category of intrinsic systems, proximal to the extrinsic areas, is sensory specific.

Isomorphic: Having a one-to-one correspondence between two sets.

Kernel: See Orthogonal Functions.

Least Action Principle: Describes the fact that a process tends toward the expenditure of least energy (see also Hamiltonian).

Least squares method: A method of fitting a line or plane to a set of observational points in such a way that the sum of the squares of the distances of the points from the line or plane is a minimum.

Linearity: When the highest power of an unknown variable is one. Within Cartesian coordinates the graph of a linear equation is a straight line.

Local Circuit Neurons: Interneurons that modify processing in dendritic networks.

Logon: A quantum of information (Gabor, 1946).

Lyapunov exponent: A measure of the average divergence between two systems evolving from two slightly differing initial states. When the divergence can be represented by an arithmetic series the systems are linearly related. When divergence is geometric, the systems are related non-linearly. When the Lyapunov exponent is positive, the trajectories of the evolution of the systems diverge and the evolution is sensitive to initial conditions and therefore chaotic.

Matrix: A set of quantities arranged in rows and columns to form a rectangular array. Matrices are used to represent relations between the quantities. The quantities are the elements of the matrix. The product of the number of rows and columns of the matrix determines its "order" or dimensionality. Matrices, like numbers, can be added, subtracted and, in general, treated algebraically according to certain laws which are, however, somewhat different from the laws of ordinary arithmetic. For instance, matrix multiplication is not cummutative.

Metric Muscular Contraction: A contraction or relaxation which shortens or lengthens the muscle without changing its tension.

Modality: Experience governed by a selective sensory input (e.g., taste; vision).

Mondrian: See Frame.

Neurons: The cellular elements composing the nervous system. Usually each neuron is composed of a cell body (perikaryon) and branches (dendrites). Ordinarily one branch, an axon, emanates from a special location (the axon hillock) in the cell body where nerve impulses are spontaneously generated. This spontaneous activity is modulated by dendritic processing. Axonal nerve impulses are thus used to determine the configurations of electrochemical processes (microprocesses) that characterize cooperative and competitive interactions within the dendritic network (the receptive fields of the neuron).

Notch filter: A narrow band filter. For example a filter used to gate out interference from 60 Hz produced by electric lights.

Occulocentric: A frame centered on the optic flow.

Operator: A mathematical function such as addition, multiplication or taking the square root.

Opponent Process: A process composed of two spatially or temporally distinct antagonistic subprocesses: for example, the color red may produce excitation when in the center of the receptive field of a visual neuron but inhibition when in the surrounding field.

Optic Array: The input which the optical and retinal sensory system can process.

Optic Flow: The changes in the optical image produced by relative movement of parts of the optical array with respect to each other or by such movement produced by movement of the organisms.

Orthogonal Functions: A polynomial in which each term of the series is independent of the others. Often referred to as Hermetian. The Fourier and Wiener series are examples of such functions.

Oscillation: A device that generates a periodic signal.

Perception: The organization of sensory input into experienced patterns.

Perisensory Systems: Each sensory specific extrinsic (projection) system is flanked by a perisensory system which, when electrically excited, produces movement of that sense organ.

Phase Space: An ideal, often multidimensional space of which the coordinate dimensions represent the variables required to specify the phase or state of a system.

Polarization: The constraining of oscillations to produce a trasverse wave to a single plane.

Polaron: A unit of measurement of polarization (in the dendritic network) which combines translational and rotational degrees of freedom. This enlarges the configural space of system variables from a two dimensional manifold to the direct product space of such a manifold and a spherical rotation group (e.g., $SO(3)$).

Polynomial: An algebraic series, representing the function of one or more variables, consisting of the sum of terms whose factors are constants, positive integral, or zero powers of the variables.

Power Spectrum: A real function composed of the squares of Fourier coefficients (which are complex numbers having both a real and a virtual value).

Quadriture: In performing a Fourier analysis (decomposition) the wave form of each frequency is entered into the calculation in both its sine and cosine form. As these differ by 90°, a coefficient representing the amplitude of the intersection between sine and cosine wave forms (the "interference" between them) gives an accurate discrete measure—the quadriture—of the frequency of the wave form.

Quaternion: A generalized complex number that is the sum of a real number and a vector. Quaternions depend on one real and three imaginary units, the third of which is the product of the first two. Furthermore, multiplication over the field of quaternions is not commutative.

Random Walk: The random walk, as its name indicates, is a stochastic, stepwise procedure in which each step discerns a nearest neighbor. See Search Strategies.

Receptive Field: That extent of the *environment* which excites a neuron through its dendritic connections.

Regression: The expected values of one random variable conditional on the given values of another random variable. The best regression line is drawn using the least squares method.

Scalar: A quantity fully described by a number.

Search Strategies: Random Walk, Hill Climbing, and Gradient Descent are commonly used techniques used in achieving optimization, i.e., in searches for paths demanding least energy or entropy.

Set: Any collection of quantities that belong to a well defined category.

Soliton: A quantum unit for a solitary wave of energy caused by a single perturbation. Solitons appear when exact solutions of the classical field equations are quantized. A soliton wave, in contrast to a classical wave, retains the same amplitude and frequency as it disperses from its origin.

Spaces: In mathematics, the area or volume enclosed by dimensional coordinates.

Spatial Frequency: A measure of the density of periodic events across space. Note that density per se expressed as frequency is neither spatial nor temporal.

Spatial Summation: When signals occurring in separate neurons converge onto a common neuron, their amplitudes can sum (add or subtract). In a linear system, spatial summation results in superposition.

Spectrum: Any distribution of a property such as the frequencies of wave forms.

Stochastic Process: A process that generates a series of random values of a variable and builds up a particular (e.g., Poisson) statistical distribution.

Superposition: The algebraic sum of the individual amplitudes of waves passing through the same region. This sum constitutes a node in an interference pattern.

Symmetry: Correspondence in the relative positions of parts (or terms) on opposite sides of a median line or plane, or distributed about a point or axis.

Synapses: A type of chemical connection between the discontinuities that define neurons from one another.

Tangent: A straight line or plane that touches a surface without cutting through it. The tangent function, like the sine and cosine functions, is periodic, repeating itself every 180°.

Temporal Frequency: A measure of the density of periodic events across time. Note that density per se expressed as frequency is neither spatial nor temporal.

Temporal Summation: When the effects of signals arriving at a neural junction accumulate, temporal summation of their amplitudes results.

Tensor: An invariant specified by components in each of two coordinate systems. The components (usually vectors) of one system can be transformed into those of the other by a specified set of equations involving partial derivatives. The degree of complexity of the tensor is denoted by a superscript. When the tensor superscript is 1, the tensor is a vector; when the superscript is 0, the tensor becomes a scalar.

Tonic Muscular Contraction: A contraction in which no lengthening or shortening of the muscle occurs.

Top-down: Analysis which begins with a higher level of description and ends with a description of relationships among presumably relevant components.

Torus (Toroid): A closed curved surface with a hole in it; like a doughnut or the innertube of a tire.

Transfer function (transformation): Any function that maps one set of quantities into another.

Vector: A measure of a quantity that has direction.

Wiener polynomial: See Orthogonal functions.

Author Index

Grillner, S., 126, 147
Gross, C., 99, 101, 119, 193, 195
Gross, C. G., 13, 106, 170, 172, 193
Grossman, M., 179
Grueninger, W. E., 216
Gu, 43
Guilbaud, G., 214

H

Hall, M., 174
Halper, F., 59
Hameroff, S. R., 17, 35, 70, 87, 270, 272, 287
Hamilton, W. R., 17, 35, 70, 87
Hammond, P., 74
Harrington, M. J., 333
Harris, C. S., 29, 98
Hart, E., 88
Harter, M. R., 91
Harth, E., 90
Hartley, R. V. L., 30
Hastorf, A. H., 199, 217
Hatfield, G., 114
Hayek, F. A., 239
Head, H., 173, 179, 212
Hearst, E., 205, 208
Hebb, D. O., 9, 16, 87
Hecht, S., 53
Heckenmueller, E. G., 89
Heggelund, P., 158
Heilman, K. M., 149
Held, R., xx, xxvi, 49, 93
Helmholtz, H. von, 23, 25, 58, 93, 104, 239, 249
Henneman, E., 147
Henry, G. H., 75, 78, 80
Hering, E., 104
Hertz, R. J., 215, 220
Hiley, 277
Hiley, B. J., 27, 277
Hillyard, no initial, 249
Hillyard, S. A., 249
Hinton, G. E., xvi, 26, 32, 40, 42, 219, 342
Hirsch, H. V. B., 88
Hochberg, J., xxvii, 342
Hoffer, J. A., 123, 146
Hoffman, K. P., 75
Hoffman, W. C., 22, 110, 116, 117, 123
Hofstadter, L., 230
Homskaya, E. D., 247

Hopfield, J. J., 32, 40, 42, 237
Horvath, F., 143, 253
Hosford, H. L., 88
Houk, J. C., 146, 147
Hubel, D. H., 9, 12, 59, 75, 79, 88, 98, 106, 122, 141, 257
Huber, G. C., 37, 152
Hubner, M., 35
Hudspeth, W. J., 3, 180, 184
Hunt, S. C., 244
Hurlbert, A., 105
Hurvich, L., 104
Hyden, H., 87
Hyvarinen, J., 122

I

Ickes, B. P., 116
Isaacson, R. L., 231, 235, 236
Ito, M., 127, 130
Ivanoff, V. A., 13, 76
Ivy, 224
Iwai, E., 228
Izmailov, Ch. A., 105, 357

J

Jackson, J. H., 173
James, W., 165, 230
Jameson, D. 104
Jami, L., 147
Jansson, G., 56, 109
Jasper, H., 156
Jennings, R. J., 98
Jervey, J. P., 181
Johansson, G., 56, 96, 97, 109
John, E. R., 10, 254, 343
Jones, L. A., 122
Jones, R. S., 22, 180, 261
Julez, 15
Julez, B., 26, 78
Jung, R., 9

K

Kaada, 216
Kaada, B. R., 215, 240
Kamback, M. C., 79, 81, 82, 244, 254
Kameda, K., 137
Kant, E., xxiii
Kaufman, L., 106, 107, 133

Subject Index